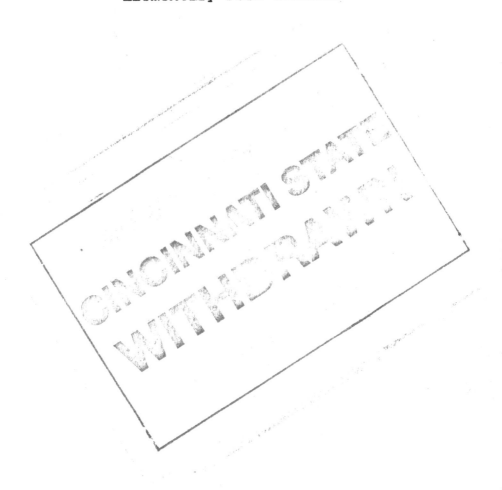

ELEMENTARY
FOOD SCIENCE

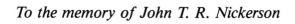

To the memory of John T. R. Nickerson

ELEMENTARY FOOD SCIENCE

Third Edition

Louis J. Ronsivalli

Former Director
Northeast Utilization Research Center
Gloucester, Massachusetts

Ernest R. Vieira

Chairman, Department of Food Science
and Nutrition
Essex Agricultural and Technical Institute
Hathorne, Massachusetts

An **avi** Book
Published by Van Nostrand Reinhold
New York

An AVI Book
(AVI is an imprint of Van Nostrand Reinhold)

Van Nostrand Reinhold
115 Fifth Avenue
New York, New York 10003

Chapman and Hall
2-6 Boundary Row
London, SE1 8HN, England

Thomas Nelson Australia
102 Dodds Street
South Melbourne 3205
Victoria, Australia

Nelson Canada
1120 Birchmount Road
Scarborough, Ontario M1K 5G4, Canada

16 15 14 13 12 11 10 9 8 7 6 5 4 3 2 1

Library of Congress Cataloging-in-Publication Data

Ronsivalli, Louis J.
    Elementary food science/Louis J. Ronsivalli, Ernest R. Vieira.—
3rd ed.
        p.   cm.
    Rev. ed. of: Elementary food science/John T. Nickerson, Louis J.
Ronsivalli. 2nd ed. © 1980.
    "An AVI book."
    Includes bibliographical references and index.
    ISBN 0-442-00532-6
    1. Food handling.   2. Food industry and trade.   I. Vieira, Ernest
R.   II. Nickerson, John T.   Elementary food science.   III. Title.
TX537.R66   1991
641.3—dc20   91-32532

Contents

Preface

Food science is a subject that requires a broad interpretation. As an area for study or practice, it cannot be described as a scientific discipline in the same strict sense that is used to describe biology, chemistry, physics, or mathematics because it employs all of these disciplines and a good deal more. Food science has been classified as an applied biological science, obviously because of the biological nature of foods; but that classification is too limiting, since many of the activities of practicing food scientists are more accurately classified as analytical chemistry, chemical engineering, microbiology, nutrition, toxicology, and so on. Prior to the establishment of university curricula in food science, the first food science practitioners were drawn from such fields as chemistry, chemical engineering, bacteriology, and biology. Also, because the earliest activities of food scientists emphasized the application of the latest technological developments to all aspects of food production, the activity was largely described as food technology, and many of the newly formed departments of universities that offered courses in the study of foods were called food technology departments. But much basic work was required to understand the characteristics of foods and the factors that affected these characteristics. Subsequently, there developed a distinction between food science (which involved basic studies) and food technology (which involved the application of technological developments to all aspects of food handling). The term *food technology* is used less frequently now, and many of the universities have renamed their departments food science departments.

Food science is one of the most relevant and most important areas of human endeavor of our time. While this statement is elaborated on in Chapter 1, it is appropriate to simply state here that the study of the history of foods, one of people's vital needs, reveals its dominating role in the evolution of humans. It has been postulated that the greatness achieved by the United States as a leading world power resulted directly from its technological developments in agriculture, which more than quadrupled food-producing efficiency, freeing up manpower and providing incentives for industrialization.

The authors believe that a text in elementary food science serves a number of purposes. It serves students in two-year courses in vocational schools or technical colleges who aspire to an associate degree in food technology. It serves students in the first year of universities in curricula that lead to a bachelor's degree in food science. It is also helpful to science students who aspire to degrees in related fields (e.g., medicine). Parts I and II of the text have been purposely presented to reach a broad audience including food handlers who may not have had the necessary educational preparation to permit them to handle foods in a safe manner. The authors believe that the improper handling of foods is the primary cause for the tens of thousands of food poisonings that occur annually. Yet there is no reason for even one case to occur. In fact, it is reasonable to propose that the safety of foods and the factors that affect it should be required instruction at the high school level, because everyone will, sooner or later, either prepare foods for others or be confronted with a situation in which the safety of a food is in question.

It should be obvious that the handling of foods to be consumed by others should not be permitted by anyone except qualified people. By qualified people, we mean people who have met two criteria. The first is the assimilation of the required knowledge regarding the proper handling of foods. The second is certification by an appropriate official authority, such as the U.S. Food and Drug Administration and the U.S. Department of Agriculture, that the person has demonstrated the ability and the attitude to handle foods properly. A major aim of the book is to help its readers to gain the necessary knowledge to handle foods safely.

As with any introductory text, it is not possible to cover all of the elements of a subject as broad as food science—from the many scientific disciplines that the food scientist must absorb in order to be an effective food scientist, to the many applications of food science in government, university, and industry activities. Therefore, it can be seen that whereas the text covers about two dozen topics in food science, it is not possible to cover every aspect of food science. The Suggested Readings at the end of the volume should help fill the need for additional information on those subjects that were not covered completely or that were omitted.

The decision to add Part V to the third edition is based on the growing awareness and importance of the principles of food science and technology in today's food management and preparation methods. An understanding of these principles is invaluable to any cook, chef, baker, or foodservice manager and this knowledge should be passed on to the students of this very large and essential segment of the food industry, to prepare them properly for what lies ahead. The information here will also be useful to food scientists and their students since it will give them an insight into the needs of this large segment of the industry, without whose existence food science would have little purpose. This section of the book will also show the practicality of the scientific principles as they are put to use in today's society.

I

Interrelated Food Science Topics

1

Why Food Science?

The scientific study of food is one of people's most important endeavors, mainly because food is their most important need. It is necessary for survival, growth, physical ability, and good health. Food processing and handling is the largest of all industries. Many factors require that those scientists who choose to study foods be prepared to absorb as many of the physical and life sciences and as much engineering as possible. Among these are the chemical complexity of foods, their vulnerability to spoilage, their role as a disease vector, and the varied sources of foods. The availability, nutritional adequacy, and the wholesomeness of foods are also quite varied.

Whether we know enough of the facts to trace the development of food science from the beginning is questionable. History reports that the Romans realized, more than the Greeks, Egyptians, or any of the prior civilizations, that agriculture was a prime concern of the government. The Romans, as the Egyptians and the Greeks before them, were able to preserve a variety of foods by holding them in vinegar (with or without brine), in honey, or in pitch. Some foods were dried, either by the sun or over a fire. These civilizations also produced cheeses and wines. Yet it is generally believed that until the latter part of the eighteenth century the preservation of foods had evolved as an art handed down from generation to generation. Its development was slow, depending on accidental discovery, observation, trial and error, and attempts to reproduce and put into practice the newly found techniques. Drying, freezing, smoking, fermenting, cooking, and baking had been practiced for centuries—even by illiterates. Foods frozen accidentally in cold climates and foods dried accidentally in dry climates were observed to have a longer "shelf-life" than foods that were neither frozen nor dried. Foods that might have been put over a fire to hasten drying could easily have led to the smoking process. Thus, chance occurrences led to preservation methods that permitted people to conserve foods during times of glut so that they might survive the leaner spells. It can be said that those who made the observations and realized their impact, then put their interpretations to the test until the new practice was proven, were the first food scientists. Spallanzani (1765) and Appert (1795) were among the first to apply the quasiscientific methods for preserving foods, and in 1809, Appert won a prize from the French government for developing a thermal processing technique for foods to be used by the military. Appert is credited with developing the canning process. Because of the scarcity of scientific information, Appert had to employ trial and error tactics, but his records attest to the accuracy of his observations and conclusions and show that he applied the scientific approach to gain his outstanding achievement, even though he did not know why his method worked.

It was not until the discoveries of Pasteur in 1850 and the work of other microbiologists, such as Prescott and Underwood in 1895, that people learned that bacteria spoiled food and why thermal processing prevented food spoilage.

By 1875, people had learned to preserve foods by artificial refrigeration using first, natural ice, and later, manufactured ice, to preserve fish and meats. They also learned that brine could be made colder than $32^\circ F$ ($0^\circ C$), and this enabled them to freeze foods. By 1890, mechanical refrigeration had come into wide use, opening the way to the frozen storage of foods. Quick freezing was first used in 1924 to preserve fish. During the period 1932–1934, Clarence Birdseye, with laboratories in Gloucester, Massachusetts, developed over a hundred different frozen food items, and this achievement won for him the reputation and the credit for the beginning of the quick-frozen food industry. One of the most important ensuing technological developments was the invention of the fish blocks by Birdseye technologists. This is considered by many to have revolutionized the fish processing industry.

In 1898, it was noted that bacteria were destroyed by exposure to radioactive salts of radium and uranium. By 1930, the use of ionizing radiations to preserve food was patented by O. Wust. However, the irradiation preservation of foods was not actively investigated until the team of Proctor, Van de Graaf, and Fram from the Massachusetts Institute of Technology undertook the project in 1943.

Modern technology has made possible such controlled, automated drying processes and sophisticated modifications as freeze-drying, drum drying, spray drying, and fluidized-bed drying. Controlled, automated versions of thermal and refrigeration processes have also been developed. Radiation processing (by electron-, X-, and gamma-rays), microwave processing, and aseptic canning have also been introduced.

Use of microwaves for processing foods is the most influential technical advancement in the food industry since Nicholas Appert developed canning.

A high percentage of new products developed in recent years utilizes micro-wave technology in preparation, and the fast-paced life-styles of the American population demands it. Microwave heating that was applied initially for home use has significant applications in industry, especially for thawing and tempering (near thawing) of large frozen portions such as shrimp and fish blocks, and large cuts of meat.

Though many food processes alter foods so that the finished product is more palatable or otherwise more acceptable (to some at least) than the original raw material (sauerkraut, tuna, wine, roquefort cheese, etc.), in many cases it is desirable that preservation processes do not alter the food (fish fillets, beef steak, pork chops, etc.). Only refrigeration can preserve most foods without altering them substantially.

FOOD—OUR MOST IMPORTANT NEED

The U.S. government recognized the importance of food when the U.S. Department of Agriculture (USDA) was formed in 1862 under President Abraham Lincoln and especially later when congressional advocates for the department urged that it be made an executive department to be headed by a secretary and member of the cabinet. Their recommendation followed their conclusion that "Agriculture, the single most important economic activity in the nation, should be represented in the innermost council of government." In 1889, the USDA was elevated to cabinet status.

It is universally accepted that people's basic needs are food, clothing, and shelter. Of course, such a list ignores the need for oxygen and water, two critical requirements, but this is understandable since we take for granted the presence of adequate amounts of oxygen in the air we breathe, and we are ever aware of the copious supplies of water in the many rivers, lakes, and wells in most parts of the world. It is only lately that a concern for water supplies is evident. It should be quite clear that food is listed before clothing and shelter because it is the most important of the three. In fact, like oxygen and water, food is a critical need without which humans cannot survive. Clothing and shelter, on the other hand, are not critical to survival, although their availability makes life more convenient and permits life in areas where the climate would be intolerable without them. Clothing may last for relatively long periods (months or years) and shelters may last for decades or even a lifetime; therefore, people have had to spend relatively little time in the procurement of these needs. The need for food, however, is relentless, and we are reminded to eat by the hunger sensations we feel at least three times each and every day. Little wonder that primitive humans, the hunters, spent a large part of their time foraging for food! Technological advances have made it possible for inhabitants of developed countries to spend considerably less time than ever before to earn enough to buy the food they need.

The availability of an abundant supply of food does not necessarily guarantee survival unless the food is nutritionally complete and contains no deleterious substances. Unfortunately, serious and sometimes fatal illnesses result from diets that lack sufficient proteins, vitamins, or other nutritional components. Serious adverse consequences may also result from the consumption of foods containing such harmful substances as infectious microbes, microbial toxins, viable parasites, allergenic agents, and a large number of chemical toxins. Thus, throughout human evolution people have had to concentrate on many factors affecting foods. They have had to increase the efficiency of food procurement to ensure a sufficient availability; to learn ways to preserve foods to carry them through times of scarcity or crop failures; and to learn specific processing methods such as baking, pickling, and fermenting to increase the variety and desirability of food. Also, people have had to learn the rudiments of the nutritional and medical aspects of food diets to maintain their health, and to learn how to minimize food-borne illnesses. However, we have a long way to go, and the little that we already know about foods only serves to make us aware of their complexity and of the ponderous work that needs to be done in food science.

Military leaders, throughout history, have been cognizant of the role of food in a military operation. An abundance of food has always been and will always be necessary to maintain the morale of the soldiers and to sustain invasion tactics; but the nature of the foods is also important, since the mobility of an army is affected by the mass of material it must carry. Thus, dried, compact foods enhance mobility. One of the outstanding facets of the military successes of Genghis Khan was the mobility of his army of mounted soldiers. With only a very scant food supply he was able to engage in swift cavalry attacks over long periods, which often caught his enemies off guard, too bewildered to rally an effective defense. Marco Polo is credited with reporting the Khan's solution to his food supply problem. Apparently, each of the Khan's horsemen carried two leather bags—one larger than the other. In the large one, he carried dried milk—produced by drying fluid milk in the sun during periods of rest. When sufficient dried milk was produced, the horsemen were prepared to start an offensive. During each morning of the offensive, some dried milk and water were put into the small bag wherein the dried milk was rehydrated, helped, in some measure, by the agitation resulting from the motion of the horse. The rehydrated milk was consumed at some time during the day. With a supply of dried milk, the lightly equipped army of the Khan could cover long distances in weeks, and when the supply of milk was exhausted, the men were able to continue, when necessary, by employing one more innovative technological tactic. They bled their horses once each day, taking about one pint of the animal's blood, which they drank for nourishment. It is reported that the army was able to continue for at least one additional week by this scheme.

It was because Napoleon recognized the importance of food preservation to maintain a dependable food supply during a war that he offered a reward for the development of a canning process that motivated Appert to his great achievement. And it is speculated that the same motive resulted in the establishment of the U.S. Department of Agriculture in 1862 during the early part of the U.S. Civil War.

The full impact of a concerted technological effort in the food logistics for the military was first evident during World War II, when American troops were equipped with light, compact, nutritionally balanced food packets that could sustain them during a military action. The proven value of the application of food science for military purposes has resulted in a continuing effort by food scientists at the U.S. Army Natick Development Center, Natick, Massachusetts, whose efforts are augmented by those of industrial and academic scientists.

FOOD SCIENCE AND HEALTH

The optimum physical and mental functioning of the body is dependent on the nutritional quality of the foods it receives. Humans have observed this from the beginning of time, and certain diets have evolved as a result of these observations. The analysis and planning of diets were not possible until food science became established to a degree and produced the basic information that made these activities possible. From the knowledge acquired through the development of food science emerged conclusions that resulted in the classification of foods into nutritional groups, representatives of which are considered to be necessary in all diets to ensure the intake of a recommended minimum of protein, carbohydrates, vitamins, minerals, and so on. Evidence of the links between diets and certain symptoms of ill health became easier to obtain as food science developed, and the potential of specific diets in corrective and preventive medicine has been gradually recognized and is now effectively practiced. For example, people suffering from atherosclerosis are advised to eat more of the white meats of poultry (about 2% fat) and the extra lean fishes such as cod (about 1% fat) for their protein sources, in order to lower their fat and cholesterol intakes.

FOOD—THE LARGEST OF ALL INDUSTRIES

Food is not only our most important need, but the food industry is the largest of all industries, employing tens of millions of people in growing, fishing, processing, transportation, storage, distribution, marketing, and so on. Tens of millions more people are required to service the needs of this industry and the people that operate it by providing the required facilities, housing, equipment, transportation, financing, utilities, and communications. The retail value of the U.S. food industry is hundreds of billions of dollars (about one-fifth of all sales), and conglomerates engaged in the food industry have annual sales in billions of dollars each.

THE IMPACT OF FOOD SCIENCE ON SOCIETY

Perhaps the greatest impact of food science on society has come in the area of agriculture. The earliest development of agriculture changed nomadic societies to settled ones, because farming is more readily done on cultivated land or land that already has been used as a farm. Once the idea of farming the same piece of land was conceived, permanent shelter became more practical and the forerunners of modern-day houses were built. The protection of farms was important enough to cause farmers to group together and to establish boundaries, and tiny hamlets, the forerunners of modern-day towns and cities, were formed. But even as the art of agriculture improved in efficiency so that increasingly less farmers were able to produce enough food to feed the population, farming efficiency as late as 1862 was only about 4.5—that is, it took 2 farmers to produce the food requirements for 9 people. Within a hundred years, the U.S. Department of Agriculture, in collaboration with land-grant colleges, farmers, and state extension agencies, increased the farming efficiency dramatically to 26—that is, it took only 1 farmer to produce the food requirements of 26 people. This accomplishment released a large proportion of the population to engage in other efforts such as manufacturing, construction, transportation, education, research, and medical services. Because of the added manpower that the United States was able to direct in other fields, it became transformed from a fledgling nation to the largest food-producing one, the leading industrial one, and the world's strongest political and military power.

We are in an era where food and what is done to it are oftentimes topics for newspapers and other public communication media. Some of the publicity is authoritative and authentic, but some of it is less than authentic, even misleading and deceptive. In addition, the public is confused by the vacillation of authorities concerning the potential hazard of additives and contaminants that are intentionally or unintentionally added to foods. The public is alarmed by the incessant warnings by authorities and pseudoauthorities against a variety of food additives, and it is bilked mercilessly by misleading assertions on the purity of organically grown foods and on the properties of certain foods that cause a decrease in obesity. Even in well-meaning drives to substitute oleomargarine for butter to lower the risk of heart disease, the public is misled to a degree. There is an awareness that public education on food science is sorely lacking, and the Institute of Food Technologists (the national society for food scientists) has contributed much in attempts to remedy this. Professors of food science at a number of universities and scientists in private industry have also set up public education programs. As a result of the efforts of these dedicated people, a number of informative publications have been issued and are available to the general public.

The Institute of Food Technologists has published overview and short articles on many subjects such as

food irradiation   foodborne microorganisms
biotechnology   microwaves in the food industry
plastic packaging   artificial intelligence (computers)

The Food Science and Nutrition Department at the Essex Agricultural and Technical Institute has written a series of short articles on diet and nutrition that include

"Turkey Business" (all you ever wanted to know about turkeys but were afraid to ask)
"Tis the Season to Be Jolly" (alcohol—its use and dangers)
"When the Losers Are the Real Winners" (sensible weight-loss methods)
"Chocolate—the Food for Lovers" (a Valentine's Day special)

Other subjects covered in the series include nutrition in athletics, coronary heart disease, food labeling, and nutrition for life. For more information on these articles, you may write to

The Institute of Food Technologists
221 North LaSalle Street
Chicago, IL 60601

and

Food Science Department
Essex Agricultural and Technical Institute
Hathorne, MA 01937

Other organizations have contributed to consumer awareness programs. Two of these are the American Council on Science and Health, 1995 Broadway, New York, NY 10023 and the Council for Agricultural Science and Technology, 137 Lynn Ave. Ames, IA 50010.

FOOD SCIENCE AS A PROFESSION

Food science may well be among the most important, the most timely, and the most relevant professions of our time. It is most important because it is the device by which we can control the availability, the nutrition, and the wholesomeness of food—the one commodity that is critical to human survival. It is timely because the gap between the accelerating food demand and inadequate food supply, on a worldwide basis, continues to widen and because the future looks even more bleak. Its relevance is apparent in some of the universities where special, practical courses in food science are available as electives to nonscience majors. This idea, that seemed worthy only because the subject matter appeared both relevant and timely to a few professors, has resulted in a positive student response that has surpassed all expectations. At the several universities involved, specially designed courses have attracted hundreds to thousands of students. Exposure to food science via these courses has resulted in the transfer of a few of the students from other fields to food science. There are more than forty universities and colleges that offer degrees in food science up to the Ph.D. level. Some schools offer associate degrees (AAS) in food science. Graduates of these courses are able to perform many of the professional duties in industry that would otherwise have to be performed by food scientists at the bachelor level.

Food science is not a discipline such as chemistry or mathematics. It is rather a mixture of disciplines, with emphasis placed on the food-related aspects of the disciplines. Thus, the food science student concentrates on the microbiology of foods, the biochemistry of foods, the rheology of foods, the applications of engineering principles to food processing and food preservation, and so on, but he or she also studies some disciplines and some courses without emphasis on food-related aspects. The latter include mathematics, inorganic chemistry, and basic physics. In some schools, laboratory courses include considerable training in the use of food processing equipment, such as a variety of heat exchangers, driers, homogenizers, comminuters, and sealing machines. Thus, it should be obvious that an engineering ability is useful for aspiring food scientists. The reasons for the broad academic preparation required by food scientists are as follows:

• Foods, originating from animals and plants, are complex biochemical systems that continue to undergo change (mainly deteriorative) at rates that depend on such environmental conditions as temperature, humidity, and presence of oxygen.

- Foods are generally contaminated with a variety of microorganisms that subsist on the food components, creating changes in proteins, fats, and carbohydrates that result in the formation of sometimes offensive, sometimes toxic, sometimes desirable by-products.
- The food scientist may want to employ certain food additives to rectify nutritional deficiencies, to prevent the development of certain microbial toxins (e.g., botulinum toxin), to prevent spoilage, to improve texture, and so on.
- The food scientist needs to be proficient in plant operations and have a knowledge of process equipment and processes.
- The food scientist must be concerned with pesticide and fertilizer residuals, as well as compounds of mercury and other elements; this is the case even when the presence of the contaminating material is as low as parts per million and less.
- The food scientist needs to know something about parasites, insects, and other foreign materials. In the literature search, the chemist goes to the *Chemical Abstracts,* the biologist goes to the *Biological Abstracts,* but the food scientist very often covers all or most of the abstracts.

The professional society for food scientists is the Institute of Food Technologists (IFT). The *1990 Directory* of that society lists a membership of about 23,000. Affiliated with the IFT are about 8,000 food companies, educational institutions, research and development companies, and so on.

2

Nutrition

Nutrition may be defined as a series of processes by which an organism takes in and assimilates food to promote growth, to expend energy, to replace worn or injured tissue, and to prevent some diseases. However, nutrition encompasses many processes, and thus, it may be given many definitions. Mendel, among others, has been quoted as defining nutrition as "The Chemistry of Life." Mendel's definition may be most appropriate from the scientist's point of view, because the processes by which food components are assimilated, converted, and utilized are understood and properly managed only when their chemistry is understood. Now, much of the chemistry of life is understood reasonably well, and most nutritional deficiencies could be easily diagnosed and successfully treated. Nutritional requirements and food energy values are well known, and the public is becoming better informed about these and vitamin and mineral needs, as well. Still, the interrelationships among food constituents, particularly as related to metabolism, and the delicately balanced chemistry of the body sometimes place a thorough understanding of nutrition well beyond our present capabilities. Therefore, although the mechanisms for studying specific aspects of nutrition are presently available (e.g., calorimetry for determining food energy values), many aspects of nutrition can be studied only by observing the organism's total response (e.g., long-term animal feeding studies for determining if a food additive might have adverse effects on the consumer).

Knowledge, in the field of nutrition, is relatively new, especially regarding the vitamins and some trace elements, and medical practitioners are not always as well informed in nutrition as they should be. Consequently, while information on the early symptoms of nutritional deficiency is often available, some cases of dietary inadequacies may go unnoticed to the detriment of those involved.

The need to maintain a nutritionally adequate diet has spurred the development of data relating to dietary needs. The Food and Nutrition Board of the National Research Council has published a table of recommended dietary allowances that are considered adequate for optimum body functioning (see Table 2-1). When the dietary intake is insufficient for short periods, body reserves may be substituted, especially for energy needs, but eventually, the body must be replenished with essential food components. When the dietary intake is insufficient for long periods, diseases resulting from inadequate nutrition develop, as described in Table 2-2.

By gross analysis, in terms of food components, humans have been reported to consist of approximately 18% protein, 0.6% carbohydrate, 15.5% fat, 3% minerals, 0.000001% vitamins, and the rest (about 63%) water. It is considered by many experts in nutrition that the body requires daily helpings of food from certain basic foods groups that include: (1) meats, poultry, fish, eggs, and beans; (2) green and yellow vegetables; (3) milk, cheeses, and other dairy products; (4) breads and cereals; and (5) fruits.

While water has no nutritional value, it nevertheless plays an important role in nutrition. As a major component of the body's transport system (blood and lymph), it is instrumental in the distribution of energy components to the points of need and in the collection and removal of metabolic waste products through the kidneys, the sweat glands, and the lungs. Therefore, the body must maintain an adequate amount of water (about two-thirds of the body weight) in order to function properly. Water enters the body as drinking water and as a major component of most foods and beverages. It is estimated that for proper body functioning, a person eliminates, and therefore requires, more than 2 qt of water each day. Over one half of the intake should be in the form of drinking water.

With modern technological advances it is possible to ensure sufficient vitamin and mineral intake through the availability of capsules that contain concentrated amounts of these nutrients. However, it is desirable that nutrients be derived from foods rather than pills, since foods contain many additional components, the benefits of which may not be fully understood. Studies have shown that it is better to obtain vitamin C requirements from citrus fruits than from vitamin tablets, since oranges, for example, contain other nutritional components, such as bioflavonoids, that may serve an important function in the biological processes of the body. Thus, if vitamin C tablets are used in place of citrus fruits, the body may sustain a lack of components that may have adverse effects on the physiological functions of the body without giving any clue as to the causes of undesirable body responses. The same has been suspected for the substitution of synthetic vitamin A for fish

TABLE 2-1.   Recommended Dietary Allowances, Revised 1989[a]
(Designed for the maintenance of good nutrition of practically all healthy people in the United States)

Category	Age (years) or Condition	Weight[b] (kg)	(lb)	Height[b] (cm)	(in)	Protein (g)	Vita-min A (μg RE)[c]	Vita-min D (μg)[d]	Vita-min E (mg α-TE)[e]	Vita-min K (μg)
									Fat-Soluble Vitamins	
Infants	0.0–0.5	6	13	60	24	13	375	7.5	3	5
	0.5–1.0	9	20	71	28	14	375	10	4	10
Children	1–3	13	29	90	35	16	400	10	6	15
	4–6	20	44	112	44	24	500	10	7	20
	7–10	28	62	132	52	28	700	10	7	30
Males	11–14	45	99	157	62	45	1,000	10	10	45
	15–18	66	145	176	69	59	1,000	10	10	65
	19–24	72	160	177	70	58	1,000	10	10	70
	25–50	79	174	176	70	63	1,000	5	10	80
	51+	77	170	173	68	63	1,000	5	10	80
Females	11–14	46	101	157	62	46	800	10	8	45
	15–18	55	120	163	64	44	800	10	8	55
	19–24	58	128	164	65	46	800	10	8	60
	25–50	63	138	163	64	50	800	5	8	65
	51+	65	143	160	63	50	800	5	8	65
Pregnant						60	800	10	10	65
Lactating	1st 6 months					65	1,300	10	12	65
	2nd 6 months					62	1,200	10	11	65

Source: From Recommended Dietary Allowances, Revised 1989. Food and Nutrition Board, National Academy of Sciences–National Research Council, Washington, D.C.

[a]The allowances, expressed as average daily intakes over time, are intended to provide for individual variations among most normal persons as they live in the United States under usual environmental stresses. Diets should be based on a variety of comon foods in order to provide other nutrients for which human requirements have been less well defined. See text for detailed discussion of allowances and of nutrients not tabulated.

[b]Weights and heights of Reference Adults are actual medians for the U.S. population of the designated age, as reported by NHANES II. The median weights and heights of those under 19 years of age were taken from Hamill et al. (1979, see pages 16–17). The use of these figures does not imply that the height-to weight ratios are ideal.

Summary Table: Estimated Safe and Adequate Daily Dietary Intakes of Selected Vitamins and Minerals[a]

Category	Age (years)	Biotin (μg)	Pantothenic Acid (mg)
		Vitamins	
Infants	0–0.5	10	2
	0.5–1	15	3
Children and	1–3	20	3
adolescents	4–6	25	3–4
	7–10	30	4–5
	11+	30–100	4–7
Adults		30–100	4–7

Source: From Recommended Dietary Allowances, Revised 1989. Food and Nutrition Board, National Academy of Sciences–National Research Council, Washington, D.C.

[a]Because there is less information on which to base allowances, these figures are not given in the main table of RDA and are provided here in the form of ranges recommended intakes.

| Water-Soluble Vitamins | | | | | | Minerals | | | | | | | |
Vita-min C (mg)	Thia-min (mg)	Ribo-flavin (mg)	Niacin (mg NE)[f]	Vita-min B$_6$ (mg)	Fo-late (µg)	Vita-min B$_{12}$ (µg)	Cal-cium (mg)	Phos-phorus (mg)	Mag-nesium (mg)	Iron (mg)	Zinc (mg)	Iodine (µg)	Sele-nium (µg)
30	0.3	0.4	5	0.3	25	0.3	400	300	40	6	5	40	10
35	0.4	0.5	6	0.6	35	0.5	600	500	60	10	5	50	15
40	0.7	0.8	9	1.0	50	0.7	800	800	80	10	10	70	20
45	0.9	1.1	12	1.1	75	1.0	800	800	120	10	10	90	20
45	1.0	1.2	13	1.4	100	1.4	800	800	170	10	10	120	30
50	1.3	1.5	17	1.7	150	2.0	1,200	1,200	270	12	15	150	40
60	1.5	1.8	20	2.0	200	2.0	1,200	1,200	400	12	15	150	50
60	1.5	1.7	19	2.0	200	2.0	1,200	1,200	350	10	15	150	70
60	1.5	1.7	19	2.0	200	2.0	800	800	350	10	15	150	70
60	1.2	1.4	15	2.0	200	2.0	800	800	350	10	15	150	70
50	1.1	1.3	15	1.4	150	2.0	1,200	1,200	280	15	12	150	45
60	1.1	1.3	15	1.5	180	2.0	1,200	1,200	300	15	12	150	50
60	1.1	1.3	15	1.6	180	2.0	1,200	1,200	280	15	12	150	55
60	1.1	1.3	15	1.6	180	2.0	800	800	280	15	12	150	55
60	1.0	1.2	13	1.6	180	2.0	800	800	280	10	12	150	55
70	1.5	1.6	17	2.2	400	2.2	1,200	1,200	320	30	15	175	65
95	1.6	1.8	20	2.1	280	2.6	1,200	1,200	355	15	19	200	75
90	1.6	1.7	20	2.1	260	2.6	1,200	1,200	340	15	16	200	75

[c] Retinol equivalents. 1 retinol equivalent = 1 µg retinol or 6 µg β-carotene. See text for calculation of vitamin A activity of diets as retinol equivalents.

[d] As cholecalciferol. 10 µg cholecalciferol = 400 IU of vitamin D.

[e] α-Tocopherol equivalents. 1 mg d-α tocopherol = 1 α-TE. See text for variation in allowances and calculation of vitamin E activity of the diet as α-tocopherol equivalents.

[f] 1 NE (niacin equivalent) is equal to 1 mg of niacin or 60 mg of dietary tryptophan.

| Category | Age (years) | Trace Elements[b] | | | | |
		Copper (mg)	Man-ganese (mg)	Fluoride (mg)	Chromium (µg)	Molybdenum (µg)
Infants	0–0.5	0.4–0.6	0.3–0.6	0.1–0.5	10–40	15–30
	0.5–1	0.6–0.7	0.6–1.0	0.2–1.0	20–60	20–40
Children and	1–3	0.7–1.0	1.0–1.5	0.5–1.5	20–80	25–50
adolescents	4–6	1.0–1.5	1.5–2.0	1.0–2.5	30–120	30–75
	7–10	1.0–2.0	2.0–3.0	1.5–2.5	50–200	50–150
	11+	1.5–2.5	2.0–5.0	1.5–2.5	50–200	75–250
Adults		1.5–3.0	2.0–5.0	1.5–4.0	50–200	75–250

[b] Since the toxic levels for many trace elements may be only several times usual intakes, the upper levels for the trace elements given in this table should not be habitually exceeded.

TABLE 2-2.   Some Diseases Due to Malnutrition

Name of Disease	Cause	Manifestations
Kwashiorkor and marasmus	Protein and calorie deficiency	Growth retardation, impaired mental development, edema, enlarged liver, pigment changes in skin, low serum proteins, enzyme deficiency
Xerophthalmia and keratomalacia	Vitamin A deficiency	Night blindness, infection of eye with loss of vision, skin changes (hyperkeratosis)
Anemias	Deficiency of iron, folic acid or vitamin B-12	Pallor, weakness, heart failure, low hemoglobin and red cell count
Endemic goiter	Iodine deficiency	Thyroid enlargement, cretinism
Beriberi	Thiamin deficiency	Peripheral neuritis, central nervous system disturbances, heart disease
Ariboflavinosis	Riboflavin deficiency	Cheilosis, glossitis, seborrheic dermatitis
Pellagra	Niacin-tryptophan deficiency	Dermatitis, mental changes, diarrhea, inflammation of gastrointestinal tract
Scurvy	Vitamin C deficiency	Hemorrhages, improper growth of bone and supporting tissue, anemia
Rickets	Vitamin D deficiency	Improper bone growth, abnormal calcium and phosphorus metabolism, skeletal deformities

liver oil. It is now believed that the fish liver oil contains beneficial nutrients that are not present in the synthetic vitamin A formulations. However, it must be remembered that the content of any of the nutrients in foods is limited and that therapeutic needs for specific nutrients are sometimes so great that they can only be filled through the use of concentrated formulations.

An insight into nutrition can be gained by a consideration of the important food substances (protein, carbohydrates, fats, vitamins, and minerals) and we will facilitate their presentation by classifying them mainly on the basis of their chemical characteristics and/or general behavior.

PROTEINS

Proteins are the chief organic constituents of muscles and other tissues. Proteins are major components of the enzymes that regulate and carry out the general metabolism and functional processes of living things. Proteins are part of the intracellular and extracellular structure of animals; they make up the structure and composition of many hormones and antibodies (disease-resisting components), and are concerned with many other factors involved with body functions. Proteins contain nitrogen, carbon, hydrogen, oxygen, and sometimes sulfur and phosphorus. All proteins contain nitrogen at a level of about 16%. The analysis for proteins is determined indirectly by analyzing for protein nitrogen, then multiplying the results by 6.25 to determine the actual amount of protein analyzed. All proteins are composed of amino acids having the general formula

$$R-CH \cdot COOH$$
$$| $$
$$NH_2$$

where R could represent any one of a variety of chemical structures. In the simplest amino acid (glycine), R represents one hydrogen atom—thus, the formula for glycine is

$$H-CH \cdot COOH$$
$$|$$
$$NH_2$$

In larger amino acids, the R could represent a complex structure such as in methionine

$$CH_3 \cdot S \cdot CH_2 \cdot CH_2 \cdot CH \cdot COOH$$
$$|$$
$$NH_2$$

In proteins, amino acids are chiefly linked together to form peptides by a peptide bond (—CO—NH—). The bond links the carboxyl group (COOH) of one amino acid with the amino group (NH_2) of another amino acid with the release of one molecule of water.

Because proteins contain carbon, they can be used as fuel since part of the molecule can be oxidized, sometimes involving deamination, to supply energy.

Proteins are required by humans for growth (protein synthesis) and for repair and maintenance of cells. Since mature adults have, in essence, ceased to grow, their protein requirement is less, per unit weight, than that of those who are still growing.

While the human requires proteins, all proteins are not of a suitable composition to supply the needs of the body, especially that of the growing child. Generally, animal proteins are complete proteins or of a composition that can supply all the body requirements, while vegetable proteins are not complete. Some animal proteins are more complete than others. Proteins are complete or not complete, depending on the amino acids (the prime components of proteins) they contain. Humans require a source of ten amino acids (the essential amino acids). There are many amino acids not required by humans. The chief difference between essential and nonessential amino acids is that humans cannot synthesize the essential amino acids in their bodies or, as in some cases, not in sufficient amounts. Therefore, essential amino acids must be obtained from the diet.

Most proteins are evaluated against egg albumin, considered to be a complete protein. However, fish, meats, poultry, and milk are considered to supply the essential protein components for growth and repair of cells. If proteins are to be obtained from vegetable sources alone, the human must have a diet that includes a variety of different vegetable foods.

The ten amino acids essential for humans are leucine, isoleucine, lysine, methionine, arginine, phenylalanine, histidine, threonine, tryptophan, and valine. Among these it should be noted that the body can utilize phenylalanine to form tyrosine but cannot form phenylalanine from tyrosine. Also, the body can form cystine or cysteine from methionine but cannot form methionine from cystine or cysteine.

Certain amino acids have a particular function in the body:

Glycine (nonessential) is utilized by the liver to detoxify certain components of foods, such as benzoic acid. It may also be involved in the synthesis of several body components, such as the bile acids. Glutamic acid (nonessential) may act as a source material for the synthesis of other amino acids.

Histidine (essential) is needed for growth and for the repair of human tissues and is converted to a substance that stimulates the secretion of hydrochloric acid in the stomach to facilitate gastric function.

Proline and hydroxyproline (nonessential amino acids) contain a structure found in hemoglobin (blood pigment) and in the cytochromes (compounds essential for oxidation and reduction reactions in the body).

Arginine (essential) is required for the detoxification of ammonia and amines resulting in the production of urea. It is often classified as nonessential because it can be synthesized from other amino acids in the body although, too often, in insufficient amounts.

Phenylalanine and tyrosine are used by the body to make the hormones adrenaline and thyroxine and are also involved in the formation of melanin, a pigment present in the skin, hair, and parts of the eye.

Tryptophan is an amino acid from which a substance involved in the constriction of blood vessels is formed, and is present in components of blood involved in clotting.

Cystine, cysteine, and methionine are sources of a part of the structure of insulin and the keratin of hair and are involved with oxidation-reduction reactions in the body.

While proteins eaten in excess of that required for growth or cellular repair may be utilized as a source of energy, it is not considered that they are efficiently utilized for this purpose.

CARBOHYDRATES

In order to carry out its day-to-day physiological functions and maintain a constant body temperature (invariably in an environment of changing temperatures, usually less than that of body temperature), the body requires a constant source of energy. Beyond its continuing maintenance needs for energy, the body periodically needs relatively larger amounts of energy to do work or to engage in other vigorous physical activities. Humans derive their energy mainly from carbohydrates (55–65%), although they can also utilize fats and proteins for this purpose.

The carbohydrates are a class of chemical compounds that consist of carbon, oxygen, and hydrogen. The carbohydrates that are important in nutrition include the sugars, the starches, the dextrins, and glycogen. Cellulose, pectin, and other carbohydrates are not important nutritionally.

Sugars

Sugars, important in nutrition, consist of monosaccharides, having the general formula $C_6H_{12}O_6$, and disaccharides, having the general formula $C_{12}H_{22}O_{11}$. Although the monosaccharides consist of 3-carbon sugars (trioses), 4-carbon sugars (tetroses), 5-carbon sugars (pentoses), and 6-carbon sugars (hexoses), only the latter are important in human nutrition as sources of energy.

Glucose, a 6-carbon sugar, is one of the simplest carbohydrates found in foods. While many foods contain traces of glucose, it is found in significant amounts only in fruits, such as grapes. Fructose, also a 6-carbon sugar, is found in fruits and honey. Both of these sugars can be utilized by the body as a source of energy.

Sucrose (the ordinary table sugar derived from sugar cane and beets) is a 12-carbon sugar that is broken down in the intestine to glucose and fructose, hence utilized as a source of energy.

Lactose, the 12-carbon sugar present in milk, is broken down in the intestine to glucose and galactose (6-carbon sugars), both of which can be used as sources of energy.

Starches

Starches are carbohydrates that are storage materials in the seeds and roots of many plants. Corn, wheat, rice, and other grains, as well as potatoes and other rootlike vegetables, contain significant amounts of starch. Starch is made up of many units of glucose linked together in different forms. In the intestine, starch is broken down to glucose and utilized as a source of energy.

Cooking (moist heat) causes starch grains to swell and rupture, thus converting starch to a form that is readily digested.

In the body, much of the glucose may be utilized directly as a source of energy, but some of it is converted into fat, the muscles utilizing fatty acids indirectly as fuel for energy. Excess carbohydrates, not required for energy, when ingested (eaten) will be stored in the body as fat.

Dextrin

Dextrin is an intermediary breakdown product of starches. It is produced in the body by the action of saliva and pancreatic juice on starch, and its presence in the intestine is considered beneficial to the digestive process.

Glycogen

Glycogen is produced in the liver from glucose (the end product of carbohydrate digestion), and it is stored in the liver, as well as in the muscles where it is available for immediate use as energy. Both the liver and the muscles can store only a limited amount of glycogen; therefore, when an excess of carbohydrates is ingested, there will be a tendency to develop an excess of glycogen. The excess carbohydrates will then be converted to fat and stored in the body as fat. The body maintains an equilibrium between glucose, the energy-producing sugar, and glycogen, which can be converted to glucose as the glucose in the blood is used up to produce energy. The production of energy from glucose involves oxidation of the sugar with the release of water and carbon dioxide, which are easily removed from the body.

$$\text{Glucose} + \text{oxygen} \rightarrow \text{energy} + \text{carbon dioxide} + \text{water}$$

$$C_6H_{12}O_6 + 6O_2 \rightarrow E + 6CO_2 + 6H_2O$$

Fibers

Dietary fiber includes the nondigestible carbohydrates. These may be either water-soluble or water-insoluble. Both have nutritional significance. The water-insoluble group that includes wheat products and wheat bran is believed to reduce chances of colon cancer by increasing bulk and diluting the effect of secondary bile acids. The water-soluble fibers such as those found in the brans of some cereals (e.g., oats and rice) and in pectin are believed to lower the levels of serum cholesterol by binding with bile acids and causing removal of cholesterol in the feces. While claims may be made for cholesterol-level-lowering properties of brans from different grains (e.g., the bran from oats and the bran from the psyllium seed, which have much higher amounts of bran than that of other grains), the more productive course for trying to control cholesterol levels is to limit the consumption of foods that are high in cholesterol and high in fats. The consumption of fiber is recommended, although not to excess. It appears that excessive amounts of dietary fiber may interfere with the retention of minerals required by the body.

FATS

Fats are glyceryl esters of fatty acids (see Chapter 24). Fats, as do carbohydrates, contain the elements carbon, oxygen, and hydrogen, but the proportion of oxygen in fats is less, and it can be said that fats are fuel foods of a more concentrated type than are the carbohydrates. Carbohydrates and fats are interchangeable as fuel foods, but it can be shown, by calorimetry, that fats produce more than twice the heat energy produced by carbohydrates. One gram of fat yields 9 Cal, while 1 gram of carbohydrate yields 4 Cal. An additional advantage of fat from the viewpoint of energy availability is that it stores well in large amounts in adipose tissues. Thus fat, considered to be a reserve form of fuel for the body, is an important source of calories. Paradoxically, this is not advantageous in affluent societies where the problem is not the availability of food for energy, but rather the health hazard of obesity.

Fats may occur in foods as materials that are solid at room temperature or as oils that are liquid at room temperature. Solid fats contain comparatively small amounts of fatty acids with two or more groups of adjacent carbons that are not fully saturated with hydrogen. That is, these carbons could accept another hydrogen: $-CH_2-CH_2-$(saturated), $-CH=CH-$(unsaturated).

Vegetable and marine fats (fish oil, whale oil, etc.) tend to contain unsaturated fatty acids, hence are oils and liquid at room temperature, whereas the fats of most land animals (cattle, hogs, poultry) contain comparatively large amounts of saturated fatty acids, and therefore are solid at room temperature.

Small amounts of three fatty acids, linoleic acid: $CH_3-(CH_2)_4-CH=CH-CH_2-CH=CH-(CH_2)_7-COOH$; linolenic acid: $CH_3-CH_2-CH=CH-CH_2-CH=CH-CH_2-CH=CH-(CH_2)_7-COOH$; and arachidonic acid: $CH_3-(CH_2)_4-CH=CH-CH_2-CH=CH-CH_2-CH=CH-CH_2-CH=CH-(CH_2)_3-COOH$ are considered to be essential to life and health. Vegetable oils (excepting coconut and olive oils) contain considerable amounts of linoleic and linolenic acids, and the human body is able to synthesize arachidonic acid from the former two fatty acids.

There are a number of phospholipids similar to fats in that two of the alcohol groups (R—OH) of glycerine are esterified to fatty acids while the third alcohol group is esterified to a side chain containing phosphorus and nitrogen. While these compounds are found in animals, their exact function is not known.

Another substance, sphingomyelin, is an important constituent of nerves and brain tissues. This is a kind of lipid in which glycerol is replaced by a long-chain alcohol containing nitrogen.

There are a number of sterols that have important functions in the body. These are very complex chemical compounds containing an alcohol group to which fatty acids can be esterified. The sterol cholesterol is involved in the composition of bile salts, which play a role in the emulsification of fats in the intestine, hence, in the digestion of fats. Ergosterol, another sterol, may be converted to vitamin D in the body under the influence of sunlight or ultraviolet light.

When fats are ingested, they are either hydrolyzed to glycerine and fatty acids by the enzyme lipase in the small intestine and reformed into fat in the intestinal wall, or they are emulsified and absorbed as such. If fats are to be utilized for energy, they will be oxidized to carbon dioxide and water through a complex process involving a number of enzymes, while small amounts of fat may be excreted as waste. Excess fats not required for energy, when eaten, are eventually deposited as such in the body.

It has been estimated that a large proportion of the deaths in this country are diet-related. Leading the causes are heart attack, stroke, and other coronary problems. Obesity and serum cholesterol levels are contributory factors in both of these diseases. With these facts in mind, it is very important to be aware of the amounts and types of fat that are ingested daily. Unsaturated fats that have been hydrogenated, such as in margarine, have been considered to be healthier than naturally saturated fats, such as in butter, for minimizing the risk of cardiovascular disease. Yet, recent experiments have yielded results suggesting that the hydrogenation process, through a chemical rearrangement of the fatty acids from their cis forms to trans forms, may make hydrogenated fats more harmful than naturally saturated fats.* This area requires further exploration.

---

*Unsaturated fatty acids (which include vegetable oils) are classified as stereoisomers because of the different spatial (three-dimensional) arrangements of the atoms that can occur among isomers. (Isomers are compounds that are chemically different, but have similar molecular formulas). Unsaturated fatty acids are further classified as geometrical stereoisomers because their molecules are recognized as having a plane of demarcation that divides them into two portions. When certain functional groups are on one side of the plane, such a molecule is said to be in the cis form. When the molecule is rearranged so that the functional groups then lie on both sides of the plane, the molecule is said to be in the trans form. For example:

2-butene

CH_3—C—H CH_3—C—H
‖   ‖
CH_3—C—H   H—C—CH_3
cis form   trans form

VITAMINS

There are a number of vitamins required in small amounts by the human body for sustaining life and good health. Some are fat-soluble; others are water-soluble. The recommended dietary allowances (RDA) for the vitamins and minerals described below are shown in Table 2-1.

Vitamin A

Vitamin A is a fat-soluble vitamin. It is found only in animals, although a number of plants contain carotene, from which vitamin A can be produced in the body once the plants containing carotene are eaten. Vitamin A may be formed in the body from the yellow pigments (containing carotene) of many fruits and vegetables, especially carrots. Vitamin A is also found in the fats and especially in the liver oils of many saltwater fish. Vitamin A is required for vision. Epithelial cells (those cells present in the lining of body cavities and in the skin and glands) require vitamin A. This vitamin is also required for resistance to infection. Deficiency of vitamin A may cause impairment in bone formation, impairment of night vision, malfunction of epithelial tissues, and defects in the enamel of teeth.

Whereas vitamin A doses are popularly expressed in international units (IU), it has been reported that the studies upon which IUs were established did not take into account the poor absorption and bioavailability of carotenoids. Therefore, retinol equivalent (RE) units are preferred. To convert from one to the other, 1 IU = 0.3 RE. The definition for RE is given by the Food and Nutrition Board:

$$1 \text{ RE} = 1 \ \mu g \text{ of all-trans retinol} = 6 \ \mu g \text{ of all-trans}$$

$$\beta\text{-carotene} = 12 \ \mu g \text{ of other provitamin A carotenoids}$$

Vitamin D

Vitamin D (calciferol or activated ergosterol) is fat-soluble. This vitamin is necessary for normal tooth and bone formation. Deficiencies in vitamin D result in rickets (deformities of bone, such as bow-legs and curvature of the spine) and teeth defects. Fish oils, and especially fish liver oils, are excellent sources of vitamin D. The human body is also able to synthesize this vitamin from components of the skin through exposure to ultraviolet light or sunlight. Vitamin D is routinely added to milk.

Vitamin E

Vitamin E, of which there are four different forms (the tocopherols), is fat-soluble.

The four tocopherols have the same name except with the prefixes alpha-, beta-, gamma-, and delta- (the first four letters of the Greek alphabet). The four compounds are closely related, with some difference in the molecular weights and in the position and number of certain molecular constituents. This vitamin is an antioxidant that serves to prevent the oxidation of some body components, such as unsaturated fatty acids, and is necessary for reproduction. Almost all foods contain some vitamin E, although corn oil, cottonseed oil, margarine, and peanut oil are especially good sources of this vitamin.

While the symptoms for vitamin E deficiency in humans are not clearly established, experiments with various animals have shown that vitamin E deficiency has an adverse effect on reproduction with apparent irreversible injury to the germinal epithelium. Other symptoms noted in animal studies include injury to the central nervous system, growth retardation, muscular dystrophy, and interference with normal heart action.

Vitamin K

Vitamin K is also fat-soluble. It is essential for the synthesis of prothrombin, a compound involved in the clotting of blood. Cabbage, spinach, cauliflower, and liver are especially good sources of vitamin K, although moderate amounts are found in many other vegetables, as well as in cereals.

The significant symptom of vitamin K deficiency in humans and in animals is the loss of the ability of the blood to clot which is, of course, a dangerous condition that can result in death whenever bleeding from cuts occurs. It is believed that humans ordinarily receive adequate amounts of vitamin K in the diet.

B Vitamins

The B vitamins are water-soluble. Thiamin—vitamin B-1—is involved in all bodily oxidations that lead to the formation of carbon dioxide. It is necessary for nerve function, appetite, and normal digestion. It is also required for growth, fertility, and lactation. The symptoms of vitamin B-1 deficiency are retardation of growth, palpitation and enlargement of the heart, hypertension, and beriberi (see Table 2–2). The various effects of a disturbance of the nerve centers such as forgetfulness or difficulty in thinking are other manifestations of vitamin B-1 deficiency.

This vitamin is often lacking in the diet because much of the naturally occurring amounts of it in food are destroyed during the processing of the food. The adult requirement of vitamin B-1 is related to the food (calorie) intake. Fresh pork is an excellent source of vitamin B-1, and the heart, liver, and kidneys of pork, beef, and lamb are fair sources.

Riboflavin—vitamin B-2—is water-soluble. This vitamin makes up a part of enzyme systems involved in the oxidation and reduction of different materials in the body. Deficiency of riboflavin generally results in growth retardation and may result in vision impairment, scaling of the skin, and lesions on mucous tissues. Neuritis is another deficiency effect. The minimum intake of riboflavin for an adult is about 2.0 mg per day. The liver and kidney of pork, beef, and lamb are excellent sources of riboflavin, and the heart of these animals is a good source. Fair amounts of riboflavin are found in the muscular tissues of pork, beef, and lamb, while more is found in veal.

Niacin (nicotinic acid) is another B vitamin. This compound is part of an enzyme system regulating reduction reactions in the body. It is also a compound that dilates blood vessels. Deficiency of niacin causes pellagra (a disease that causes diarrhea, dermatitis, nervous disorders, and sometimes death). The requirement for niacin is about ten times that for thiamin. Beef, hog, and lamb livers are excellent sources of niacin. Other organs and the musculature of these animals are good to fair sources.

Pyridoxine (vitamin B-6) is part of the enzyme system that removes CO_2 from the acid group (COOH) of certain amino acids and transfers amine groups (NH_2) from one compound to another in the body. It is also needed for the utilization of certain amino acids. Deficiency manifestations are dermatitis around the eyes, eyebrows, and angles of the mouth. There may also be a sensory neuritis, and a decrease in certain white blood cells and an increase in others. Bananas, barley, beef and beef organs, cabbage, raw carrots, yellow corn, lamb and the organs of lamb, malt, molasses, peanuts, pork and the organs of hogs, potatoes, rice, salmon, sardines, tomatoes, tuna, wheat bran and germ, flour, and yams are good to excellent sources of pyridoxine.

Biotin is reported to be a coenzyme in the synthesis of aspartic acid, which plays a part in a deaminase system and in other processes involving the fixation of carbon dioxide. Deficiency of this compound is unusual, but can be demonstrated by the feeding of raw egg white, which contains the substance, avidin, which ties up biotin. Deficiencies of biotin cause scaling skin, skin lesions, and a deterioration of nerve fibers. Due to the production of biotin by the microbial flora of the intestines, the requirement for this compound is not known. Liver is an excellent source of biotin, and peanuts, peas, beans, and whole cooked eggs are good sources.

Pantothenic acid, a vitamin required for normal growth, nerve development, and normal skin is a component of enzyme systems involved in metabolism (e.g., acetylation processes). It is believed, and there is evidence, that pantothenic acid is intimately related to riboflavin in human nutrition. Deficiency symptoms can be successfully treated with either compound. Deficiencies of this vitamin cause degeneration of nerve tissues with resulting muscular weakness, numbness, and malaise. Scaling skin and dermatitis, diarrhea with bloody stools, and ulceration of the intestine are also deficiency symptoms. The organs of animals (liver, heart, brain, kidney), and eggs, whole wheat products, and peanuts are excellent sources of pantothenic acid. The muscular tissues of animals, cheese, beans, cauliflower, broccoli, mushrooms, and salmon are very good sources of this vitamin.   ·

Folic acid is required for the formation of blood cells by the bone marrow and is involved in the formation of the blood pigment hemoglobin. It is also required for the synthesis of some amino acids. Deficiency symptoms involve pernicious anemia. Nuts, dried beans, turnips, lentils, corn, and shredded wheat are good sources of this vitamin, while liver and wheat bran are excellent.

B-12 (cobalamine) is a very complex chemical compound. This vitamin is required for the normal development of red blood cells, and a deficiency in it causes acute pernicious anemia and a variety of other disorders. The exact requirement of vitamin B-12 is yet unknown, since some B-12 is synthesized by bacteria in the intestine. The organs of animals are excellent sources of vitamin B-12 and the muscles of warm-blooded animals and fish are good sources.

Ascorbic Acid

Ascorbic acid or vitamin C is required for the formation of intercellular substances in the body, including dentine, cartilage, and the protein network of bone. Hence, it is important in tooth formation, the healing of broken bones, and the healing of wounds. It may be important to oxidation-reduction reactions in the body and to the production of certain hormones. Deficiency of vitamin C causes scurvy (spongy gums, loose teeth, swollen joints, hemorrhages in various tissues, etc.) and impaired healing of wounds. Orange juice is an excellent source of vitamin C. Tomato juice, if it has been processed properly, is a fair source of this vitamin. Green peppers, cabbage, broccoli, and brussels sprouts are excellent to good sources of vitamin C, while other vegetables such as peas, spinach, and lettuce are good to fair sources. Many fruits contain fair amounts of vitamin C.

MINERALS

A number of minerals or elements are required for normal body functions. Iron is required, since it is an essential part of both the blood pigment, hemoglobin, and the muscle pigment, myoglobin. Some body enzymes also have a composition that includes iron. Deficiencies of iron cause anemia. Liver, animal muscle tissues, eggs, oatmeal, wheat flour, cocoa, and chocolate are good sources of iron. Approximately 10.0 mg of iron are required daily.

Iodine is required by all vertebrate animals, including the human, since it is a component of the hormone, thyroxine, produced by the thyroid gland. This hormone regulates metabolic levels. Deficiency of iodine leads to low level metabolism, lethargy, and goiter. Requirements of iodine are believed to be about 0.1 mg daily. Sea food and saltwater fish are the best sources of iodine. In areas where the water is known to be deficient in iodine, iodized table salt may be used in place of regular table salt.

Sodium is required by the human, as it is part of all of the extracellular fluids of the body. Since table salt is used by essentially all people, there is little likelihood of deficiencies except in diseases involving prolonged vomiting or diarrhea.

The consumption of salt and other sodium sources should be limited. Sodium has been shown to lead to hypertension (high blood pressure) and it is recommended to keep daily consumption levels to between 1100 and 3300 mg. The average in the typical American diet is closer to 6000 mg.

Potassium is present in body cells and is associated with the function of muscles and nerves and with the metabolism of carbohydrates. Deficiency of potassium is unusual except in cases of disease involving prolonged diarrhea. Sources of potassium include meats, eggs, oranges, and bananas.

Phosphorus, an important component of bones and teeth, is also associated with essential body lipids, and its intake should be in a ratio 1:1 calcium/phosphorus. Sources of phosphorus are meats, fish, eggs, and nuts.

Calcium is required for bone and tooth structure and is necessary for the function of nerves and muscles. Calcium is also required for the clotting of blood. Deficiencies of calcium may lead to weak and flaccid muscles. Milk, cheese, sardines, and canned salmon are especially good sources of calcium.

Magnesium is a minor component of bones and is present in soft tissue cells. Deficiency of magnesium is unusual, since most vegetables, cereals and cereal flours, beans, and nuts contain adequate amounts to take care of daily requirements.

All body proteins contain sulfur, for it is a component of some amino acids. Certain vitamins also contain sulfur, required for the function of some enzyme systems. Meats, fish, cheese, eggs, beans, nuts, and oatmeal are all good sources of sulfur.

Fluorine is present in body tissues in trace amounts and helps to prevent tooth decay. Drinking water is the chief source of fluorine and fish is also a good source of this element. In high concentrations, fluorine is poisonous.

Copper is required for some body enzyme systems and is present in trace amounts in all tissues. Like fluorine, copper is poisonous in high concentrations. Fruits, beans, peas, corn, flour, rye, oats, eggs, liver, fish, and oysters are adequate sources of copper. Dietary deficiency of copper is unknown.

Cobalt is a component of vitamin B-12, the only compound present in the body known to contain this element. Very small amounts of this mineral are, therefore, required. Sufficient amounts of cobalt are present in most foods, and some may be absorbed from cooking utensils. Excessive amounts of cobalt cause toxic effects. Dietary deficiency of cobalt is unknown.

Zinc and manganese are present in all living tissues. Most human diets contain 10–15 mg of each metal per day. Both metals are important components of a number of enzyme systems. Dietary deficiency of either zinc or manganese is uncommon because of their ubiquity in foods. However, there are recorded cases of the effects of deficiencies of each element. A deficiency in zinc has been attributed to dwarfism, gonadal atrophy, and possible damage to the immune system. A deficiency of manganese in experimental animals resulted in bone disorders, sexual sterility, abnormal lipid metabolism, and even toxicity.

Selenium, molybdenum, and nickel are all found in trace amounts in the body. Selenium helps depress the symptoms of vitamin E deficiency, as well as muscular dystrophy in animals. Nickel has a role in physiological functions. Molybdenum is involved in oxidative and catabolic enzyme reactions. In excessive amounts, it results in copper deficiency. The molybdenum/copper balance can be restored by treatment with sulfur. Deficiencies of these metals are not common for humans.

Vanadium deficiencies for humans are not known; however, deficiencies of this element in birds and animals result in growth retardation, deficient lipid metabolism, impairment of reproductive function, and bone growth retardation.

Silicon is found in unpolished rice and grains and is quite prevalent in beer. Certain diseases involving connective tissue are believed to result when it is not present in adequate quantities. The required amounts for humans are not known.

Tin, occurring naturally in many tissues, has been found necessary for the growth of rats. It is believed essential to the structure of proteins and possibly other biological components. As it is present in most foods, tin deficiencies should not occur except possibly in foods that undergo refinement processes.

Chromium plays a physiological role thought to be related to glucose metabolism—perhaps by enhancing the effectiveness of insulin. While it is a normal body component, its content decreases with age.

Aluminum, boron, and cadmium are also found in trace amounts in the human body, but neither their roles nor the effects of their deficient or excessive amounts are known. Although the affected areas of the brain of those afflicted with Alzheimer's disease have been found to contain excessive amounts of aluminum, the effect of this abnormality on the disease or vice versa is not yet clear.

3

Sanitary Handling of Foods

Food must be handled sanitarily in order to prevent the growth of microorganisms already present and to prevent further contamination if we are to stop the million or more cases of food poisoning that occur each year in the United States. Sanitary handling involves personal hygiene as well as sanitary procedures.

PERSONAL HYGIENE

Rules of personal hygiene that must be strictly observed by food handlers are reasonable and require little more than common sense and awareness.

1. Persons with communicable diseases, including skin infections, should never be allowed to handle foods to be consumed by others. Obviously, this means that all food handlers must undergo periodic physical examinations to establish this qualification.
2. Food handlers should observe physical cleanliness and should wear clean (preferably white) work uniforms (no jewelry).
3. They should keep the head covered, the fingernails short and clean (no nailpolish).
4. When possible, gloves should be worn, but whether or not gloves are worn, the hands should be washed and dipped in a disinfectant prior to handling food. The hands should be rewashed any time they are used for anything else prior to handling food again.
5. When handling foods, the hands should not touch the mouth, nose, or other part of the body, especially body openings, since these are possible sources of pathogens. Remember that the hands are involved in most instances of personal contamination of foods.

6. During work, food handlers should neither smoke, drink, nor eat in the work area.
7. Pets and other animals do not belong in the food-processing area.
8. Sneezing and coughing should be confined to a handkerchief, and in fact, the individual should leave the work area when either is imminent. After using a handkerchief, the hands are to be rewashed.
9. Cloths should not be used for cleaning.
10. Foods that appear to be unwholesome, or that may contain unacceptable contaminants, should not be handled.

SANITATION IN THE HOME

The home should be kept clean by periodic cleaning and by setting rules of conduct for members of the household such as discouraging litter and encouraging use of ash trays (if discouraging smoking is unsuccessful). The surfaces should be kept dust-free, preferably by vacuum cleaning, and surfaces that contact foods should be of easily cleaned material such as plastics and stainless steel. Tableware, such as knives, and pots and pans should have handles of metal or plastic rather than wood. Tableware and utensils should be cleaned as soon after use as possible and should not be left uncleaned for long periods either in the sink or on the counter, since bacteria will grow and may become airborne to contaminate other food. Tableware and utensils should be washed in hot water and detergent and rinsed, then immersed in hot water (that has been heated to a minimum of 170°F [76.7°C]) for at least ½ minute.

In foodservice establishments, it is a violation of federal law to use a product as a chemical sanitizer unless it is Environmental Protection Agency (EPA) registered. Some household bleaches have EPA registration and the accuracy of all claims on the label have been proven. Follow the directions for sanitizing carefully. To sanitize dishes and other food utensils, the Food and Drug Administration (FDA) recommends a solution of 50 ppm available chlorine as a hypochlorite. After washing and rinsing, the utensils must be submerged in the warm (75°F [24°C] or higher) solution for 1 minute. For countertops, cutting boards, or equipment that cannot be submerged, spray or wipe with a solution of twice the strength above (100 ppm available chlorine as a hypochlorite), and allow to air-dry.

Automatic dishwashers may be used with confidence, since they clean effectively and since the temperature of the water can be raised to a higher level than can be tolerated in hand washing. Keep the refrigerator and freezer clean and free from odors. Keep a clean house and enforce the habits that keep it clean, and members of the household will be prompted to help keep it clean. The home should be kept free from rodents and other pests, such as roaches and flies, by a strict preventive program and by a continuing check for indications of the presence of these undesirable elements. When they are present, concerted efforts to eliminate them should not be spared.

Care of food in the home involves precautions in a number of areas. Approximately 88% of all cases of food poisoning can be traced to handling of food at improper temperatures. Food must be kept out of the temperature "danger zone" (Fig. 3-1) in all phases of preparation (purchase, transport, preparation, service, and storage).

When shopping for foods, shop at clean stores where employees observe the rules to be found earlier in this chapter. Shop for the perishable foods (e.g., milk, meat, fish) last, and do not delay going home once the shopping has been completed. Remember that bacteria (which spoil foods) grow to very large numbers in just hours while in a warm car. Once home, the perishable foods should be unpacked immediately and transferred quickly to the refrigerator or freezer.

Perishables should be kept in a refrigerator held at as low a temperature (above freezing) as possible. Remember that the most important deterrent to food spoilage is low temperature. The refrigerator should be kept at temperatures in the range 32°-38°F (0°-3.3°C), preferably on the lower side of the range. Frozen foods should be held at 0°F (−17.8°C) or below. Neither the refrigerator nor the freezer can lower the temperature of bulk foods quickly enough, and spoilage occurs during the period of cooling; therefore, when the bulk of foods can be reduced it should be done. Large pots of stew, bulk hamburger, and large cuts of meat, could all be divided and put in small containers. Cooling food quickly helps to avoid spoilage (see Fig. 3-2).

Packaging of the foods is important, especially in impervious films, to minimize freezer burn, oxidative deterioration, and dehydration. Refrigerated foods should be covered, except for ripe fruits and vegetables. All cooked foods, meats, fish, cold cuts, bacon, frankfurters, should be packaged before refrigerating. Nuts should be packaged and refrigerated to slow down the oxidation of their fats, which leads to rancidity. Greens (e.g., spinach) should be refrigerated unwashed. It should be remembered that fresh foods should be used as soon as possible. Fresh foods, with some exceptions, deteriorate rapidly. Some foods are best held at room temperature and these include baked goods (to hold for more than two days, they should be frozen), unripe fruit, and bananas. When meats, eggs, poultry, fish, and other perishable foods are to be held, it should be remembered that the safe holding temperatures are those below 45°F (7.2°C) and those above 140°F (60°C).

Meals that are consumed following their preparation are not likely to be responsible for food poisoning. On the other hand, meals that are consumed hours after preparation, such as is customary at picnics and outings, should be supervised by knowledgeable people. This is especially true of salads con-

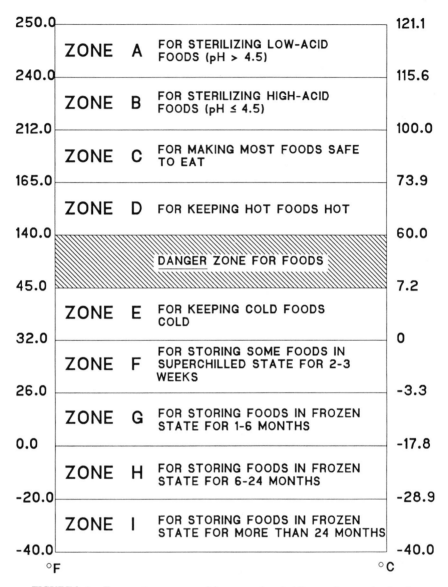

FIGURE 3-1.   Temperature zones used for processing, holding, and preserving foods.

taining eggs, chicken, or turkey, or products made from them. Prepared foods that are not to be used for long periods should be immediately refrigerated and reheated, if necessary, just prior to use. Some products such as puddings, custards, and eclairs should be held under refrigeration at all times. Home freezers are not of sufficient capacity to flash-freeze stuffed

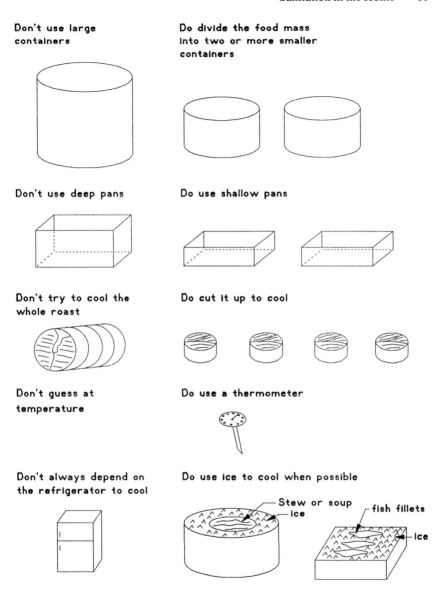

Don't use large
containers

Do divide the food mass
into two or more smaller
containers

Don't use deep pans

Do use shallow pans

Don't try to cool the
whole roast

Do cut it up to cool

Don't guess at
temperature

Do use a thermometer

Don't always depend on
the refrigerator to cool

Do use ice to cool when possible

Stew or soup
ice

fish fillets

ice

FIGURE 3-2.   Do's and don'ts for the safe cooling of foods.

poultry, chicken, and especially turkey, and, therefore, poultry should not be stuffed prior to freezing. Instead it should be stuffed prior to cooking. Leftovers should be used as soon as possible; this is especially true of salads, chicken, and other perishables. If, due to odor or other indicator, there is any doubt about the safety of a food, it is best to discard it unless advice can be obtained from a food scientist. Extreme care must be taken with foods to be taken on a picnic or outing.

1. Precool all perishable foods, including ingredients for salads, preferably in a refrigerator.
2. Heat all foods, to be served hot, to at least 165°F (73.9°C).
3. Keep cold foods cold (45°F [7.2°C] or below) and hot foods hot (140°F [60°C] or above) until served.

It is best to refrain from handling pets while preparing foods.

FOODSERVICE SANITATION

It has been reported that about 111 million meals per day are served in approximately 464,000 restaurants in the United States. The U.S. Public Health Service has reported that about two-thirds of all reported food poisonings result from meals served in restaurants. In terms of numbers, no one can be sure, since only a small percentage of all food poisonings is ever reported. One thing is known, and that is the number is very high, with some estimates indicating that it is about one million per year. Thus, sanitation in restaurants requires considerable improvement, since it is known that nearly all food poisonings are avoidable. The main reason for food poisoning is the poor attitude of some workers and the ignorance of others. Therefore, it must be the responsibility of the managers and owners of restaurants to employ only those with healthy attitudes and to make sure that they have been properly educated. Attitude has to be the most important criterion for employment, since the education part is simply a matter of a little time and effort. On the other hand, no amount of education in sanitation can improve an unhealthy attitude. People with unhealthy attitudes *must* be removed from food handling responsibilities. The problem is aggravated by the fact that restaurants are visited by large numbers of people over short periods (taxing the cleaning and food handling efforts of the facilities) and by the fact that some of the customers are bound to have communicable diseases.

Whereas restaurants outnumber other feeding establishments (e.g., hospitals and school and industrial cafeterias), in the latter, about 97 million meals are served daily.

The number of people involved in serving meals in restaurants and institutions is estimated to be 8.0 million. Whether food is to be prepared and served in restaurants or in institutional cafeterias, safety precautions and sanitary procedures are very similar.

In general, the floor plan of an area where people are fed need not be special except that it can be easily cleaned and kept clean. The surrounding area should be pleasant; the floor should carpeted and of a type that is easy to clean thoroughly.

It should be mandatory to use only potable (drinkable) water in foodserving establishments. If nonpotable water is used for cooling refrigeration units in walk-in refrigerators, for example, this water should not be connected with the potable water system, and the pipes should be painted with some identifying color.

In the food preparation and utensil-cleaning areas, the floors should be constructed of acid-resistant unglazed tile or of epoxy or polyester resin on a suitable base material. Also, the floor should be sloped to drains to facilitate cleaning and prevent the accumulation of water. Drains should be separate from toilet sewer lines to a point outside of the building and should be so constructed as to prevent the possibility of backup into the building. The walls of food preparation and utensil cleaning areas should be constructed of smooth glazed tile to distances equivalent to splash height, since this type of construction makes for easier and more effective cleaning. The junction of the walls and floor should be coved or curved, which also facilitates cleaning, there being no angled corners where food materials can lodge.

The surfaces of benches and tables in food preparation areas should be of stainless steel or plastic, since such materials are impervious, noncorrodible, and easy to clean. For the same reason, cooking utensils, including steam kettles, should be constructed of stainless steel.

Areas in which steam cooking, steam cleaning, or deep-fat frying is done should be provided with hoods and exhaust fans to the outside. Hoods should be constructed of stainless steel for ease in cleaning and should be equipped with traps to prevent condensed moisture from running back into foods being prepared.

Cutting boards should be constructed of plastic, preferably Teflon, as such material is easy to clean, does not absorb water, and does not foster bacterial growth.

Walk-in refrigerators should have floors constructed of unglazed tile that are sloped to drains to facilitate cleaning. The drains should not empty directly into the sewerage system. Instead, they should empty into a sink or other container that empties in turn into a drainage system, so there is no possibility of backup into the refrigerator. The walls and ceilings of walk-in refrigerators should be constructed of glazed tile to facilitate cleaning.

Wash basins, soap, hot and cold water, and a container of disinfectant (preferably a solution of one of the iodophors) together with paper towels should be present in the food preparation, utensil washing, and food exit areas to make certain that anyone having left his or her particular operation washes, disinfects, and dries his or her hands prior to resuming work.

The management of foodserving establishments should obtain raw food materials only from reliable sources. It should also determine that the water to be used for drinking, cooking, and cleaning is potable.

The precautions to be used in cooking foods are no different from those that have been given for household food safety, but if foods, including gravies, are to be held on steam tables, the temperature of all parts of the food should never fall below 145°F (62.8°C), and preferably not below 150°F (65.6°C). Also, any food container held on steam tables should be emptied, removed, and replaced with a new container of the particular food instead of being partially emptied and refilled with more food.

If leftover cooked foods are to be refrigerated, they should be placed in covered impervious containers (plastic or metal) and labeled. A card catalog of leftover foods should be maintained so that such materials may be thrown away if held for periods of more than four days at temperatures of 38°F (3.3°C) or above.

If cream-filled pastries, such as eclairs or pies, or salads, such as potato, tuna fish, crab meat, or chicken, are to be held in the refrigerator or in display cases, the temperature of such storage areas should be 38°F (3.3°C) or below.

Personnel with boils or pus-producing infections on their hands should not be allowed to handle foods or to clean utensils or equipment. Any personnel known to have had a recent intestinal ailment should be excused from work until such a period as it can be determined that he or she is not infective.

All garbage and waste materials should be held in leakproof metal or plastic containers with tight-fitting covers when held on the premises of the foodserving establishment. Rubbish should also be held in this manner. After emptying, each container should be cleaned inside and outside, and the water used for such cleaning disposed of in the sewerage system. Such containers should be washed in an area well separated from that used for washing utensils; containers of garbage and trash should be stored in verminproof rooms, well separated from the food preparation and serving areas. The floor of such storage rooms, and the walls up to distances of splash height, should have an impervious easy-to-clean surface. Storage areas of this type should be cleaned periodically. Care should be exercised to see that rodents and insects do not become established in waste storage areas.

An effective method of sanitizing glasses, chinaware, and utensils is to wash in water at least at 120°F (48.9°C) with detergent followed by rinsing, then immersing in clean water at 170°F (76.7°C) for 0.5 min. Immersion for 1 min in a solution containing 50 ppm available chlorine or 12.5 ppm of an iodophor, in each case at a temperature not below 75°F (23.9°C), may be substituted for the hot-water dip for purposes of sanitizing utensils and tableware.

For a typical foodservice facility, see Figure 3–3.

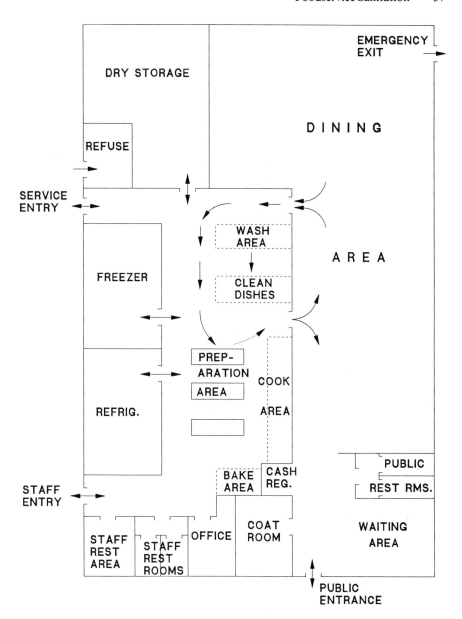

FIGURE 3-3.   Simplified floor plan for a well-organized foodservice operation.

PLANT SANITATION

Plant sanitation is necessary, first because it is a law (see sections 402(a)(3) and 402(a)(4) of the Food, Drug and Cosmetic Act), and second because it is good ethics, good economics, and we all expect it.

An important part of plant sanitation is the establishment of a strict quality control over the incoming raw materials. No amount of plant sanitation can remain effective if incoming materials are allowed to bring in contaminants.

Many of the factors concerned with food safety in plants manufacturing food products are the same as those indicated for food preparation and serving establishments. There are some additional considerations, however.

Plant Exterior

The surroundings for food plants should be neat, trim, and well landscaped. There are several reasons for this. Nice surroundings have a good psychological effect on those who work within. If the environs are well kept, the personnel working there are much more apt to try to keep things neat and clean on the inside. If the surroundings are dirty or cluttered, those working in the plant are apt to become careless in matters concerned with general sanitation. All parking spaces, roadways, and walks should be paved so that dust contamination of the air will be minimized, and contamination, such as animal droppings, will be washed away with each rain rather than be soaked into the ground to be airborne during dry spells. The area surrounding a food plant, including platforms, should not be used for storing crates, boxes, or machinery, since these materials may become a harborage for rodents that may eventually find their way into the plant. There should be no area around the plant where the landscaping allows potholes or depressions of any kind in which water may accumulate and become a breeding place for insects that then may become established within the plant. Food materials, ensilage piles, or other organic wastes should not be present in any exposed area near the plant, since they attract and become breeding places for insects, especially flies, which are difficult to control in food plants, even in the best conditions. There should be no neighboring plants, such as chemical, sewage, poultry, or tanneries, that may transfer bacteria or chemicals to the food plant.

Plant Construction

Food manufacturing plants are best constructed of brick or concrete, since wood is difficult to maintain in a clean and sanitizable condition and is more vulnerable to invasion by rodents, birds, and other pests. If the plant is constructed of wood, the foundation should be "rat-stopped" (constructed of cement to a distance of several feet below and above the ground). The walls and roof junction of the food plant should be weatherproof and impenetrable by insects. In food-processing or utensil-washing areas, the junction of the wall and floor should be curved and have no angled corners, in order to facilitate cleaning. Window ledges should be slanted to prevent their use by personnel for storage of materials. The floor should be made of acid-resistant unglazed tile or of epoxy resin material, an epoxy tile grout laid on cement, for instance. The floor should be sloped to drains so that water does not accumulate. A cement surface is undesirable, since it tends to become pitted, leaving areas where water and food scraps accumulate and where bacteria may grow to large numbers, thus becoming sources of bacterial contamination and putrid odors, as well. The walls should be covered with glazed tile at least up to distances of splash height, in order to facilitate cleaning.

Raw materials should be separated from areas producing the finished product by a solid nonleaking wall (no openings, no doors) or by using separate buildings. The boiler room must also be separate and closed off. Each entryway to the area producing the finished product should be equipped with a shallow pan containing a disinfectant, so that those who enter the area must step into the pan, thus disinfecting their shoes or boots.

Equipment

Food-processing equipment should be so designed that all surfaces contacting foods are smooth, relatively inert, nonabsorbent, easily reached for cleaning, and of materials that are easily cleaned and sanitized. Moreover, it is desirable that as much of the equipment as possible can be cleaned without disassembling, but that disassembly to the required degree is possible and easily done. These specifications are desirable because they ensure that sanitation of equipment is possible and because sanitation can be accomplished quickly, effectively, and inexpensively. They are also desirable because they do not contribute to delaying tactics on the part of employees.

The equipment, benches, and machinery used in food-processing and utensil-cleaning areas should be of such materials and design as to make cleaning as easy as possible. Surfaces should be smooth (about 150 grit). Cutting boards, knife handles, and shovel handles, should be of hard plastic or other materials impervious to water. Black and cast irons and ordinary steel may be used for equipment that has no contact with foods, such as retorts and can sealers. However, since these materials have rough surfaces and are subject to corrosion and are difficult to clean, their surfaces should not come in contact with food materials. While the surface of new galvanized iron is corrosion-resistant, the zinc covering soon wears off, exposing the iron, which can corrode. Also, zinc may cause a discoloration of certain foods. For these reasons, galvanized iron is not acceptable as a surface for contact with foods. Copper is used in steam kettles for the manufacture of certain foods like jams and jellies, because it is a good conductor of heat. When used in processing other foods, it must be kept scrupulously clean, however; otherwise, oxides accumulate, accelerating the destruction of vitamin C and the oxidation of fats.

Alkaline materials used on copper equipment may cause a discoloration of foods. It is generally undesirable to use copper in food-processing equipment, even though it is among the best conductors of heat available. Monel metal, an alloy consisting mainly of nickel and copper, is suitable for food-processing equipment but is expensive. Aluminum conducts heat well but is subject to corrosion when contacting alkaline materials or fruit acids. Glass is used for piping for the transportation of liquids, such as milk, and such piping can be cleaned in place without dismantling. It is not suitable for lining metal equipment, nor is enamel, being subject to chipping, thus exposing the metal, which may then corrode. Glass or enamel chips may also become incorporated in the food. Rubber is used for conveyor belts that transport materials, but rubber is not easily cleaned and belts lined with Teflon or a suitable metal are preferable to those lined with rubber. Stainless steel is doubtless the most suitable material for the construction of equipment that contacts food. It is noncorrosive and easily cleaned and sanitized. A special stainless steel may be required for areas contacted by chlorides, such as those occurring in sea water or brine.

Piping and pumps should have no threaded joints where food can accumulate. Sanitary design for such equipment calls for flush joints held together by clamps, allowing thorough cleaning and sanitizing. Pipes that carry food materials should have no dead ends that cannot be cleaned and where food materials can accumulate and decompose. With such construction, surges on the line cause decomposed material to enter the mainstream of the food material passing through the pipes. Pipes should not be joined to tanks or hoppers, so that the pipe end extends into the tank itself. In such cases, when the liquid falls below the level of the pipe, some food remains in the pipe end where it may decompose and eventually contaminate new material entering the tank. Tanks, flumes, thermometer wells, pots, and pans should have only curved corners and junctions of sides and bottom in order to facilitate cleaning.

Personnel Facilities

Locker rooms should be provided, separate for male and female personnel, and a sufficient number of lockers should be available to provide one for each worker so that outside clothing may be stored. These locker rooms should be kept clean and tidy.

Separate toilet rooms with self-closing doors (that do not open directly to processing area) should be provided for men and women workers. Toilet rooms should have wash bowls with hot and cold running water, soap dispensers, paper towels, and containers for refuse. The minimum number of toilets and wash basins is given in Table 3-1. Urinals may be substituted for toilets in the men's rooms on a one-to-one basis, but the number of toilets must never be fewer than two-thirds of the number given in Table 3-1. The hand-washing units should be of the foot-activated type.

If personnel are to eat lunches at the plant, a room separate from other rooms, including locker rooms, should be provided for this purpose. This room should be kept clean and sanitary. Drinking fountains should never be located in toilet rooms.

All personnel working in food-processing or utensil-cleaning areas should be provided with clean outer uniforms daily.

In processing or utensil-cleaning areas, there should be wash basins, a container of disinfectant (preferably a weak solution of an iodophor), and paper towels so that those in charge can make sure that workers wash and disinfect their hands before returning to work once having left their particular area of operation. This is of great importance to good food plant sanitation.

Food-processing plants must have adequate light to ensure that employees can perform their duties effectively. Table 3-2 cites the minimum light requirements to carry out different operations in the plant.

Food-processing plants should have good ventilation with filtered air, to reduce the atmospheric humidity, and hence the amount of condensation, which if allowed to occur, promotes the growth of bacteria and molds on the surfaces of walls, ceilings, floors, equipment, utensils, foods, and so forth.

TABLE 3-1.   Required Lavatory Facilities

Number of Employees	Minimum Number of Toilets	Minimum Number of Wash Basins
1–9	1	1
10–24	2	1
25–49	3	2
50–74	4	3
75–100	5	4
>100	5 + 1/30 additional employees	4 + 1/50 additional employees

TABLE 3-2.   **Minimum Light Requirements for Food**
Processing Plants

Operation	Minimum Light (Ft-Candles)
Sorting, grading, inspection[a]	50
Processing, active storage	20
Instrument panels, switchboards	10
Toilet rooms, locker rooms, etc.	10
Dead storage	5

[a]Local lighting for inspection may have to be as high as as 100–150 ft-candles, depending on the type of inspection performed.

Storage

Dry materials such as breadings and flour, to be stored, should be held in a room constructed of materials, such as brick or cement, which do not allow the entrance of insects and rodents. Such rooms should be refrigerated to about 50°F (10°C) to prevent the hatching of eggs and the development into adult insects, should viable insect eggs be present.

Cleaning the Plant

All floors, walls, benches and tables, conveyors, hoppers, fillers, kettles, and utensils used for processing foods should be thoroughly cleaned and sanitized at least once, and preferably twice, per 8-hour working shift. Large plants should have cleaning crews with a foreman. A list of approved cleaning compounds was published by the U.S. Department of Agriculture in 1987, and it is available from that agency. The water used for cleaning should be potable and have a temperature of about 130°–140°F (54.4°– 60.0°C). The type of detergent used in cleaning should be suitable to remove the type of soil that will be encountered. Depending on the application, detergents should have certain properties. In general, detergents should not be corrosive. When used in hard water, they should not form precipitates. They should have good wetting, and in many cases emulsifying, properties. They should be good solvents for both organic and inorganic soils. They should saponify fats and have good dispersal and deflocculating properties. They should not form residual films on surfaces. High-pressure water and high-pressure steam can be used to flush hard-to-reach places with detergent.

Chemical agents used for controlling microbes include bacteriostats, which prevent the growth and spread of bacteria, and bactericides, which not only stop bacterial growth, but also destroy the bacteria. Some agents are bacteriostatic in small amounts and bactericidal in large amounts. Effective sanitation programs should be concerned mainly, if not completely, with bactericides that include compounds in the following chemical classes: halogens, phenolics, quaternary ammonium compounds, alcohols, carbonyls, and miscellaneous others. The halogens, chlorine and iodine, are considered to be the most important sanitizing agents known. Such common uses as chlorination of drinking water and iodine treatment for cuts make these compounds familiar. Phenolics, such as cresol, are considered to be also very good sanitizers; however, they have some disadvantages, among which are high irritation characteristics and relatively high cost. Quaternary ammonium compounds, while effective in the control of algae and some bacteria, are relatively ineffective against a variety of microbes that are not resistant to the halogens and phenolics. Alcohols are not as effective as generally believed, and while some carbonyls, such as formaldehyde, are effective, they are also hazardous to use. There are other miscellaneous sanitizers, but they are generally low in effectiveness and high in cost.

After cleaning and rinsing with hot water, equipment should be immersed for about 1 min or rinsed with a solution of an iodophor containing 12.5 ppm of available iodine. Iodophors, or "tamed iodines," are combinations of iodine and surface active agents that have the sanitizing advantages of iodine with minimized disadvantages of iodine. Iodine by itself is not very soluble in water, has a high vapor pressure, is corrosive, and leaves a stain. In combination with surfactants, these undesirable properties are minimized. A solution containing 50 ppm of available chlorine at a temperature not below 75°F (23.9°C) may be substituted. All equipment so constructed as to hold liquids should be thoroughly drained after cleaning and sanitizing, and containers, such as pans, should not be nested after cleaning and sanitizing, since this prevents draining and evaporation of moisture and thus provides moisture in which bacteria may grow. For a summary of the properties of sanitizing agents see Table 3-3.

Water Supply

The water supply should be adequate for filling the plant's needs. All water that may contact either foods or surfaces that may be contacted by foods must be of potable quality (safe for drinking). The water used for cleaning should be of adequate temperature and pressure and supplied via a plumbing system of adequate capacity and in conformance to building codes.

Sewage Disposal

Sewage disposal must be through a public sewerage system or through a system of equal effectiveness in carrying liquid disposable waste from the plant.

TABLE 3-3.   Advantages and Disadvantages of Three Important Classes of Sanitizers

Hypochlorites (Liquid)	Iodophors	Quats[a]
Advantages		
Inexpensive	Stable	Stable
	Long shelf-life	Long shelf-life
Active against all microorganisms	Active against all microorganisms except bacterial spores and bacteriophage	Active against many microorganisms, especially the thermoduric types
Unaffected by hard water salts	Unaffected by hard water salts	Form bacteriostatic film
Water treatment	Noncorrosive	Prevent and eliminate odors
Active against spores	Not irritating to skin	Nonirritating to skin
Active against bacteriophage	Easily dispensed and controlled	Noncorrosive
Easily dispensed and controlled	Acid nature prevents film formation	Stable in presence of organic matter
Not film forming	Concentration easily measured by convenient field test	Easily dispensed and controlled
	Visual control (color)	Stable to temperature changes
Concentration easily measured by convenient field test	Good penetration qualities	Good penetration qualities
	Spot-free drying	May be combined with nonionic wetting agents to formulate detergent sanitizers
Disadvantages		
Short shelf-life	Not as effective against spores and bacteriophage as hypochlorites	Incompatibility with common detergent components
Odor	Expensive	Germicidal efficiency varied and selective
Precipitate in iron waters	Should not be used at temperatures exceeding 120°F (48.9°C)	Slow in destruction of coliform and Gram-negative psychrophilic bacteria (like *Pseudomonas*)

TABLE 3-3. *(continued)*

Hypochlorites (Liquid)	Iodophors	Quats[a]
	Disadvantages	
Corrosiveness on some metals	Germicidal action adversely affected by highly alkaline water or carryover of highly alkaline detergent solutions	Expensive Slow to dissipate (residual problem) Objectionable film on surfaces treated Foam problem in mechanical application
Use concentration 200 ppm Cl_2	25 ppm I_2	220 ppm quat

Courtesy of Klenzade Division, Ecolab, Inc.

[a]Quaternary ammonium compounds

The sewerage system must conform to building codes and in no way be a source of contamination to the products, personnel, equipment, or plant. Drains must be sufficient to ensure the rapid and complete transfer of all wash water, spilled liquids, and so on, to the sewerage system.

SANITATION IN RETAIL OUTLETS

Most regulations applicable to foods in retail stores are the same as those which are applied in food manufacturing plants, but there are some precautions especially applicable to retail outlets. Fresh uncut meats should be stored in a walk-in refrigerator with walls and ceilings of glazed tile to facilitate washing and cleaning. The floor should be constructed of unglazed tile and sloped to drains. The temperature of the meat storage room should be held at 32°–37°F (0°–2.8°C). Carcasses or sides should be hung on hooks attached to rails. Sawdust should not be used on the floor since this creates dust, which is, to some extent, a source of contamination.

The room where meat is cut into retail portions should have the same wall, ceiling, and floor construction as does the meat storage area. Benches used for cutting meat should have surfaces of stainless steel, and cutting boards should be made of a plastic material, preferably Teflon, which is impervious and easily cleaned and sanitized. The temperature of this room should be about 50°F (10°C), since personnel find it difficult to work at lower temperatures. However, a low relative humidity must be maintained in the cutting area; otherwise the meat will condense moisture (sweat), which will facilitate the growth of spoilage bacteria. Also, neither cut nor uncut meat should be allowed to accumulate in this area but should be moved back into the storage area or into display cases as soon as possible. The meat-cutting area should be cleaned and sanitized at least once per 8-hr working period and should follow essentially the same methods as indicated earlier for food manufacturing plants.

In the grinding of meat, such as hamburger, separate grinders (or grinder heads) should be used for beef and pork. The reason for this is that pork may contain an infective roundworm, which causes the disease known as trichinosis in humans. In pork, this is usually taken care of by cooking to a temperature that destroys the worm cysts. Hamburger, however, is sometimes eaten undercooked or only lightly heated, in which case the cysts would not be destroyed. If, therefore, the same grinder is used for beef and pork, small pieces of pork containing cysts may contaminate the ground beef. It seems reasonable that a grinder head be used for pork, then washed and used for beef without any hazard. However, there is always the chance that the grinder head will not be thoroughly washed.

Retail display cases for cut meats, chicken, cooked and fresh sausage products, bacon, and cold cuts should be held at temperatures of 32°–38°F (0°–3.3°C) and should be of the closable variety. Also, personnel in charge of display cases should make certain that products move more or less in the order of "first in first out" and that no item remains in the display case for long periods of time.

Large or small canned hams of the type requiring refrigeration should be held, at all times, at temperatures of 38°F (3.3°C) or below. They should *never* be displayed in general store areas, aisles, or windows where there is no refrigeration. Unfortunately, retail outlets do not always observe safe practices.

Fresh produce is often times poorly handled in retail outlets. The cells of such foods continue to respire after they are harvested, and the higher the temperature at which they are held the faster the rate of respiration. Respiration brings about chemical changes in fresh produce that cause a deterioration of quality. Loss of sweetness, loss of succulence, toughening, and the development of off-flavors are some of the changes that may take place in fresh produce because of respiration. For instance, sweet corn on the cob, freshly picked, then held at 35°F (1.7°C) is perfectly good in taste and texture after 15 days of storage. At high temperatures, its quality will be lost in a few hours. Storage areas for fresh produce should be clean and held at 32°–37°F (0°–2.8°C). Potatoes, turnips, and cabbages should be held at about 50°F (10°C), since cabbage and turnips stand up well at this temperature, and potatoes convert starch to sugar at 40°F (4.4°C) or below—becoming sweet. Most fresh produce should be displayed in an area or cabinet held at 32°–37°F (0°–2.8°C) or partially surrounded with ice, since such temperatures maintain quality. A possible exception is lettuce which, if held in ice, must be held in tempered ice (temperature brought up to 32°F [0°C]); otherwise, the produce may freeze, causing the leaves to wilt.

Fish and shellfish, such as shucked clams, oysters, scallops, and shrimp, should be held in a display case surrounded by ice. This provides a temperature of about 33°F (0.6°C) and is the best way to maintain this low temperature, without freezing, for products that are extremely perishable.

Milk, cream, sour cream, cheeses, and butter should be held in an open-top display case, the temperature of which is held at 32°-37°F (0°-2.8°C).

Frozen foods, which are not indefinitely stable, are rarely handled under satisfactory conditions in retail stores. At −30°F (−34.4°C), frozen foods deteriorate at an extremely slow rate. At 0°F (−17.8°C), many foods will have a storage life (no noticeable loss of quality) of at least 6 months, and some foods have a storage life of at least 1 year at this temperature. As the storage temperature is raised above 0°F (−17.8°C), for each 5 degrees F (2.8 degrees C), the rate of deterioration is approximately doubled. Thus, a product that has a storage life of 6 months at 0°F (−17.8°C) will have a storage life of only 3 months at 5°F (−15°C). When frozen foods are delivered to the retail store, they should not be allowed to stand on platforms or in a room at high temperature but should be immediately placed in the frozen storage room. The frozen storage room should always be held at a temperature of 0°F (−17.8°C) or below, preferably at −20°F (−28.9°C). Display cases used for holding frozen foods in the retail area should be of the open-top type, or of the enclosed shelf type. Shelf-type display cases for frozen foods are not suitable unless they are enclosed by doors. The reason for this is that cold air is heavier than warm air; hence, in the open-top case the cold air tends to remain in the area where the foods are held. Shelf-type frozen food cases must be refrigerated by blowing cold air out and over the product. Since this air is heavier than warm air, it tends to flow outward and downward into the room. In display cases of this kind it is, therefore, difficult to maintain temperatures of 0°F (−17.8°C) or below around the entire product. Those items in front where warm air has access are usually surrounded by air temperatures much higher than 0°F (−17.8°C), and hence are subjected to an accelerated rate of deterioration.

Canned foods require some consideration in retail handling. To begin with, the buyer of canned foods for a retail outlet should have the knowledge, or employ personnel with the knowledge, to determine whether or not these products have been sufficiently heat processed for safe consumption. That means that the foods must be heated to the point where all spores of the bacterium known as *Clostridium botulinum* have been destroyed. Actually, in order to prevent spoilage (not disease) by other bacteria, canned foods should be heated beyond the point at which all disease-causing bacteria will have been destroyed.

An adequate backlog of canned foods must be available to the retail store. This means that there must be a warehouse where canned foods are stored. Such warehouses should be held at temperatures not above 75°F (23.9°C), because bacteria known as thermophiles, which are difficult to destroy by heat, may be present as spores in an occasional can of food. These bacteria do not cause disease, but they can cause spoilage of canned foods. Since they are so heat resistant, it would take excess heating to reach the point where all of the thermophilic spores would have been destroyed should they be present. It is fortunate that these bacteria grow only at high temperatures (usually well above 75°F [23.9°C]). For this reason, the temperature of the warehouse where canned foods are stored should be regulated as previously stated. Nor should the storage warehouse for canned foods be held at temperatures below 50°F (10°C), for if this is done, when higher temperatures are reached in this area or when the cans are placed in the retail outlet at higher temperatures, moisture may condense on the surface (the cans may sweat) and cause rusting of the outside surface, which discolors the label and is otherwise unsightly, and it may eventually weaken the can to permit microbial invasion of the contents.

Canned foods, both those stored in the warehouse and those held in retail stores, should be handled on a first-in, first-out basis. The reason for this is that while most canned foods have a relatively long storage life, they are not indefinitely stable. The usual type of deterioration after long periods of storage is due to internal corrosion of the container, which results in a swelled can or in leakage. Deterioration of this type is most often encountered in acid foods, such as tomato products, in which case internal corrosion produces hydrogen gas causing the can to swell. The food in this case may be perfectly edible, but consumers would be running a risk to eat the food from a swelled can since they cannot be sure that the cause of the swelling was not due to gas produced by some disease-causing bacterium. Also, swelled cans sometimes burst, causing the product to be spread over a wide area, creating a considerable mess and bad odors.

THE HAZARD ANALYSIS AND CRITICAL CONTROL POINT SYSTEM (HACCP)

HACCP, a system for assuring the safety of foods, was developed in 1971 in a cooperative effort by the U.S. Army Natick Laboratories, the National Aeronautics and Space Administration, and the Pillsbury Co. The system employs seven elements:

1. Assess potential hazards in all stages of food production, from growing to the finished products.
2. Determine critical points (CCP) where controls are necessary to eliminate or reduce hazards.

3. Establish requirements to be met at each CCP.
4. Establish procedures to monitor each CCP.
5. Establish corrective actions when monitoring uncovers deviations from plan.
6. Establish record-keeping procedures.
7. Establish procedures to monitor effectiveness of HACCP.

HACCP is widely accepted and recommended for all food production, handling, and distribution.

4

Regulatory Agencies

A major evolution in modern societies is the widespread use of food produced and often preserved in areas remote from the consumer. Since consumers do not know how the food was handled, they do not know if it is safe to eat. (In ancient times, slaves and animals were sometimes compelled by their masters to eat food of questioned safety before it was eaten by their masters.) Thus, as the entire population presently requires protection, it is a proper government function to determine the wholesomeness and purity of foods and to protect the consumer against economic fraud as well as health hazard. Yet government seldom assumes this responsibility spontaneously, and protective regulatory legislation is passed and enforced only after consumer-oriented persons or groups stimulate broad public support for government action.

In the United States, the basic regulation covering the safety and legitimacy of commercial foods was not enacted until several states had already passed laws to protect consumers against adulterated and misbranded food and drugs within their own states. It was not until 1906 that the Federal Food and Drug Act was passed, due to the efforts of dedicated people, such as Dr. Harvey W. Wiley. Dr. Wiley is given credit for the enactment of the first federal regulation covering safe and pure foods and drugs. Subsequent additions to federal regulations have followed.

There are several federal agencies for regulating foods and food products sold in the United States, but only three have enforcement authority. These are the Food and Drug Administration (Department of Health, Education and Welfare) and the Meat Inspection Division and Poultry Inspection Service, both of which come under the Department of Agriculture.

THE FOOD AND DRUG ADMINISTRATION

The Food and Drug Administration (FDA) is probably the most important enforcement agency since it regulates all our foods except meat and poultry and, in some instances, can even regulate these products. There are two general regulatory categories: adulteration and misbranding. A food is adulterated if (1) it is filthy, putrid or decomposed, (2) it is produced in unsanitary conditions, (3) it contains any substance deleterious to health. A food is misbranded if (1) it is a food for which standards of identity have been written and it fails to comply with these standards, (2) it is wrongly labeled, (3) it fails to meet the regulations for fill of container.

Adulteration

Adulteration is not difficult to determine since there are tests that can be made to detect sources of contamination such as rodents (hairs, pellets, or urine), insects, dirt, and other detritus. Also, if a food is putrid, this can be detected by the ordinary human senses, a fact that is well known and accepted. However, the detection of decomposition is not easy and often scientists do not agree on what constitutes decomposition of a particular food. Citations based on the decomposition of a food, therefore, frequently have to be settled in court.

Regarding additives that may be present in foods, the administration and the industry know that certain chemicals are toxic and cannot be added to foods at all. The FDA has a GRAS (generally regard as safe) list that specifies which chemicals may be added to foods and, in many instances, how much may be added to a particular food. Many compounds on this list come under what is called the Grandfather Clause, these chemicals having been used in foods for years with no apparent ill effect. For some chemicals that can be added to foods and for any new chemical that will be added, tests have been or will be made by feeding several kinds of animals (e.g., rats, dogs, mice, guinea pigs) a diet containing the chemical over a period of several generations. The results of such tests are determined by observations on the weight and general health of the animals, as well as their ability to breed, and on autopsies and chemical tests for specific enzyme activities, and so on. Time, trained personnel, and special facilities are required for testing a new food additive. This is a very expensive process, requiring, as a rule, the outlay of several hundred thousand dollars, and no producer of such a new compound is apt to initiate such testing, which must satisfy the FDA, unless he is certain that the new additive will provide specific advantages and have great utility.

It is difficult to enforce the section of the law prohibiting substances that may be deleterious to the health of the consumer. For example, pathogenic bacteria, such as the *Salmonella* organisms often present in food, can cause disease and even death. The FDA and food scientists know that poultry and other foods generally contain these organisms but are unable to control the situation. If enforcement were attempted, for instance, in the case of poultry, the whole industry would be shut down, since approximately 25% of the product contains salmonellae. The testing for this group of organisms requires at least two days to obtain results, another factor that serves to impede enforcement. This regulation, therefore, should probably be changed or reworded, since laws that cannot be enforced are useless and lead to unsatisfactory practices.

Foods found to be adulterated are seized by the FDA and destroyed.

Misbranding

If a standard of identify has been set up for a particular food, the food can only contain the ingredients specified in the standard. If the food is found to contain other ingredients or additives, it will be seized and destroyed. As an example, sulfur dioxide is allowed in some foods and might be used to provide good color in ketchup. However, there is a standard of identity for ketchup in which sulfur dioxide is not included. Therefore, if ketchup were found to contain sulfur dioxide, it would be seized and destroyed. Foods for which a standard of identity has been established and that do not conform to these standards are destroyed on the premise that they have no identity. Standards of identity have been set up for some bakery products, cacao products, cereal flours and related products, alimentary pastes, milk and cream, cheeses, processed cheese, some cheese foods and spreads, some canned fruits, fruit preserves and jellies, some canned shellfish, eggs and egg products, oleomargarine, some canned vegetables, canned tomatoes, tomato products, and other foods. A food that is misbranded may be wrongly labeled as to weight, portions, or ingredients if no standard of identity has been established for it. If wholesome, wrongly labeled products need not be destroyed. Instead, they can be relabeled to comply with ingredients, weight, and so on, and sold. If the product fails to meet the "fill of container" requirement, it may be relabeled to specify this fact and sold under the new label.

It should be noted that, theoretically, the FDA can regulate only those foods that are shipped interstate (from one state to another), but there are ways to get around this. For instance, if a company ships one food interstate but not another, both foods may come under the jurisdiction of the FDA.

The U.S. Public Health Service

The U.S. Public Health Service has regulatory authority over the sanitary quality of drinking water and foods served on interstate and international carriers (airlines, trains, etc). This agency carries out research and surveillance on food-borne diseases (infections and intoxications) and sanitary processing and shipping of foods. It is now a part of the FDA. In cooperation with state regulatory agencies, it sets up standards for coastal waters from which bivalve shellfish, such as oysters and clams, may be harvested for consumption. It also sets up specifications for waters from which bivalves may be harvested and then subjected to purification procedures or relayed in approved waters. It also helps set up standards for the bacteriological quality of the bivalve shellfish and for shellfish-growing waters. Shellfish dealers are registered and must keep records indicating the area from which bivalves were harvested, from whom they were purchased, and to whom they were sold. The state and the Public Health authorities keep a list of approved shellfish dealers. It is up to the state authorities to make sanitary surveys of the bivalve growing areas and bacteriological tests of the waters of shellfish-growing areas and of the shellfish. If a particular dealer does not comply with regulations, he is taken off the approved list and any product that he ships interstate will be seized by the FDA. It is also probable that state authorities would seize his product shipped intrastate. Also, if the state program for shellfish sanitation does not meet the requirements of the Public Health Service, all producers within the state are taken off the approved list and no bivalve product can be shipped interstate.

The Public Health Service also sets up standards for milk and cream together with state authorities. This includes the control of disease in dairy herds, the management and milking of herds, the bacteriological quality of raw milk and cream and certified milk, pasteurization procedures including time and temperatures, and the bacteriological quality of pasteurized milk and cream.

The FDA has the power to inspect any food processing or food handling plant and to close any plant it considers to be unsanitary or to be adulterating foods in any way. FDA inspectors inspect some food plants but do not have the personnel to inspect them all even annually. Most enforcement results from chemical or bacteriological analyses of some product. If according to their analysis a product is found to be adulterated, it will be seized and destroyed, either with or without court hearings. In a case where the FDA learned that a certain boat, without freezer capacity, had been fishing for an extraordinarily long time prior to landing its catch, the FDA inspectors waited until the product was filleted, packaged under a particular label, and frozen, then seized the product. This resulted in a court case in which the FDA convinced the judge that the product was decomposed. The product was destroyed and the producers fined.

THE MEAT INSPECTION BUREAU

The Federal Meat Inspection Act, made law in 1906, is administered by the United States Department of Agriculture (USDA) through its Meat Inspection Bureau, a branch of the Agriculture Research Service. This law regulates the safety of meats (beef, pork, lamb) entering into interstate commerce. The Meat Inspection Bureau is also an enforcement agency. It differs from the FDA in that most of the regulation is carried out by inspectors stationed at the plant processing the food. They deal with any food that contains more than a small percentage of meat. When cattle, hogs, or sheep are slaughtered, one or more inspectors (who are veterinarians) must be stationed at the slaughtering plant if any parts of such products are to be shipped interstate. The animals may be inspected prior to slaughter, and if diseased, are destroyed. However, the main inspection comes after slaughter. As the animals are slaughtered, the carcass, entrails, and organs are tagged and identified with a particular carcass. The veterinarian inspectors test the viscera to determine whether or not the animals were diseased. Diseased animal carcasses including organs and entrails are covered with a dye and must be disposed of as tankage and not used for human consumption. (Tankage is slaughterhouse waste that is heat processed and dried and used as fertilizer.)

The Meat Inspection Bureau also has "lay" inspectors. These inspectors have some training but are not veterinarians. Lay inspectors deal primarily with those plants or areas of plants where meat is cut into portions for further processing or for shipment as fresh cuts; where sausages (fresh sausage, frankfurters, bologna and other cooked sausage, dried sausage, etc.) are produced; and where hams, shoulders, and bacon are cured, smoked, and so on. Lay inspectors determine that processing rooms and equipment are clean and sanitary before work is started, and if not satisfactory, the room is tagged and cannot be used for processing until cleaned and sanitized to the satisfaction of the inspector.

The Meat Inspection Bureau maintains lists of approved ingredients for cured and processed products, and it is part of the inspectors' job to determine that nothing is added to processed products that is not on the approved list. Inspectors also check the amounts of some approved materials added to processed products. The Meat Inspection Bureau has laboratories that make some analyses. For instance, a certain amount of water can be added to some cooked sausages or to cured hams. The amount of water allowed is specified (e.g., 10% of the finished product in frankfurters). In frankfurters, the added water gets into the product as ice during the cutting of the meat, one of the reasons for adding water in this case being that of keeping the ingredients (the meat emulsion) cool during cutting, which improves the quality of the finished product. The inspector cannot tell exactly how much water is being added during the cutting, but if he becomes suspicious he will take samples of the finished product, ship them to a bureau laboratory, and have them analyzed for added water. In any case, samples for analysis may be taken periodically from processing plants. The same kind of inspection and analysis may be used for other processed products, including hams.

States also have inspectors who regulate the slaughter and processing of meats that are used intrastate and not shipped interstate. However, such inspection in the past has been far from adequate. In recent years federal authorities decided improvement in the inspection and regulation of local slaughtering and meat-processing plants was essential, and this improvement is presently being implemented.

The USDA periodically inspects (at least twice a year) "custom" slaughter houses (those that slaughter but do not sell the meat). When the plants start selling meat wholesale or retail, the USDA will inspect more frequently. The inspections will be done for sanitation, adherence to USDA standards, and a USDA veterinarian will inspect the carcasses for disease.

The USDA also has a Total Quality Control (TQC) program in which a plant sets up its own regulations that are at least as stringent as those set by the USDA. The plant personnel conduct inspections and keep the records. USDA inspectors will inspect the plants regularly and will check all records closely.

THE POULTRY INSPECTION SERVICE

The Poultry Inspection Service, similar in scope and operation to the Meat Inspection Bureau, is responsible for the inspection of poultry products. An agency within the USDA, it ensures that all poultry sold in interstate commerce is processed in U.S. government-inspected plants and is wholesome. Although poultry inspection is mandatory, the grading of poultry products is voluntary on the part of the processor. Poultry is inspected prior to dressing, during evisceration, during packing, and after packing.

OTHER REGULATORY AND/OR INSPECTION AGENCIES

There are some inspection agencies the activities of which are of a regulatory nature but they are not necessarily enforcement agencies. One of these is the Voluntary Inspection Service of the U.S. Department of Commerce. It is administered by the Department's National Marine Fisheries Service, National Oceanic and Atmospheric Administration. If a fish processor so desires, he may have an inspector stationed in his plant on a permanent basis to assess the premises for sanitary conditions, determine that wholesome ingredients are used, and grade the product. As previously stated, this is an entirely voluntary service, and the processor must pay whatever costs are involved in such an inspection. With this type of inspection, the product is evaluated and graded as A, B, or C in quality, the last grade being the lowest acceptable quality. The packer can label the product accordingly.

Continuous inspection is available for certain canned and frozen fishery products. While the inspectors do not inspect every fish, they do inspect a sufficient number so that all lots of fish are sampled, and since each lot is relatively uniform in quality, unacceptable fish are bound to be identified. This is also true for canned fish. The inspection of frozen fish products does not permit the same degree of confidence, since frozen products are manufactured from blocks of frozen fish or shellfish, usually prepared and frozen outside the United States. It is true that the inspection service can and does sample the finished product to determine quality, but this can only be a spot check that is not adequate to evaluate the quality of the whole pack. There is another reason why grading canned fish is more effective than grading frozen fish. Once the canned product has been processed, the quality does not change to any extent. This is not the case with frozen foods. Frozen fishery products are not indefinitely stable even at 0°F (-17.8°C). At higher temperatures they deteriorate at a much faster rate. It is unfortunate that while manufacturers tend to freeze and store fishery products to a temperature of 0°F (-17.8°C) or below, those who transport such products and especially retailers, during the handling and display of fishery products, tend to hold products at temperatures well above 0°F (-17.8°C). For this reason a frozen fishery product labeled grade A may actually be grade C or substandard by the time that it reaches the consumer.

The USDA has a grading service for fruits, fruit juices, and vegetables, both canned and frozen. Again, for canned fruits and vegetables, the grading is quite effective, but for frozen products the same objections are applicable as to frozen fishery products. To make the grading of frozen foods effective, the temperatures at which these products are shipped, the temperatures at which they are handled and stored at the retail level, and especially the temperatures at which frozen foods are held during display at the retail level must be regulated.

The Environmental Protection Agency (EPA) authorizes and regulates the use of pesticides and other environmental contaminants, and it monitors compliance and provides technical assistance to the states.

The Internal Revenue Service (IRS) enforces, with FDA collaboration, the Federal Alcohol Administration Act and other pertinent regulations that control the commerce of alcoholic beverages (e.g., whiskey, wine, beer, brandy).

The National Bureau of Standards (NBS) is responsible for setting the official standards for units of weights and measures for all commercial products, including foods.

The Office of Technical Services (OTS) issues voluntary "Simplified Practices Recommendations" in order to limit types and sizes of packages, bags, and jars used as food containers.

The Federal Trade Commission (FTC) enforces the provisions of the FTC Act, which prevents unfair and deceptive trade practices.

The regulation and standardization of foods in international trade represent a prodigious and nearly impossible task. Yet the benefits to be derived are of such magnitude that they merit the necessary efforts to achieve them. The Codex Alimentarius Commission, an international organization, has been formed by over 90 countries to establish food standards. Its importance is recognized when we are told that the U.S. FDA detains about 40% of the imported foods that it checks. What of the food shipments that escape inspection? What proportion of the imported foods is mislabeled? What proportion contains harmful substances or is contaminated or adulterated? It is because of these considerations that the FDA detains so much of the imported foods that it checks. The member countries of the Codex Alimentarius send their experts to the international meetings, held in Rome, to help formulate the quality standards that are more strict in some aspects than those of many countries. For example, the International standards require the listing of all ingredients in food formulations. The work done by this international body, slow though it is, should facilitate trade among the member countries, and the risks of food-borne illness and deceptive practices should be substantially reduced.

5

Food Additives

DEFINITION OF FOOD ADDITIVES

Food additives may be defined as chemical substances deliberately added to foods, directly or indirectly, in known and regulated quantities, for purposes of assisting in the processing of foods, preservation of foods, or in improving the flavor, texture, or appearance of foods.

The term does not include chance contaminants. An additive may be reactive or inactive; it may be nutritive or nonnutritive; it should be neither toxic nor hazardous. Some substances, such as pesticides and packaging components, are added to foods unintentionally, and these are, of course, undesirable, and may be hazardous to health. Because of their toxicity, their presence is closely regulated by strict government tolerances.

Many food additives are classified as GRAS ("Generally Regarded As Safe") additives. Additives are classified as GRAS when they have been used without apparent harm for long periods, long before regulations were put into effect.

PHILOSOPHY OF FOOD ADDITIVES

Foods are made entirely of substances that, in the pure form, can be described as chemicals or chemical compounds. It is important to note that our knowledge of the composition of foods, because of its complexity, is by no means complete. For instance, it is reported that one of the most important of humans' natural foods, human milk, contains several hundred chemical compounds.

Unfortunately, the interpretation of the word *chemical* is too often inaccurate. Thus, some consumers are apprehensive about purchasing a food that is preserved by treating it with a chemical with which they are unfamiliar. However, a number of foods may be preserved with table salt, which is a chemical. Consumers are not apprehensive about using salt as a preservative, because they are familiar with it, at least for adding taste and sometimes for bringing out the flavor in foods, yet table salt is definitely a chemical, having the name, sodium chloride, and the formula, NaCl. Refined sugar, vinegar, spices, and other substances that are routinely added to foods are also chemicals or mixtures of chemicals, and we do not question the use of these, either. The characteristics of chemicals that we use with confidence are: (1) familiarity and (2) frequent use. The characteristics of chemicals that arouse skepticism in consumers are that they are uncommon and unfamiliar.

A large number of chemical additives are unfamiliar, and there is a need for regulatory agencies to question their use from the standpoint of safety. Obviously then, we should not fear the use of chemicals, but we do need to screen them for safety when their effects on human health are not known. Some lessons have been learned along these lines. For example, indiscreet use of certain additives used for coloring candy and popcorn was reported to have caused diarrhea in children resulting in the removal of these dyes from the FDA approved list of additives. There are a number of related ideas that must be remembered when dealing with food additives:

- All foods are composed of chemical compounds, many of which can be extracted and added to other foods, in which case they are classified as additives.
- Any additive or chemical compound can be injurious to health when particularly high levels of that compound are added to foods.
- Any additive or chemical compound can be safe to use when particularly low levels of that compound are added to foods.
- It is necessary to evaluate each additive for its usefulness and toxicity in a sensible, scientific way, regardless of how safe its proponents say it is and how toxic its opponents say it is.

The use of radiation for preserving foods has been declared an additive, and whether or not it should be approved by the FDA makes it the prime example of extreme opposition and extreme favor. Quite often, the tendency to take a strong position for the use of an additive might make a proponent overlook or rationalize undesirable investigative facts concerning the additive. On the other hand, opponents tend to make irrational demands of investigators to prove the safety of an additive; for example, opponents to the use of radiation for preserving foods have suggested that radiation should not be approved for preserving foods until all possible chemical effects of the process have been identified. This, without going into detail, is an impossible task. It would be just as impossible to identify all the chemical effects of frying food and of baking food.

Given present capabilities, our most reasonable evaluation of an additive for safety can be made through conventional animal feeding studies. The overall physiological effects that an additive may have on animals of two or three different species over a specified number of generations is the most comprehensive, as well as the most reliable, way to evaluate the safety of a food additive.

It should be remembered that chemical materials cannot be added to foods unless their use, in the quantities added, has been approved by the FDA. Moreover, additives are tested for toxicity in concentrations much greater than those allowed in foods. It should also be remembered that most food additives are components of natural foods and that without these additives the quality of many foods would be greatly inferior to those to which we have become accustomed. The shelf-life or availability of many foods would also be greatly limited were all additives to be eliminated from foods. Food additives are difficult to classify mainly because they overlap each other in numerous combinations of effects. It should be remembered, therefore, that the following classification is not a precise one.

ANTISPOILAGE AGENTS

Although foods can be sterilized (as by heat processing) and contained in such a way as to prevent contamination by microbes during storage, it still is often necessary in some cases to forego sterilization, thus making it necessary to take other steps to prevent microbial degradation of the food. Foods can be protected against microbial attack for long periods (months to years) by holding them at temperatures below freezing (see Chap. 13). They can be preserved for shorter periods (several days) by holding them in ice or in a refrigerator at temperatures in the range 32°- 46°F (0°-7.8°C) (see Chap. 12). Foods can also be preserved by altering them to make them incapable of supporting microbial growth. Drying is an example of this type of preservation. Foods must also be preserved against color and texture changes.

Quite often it is either impossible or undesirable to employ conventional preservation methods, and a large variety of food additives is available for use, alone or in combination with other additives or with mild forms of conventional processes, to preserve foods. Usually, preservatives are used in concentrations of 0.1% or less. Sodium diacetate and sodium or calcium propionate are used in breads to prevent mold growth and the development of bacteria that may produce a slimy material known as rope. Sorbic acid and its salts may be used in bakery products, cheeses, syrups, and pie fillings to prevent mold growth. Sulfur dioxide is used to prevent browning in certain dried fruits and to prevent wild yeast growth in wines used to make vinegar. Benzoic acid and sodium benzoate may be used to inhibit mold and bacterial growth in some fruit juices, oleomargarines, pickles, and condiments. It should also be noted that benzoic acid is a natural component of cranberries.

Salt is an excellent microbial inhibitor, mainly due to its suppression of the water activity (see Chap. 11) of the material to which it is added. Its effectiveness is enhanced when the food is also dried or smoked or both. Smoking also imparts a partial preservative effect.

Weak acids, such as sorbic acid, or salts of weak acids, benzoates, propionates, nitrites, certain chelating agents (chemicals that tie up metals and prevent the catalytic action of metals), and other chemical additives are effective preservatives. Natural spices also have antimicrobial properties. Antibiotics, relatively new antimicrobial agents, have been used as food additives and are still used to preserve animal feeds and human foods in some countries. Their use in human foods is banned in the United States and in some other countries.

Since many antimicrobial agents are generally toxic to humans, their use must be regulated not to exceed established levels beyond which they are hazardous to human health.

Nitrites, proven inhibitors of *Clostridium botulinum,* and nitrates are added to cured meats, not only to prevent botulism, but also to conserve the desirable color as well as add to the flavor of the products.

ANTIOXIDANTS

Antioxidants are food additives used, since about 1947, to stabilize foods that by their composition would otherwise undergo significant loss in quality in the presence of oxygen. Oxidative quality changes in foods include the development of rancidity from the oxidation of unsaturated fats resulting in off-odors and off-flavors and discoloration from oxidation of pigments or other components of the food.

Although it would seem relatively simple to prevent oxidation of foods by proper packaging and precautions during handling, the facts are (1) that oxygen is difficult to exclude from food systems, especially since it is often closely associated with the food and (2) that only minute amounts of oxygen are sufficient to degrade the food.

There is a large number of antioxidants, and although they may function in different ways, the net effect of each is to prevent, delay, or minimize the oxidation of foods to which they are added. One of the ways by which some antioxidants function involves their combination with oxygen. Others prevent oxygen from reacting with components of the food. When only a limited amount of oxygen is present, as in a hermetically sealed container, it is possible for some antioxidants to use up all of the available free oxygen, because they have a relatively great affinity for it. Some antioxidants lose their effectiveness when they combine with oxygen; therefore, there is no advantage to using this type of antioxidant unless the food is enclosed in a system from which oxygen or air can be excluded. In the use of antioxidants, it should be kept in mind that other precautions are necessary to minimize oxidation, since heat, light, and metals are prooxidants, that is, their presence favors oxidative reactions. Many of the antioxidants used in commerce occur naturally in foods (e.g., vitamin C, vitamin E, citric acid, amines, and certain phenolic compounds). However, the amines and the phenolic compounds can be toxic to humans in low concentrations; therefore, they and the synthetic antioxidants require strict regulation of their use in foods. It should be pointed out that the potency of the naturally occurring antioxidants is not as great as that of the commonly used synthetic antioxidants. The antioxidants that are considered to be the most effective and therefore are most widely used are butylated hydroxyanisole (BHA), butylated hydroxytoluene (BHT), and propylgallate. These are usually used in formulations that contain combinations of two or all three of them, and often in combination with even a fourth component, very often citric acid. The main purpose in adding citric acid is for its action as a chelator (a chelator ties up metals, which thereby prevents metal catalysis of oxidative reactions).

Fats and shortenings, especially those used in bakery goods and fried foods, are subject to oxidation and the development of rancidity after cooking. To prevent this, chemical antioxidants in concentrations up to 0.02% of the fat component may be added.

The use of antioxidants is regulated by the Food and Drug Administration and is subject to other regulations, such as the Meat Inspection Act and the Poultry Inspection Act. Their use is limited so that the maximum amount that can be added is generally 0.02% of the fat content of the food; there are some exceptions to, and variations of, that rule.

NUTRIENTS

The need for a balanced and ample nutrient intake by the human body is well known. Although nutrients are available in foods, losses of fractional amounts of some of them through processing, and increasing frequencies of improper dieting, have led to the practice of adding minimum daily requirements, or sizable fractions of minimum daily requirements, of a number of nutrients to popular foods, such as breakfast cereals, baked goods, pasta products, and low-calorie breakfast drinks. Nutrient additives include mainly vitamins, proteins, and minerals.

Vitamin D is an exceptional example of the value of the food additive concept. The major source of vitamin D for humans lies in the existence of a precursor compound lying just under the skin that converts to the vitamin form when we are exposed to the radiant energy of the sun. However, in many cases, exposure to the sun is sporadic and insufficient, especially in areas where there is normally insufficient sunshine or in cases where outdoor activities are of insufficient duration. Thus, vitamin D is added to nearly all commercial milk in a ratio of 400 U.S.P. units per qt (0.95 liter). (Vitamins A, C, and some of the B vitamins are added to some foods.)

The addition of protein concentrate (produced from fish or soybeans) to components of the diet of inhabitants of underdeveloped countries has been used successfully to remedy the high incidence of protein malnutrition. It should be noted that soybean protein is incomplete and requires the addition of some amino acids in which it is deficient. Children, especially, succumb in large numbers to the disease, *kwashiorkor,* that results from insufficient protein intake.

Among minerals, iron has received major attention as a food additive, mainly because of its role in preventing certain anemias.

FLAVORINGS

Flavorings are compounds, many of which are natural, although there are also many synthetic ones, that are added to foods to produce flavors or to modify existing flavors. In the early days of human existence, salt, sugar, vinegar, herbs, spices, smoke, honey, and berries were added to foods to improve their taste or to produce a special, desirable taste. The range of natural and synthetic flavoring available to the modern food technologist is very large. Essential oils form a major source of flavorings. Essential oils are odorous components of plants and plant materials that are the characteristic odors of the materials from which they are extracted. Because of the large production of orange juice, quantities of essential oil of orange are produced as by-products. For this reason, there is little need for the production of synthetic orange flavoring.

Fruit extracts have been used as flavorings, but these are relatively weak when compared to essential oils and oleoresins. An oleoresin is a solvent extract of spices from which the solvent, usually a hydrocarbon, has been removed by distillation. Because of their weak effects, fruit extracts may be intensified by combining them with other flavorings.

Synthetic flavorings are usually less expensive and more plentiful than natural flavorings. On the other hand, natural flavorings are often more acceptable. However, they are quite complex and difficult to reproduce synthetically. In fact, one of the problems with natural flavorings is that they may vary according to season and other uncontrollable variables. Synthetic flavorings, however, can be reproduced quite accurately. Many artificial flavors, such as amyl acetate (artificial banana flavor), benzaldehyde (artificial cherry flavor), and ethyl caproate (artificial pineapple flavor), are added to confectioneries, baked products, soft drinks, and ice cream. These flavorings are added in concentrations of 0.03% or less.

FLAVOR ENHANCERS

Flavorings either impart a particular flavor to foods or modify flavors already present. Flavor enhancers intensify flavors already present, especially when the desirable flavors are relatively weak. Monosodium glutamate (MSG) is one of the best known and most widely used flavor enhancers. This compound occurs naturally in many foods and in a certain seaweed that was used for centuries as a flavor enhancer for soups and other foods. It is only within the last hundred years that the reason for the effectiveness of the seaweed was discovered to be MSG. The way in which MSG enhances flavor is not yet understood. While it is effective at relatively low levels (parts per thousand), there are other compounds called flavor potentiators that also enhance flavors but are extremely powerful, effective in parts per million and even per billion. These compounds have been identified as nucleotides, and their effect is attributed to their synergistic properties (properties that intensify the effect of natural flavor components).

ACIDULANTS

From the root word, *acid,* in acidulants, one can conclude that this class of compounds tends to lower the pH of any food in which the compounds are incorporated. They also enhance desirable flavors, and in many cases, such as in pickled products, are the major taste component. Vinegar (acetic acid, CH_3COOH) is added to relishes, chili sauce, ketchup, and condiments as a flavor component and to aid in the preservation of these products. Since the microbial spoilage of food is inhibited as the pH of a food is lowered, acidulants are used for that purpose in many cases. Many acidulants occur naturally in foods (e.g., citric acid in citrus fruits, malic acid in apples, acetic acid—the major component of vinegars; figs contain all three acids). Tartaric acid is widely used to lend tartness and enhance flavor. Citric acid is widely used in carbonated soft drinks. Phosphoric acid is one of the very few inorganic acids used as an acidulant in foods. It is widely used, comprising 25% of all the acidulants in foods. Citric acid accounts for 60% of all acidulants used in foods.

In addition to their preservative and flavor enhancing effects, acidulants are used to improve gelling properties and texture. Acidulants are also used as cleaners of dairy equipment.

Acidulants may be used in the manufacture of processed cheese and cheese spreads for the purpose of emulsification as well as to provide a desirable tartness.

Acid salts may be added to soft drinks to provide a buffering action (buffers tend to prevent changes in pH) to prevent excess tartness. In some cases, acid salts are used to inhibit mold growth (e.g., calcium propionate is added to bread to prevent mold growth).

ALKALINE COMPOUNDS

Alkaline compounds are compounds that raise the pH. Alkaline compounds, such as sodium hydroxide or potassium hydroxide, may be used to neutralize excess acid that can develop in natural or cultured fermented foods. Thus, the acid in cream may be partially neutralized prior to churning in the manufacture of butter. If this were not done, the excess acid would result in the development of undesirable flavors. Sodium carbonate and sodium bicarbonate are used to refine rendered fats. Alkaline compounds are also added to chlorinated drinking water to adjust the pH to high enough levels to control the corrosive effects of chlorine on pipes, equipment, and so forth. Sodium carbonate is also used in conjunction with other compounds to reduce the amount of hardness in drinking water. Sodium hydroxide is used to modify starches and in the production of caramel. Sodium bicarbonate is used as an ingredient of baking powder, which is used for baked products. It is also a common household item used in a variety of cooking recipes. Alkaline compounds are used in the production of chocolate and in the adjusting of acidity levels in grape juice and other fruit juices that are to be fermented in the production of wine.

It is important to note that some alkaline compounds, such as sodium bicarbonate, are relatively mild and safe to use, while others, such as sodium hydroxide and potassium hydroxide, are relatively powerful reagents and should not be handled by inexperienced people.

SWEETENERS

Sweetening agents are added to a large number of foods and beverages. Table sugar (sucrose), the most commonly used sweetener in this country, and corn sugar and syrup, are covered in Chapter 23 and therefore will not be described in any detail here. Sweeteners include other sugars, as well as an abundance of natural and synthetic agents of varying strengths and caloric values.

Many sweeteners are classified as nonnutritive sweeteners. While this classification might imply a lack of nutritional value, the implication is correct only in a relative sense. That is, the caloric value of a nonnutritive sweetener, like aspartame, for example, is about 4 Cal/g as it is for sugar; however, since it takes only 1 g of aspartame to provide the same sweetness level as about 180 g of sugar (sucrose), it can be seen that the caloric contribution of aspartame is only about 0.5% that of sucrose. It is on this basis that nonnutritive sweeteners are classified.

The presently approved sweeteners are saccharin, fructose, glycyrrhizin, xylitol, mannitol, sorbitol, acesulfame, and aspartame. A group of sweeteners that may have some probability of FDA approval in the future includes cyclamates and neo-DHC (neohesperidin dihydrochalcone). A third group of sweeteners, having only a low probability of FDA approval, includes acetosulfam, D-6-chlorotryptophan, and a nondialyzable, water-soluble extract of the tropical serendipity berry. The miracle berry (different from the serendipity berry) has been included in this last group, but there is no evidence of a sweet principle in the miracle berry.

Fructose

Of the other natural sugars used by humans, fructose (also known as levulose), a monosaccharide ($C_6H_{12}O_6$), is the sweetest (nearly twice as sweet as the table sugar, sucrose); and it is the most water-soluble of the sugars. It is hygroscopic, making it an excellent humectant when used in baked goods. The value of a humectant in baked goods is that it retards their dehydration. Solutions of fructose have a low viscosity that results in lower "body" feel than sucrose but in greater flexibility of use over a wide range of temperatures. Because of its greater solubility and more effective sweetness than sucrose, fructose is a better alternative to sucrose when very sweet solutions are required, as fructose will not crystallize out of solution, whereas sucrose will. Fructose has sometimes been called the fruit sugar, since it occurs in many fruits and berries. It also occurs as a major component in honey, corn syrup, cane sugar, and beet sugar. In fact, sucrose, a disaccharide, is composed of glucose and fructose. Of these two components, the glucose moiety cannot be metabolized by diabetics, and it is for this reason that the ingestion of sucrose cannot be tolerated by diabetics. Fructose, on the other hand, does not require insulin for its metabolism and can, therefore, be used by diabetics with no concern. Its use also appears to reduce the incidence of dental caries. When used with saccharin, it tends to mask the bitter aftertaste of saccharin. As it apparently accelerates the metabolism of alcohol, it has been used to treat those suffering from overdoses of alcohol. It has been recommended as a rapid source of energy for athletes and, in combination with gluconate and saccharin, as an economic, effective, safe, low-calorie sweetener for beverages.

Molasses

Molasses can be considered a by-product of sugar production (see Chap. 23). The use of molasses as a sweetener in human foods is largely in baked goods that include bread, cookies, and cakes. In addition to sweetening, molasses adds flavor and acts as a humectant. It is also used in baked beans and in the production of rum and molasses alcohol. (The greatest use of molasses, however, is in the production of animal feeds.) Molasses comprises about 60% sucrose, but the sucrose content can be lower, depending on the grade of the molasses and on the raw material from which it was produced. Thus, the sucrose content of cane blackstrap (the final fraction of cane molasses) is only about one-half that of beet blackstrap (the final fraction of beet molasses). The fractions produced before the blackstrap are of higher grades and are those usually used for human consumption. Blackstrap generally is used for industrial purposes.

Honey

Honey, a natural viscous syrup, comprises mainly invert sugar. It is produced from the nectars of flowers, which is mainly sucrose, by the action of an invertase enzyme that is secreted by the honey bee. Honey is used as a direct sweetener, as an additive in a number of products, including baked goods, as well as other ways. It is relatively expensive.

Invert sugar, corn sugar, and corn syrup are covered in Chapter 23 and will not be covered here.

Maple Sugar

Maple sugar is produced from the sap of the sugar maple tree. It comprises mainly sucrose and small amounts of other sugars, including invert sugar. Maple sugar is used in the manufacture of candies, fudge, baked goods, and toppings. It is among the most expensive of sweeteners.

Lactose

Lactose ($C_{12}H_{22}O_{11}$), the sugar component of mammalian milks, is less sweet and less water-soluble than sucrose. While babies and young children generally are able to metabolize this sugar, some are unable to do so. The ability to metabolize the sugar appears to decrease with age. When a person is unable to metabolize lactose, the ingestion of milk may cause intestinal discomfort, cramps, and diarrhea. The major source of lactose is whey, a cheese by-product. Because lactose is not as sweet as sucrose, larger amounts can be used in those foods in which the texture benefits from a high solids content.

Maltose

Maltose ($C_{12}H_{22}O_{11}$) or malt sugar is produced during the malting process in brewing (enzyme conversion of starch). It is converted to alcohol by the action of yeasts through an intermediate conversion to dextrose. This sugar is much less sweet than sucrose, and it is used mainly in the manufacture of baked goods and infant foods.

Saccharin

Saccharin, the imide of o-benzosulfonic acid, is used as a sodium or calcium salt. It is about 300 times sweeter than sucrose (table sugar). It may leave a bitter aftertaste, and its safety has been questioned as a result of some animal feeding tests. As an intense sweetener it is useful for diabetics, and it reduces the incidence of dental caries.

Cyclamate

Cyclamate had been used as a nonnutritive sweetener prior to its removal from the FDA approved list of additives. In many cases, it was used together with saccharin. Cyclamate is not as sweet as saccharin by weight, but it is about 30 times sweeter than sucrose. Like saccharin, it has been used as the sodium or calcium salt.

Aspartame

Aspartame is the common name for aspartyl-phenylalanine. It is a combination of the two amino acids from which its name is derived. First produced in 1969, it is reputed to be about 180 times sweeter than sucrose. Like cyclamate, it was approved and later banned by the FDA. Exhaustive evidence of its safety has been presented by animal testing and by definition of its metabolic fate in animals and humans. It was subsequently reinstated, as safe for use, by the FDA.

Unlike saccharin and cyclamate, aspartame leaves no bitter aftertaste. It is quite expensive, about 200 times more so than sucrose, but as it is about 180 times sweeter than sucrose, its cost for obtaining a given unit of sweetness is not much more.

Xylitol

Xylitol is a polyhydric alcohol having the formula $C_5H_7(OH)_5$. It is presently used in chewing gum, mainly because of its noncariogenic property (it has not been found to cause tooth decay). It occurs naturally as a constituent of many fruits and vegetables, and is a normal intermediary product of carbohydrate metabolism in humans and in animals. Commercially, it is produced by the hydrolysis of xylan (which is present in many plants) to xylose, which is then hydrogenated to produce xylitol. The xylitol is then purified and crystallized. Xylitol imparts a sweet taste, which also appears to have a cooling effect. As it is not metabolized by many microorganisms, it is quite stable.

Sorbitol

Sorbitol is a polyhydric alcohol ($C_6H_8(OH)_6$) that is found in red seaweed and in fruits (apples, cherries, peaches, pears and prunes). It was first isolated from the sorb berries of the mountain ash; hence, its name. It is used as an additive because of its humectant property as well as its sweetening effect. It is used in cough syrup, mouthwashes, and toothpaste. Another of its desirable properties is that it is not easily fermented by microorganisms. Because sorbitol is largely transformed to fructose by liver enzymes in the body, it is tolerated by diabetics, since fructose is not dependent on the availability of insulin for its metabolism. Sorbitol can be produced industrially by the electrochemical reduction or catalytic hydrogenation of glucose. However, sorbitol should not be used as the sole sweetener, because its low sweetness intensity would require the ingestion of such amounts of sorbitol as to result in the conversion of fructose into glucose.

Mannitol

Mannitol is a polyhydric alcohol having the formula $C_6H_8(OH)_6$. It is used in chewing gum, pharmaceuticals, and in some foods. It is a naturally occurring sweetener in many plants, algae, and molds. It occurs in the sap of the manna tree, an ash native to southern Italy, and can also be made by the reduction of either of the monosaccharides, mannose or galactose. Industrially, it is produced by electrochemical reduction or catalytic hydrogenation methods. While it is similar to sorbitol in many respects, it is less soluble than sorbitol.

Serendipity Berry

The serendipity berry contains the most intense natural sweetener known. It is the fruit of the plant *Dioscoreophyllum cumminsii,* indigenous to Africa.

While the berry is too sweet to have found use among the natives (it is about 1000 times sweeter than sucrose), parts of the plant are eaten. The water-soluble sweet principle occurs in the pulp of the small fruit (about ½ in. or slightly more than 1 cm in diameter). There is no known use of this naturally occurring sweetener at present. Its chemical structure has not been identified as yet. It appears to be associated with the fruit's protein fraction, but it is believed to be other than proteinaceous.

Miracle Fruit

Miracle fruit, a berry from the plant *Synsepalum dulcificum,* is also indigenous to Africa. While the sweetness value of this berry is in question because it does not always appear to impart sweetness, it has been studied for its sweetness value. In our own experiment with the extract of miracle fruit, performed by placing the extract in the mouth, we found that lemons tasted sweet and not at all acidic but that the extract did not sweeten coffee or other unsweetened foods. We also found that sweetening lemons required about ½ hr before taking effect and that the effect lasted for only about 3 hr. Thus, adding this agent to lemon juice will not make the juice sweet. The juice will only taste sweet about ½ hr after the mouth has been coated with miracle fruit extract. It has been proposed that the effect of this berry's extract is not to sweeten but to numb the ability of the taste buds to detect acidity, allowing the sugar in the lemon to come through.

Dihydrochalcones

Dihydrochalcones are intensely sweet compounds obtained by the hydrogenation of chalcones found in naringin and neohesperidin, two flavanones occurring naturally in grapefruit and oranges. The sweetness levels of the dihydrochalcones vary, but the average is estimated to be about 1000 times sweeter than sucrose. This class of compounds imparts a cooling effect as well as a lingering sweetness effect, desirable characteristics for use in chewing gum. However, there may be a time lag before the sweetness of these compounds is felt; therefore, saccharin is used in combination with them to provide the immediate sweet taste.

Other Sweeteners

A relatively new sweetener called SRI oxime V is prepared from perillartine, an aldoxime. It is reported to be over 400 times sweeter than sucrose and to have no adverse aftertaste, as does saccharin. It would appear to have broad application as a sweetener, although there are no reports of any use thus far.

Sucaryl is a nonnutritive sweetener produced as a salt of sodium or calcium (the latter for the benefit of those who must exclude sodium from their diets).

Glycyrrhizin, a natural sweetener, is 50 times sweeter than sucrose. It is a flavor potentiator on the GRAS list since 1973. A triterpenoid glycoside from the licorice root, it has a licorice flavor.

Thalose is not a sweetener, but it enhances the sweetness of sucrose. Therefore, with its addition, the amount of sucrose required to arrive at the desired level of sweetness can be lowered by about 10%.

Acetosulfam is a synthetic sweetener that tastes similar to saccharin but has only one-half the sweetening effect of saccharin.

D-6-Chlorotryptophan is reported to be about 1300 times sweeter than sucrose. It has no aftertaste or toxicity.

Stevioside is a naturally occurring sweetener having a sweetening effect 300 times greater than sucrose.

Dulcin is several hundred times sweeter than sucrose, but is may never be used because of its toxicity. It is produced by heating p-phenetidine with urea or by reacting p-phenetidine hydrochloride with potassium cyanate.

STARCHES

Although starches differ from each other somewhat, depending on the plant from which they are extracted, they are sufficiently similar chemically to be often classified together as starch. The two basic starch polymers are amylose and amylopectin. Starch is used as a source of carbohydrate, and because it is relatively inexpensive, is often used as an extender. Its properties also make it useful as a thickening agent. The major source of starch is corn, but some starch is also produced from sorghum, potatoes, and wheat.

GUMS

Gums, a class of complex polysaccharides, are defined as materials that are dispersible in water and capable of making the water viscous. Many gums occur naturally in certain land and sea plants. Examples are gum arabic and agar. Many gums, such as the cellulose derivatives, are modified or semisynthetic, and some gums, such as the vinyl polymers, are synthetic. Gums are used to stabilize ice cream and desserts, thicken certain beverages and preserves, stabilize foam in beer, emulsify salad dressings, and form protective coatings for meat, fish, and other products. Gums add "body" and prevent settling of suspended particles in chocolate milk, ice cream, and desserts. They may also prevent the formation of large ice crystals in frozen desserts. A significant potential for the use of gums lies in the production of certain low-calorie foods. For example, the oil(s) in salad dressing can be replaced with gums to result in a product with the normal appearance, texture, and taste but without the calories normally associated with the product.

ENZYMES

Enzymes occur naturally in foods, and their presence may be beneficial or detrimental, depending on the particular enzyme (see Chap. 8 for information on enzymes). When the presence of enzymes is undesirable, steps are taken to inactivate them. When their presence is desirable, either the enzymes or sources of them are intentionally added to foods. Thus, the enzyme papain (from the papaya fruit) is added to steak to tenderize it. Many of the useful enzymes used in food processing are produced by microbes; consequently those microbes producing the desired enzyme(s) may be added intentionally to food materials. For example, specific yeasts are intentionally added in the production of bread, beer, or cheese.

The use of enzymes as food additives presents no problem from the standpoint of safety, since enzymes occur naturally, are nontoxic, and are easily inactivated when desired reactions are completed. Enzymes called amylases are used together with acids to hydrolyze starch in the production of syrups, sugars, and other products.

Invertase

Certain enzymes, such as invertase, split disaccharides, such as sucrose (table sugar), to lower sugars (glucose and levulose). Invertase has many applications, and is used, for example, to prevent crystallization of the sucrose that is used in large amounts in the production of liqueurs. Without invertase, the liqueurs would appear cloudy.

Pectinase

Pectinases are enzymes that split pectin, a polysaccharide that occurs naturally in plant tissues, especially those of fruit. Pectin holds dispersed particles in suspension, as in tomato juice. Since it is desirable to keep the thick suspension in tomato juice, the pectinases that occur naturally in it are inactivated by heat. On the other hand, products such as apple juice are customarily clear, and this is accomplished by adding commercial pectinase to the product, which degrades the pectin in the apple juice, resulting in the settling out of the suspended particles, which are then separated from the clear juice. In the manufacture of clear jellies from fruits, it is first necessary to add pectinase to destroy the naturally occurring pectin in order to clarify the juice. Once the juice has been clarified, pectin has to be added to produce the thick consistency of jelly. The pectinase that was added in the first place must be inactivated as part of the process; otherwise the enzyme would also break down the pectin that is added to produce the thick consistency.

Cellulase

Cellulases are enzymes that can break down cellulose, said to be the most abundant form of carbohydrate in nature. Cellulose, the principal structural material in plants, is insoluble in water and is indigestible by humans and many animals. Ruminants are able to digest cellulose because of a cellulase (produced by microorganisms in the large stomach) contained in their gastric juice. Commercial applications of cellulases are not widespread at present. Cellulases are used for tenderizing fibrous vegetables and other indigestible plant materials for the production of foods or animal feeds. They have other minor uses, as well.

Protease

Proteases are enzymes that break down proteins, polypeptides, and peptides. Peptides are the structural units of which polypeptides consist, and polypeptides are larger structural units that make up the protein. There is a large variety of specific proteases, and each of them attacks protein molecules at different sites, producing a variety of end products. Proteases are used to produce soy sauce from roasted soybeans, cheese from milk, and bread dough from flour. They are also used to chill-proof beer (untreated beer develops an undesirable haze when chilled) and to tenderize meats. Proteases are widely used in the food industry, but they are reported to have even wider use in nonfood applications.

Lipase

Lipases, the lipid (fat or oil) splitting enzymes, have limited commercial application, with oral lipases having the widest. Lipases prepared from oral glands of lambs and calves are used in a controlled way in the production of certain cheeses and other dairy products, as well as lipase-treated butter fat used in the manufacture of candies, confections, and baked products. Lipases are also used to remove fat residuals from egg whites and in drain cleaner preparations.

Glucose Oxidase

Glucose oxidase is an enzyme that specifically catalyzes the oxidation of glucose to gluconic acid. This reaction is important in preventing nonenzymatic browning, since glucose is a reactant in the undesirable browning reaction. The most important application of this enzyme is in the treatment of egg products, especially egg whites, prior to drying. Eggs treated with this enzyme before they are dried do not undergo nonenzymatic browning during storage, since the sugar has been removed. In some cases, the enzyme is added to remove traces of oxygen to prevent oxidative degradation of quality. Examples of this type of application are bottled and canned beverages (especially beer and citrus drinks) and mayonnaise.

Catalase

Catalases are used to break down hydrogen peroxide to water and oxygen. Therefore, catalases are used when the presence of hydrogen peroxide is undesirable or when hydrogen peroxide is used for specific purposes, such as in bleaching, but them must be removed from the system. Examples of the latter case are the uses of hydrogen peroxide for preserving milk in areas where heat pasteurization and refrigeration are unavailable and in the manufacture of cheese from unpasteurized milk. Hydrogen peroxide is produced when sugars are enzymatically removed from eggs to prevent browning during the spray-drying process (see Chap. 17). Catalase is used to convert the unwanted H_2O_2 to water and oxygen.

SEQUESTRANTS

The role of sequestrants is to combine with metals, forming complexes with them and making them unavailable for other reactions.

$$M + S \rightarrow MS$$

where
    M = metal
    S = sequestrant
    MS = complex

Sequestrants, as many other additives used for enhancing specific properties of foods, occur naturally in foods. Many sequestrants have other properties; for example, citric, malic, and tartaric acids are acidulants but they also have sequestering properties.

Since metals catalyze oxidative reactions, sequestrants can be considered to have antioxidant properties. Thus, they stabilize foods against oxidative rancidity and oxidative discoloration. One of the important uses of sequestrants as additives is to protect vitamins, since these important nutrients are especially unstable to metal catalyzed oxidation. Sequestrants are used to stabilize the color of many of the canned products and they help stabilize antioxidants. Sequestrants are especially helpful in stabilizing the color and the lipids in canned fish and shellfish. Since fish and shellfish naturally contain relatively high concentrations of metal, these products normally have poor color stability, and the lipids tend to rancidify during storage.

Sequestrants are also used to stabilize the flavors and odors in dairy products and the color in meat products.

POLYHYDRIC ALCOHOLS

Many polyhydric alcohols (also called polyols) are used to improve texture and moisture retention because of their affinity for water. Many polyols are present in foods naturally, with glycerine being the predominant one. However, only four of the many polyols are allowed as food additives. They are glycerine, sorbitol, mannitol, and propylene glycol. All but the last have a moderately sweet taste (see section on sweeteners), though none are as sweet as sugar. Propylene glycol has a somewhat undesirable bitter taste, but is not unacceptable in small amounts. Sorbitol imparts a cooling sensation. Glycerine, on the other hand, imparts a heating sensation.

Polyols are used in the production of dietetic beverages, candy, gum, and ice cream to contribute to texture as well as to sweetness. These compounds have a less adverse effect on teeth than sugar, due to the fact that they are not fermented as quickly as sugar and are usually washed away before they can be utilized by microorganisms.

SURFACE ACTIVE AGENTS

Surface active agents affect the physical force at the interface of surfaces. Commonly called surfactants, they are present in all natural foods, since by their nature they play a role in the growth process of plants and animals. They are defined as organic compounds that affect surface activities of certain materials. They act as wetting agents, lubricants, dispersing agents, detergents, emulsifiers, solubilizers, and so forth. One use for wetting agents is to reduce the surface tension of materials to permit absorption of water by the material. An example of their use is chocolate mixes used in the home to prepare chocolate milk by adding water.

Dispersions of materials depend on the reduction of interfacial energy, and this can be accomplished by certain surfactants.

Surfactants are used in the production of foods to prevent sticking, such as in untreated peanut butter. Surfactants are also used in cleaning detergents used on food equipment, and they can stabilize or break down foams.

Emulsifiers, such as lecithin, mono- and diglycerides and wetting agents, such as a class of chemicals known as "tweens," may be added to bakery products (to improve volume and texture of the finished products and the working properties of the dough and to prevent staling of the crumb), cake mixes, ice cream, and frozen desserts (to improve whipping properties). Except for the tweens, the chemicals cited above are natural components of certain foods.

COLORANTS

We are accustomed to specific colors in certain foods, and colors often provide a clue to the quality of the foods. Many colorants (compounds that add color to foods) are natural, and these include the yellow from the annatto seed, green from chlorophyll, orange from carotene, brown from burnt sugar, and red from beets, tomatoes, and the cochineal insect.

Some colorants, however, are derived from synthetic dyes. The synthetic dyes in use have been approved by the FDA.

Some compounds are used to produce a white color. Thus, oxidizing agents including benzoyl peroxide, chlorine dioxide, nitrosyl chloride, and chlorine are used to whiten wheat flour, which is pale yellow in color, at the end of its production cycle. Titanium dioxide may be added to some foods, such as artificial cream or coffee whiteners.

LEAVENING AGENTS

Leavening agents are used to enhance the rising of dough in the manufacture of baked products. Inorganic salts, especially ammonium and phosphate salts, favor the growth of yeasts, which produce the carbon dioxide gas that causes dough to rise. Chemical leavening agents that react to form carbon dioxide are also used in baked goods. When either sodium bicarbonate, ammonium carbonate, or ammonium bicarbonate is reacted with either potassium acid tartrate, sodium aluminum tartrate, sodium aluminum phosphate, or tartaric acid, carbon dioxide is produced. Baking powder is a common household leavening agent that contains a mixture of chemical compounds that react to form carbon dioxide, producing the leavening effect.

IONIZING RADIATION

This topic is given only minor mention, because it is not yet of significance in food processing, even though it has been demonstrated to have numerous advantages and considerable potential as a disinfesting agent as well as being a proven preservation process. It is included in this chapter only because it has been legally defined as a food additive even though it is widely recognized and widely described as a food process. For more information, the reader is referred to the book by Josephson and Peterson, 1983 (see Suggested Readings).

6

Foodborne Diseases

Almost all the factors that contribute to food disease result from ignorance of proper food-handling procedures or from the unwillingness of some individuals in food industries (including food processors) to comply with the basic guidelines for proper food handling. Thus, foodborne diseases will continue to occur at unnecessarily high rates as long as (1) food handlers do not employ strict sanitation in both their personal habits and in the maintenance of their work area and equipment, (2) foods are not properly refrigerated, (3) foods are not adequately processed, (4) cross-contamination situations are not avoided and, (5) management does not realize the importance of preventing foodborne diseases. Proper food-handling procedures include rather simple techniques, such as holding at specified temperatures, but they also include complex procedures, such as those for calculating processing times and predicting certain biochemical reactions that might result from processing modifications. Ordinarily, therefore, at some level in the food-processing stage, the services of a professional food technologist are required. Once a food has been properly processed, the remaining handling it undergoes does not require a professional food technologist, but it does require periodic quality control checks by personnel qualified in microbiology and sanitation.

Foodborne diseases are mostly caused by several species of bacteria, although viruses, parasites, amoebas, and other biological, as well as chemical, agents may be responsible.

As has been previously stated, the bacteria in food sometimes have good effects, but sometimes are undesirable in that they may result in the deterioration of foods or may cause disease in humans and other animals. The disease-causing bacteria in foods, or their end products that cause disease, are transmitted through the eating of foods. Foodborne diseases are classified as food infections and food intoxications, although the distinction between the two categories is not clear in some cases (e.g., *Bacillus cereus* and *Clostridium perfringens*).

FOOD INFECTIONS

Food infections are those in which the disease organism is carried through foods to the host (human or animal) where it actually invades the tissues and grows to numbers that cause disease.

Salmonellosis

Salmonellosis is caused when foods contaminated with *Salmonella* bacteria are eaten. At the present time, approximately 42,000 cases of salmonellosis are reported yearly. About 150 deaths annually are due to this disease. However, it is considered that only about 1% of acute digestive illnesses are reported in this country, so that actually there may be many more cases of this disease.

Typhoid fever, of which there are fewer cases than of salmonellosis, hence fewer deaths, is caused by an organism belonging to the *Salmonella* species, but this disease is usually not considered to be the ordinary salmonellosis for three reasons: (1) The ordinary *Salmonella* organisms will infect other animals as well as humans, while the typhoid germ is known to infect only humans; (2) typhoid fever is usually more severe than the ordinary salmonellosis; and (3) in healthy adults, several hundred thousand to several million ordinary *Salmonella* bacteria (cells) must be ingested (eaten) to cause salmonellosis, while the ingestion of even one typhoid cell may cause typhoid fever.

It is known that antibiotics, especially cholramphenicol or some of the modified penicillins, are effective in treating salmonellosis, but since this disease is oftentimes not called to the attention of a physician, it may cause a more severe illness than if it were treated.

The ordinary symptoms of salmonellosis are abdominal pain, diarrhea, chills, frequent vomiting, and prostration. However, there are instances in which much more severe symptoms may be encountered. The incubation period (time after ingesting the organisms until symptoms are evident) is 7–72 hr. In typhoid fever, the incubation period is 7–14 days.

Persons with salmonellosis often become carriers of the organism for a period of time after they have recovered from the disease. That is, they continue to discharge the organisms in their feces. Because of this, carriers often contaminate their hands with these organisms that may not be removed completely even after thorough washing. Hence, if carriers handle foods that are to be eaten by others, they may contaminate them with these bacteria, and in this manner, transmit the disease to others. In most cases, the carrier stage does not persist longer than 12 weeks after symptoms with salmonellosis, and for shorter periods with typhoid fever. However, there are isolated cases in which the carrier stage lasts much longer than 12 weeks, and 2–5% of those ill with typhoid fever may become permanent carriers.

The *Salmonella* bacteria are rod-shaped; they do not form spores, and thus are not especially heat-resistant. They are motile (can move about in the water, in foods, or other materials in which they are found) and will grow either with or without air (oxygen). At the present time, more than 2,000 types of *Salmonella* bacteria are known, all of which are considered to be infective to man. Obviously, these organisms are very widespread.

Whereas it is considered that many *Salmonella* bacteria must be taken in to cause the disease in a normal adult, it is known that the very old and especially the very young may contract the disease after ingesting (eating) only a few of these organisms. Therefore, any food, especially a food that can be eaten without cooking, should be kept essentially free of these bacteria.

The *Salmonella* bacteria grow at temperatures near 95°F (35.6°C), but they will also grow (more slowly at both higher and lower temperatures than this. It has also been found that many foods are suitable for the growth of these organisms and that in some foods they will grow slowly at temperatures as low as 44°F (6.7°C) or as high as 114°F (45.5°C). Moreover, since the destruction of bacteria by heat is a matter that involves both time and temperatures as well as the degree to which a food protects bacteria; temperatures as high as 140°F (60°C) may be required to bring about marked decreases in these bacteria during the cooking of some foods.

Regarding the destruction of bacteria by heat, it should be explained that as they are heated and a temperature is reached at which they are destroyed, they are not all destroyed at once. For instance, if at 120°F (48.9°C), 90% of the organisms would be destroyed in a period of 5 min, it would take 10 min to kill 99% of the organisms, 15 min to kill 99.9% of the organisms, and so on. It should be noted that if some of these *Salmonella* organisms in foods survive whatever heating they receive during cooking, and the food is thereafter held at temperatures at which they will grow [44°–110°F (6.7°–43.3°C)], especially at room temperatures, the organisms may grow again to large numbers.

Some types of cooking are not sufficient to destroy all *Salmonella* bacteria that may be present in foods. Examples of cooked foods in which these organisms may survive are scrambled, boiled, or fried eggs, meringue, turkey stuffing, oysters in oyster stew, steamed clams, and some meat dishes. Foods eaten raw or without further cooking, such as clams, oysters, milk powder, cooked crabmeat, and smoked fish, may be infective should they be contaminated with *Salmonella* bacteria. These foods should be kept free from *Salmonella* bacteria, especially since they may be eaten by young people who are quite subject to infections of this kind.

Shellfish, egg products, prepared salads, and to some extent, raw and cooked meats have often been associated with the transmission of salmonellosis. Raw shellfish may be taken from waters contaminated with *Salmonella* bacteria and cooked shellfish meats may be contaminated by humans since they are usually removed from their shell by hand. Poultry of all types, beef cattle, and hogs may have salmonellosis or be carriers of the organism causing the disease; hence under conditions of cooking in which these organisms are not destroyed, they may be transmitted to humans.

It has been reported that 2.6–7% of all fresh eggs are contaminated with *Salmonella*. The USDA recommends cooking all eggs until the yolks are solid to ensure destruction of all *Salmonellae*.

Pets, such as cats and dogs, can have salmonellosis and be carriers of the causative organism. Since this is the case, children, especially the very young, who handle materials contaminated by pets and who are very subject to contracting the disease, may contract salmonellosis from pets.

It may be wondered why animals should have salmonellosis. The reason seems to be that their feeds, especially fish meal, meat meal, and bone meal, fed to them as supplements, often contain *Salmonella* bacteria. This is also true of some of the dried types of food used for feeding pets.

Methods or procedures that would help to eliminate salmonellosis or greatly decrease the number of cases are listed in the following paragraphs.

1. Good sanitation methods and procedures in food manufacturing plants, in restaurants and institutions serving foods and in the home are essential. This includes not only the cleaning and sanitizing of equipment and utensils, the elimination of insects and rodents, and the cleaning and sanitizing of floors, walls and so on, but also the personal cleanliness of workers or those preparing and serving foods. All personnel should wash and sanitize their hands prior to handling foods once having left their working stations for any reason.

2. All foods should be held at temperatures of 40°F (4.4°C) or below when not being cooked, prepared for cooking or being served. This would not eliminate *Salmonella* organisms from foods, but it would prevent their growth in the foods so that their number would be too small to cause salmonellosis in healthy adults.

3. Foods that can be eaten without further cooking should be produced under the best conditions of sanitation, and some foods of this type, such as milk powder, should be subjected to frequent bacteriological

examination to determine that they are essentially free of *Salmonella* bacteria.

4. Where possible, foods (poultry stuffings, etc.) should be cooked to temperatures (at least 150°F [65.6°C]) at which it can be assumed that all *Salmonella* bacteria have been destroyed.

5. Egg products (dried or frozen) should be pasteurized (heated to 140°F [60°C] for 3-4 min), then cooled prior to drying or freezing.

6. Flocks of poultry known to have salmonellosis (this can be determined by testing) should be eliminated as egg producers. This can be done without economic loss since such poultry may be used as food.

7. The food, especially protein supplements, given to pets and other animals, should be treated to eliminate the *Salmonella* bacteria that infect these animals. This can be done, for instance, by pelletizing the food or supplements, a treatment that raises the temperature sufficiently to destroy many of the bacteria that might be present.

8. Animals that have died from disease should not be eaten. (This rule is sometimes not observed on farms.)

Shigellosis

Shigellosis, sometimes called bacillary dysentery, is a food infection caused by bacteria of the genus (group) known as *Shigella*. Each year, there are about 17,000 cases of shigellosis reported. There is a higher mortality rate with shigellosis than with salmonellosis.

The ordinary symptoms of shigellosis are diarrhea with bloody stools (feces), abdominal cramps, and some fever. In severe cases, the symptoms are much more complex. There are only about 10 known species or types of *Shigella* bacteria as compared with more than 2000 for *Salmonella*. However, one of these organisms, *Shigella dysenteriae*, usually causes a much more severe disease than either *Salmonella* or other *Shigella* bacteria. The incubation period (time after ingesting the bacteria before symptoms are evident) is said to be as long as 7 days with an average of 4 days.

The *Shigella* bacteria are nonmotile (do not move about in the solutions in which they live). They are rod-shaped cells that will grow in both the presence and absence of oxygen. They do not form spores.

As in the case of salmonellosis, people may become carriers of the *Shigella* organism after they have had the disease, hence may become a source of contamination or infection to others who eat foods that they have handled. However, the carrier stage with shigellosis is shorter than is the case with salmonellosis.

Shigellosis is transmitted chiefly through water or milk, but the disease has also been transmitted through the eating of soft, moist foods, such as potato salad. At the present time, it is believed that when foods become the source of the organism in *Shigella* infections they have been contaminated, directly or indirectly, with small amounts of human fecal discharges.

It has been reported that the optimum growth temperature for *Shigella* bacteria is about 98.6°F (37°C) and that the range in which growth can occur is 50°–104°F (10°–40°C). They are relatively sensitive to heat and can tolerate up to 6% salt.

Certain control methods may be noted based on the knowledge of how food and drink should be handled.

1. Since water is a known source of the organism causing shigellosis, all water used for drinking, for adding to foods or for the cleaning and sanitizing of equipment and eating utensils should be potable (drinkable). The potability of water is determined by sanitary surveys and by bacterial tests made on samples of the water. Any food-manufacturing or food-serving operation should use only water known to be potable. Municipal water supplies should be checked periodically to determine that they are not polluted (contaminated with human or animal discharges). In some cases, water from deep wells from sources not connected with the municipal water supply is used for foods and cleaning. Also, sea water is sometimes used for cleanup in food-serving or food-manufacturing operations. In such instances, management should arrange for bacterial tests to be made on such water supplies at frequent intervals to determine that they are not polluted.

2. Since it is good practice in food handling to refrigerate foods not in use, another method of controlling shigellosis is to hold foods at 40°F (4.4°C) or below at all times when they are not being served or prepared for serving.

3. It is known that humans may become *Shigella* carriers; therefore, in food-handling operations such as food manufacturing, the preparing of food for serving or the serving of food, personnel known to have had an intestinal disease should be excluded from any tasks that would bring them into direct contact with any food.

Vibriosis

Vibriosis, a disease caused by the bacterium *Vibrio parahaemolyticus*, was first identified in Japan where there were outbreaks involving the infection of many people. A few cases have been reported in the United States. Between 1978 and 1982, 164 cases were reported in the United States. This disease, unlike others that may be transferred from many foods, is contracted almost solely from seafood. With the increased consumption of seafood in the United States, this organism may gain importance in its implications in foodborne disease.

The symptoms of vibriosis are abdominal pain, nausea, vomiting with diarrhea, and occasional blood and mucus in the stools (feces). A fever involving a 1°–2°F (0.55°–1.1°C) rise in temperature is experienced in 60–70% of the cases. The period of incubation after ingestion (eating) of the organism is 15–17 hr and the symptoms last for 1–2 days. Whether or not people who have had this disease become carriers is not known.

The organism causing vibriosis is a short, curved, rod-shaped, motile cell. It grows with or without oxygen and is believed to require 2–4% sodium chloride for growth. The organism is found naturally in the ocean, and, since it grows fastest at 86°–104°F (30°–40°C), is found in highest concentrations near the shoreline during the summer months.

Raw fish and molluscs (squid, octopus) have been the foods most often involved in the transmission of vibriosis, but it is known to be present sometimes in shellfish, such as clams and oysters, and has also been found in cooked crab meat. The extent to which the latter foods may have transmitted the organism and caused the disease is not known.

The control of vibriosis would appear to involve the following precautions:

1. Since the *Vibrio* is found in high concentrations in seawater only during the period in which coastal waters are quite warm, it would appear to be preferable not to eat raw molluscs (squid, octopus, clams, and oysters) during the months of July, August, and September in temperate climates or in whatever months the coastal waters of a particular region are warmest.

2. Since *Vibrio parahaemolyticus* is quite heat-sensitive and would be destroyed by whatever cooking is necessary to remove crab meat from the shell, the presence of the organism in cooked crab meat must have been due to contamination after cooking. This indicates that good food plant sanitation is a method of controlling vibriosis. It should be noted that some plants that process marine foods use seawater for the cleaning of equipment, floors, and so forth. This should not be allowed; the use of potable fresh water that has been adequately chlorinated for the cleaning and sanitizing of food plants and food-plant equipment is a method of controlling vibriosis.

Cholera

Cholera is rarely encountered in the United States; however, sporadic cases occur during summer months along coastal areas. The outbreaks generally result from consuming inadequately cooked crabs or oysters. The risk of contracting cholera is markedly decreased by thoroughly cooking shellfish and preventing their recontamination from surfaces or containers holding raw shellfish.

In the Near and Far East, cholera causes, from time to time, much sickness and death. The symptoms of cholera include diarrhea with an abundance of watery stools, vomiting, and prostration. Eventually, since the patient is unable to retain water taken by mouth, dehydration becomes a weakening factor in the disease. Due to the rundown condition of the patient, secondary (other types) infection may set in.

The organism causing cholera is *Vibrio cholerae*. It is a short curved rod that is motile. This bacterium is aerobic (requires oxygen to grow).

Cholera is ordinarily transmitted through drinking water, but it can be transmitted through contaminated foods that have been washed in polluted water or handled by persons having the disease.

The control of cholera appears to require mainly pure water for drinking, adding to foods, and cleaning and sanitizing utensils and equipment used for the manufacture, preparation, and serving of foods.

Trichinosis

Trichinosis is not a bacterial disease. It is caused by the microscopic roundworm, *Trichinella spiralis*. Approximately 100 cases of the disease are reported in this country each year, with an indeterminate number of unreported cases. There are also a few deaths attributed to this disease each year. Trichinosis is transmitted through the eating of pork, although some wild game, such as bear, has also been known to cause trichinosis. Many of the reported cases are due to pork processed by farmers or local butchers. However, some of the products of larger packers have also transmitted this disease.

The symptoms of trichinosis vary with the number of organisms ingested. If large numbers of larvae (stage of the life cycle of the worm) are eaten, nausea, vomiting and diarrhea develop 1–4 days after the food is eaten. If only a few organisms are eaten, symptoms may be absent. On the seventh day after they are taken in, the larvae (produced by the adult worms) migrate from the intestines to the muscles, causing an intermittent fever as high as 104°F (40°C) that can last for a few weeks. The upper eyelids may swell due to the accumulation of fluids. Once the larvae have located in areas between the muscle fibers, a cyst is formed that becomes calcified. In this state, the larvae remain dormant in the body over a period of years.

The trichina organisms in meat are present as the larval stage of a roundworm, and in the human intestine, develop into adult roundworms. The adult worms unite sexually and the females produce larvae that migrate from the intestine to the muscle tissues.

The following paragraphs describe a number of ways in which trichinosis can be controlled or prevented.

1. Since the trichina larvae are destroyed by a temperature of 137°F (58.3°C), fresh pork should not be eaten unless all parts have been heated to this temperature or higher. It is a good general rule never to eat fresh pork that shows any pink or red color or that has not been heated to the point where no indication of uncooked meat fluids can be seen.

2. The USDA has several rules governing the processing of pork sold as cured products. (a) The fresh pork shall have been frozen and held at 5° to −20°F (−15° to −28.9°C) for a period of 6–30 days, the time of holding depending on the temperature at which it is held and the size of the portion of pork; (b) all parts of the cured product shall have been heated to at least 137°F (58.3°C) in ready-to-eat products; (c) for dried, summer-type sausage (Italian salami, cervelat, etc.), the product shall have curing compounds added, after which it must be held for at least 40 days at temperatures not lower than 45°F (7.2°C).

3. The cooking of garbage to be fed to hogs is considered to be a method of controlling trichinosis since uncooked pork may be present therein. Such pork might contaminate the hog eating it, thus causing it to be a source of infection to humans.

Amebiasis

Amebiasis, as trichinosis, is not a bacterial disease. A single-celled animal (an amoeba) causes amebic dysentery in humans. The organism is called *Endamoeba histolytica.*

Amebiasis varies greatly in symptoms from patient to patient and periodically in severity in the same patient. Diarrhea is a common symptom of the disease, and it may be persistent and severe, mild, or occasional. Abdominal pain, fatigue and fever are sometimes encountered. Incubation lasts from 2 days to several months, but is usually 3–4 weeks.

The control of amebiasis is essentially a matter of good sanitary procedures. (1) Drinking water, water added to foods, and water used for washing and sanitizing of equipment and utensils and for irrigation of crops should be potable. (2) Water to be used for foods or for equipment or utensils that contact foods, taken from deep wells, lakes, or ponds, should be tested periodically for bacteriological safety. Although this is not a bacterial disease, it appears to occur when bacteria indicative of pollution with human discharges are present. (3) Persons known to have had amebic dysentery should be rigidly excluded from food handling of any kind.

Other Food Infections

Tuberculosis (caused by *Corynebacterium tuberculosis*) and brucellosis (caused by *Brucella melitensis* and also known as undulant fever) are diseases that in the past were transmitted through milk but have been controlled in recent years by heat pasteurization of milk and the testing of dairy herds, which eliminated infected animals.

The ingestion of foods may be involved in infectious hepatitis when infected food handlers who are careless in their personal habits are involved in preparing and/or serving food to others, or when contaminated shellfish are eaten raw or without adequate cooking.

Streptococcal infection is quite rare and can be prevented by pasteurization.

Taenia solium (a tapeworm that may infest pork), *Taenia saginatta* (a tapeworm sometimes found in beef), and *Diphyllobothrium latum* (a tapeworm sometimes found in fish) all cause illness in humans, but none of these pose any hazard when foods are thoroughly cooked. Small worms of the genus *Anisakis* may also infect fish and cause illness in humans when the infected fish is not properly cooked.

Listeria monocytogenes has attracted attention because of two cheese-related outbreaks that resulted in cases of meningitis, miscarriage, and perinatal septicemia. *L. monocytogenes* has been implicated in well over 300 reported cases of listeriosis that resulted in approximately 100 deaths. These outbreaks also had a significant economical impact on the dairy industry, which suffered more than $66 million in losses due to product recalls. The ability of this organism to grow at refrigeration temperatures in combination with its appearance in raw and processed meats, poultry, vegetables, and seafood make it a serious threat to susceptible consumers and to the entire food industry. It has also survived the minimum high-temperature–short-time treatment for pasteurized milk (161°F [71.7°C] for 15 sec) and the standard treatment for cottage cheese manufacturing (135°F [57.2°C] for 30 min).

Yersinia enterocolitica is another psychotropic organism that has been the causative foodborne pathogen in raw and pasteurized milk, and contaminated water. Unlike *L. monocytogenes*, it is destroyed by normal pasteurization. Yersiniosis usually results in enterocolitis, characterized by diarrhea, fever, and severe abdominal pain in the lower right quadrant. This illness has been incorrectly diagnosed as appendicitis and has resulted in unnecessary appendectomies. The organism is widely distributed and outbreaks have been traced to a wide variety of foods, such as milk that had contaminated chocolate syrup added to it after pasteurization and tofu that was packed in contaminated spring water.

Campylobacter jejuni outbreaks have been linked to consumption of raw milk, cake icing, eggs, poultry, and beef. These underscore the need for thorough cooking and proper handling of raw products. *Campylobacter* is emerging as a leading cause of gastroenteritis in humans. Reduced oxygen levels are required for growth (microaerophilic) and the bacteria are destroyed easily by heat. *C. jejuni* is part of the intestinal microflora of mammals and birds and has been isolated from feces of healthy swine, cattle, dogs, cats, rabbits, rodents, chickens, turkeys, and wild birds. Fecal matter from healthy mammals and birds is probably the major source of this organism in our foods.

A strain of *Escherichia coli* (serotype 0157:H7) has become the causative agent in hemorrhagic colitis, resulting in severe abdominal cramps and watery, grossly bloody diarrhea and hemolytic uremic syndrome, which is the leading cause of acute renal failure in children. Vehicles of infection for this organism have been raw ground beef, ground beef sandwiches, raw milk, pork, lamb, and chicken. Prevention of this disease can be accomplished by proper cooking of ground beef and prevention of cross–contamination from raw foods and food handlers.

Other food infections have implicated *Bacillus cereus, Aeromonas hydrophilia, Arizona hinshawaii,* and *Plesimonas shigelloides.*

Viruses are obligate parasites and do not grow on culture media as do molds and bacteria. Viruses also do not replicate in foods and therefore numbers will not increase during storage, preparation, and transportation. Sanitary methods must be imposed to prevent contamination of foods with intestinal viruses. Foods can serve as a vehicle of infection for viruses even though the organisms do not proliferate in the food. Viral hepatitis of food origin is a good example of what can happen if proper handling methods are not carefully practiced.

FOOD INTOXICATIONS

Food intoxications are those diseases in which the causative organism grows in the food and produces a chemical substance in the food that is toxic to humans and other animals.

Staphylococcal Poisoning

The symptoms of staphylococcal poisoning are nausea, vomiting, abdominal cramps, diarrhea, and prostration. While the symptoms last, suffering may be acute, but this is usually for a period of only a few hours. Generally, the patient recovers without complications. The incubation period after ingestion or eating food containing the toxin is from 1 to 7 hr, usually 3 to 6 hr. Staphylococcal poisoning is often wrongly called ptomaine poisoning. Ptomaines are produced by bacteria in some foods when extreme decomposition occurs. Most ptomaines are not poisonous, and it is unlikely that many people would eat foods decomposed to this extent. It is probable, therefore, that ptomaine poisoning rarely occurs.

The bacterium that causes staphylococcus poisoning is *Staphylococcus aureus,* the same bacterium that causes white-head pimples, infections, boils, and carbuncles. These cells are spherical or ovoid in shape, nonmotile, and, in liquid cultures, arrange themselves in grapelike clusters, in small groups, in pairs, or in short chains. They grow best in the presence of air (oxygen), but they will also grow in the absence of air. They will grow in media or in foods that contain as much as 10% salt (sodium chloride). When these organisms grow in foods they produce a toxin that can be filtered away from the food and from the bacterial cells. The toxin is not destroyed by cooking.

Almost any food (except acid products) is suitable for the growth of *Staphylococcus aureus,* but certain foods have been most often the cause of staphylococcal poisoning. The food types most frequently involved in this disease are ham and ham products, bakery goods with egg, custard fillings, chicken products and especially chicken salad, potato salad, and cheddar cheese. The reason why ham products are frequently involved is that in their preparation they may become contaminated with *Staphylococcus aureus,* and since this product contains 2–3% salt, other bacteria that might grow and inhibit the growth of staphylococci are themselves inhibited by the salt. Also, people who handle ham and its products are apt to believe that such foods are not perishable. However, ham and ham products are perishable and should always be held at 40°F (4.4°C) or below.

The toxin produced by *Staphylococcus aureus* is not readily destroyed by heat. With most cooking methods, the organism itself would be destroyed, but if the organism has grown and produced toxin prior to cooking, the toxin would still be present. Therefore, such foods as milk powder have caused staphylococcal poisoning, yet no living staphylococci could be isolated from them. In the case of milk powder, the bacteria were destroyed during the heating required for drying the milk.

Humans are the main source of the organism causing staphylococcal poisoning. It has been found that approximately 40% of normal human adults carry *Staphylococcus aureus* in their noses and throats. Thus, the fingertips and hands often become contaminated with the organism. Also, any person having infected (containing pus) cuts or abrasions is a definite source of the organism. Cows may also be a source of *Staphylococcus aureus*, particularly if the animals have mastitis (an infection of the udder).

In foods, *Staphylococcus aureus* will grow at temperatures as low as 44°F (6.7°C) and as high as 112°F (44.4°C). In some foods (turkey stuffing), temperatures as high as 120°F (48.9°C) have sometimes been necessary to destroy the organism.

Staphylococcal poisoning usually occurs after a food has been held at temperatures that allow the organism to grow at relatively fast rates.

Methods of controlling staphylococcal poisoning are:

1. Hold all foods, when not being eaten or prepared for eating, at temperatures of 40°F (4.4°C) or below.
2. Prohibit all persons having boils, carbuncles or pussy abrasions or cuts on their hands from handling foods.
3. Require all personnel handling food in food manufacturing or food serving establishments to wash and sanitize (with such solutions as chlorine or one of the iodophors) their hands prior to performing their particular tasks.
4. Eliminate use of milk from cows with mastitis for human consumption.

Botulism

Botulism is an unusual disease occurring only rarely (about 15 cases per year in the United States) but with a high mortality rate (in the past, over 50%, but more recently, about 30%). The symptoms of botulism are vomiting, constipation, difficulty of eye movement, double vision, difficulty in speaking, abdominal distension and a red, raw sore throat. In severe cases, and this disease is usually severe, the breathing mechanism and eventually heart action are affected, often resulting in death.

There are seven types (A, B, C, D, E, F, G) of the bacterium *Clostridium botulinum* that may cause botulism in humans or other animals. The types that affect humans most often are A, B, and E. Humans are most susceptible to the toxin of types A and E. The botulinum organisms are spore formers that have some heat resistance, and they grow only in the absence of oxygen (air) or under conditions in which oxygen is quickly taken up by chemical substances (reducing compounds) present in some foods. The toxin is produced in the food by the bacteria before the food is eaten. Whereas the various types (A through F) of *Clostridium botulinum* are classified mainly by the fact that different antitoxins are required to neutralize each of the different toxins, there are some differences in the growth (cultural) characteristics of the cells of the different types. The types of *Clostridium botulinum* have different minimum temperatures for growth. Types E, F, and some B will grow at temperatures as low as 38°F (3.3°C), although growth will be comparatively slow at this temperature, while types A and B will not grow at temperatures below 50°F (10°C). The maximum growth rate for all types is at 86°-95°F (30°-35°C).

Unlike the toxin produced by *Staphylococcus aureus*, that produced by *Clostridium botulinum* is readily destroyed by heat. In foods, all botulinum toxins present would be destroyed by bringing the temperature to that of the boiling point of water (212°F [100°C]). Destruction of the toxin starts at temperatures well below 212°F (100°C). This is a fortunate circumstance, since most cases of botulism are caused by home-canned foods, many of which are heated prior to serving. This heating has no doubt saved many lives, since while the organism itself may not be destroyed by such heating, the toxin is usually destroyed, and it is the toxin, not the organism, that causes the disease.

Clostridium botulinum will not grow in acid foods (pH 4.5 or below), yet there have been some acid foods (pears, apricots, tomatoes) that have been involved in causing the disease. In such cases, it is believed that some other organism (mold, yeast or bacterium) has first grown and raised the pH of the food to the point where *Clostridium botulinum* would grow.

Botulinum toxin affects the nerves associated with the automatic functions of the body (contraction and dilation of blood vessels, breathing, heart action, etc.). At least in the case of type E poisoning, even when symptoms are recognized, the patient may be treated with antitoxin and eventually recover. With type A botulism, the situation is not so certain, and it is considered by some that once symptoms have occurred, the toxin is fixed, and antitoxin treatment does little good. Since the toxin blocks the function of the nerve synapses, the voluntary nervous system also becomes affected.

Since most cases of botulism are caused by home-canned foods, one method of control would be to make sure that all vulnerable home-canned foods are pressure cooked at times and temperatures suitable to destroy all spores of *Clostridium botulinum* that may be present. Pamphlets are available from the USDA that specify times and temperatures for sterilizing different products in different size containers.

Though extremely rare, there have been some commercially canned products that have caused botulism. All manufacturers of such products should have technical advisors who can determine that the heat processes given their products are sufficient to destroy all spores of *Clostridium botulinum* that may be present.

Since types E and F *Clostridium botulinum* will grow at temperatures as low as 38°F (3.3°C), all flesh-type foods, especially fish (since type E is often present), should be stored at temperatures below 38°F (3.3°C).

A good control precaution is to heat all canned vegetables (especially home-canned) to the boiling point prior to serving.

Infant botulism, first recognized in the 1970s, is not a foodborne disease.

However, it is caused by *Clostridium botulinum* that grows in the intestine, possibly due to the lack of the development of a normal intestinal flora, and it produces toxin there.

Perfringens Poisoning

Perfringens poisoning has sometimes been classified as a food infection and at other times as a food intoxication. Current research indicates that when this organism grows in foods, it produces a substance (an enzyme or other compound) that causes an intestinal disturbance in humans.

Perfringens poisoning is caused by *Clostridium perfringens* that like *Clostridium botulinum*, grows only in the absence of oxygen. Also, as in the case of the botulism organism, perfringens is a spore-forming bacterium, although the spores of this organism are not as heat-resistant as those of some types of the botulinum spores. The symptoms of perfringens poisoning are diarrhea and abdominal pain or colic. The illness occurs 8–22 hr after the food has been eaten, and the symptoms are of short duration (one day or less). The number of people involved in an outbreak is quite often comparatively large. In perfringens poisoning, what ordinarily happens is that meat or poultry is cooked, then held at comparatively high temperatures, then served. The spores survive the cooking since they have some heat resistance; then when the meat or gravy is held at room temperature or on a steam table where the temperature is below 140°F (60°C), the spores grow out to large numbers, causing illness.

In order to control perfringens poisoning, meats and gravies should be refrigerated at temperatures of 40°F (4.4°C) or below shortly after cooking if not immediately eaten, or be held at temperatures not lower than 140°F (60°C) in preparation for serving.

Other Food Intoxications

Other diseases may occur from the accidental accumulation of toxins in foods exposed to unusual environmental concentrations of chemical or biological toxins from polluted areas. In such cases, the toxins are not easily removed or destroyed; therefore, we must rely on our regulatory and public health agencies to make periodic inspections of foods that are suspect, as well as the area from which they are produced.

Bacillus cereus gastroenteritis is listed by some as a food intoxication because it is believed that toxin is released in the food as a result of cell autolysis. Surveys of foods and ingredients have shown high percentages containing *B. cereus*. High numbers of the viable cells are required for symptoms to develop. These include abdominal cramps, watery diarrhea, and some vom-

iting. *B. cereus* is a spore former and can survive some cooking temperatures. Quick cooling of foods, proper holding temperatures for hot foods
(140°F [60°C] or higher), and proper reheating of leftovers to at least 165°F
(73.9°C) are necessary for prevention.

Mycotoxins are produced by molds. Some are highly toxic to many animals and potentially to humans. Aflatoxins are the most widely studied of
the mycotoxins. As of 1980, 14 mycotoxins were recognized as carcinogens.
The FDA has recognized the potential danger of mycotoxins and has established allowable action levels.

II

Causes of
Food Changes

7

Microbial Activity

Foods are normally contaminated with microbes (or microorganisms). They are so small that we need a microscope to see them. Microbes include bacteria, yeasts, molds, algae, and protozoans. However, the organisms that normally contaminate and spoil foods are the bacteria, with yeasts and molds of secondary importance. This chapter deals primarily with bacteria, yeasts, and molds.

Under normal conditions, microbes feed on the food in which they live and reproduce. During their life cycles, they cause a variety of changes in foods, most of which result in a loss of the foods' quality. In some cases, the controlled growth of specific microbes can produce desirable changes, such as the change that results in the formation of sauerkraut from cabbage and wine from grapes. Microorganisms function through a wide variety of enzymes that they produce, and the changes in foods attributed to microorganisms are actually brought about by the chemical action of these enzymes.

CHARACTERISTICS OF MICROBES

The physical and biological abilities, requirements, and tolerances of microbes are factors that determine the effects of microbes on food.

Structure and Shape of Microbes

Bacteria, molds, and yeasts have rigid cell walls enclosing the cell materials and the cytoplasm, but they differ greatly in their properties. The microbes most important in the spoilage and controlled changes in food materials have various shapes (see Fig. 7-1). Many are rod-shaped and occur either as single

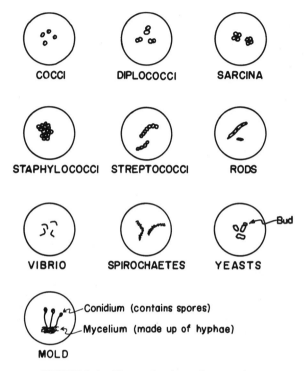

FIGURE 7-1.   Shapes of various microorganisms.

cells, as two adjoining cells, or as short chains of cells. Other bacteria are spherical in shape (cocci). Some cocci exist mainly as a grapelike cluster of cells, the staphylococci, others as a cubelike cluster of spherical cells, the sarcina. Some cocci occur in groups of two, the diplococci, or in chains, the streptococci. Some disease-causing bacteria are included in the latter two groups.

Some bacteria are curved or comma-shaped rods, the vibrios, and others are long, slender, corkscrew-shaped cells, the spirochaetes. Other bacterial groups either are not important to changes in foods or are disease-causing types (see Chap. 6).

Molds are multicellular (bacteria and yeasts are single cells) and are made up of branched threads (hyphae), consisting of chains of cylindrical cells united end to end. Some of the hyphae serve to secure nutrients from the material in which they are growing while others produce the spores that provide for reproduction, or for new mold growth. Some molds produce a mycelium (mass of hyphae) that has cross walls (septa) while others do not have cross walls in the mycelium.

Yeasts form single cells or chains of cells that may be spherical or of various shapes between the spherical and the cylindrical.

One characteristic of bacteria, yeasts, and molds is that they can exist either as active, vegetative cells or as spores. As vegetative cells, they metabolize, reproduce, cause food spoilage, and sometimes disease. They generally have a considerable effect on the environment. Their activity, however, is dependent on several environmental conditions, as we shall see later on. When conditions are unfavorable (such as high temperatures), the vegetative cells begin to die before they can reproduce, and soon all the vegetative cells die. Many microorganisms, however, also exist in the spore state, sometimes because it is a necessary step in reproduction (as in molds), so there are spores at any given time to permit the microbe to survive unfavorable conditions. In other cases, certain microorganisms, as some bacteria, exist in both the vegetative and the spore states so that when conditions become unfavorable, the spores survive.

In order for spores to survive the conditions that are destructive to their vegetative counterparts, they must have special properties. In general, spores are concentrated forms of their vegetative counterparts; thus, spores contain less water, and they are more dense and smaller than the vegetative cells. The spore wall is thicker and harder than the cell wall.

The Size of Microbes

Bacteria are comparatively small. The single cell of many bacteria is about 40 millionths of an inch (1μ) in diameter. There are, however, some types of bacteria that may be 50 or more times larger than this. Due to their small size, bacteria cannot be seen with the naked eye, and when evidence of their growth can be seen, such as when slime forms on meat, the organisms will have multiplied to very large numbers, billions of cells to each square inch (6.5 cm^2) of the meat surface.

The single cell of the mold, although not visible without magnification, is much larger than the single bacterial cell, and any significant growth of molds on foods can be seen. The visible mold comprises mycelia with or without spore heads. The spore head carries the spore that will give rise to more growth.

Yeasts vary in size from that of the more common spherical bacteria to a form several times larger than this. Like bacteria, when grown in solution, the individual cells cannot be seen, but eventually, the cell numbers will accumulate to the point where the solution becomes cloudy. There are, however, some instances in which groups of cells will form visible clumps (colonies) on foods or on the surface of solutions.

Reproduction in Microbes

Bacteria usually reproduce by fission, a transverse division across the cell to form two new cells. Under favorable conditions, this form of reproduction continues until there are billions of cells per ounce (29.6 ml) of solution or per square inch (6.5 cm^2) of surface of food material. (It should be noted that microorganisms must live in liquid material, and when they grow on food surfaces, they are actually living in the liquid available on or in the food.) There are some instances in which sexual reproduction occurs in bacteria, one cell uniting with another before division occurs, but this is not the usual circumstance and need not be discussed further here.

Under favorable environmental conditions, bacterial multiplication for some species occurs at an exceedingly rapid rate, a doubling of the number requiring about 20 min. From this standpoint, the number of cells with which a food is contaminated is very important, for if the number is high, only a few hours may be required for bacterial multiplication to reach a level that will cause food spoilage.

Molds usually reproduce by means of spores, each organism producing spores in great numbers. Mold spores are of two types: sexual spores produced by the fusion of two sex cells, or asexual spores that arise from the fertile hyphae. Most molds produce asexual spores. Asexual spores are formed on the sides or ends of hyphae threads (a conidium) or produced in a special spore case called a sporangium. Conidia contain many spores, and when a spore comes in contact with a suitable growth medium under favorable conditions, it grows to become the adult mold.

Yeasts reproduce by budding, by fission or by spore formation. In budding, a projection is formed on the original cell that eventually breaks off to form a new cell. Some types may undergo fission as do bacteria. One cell divides into two cells. Sometimes, yeasts reproduce by spore formations that may be sexual or asexual.

Motility in Microbes

Many types of bacteria are motile or are able to move about in the solutions in which they live by means of the movement of flagella, thin, protoplasmic, whiplike projections of the cell. Some bacteria, as the cocci, have no flagella and are not motile.

Molds are not motile, but they spread in vinelike fashion by sending hyphae outward.

Yeasts are not motile; consequently, they exist in relatively compact clusters, unless distributed by agitation or by some other external dispersing force.

Effect of pH on Microbial Growth

Both the growth and the rate growth of microbes are greatly affected by pH. Thus, microorganisms have an optimum pH at which they grow most rapidly and a pH range above or below which they will not grow at all. Generally, molds and yeasts grow best at pHs on the acid side of neutrality, as do some bacteria. Many species of bacteria grow best at pHs that are at neutrality or slightly on the alkaline side. Some bacteria will grow at pHs as low as 4, while others grow at pHs as high as 11. At least part of the reason why fruits are usually spoiled by molds or yeasts and flesh-type foods (meats, fish, poultry, and eggs) are usually spoiled because of bacterial growth is because of the low pH (acidic) of fruits and the near neutral pH of flesh-type foods.

Nutritional Requirements of Microbes

Microorganisms, especially bacteria, vary greatly in nutritional requirements from species to species. In the presence of particular inorganic salts, some bacteria can utilize the nitrogen in air to form proteins and the carbon dioxide in air to obtain energy or to form compounds from which they can then obtain energy. Others can utilize simple inorganic salts, such as nitrates, as a source of nitrogen and relatively simple organic compounds, such as lactates, as a source of energy. Nearly all yeasts can derive all their nitrogen from lysine, an amino acid. Some bacteria may require complex organic compounds for growth, including amino acids (the primary units of proteins), vitamins—especially those belonging to the B group—and traces of certain minerals.

It has been shown that, in some cases, not only are trace minerals necessary, but they need careful control to sustain an optimum growth rate. There is some evidence that demonstrates the ability of at least some microbes to utilize substitute elements for required ones. Sometimes, one trace element may protect microbes from the toxic effects of the presence of other elements; thus, the presence of zinc has been reported to protect yeasts against cadmium poisoning.

Molds and yeasts, like bacteria, may require basic elements (carbon, hydrogen, nitrogen, phosphorus, potassium, sulfur, etc.) as well as vitamins and other organic compounds.

Although sugar is a nutrient important to microbes, some molds and yeasts can grow well in concentrations that inhibit bacterial growth. In fact, yeasts grow extremely well in the presence of sugar.

Effect of Temperature on Microbial Growth

The optimum growth rate of microorganisms depends on the temperature; they do not grow above or below a specific range of temperatures. Again, growth temperatures vary with species, and bacteria are arbitrarily classified according to the temperatures at which they grow. Bacteria, classified as psychrophiles, grow fastest at about 68°–77°F (20°–25°C), but some can grow, although more slowly, at temperatures as low as 45°F (7.2°C), while others grow at temperatures as high as 86°F (30°C). Some will grow at temperatures as low as 19°F (−7.2°C), as long as the nutrient solution for growth is not frozen. Bacteria classified as mesophiles grow best at temperatures around 98°F (36.7°C), but some will grow at temperatures lower than 68°F (20°C) and others at temperatures as high as 110°F (43.3°C). Bacteria causing diseases of animals are mesophiles. Bacteria classified as thermophiles grow best at temperatures between 131°F (55°C) and 150°F (65.5°C), but some will grow at temperatures as low as 113°F (45°C) and others at temperatures as high as 160°F (71.1°C) or slightly higher.

It should be pointed out that whereas microorganisms grow within a given range of temperatures, their growth rate decreases greatly at the low or high temperatures of that range.

When microbes are subjected to temperatures higher than those of their growth range, they are destroyed at rates that depend on the degree to which the temperature is raised above the growth range. Some bacteria form heat-resistant spores, concentrated areas of protoplasm, within the cell. The degree of heat resistance of spore-forming bacteria varies with the species. Some types may be destroyed by raising the temperature (in the presence of moisture) to 212°F (100°C) over a period of several minutes while others can survive boiling for periods of many hours. Some may even survive temperatures as high as 250°F (121.1°C) for many minutes. Bacterial spores are the most heat-resistant living things known to humans.

In general, there are bacteria that can grow and can survive under more extreme conditions than those tolerated by any of the molds or yeasts. Molds, as a class, can grow and survive under more extreme conditions than can yeasts. On the other hand, while the growth and survival of the many species of bacteria cover a broad range of conditions, each species is highly selective, and the range of conditions under which it can metabolize is generally narrower than that of molds and yeasts.

Water Requirements of Microorganisms

Microorganisms grow only in aqueous solutions. A term, *water activity*, (a_w), has been coined to express the degree of availability of water in foods. This term is applied to all food, the ordinary fresh-type food having an a_w of about 0.99–0.96 at ambient temperatures. Low water activities, which limit the growth of microorganisms in foods, may be brought about by the addition of salt or sugar, as well as by the removal of water by drying. Under such conditions, the remaining water has been tied up by chemical compounds added to or concentrated in the food or bound to some food component, such as protein.

$$a_w = \frac{\text{equilibrium relative humidity}}{100}$$

Equilibrium relative humidity is reached in a food when the rate at which it loses water to its environment is equal to the rate at which it absorbs water from the environment.

Oxygen Requirements by Microorganisms

Some bacteria are aerobic, that is, they require oxygen (in air) for growth. Others grow best when the oxygen concentration is low (microaerophiles). Still others can grow either in the presence or absence of oxygen (facultative aerobes or facultative anaerobes). A number of bacterial species will not grow in the presence of oxygen because it is toxic to them, and these are called anaerobes.

It should be pointed out that while oxygen is toxic to anaerobic bacteria, they sometimes can grow under conditions that appear to include the presence of oxygen. The explanation for this is that organic materials (animal and vegetable matter) contain compounds that themselves tie up the available oxygen. Also, in many instances, aerobic bacteria first grow and consume the oxygen and produce reducing compounds that also combine with available oxygen, thus producing conditions suitable for the growth of anaerobic bacteria. In contrast to this, certain aerobic bacteria can utilize the oxygen in certain oxygen-bearing compounds, such as nitrates. In general, molds require oxygen for growth. Yeasts grow best in aerobic conditions, but some grow anaerobically (e.g., fermentative types) although more slowly.

Effect of Oxidation-Reduction Potential
on Microbes

The oxidation-reduction potential, expressed as Eh and measured in millivolt units, is defined as the tendency to yield electrons (become oxidized) or to capture electrons (become reduced). The greater the degree to which a substance is oxidized, the more highly positive will be its Eh value, and the greater the degree to which a substance is reduced, the more highly negative will be its Eh value. In general, aerobes require a substrate having a positive Eh, and anaerobes require a substrate having a negative Eh. The optimum Eh values for the growth of microbes vary with species.

EFFECT OF MICROBES ON FOOD

As stated earlier, bacteria, molds, and yeasts are the main causes of the spoilage of unpreserved foods, with bacteria playing the major role in the spoilage of meats, poultry, dairy, and fish products. Molds and yeasts play the major role in the spoilage of fruits and vegetables. The changes in foods due to microbial action can be classified into two types: undesirable changes and desirable changes.

Undesirable Changes

Undesirable changes can be further subdivided into (1) those that cause food spoilage, not usually associated with human disease, and (2) those that cause food poisoning whether or not the food undergoes observable changes.

Food Spoilage.   Food spoilage can be detected organoleptically. That is, we can either *see* the spoilage, *smell* the spoilage, *taste* the spoilage, *feel* the spoilage, or combinations of the four sensations. Quite often, the evidence of microbial growth is easily visible as in the case of slime formation, cottonlike network of mold growth, irridescence and greening in cold cuts and in cooked sausage, and even discrete large colonies of bacteria. In liquids, such as juices, microbial spoilage is often manifest by the development of a cloudy appearance or curd formation. The odors of spoiled protein foods are very objectionable and, in some cases, when they are intense enough, even toxic. Some of these obnoxious odors are common enough, and the compounds responsible for them are ammonia, various sulfides (as in the smell of clam flats), and hydrogen sulfide (the typical smell of rotten eggs). The tastes of spoiled foods range from loss of good characteristic taste to the development of objectionable tastes. Thus, when a pear or an orange spoils, the sweet characteristic taste of either is lost, and when milk spoils, it develops an acidic taste, sometimes also bitter. The feel of spoiled foods reflects the spoilage in different ways, depending on the type of food and the microbe involved in the spoilage, so some spoiled foods feel slimy, while others may feel mushy.

Food Poisoning.   Food poisoning may result from a variety of factors, but we are concerned with food poisoning resulting from the activity of microbes on the food. The subject is too broad to present here, and it is discussed in greater detail in Chapter 6 of this text. However, some remarks are appropriate here. Toxic compounds, such as histamine, originally classified as ptomaines, result from the microbial decomposition of proteins and, in some instances, decarboxylation of amino acids. Theoretically, some amino acids can give rise to a ptomaine derivative plus carbon dioxide. A typical example is:

$$\text{histidine} \xrightarrow[\text{decarboxylation}]{\text{microbial}} \text{histamine} + \text{carbon dioxide}$$

where histamine is the ptomaine derivative said to be poisonous.

Ptomaine poisoning, which occurs only rarely, is caused by compounds that are formed in advanced stages of spoilage (the food is putrid), whereas most food poisonings are caused either by bacterial diseases or by toxins produced in foods through bacterial growth. In many cases, foods that can cause illness have no outward signs of spoilage.

In many instances, grain used for animal feeds becomes contaminated with mold growth during storage, the molds producing toxic materials that cause diseases in the animals to which the grain is fed.

Bacteria, and especially molds, cause many diseases of vegetables and cereals as they are grown, causing economic losses, but this subject is beyond the scope of our discussion.

Desirable Changes in Foods

During the development of civilization, humans have learned how to utilize some of the products produced by the growth of certain microorganisms. The bacterial products utilized by humans are mostly produced by the bacteria that form lactic acid from sugars, although other types may form useful materials. Cultured milks (soured cream, yogurt, buttermilk, etc.) are produced through the growth of the lactic acid bacteria.

In order to obtain the curd in the manufacture of cheese, milk is cultured with bacteria that produce lactic acid, which in turn precipitates the casein, although this can be accomplished in a different way. The particular flavors and textures of many cheeses are attributed to bacterial growth during or after curd formation. Flavor and texture are influenced especially during aging or during the period in which the cheese is held in storage at a particular temperature for purposes of maturing.

The particular flavor of butter is due to the formation of small amounts of a chemical compound from sugars or citrates by the growth of lactic acid bacteria in the cream prior to churning. Pickles and olives are at least partially preserved by acid formed by bacteria when the raw materials are allowed to undergo a natural fermentation. The particular flavor and texture of sauerkraut are due to acid and other products produced by the growth of lactic acid bacteria in shredded cabbage to which some salt has been added. The typical flavor of dried-cured sausage (Italian salami, cervelat, etc.) is produced by the growth of lactic acid bacteria in the ground meat within the casing during the period in which the sausages are stored on racks and allowed to dry.

Acetic acid (vinegar) is produced from ethyl alcohol by the growth of *Acetobacter* that oxidizes the alcohol to acetic acid.

$$2(CH_3CH_2OH) \xrightarrow{O_2} 2HOH + 2(CH_3CHO) \xrightarrow{O_2} 2(CH_3COOH)$$
Ethyl alcohol   Water   Actaldehyde   Acetic acid

Various types of bread and certain other bakery products are leavened (raised) by yeasts. The yeasts, in this case, not only produce carbon dioxide, a gas that causes the loaf to rise, but also produce materials that affect the gluten (protein) of flour, causing it to take on a form that is elastic. The elasticity of the gluten is necessary to retain the gas and to support the structure of the loaf.

All alcoholic drinks are produced through the growth of different species of yeasts. This includes beer, ale, wines, and whiskeys. Whiskeys, brandies, gins, and so on are produced by distilling off the alcohol from materials that have been fermented by yeasts.

Molds are sometimes allowed to grow on sides or quarters of beef for purposes of tenderizing the meat and possibly to attain particular flavors.

Some cheeses, such as Roquefort, Gorgonzola, blue, and Camembert, owe their particular flavor and texture to the growth of molds. Under present-day manufacturing procedures, these cheeses are inoculated with molds of particular species, and incubated to allow the molds to grow and produce the desired textures and flavors.

The utilization of bacteria, molds, and yeasts to produce particular foods or beverages enjoyed by humans, in many cases results from accidental discoveries in which foods or food materials have undergone natural fermentations or changes due to the growth of microorganisms. In many cases, these natural fermentations were first used as a method of food preservation, artificial refrigeration being then unavailable. Today, these foods have become special products valued for their own particular taste and texture, even though food-handling and food-processing methods have done away with the need for preservation by natural fermentation, except in very primitive areas.

In general, it can be said that microorganisms, including bacteria, molds, and yeasts, are essential to the existence of humans and other animals on earth. Microorganisms can cause economic losses in that they cause diseases and the decomposition of animal foods. However, such decomposition is a part of the cycle that returns elements, especially nitrogen, carbon, hydrogen, and oxygen, to a form that can be utilized by living things to form new organic materials.

Antibiotics, a group of compounds successful in combating microbial infections in humans, are produced by other microbes.

8

Enzyme Reactions

THE NATURE OF ENZYMES

Enzymes, produced by living things, are compounds that catalyze chemical reactions. Reactions involving enzymes may be said to proceed in two steps. In step 1, E + S↔ES (where E = enzyme, S = substrate, and ES = unstable intermediate complex that temporarily involves the enzyme). In step 2, ES + R↔P + E (where R = a substance in the substrate that reacts with the complex, P = the final product of the reaction, and E = enzyme liberated from the complex). Their role is critical to life because they have the ability to catalyze the chemical reactions that facilitate life. Chemical reactions take place when the necessary reactants are present, but usually an energy input (activation energy) is required to start a particular reaction. The analogy usually given to illustrate this concept is that of a boulder located at the top of a hill. The boulder has the potential energy for rolling down the hill, but must first be pushed over the edge (see Fig.8-1). The potential energy of the boulder could be great, depending on its mass and altitude. It could start a rock slide or landslide involving a great amount of energy. Although the energy required to push the boulder over the edge is insignificant compared to the total energy involved in the rolling of the boulder down the hill, that initial energy (called the activation energy) is nevertheless important, for without it there would be no landslide.

It is well known that the rate at which reactions take place is dependent on the temperature, among other things. The expression that is broadly accepted as the one that most nearly relates the rate of the reaction, the activation energy, and the temperature at which the reaction proceeds is the Arrhenius equation:

$$K = Ae^{-E/RT}$$

105

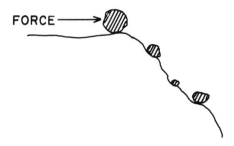

FORCE

FIGURE 8-1. Force needed to start rock slide.

where
K = rate of reaction
A = constant
e = 2.718 . . . , the base of the system of natural logarithms
E = activation energy
R = 1.99 cal/°C/mole, the gas constant
T = absolute temperature

For solution of the preceding equation, e and R are both known; K, E, and T are values that may be known or need to be found. A is the orientation factor. It is associated with the probability that the reactive sites of reactants are properly oriented for reacting with each other.

Since reactions can proceed more rapidly at higher temperatures but quite often have to accelerate within a system of constant temperature, as within our bodies, only by the action of enzymes can this occur. Enzymes are produced by living things from the lowest single-celled members to the highest, most complex members of the plant or animal kingdoms, including humans. All life depends on enzymes to convert foods or nutrients to a form in which they can be utilized and to carry out cellular functions.

In composition, enzymes always contain a protein. They may also contain or require complex chemical compounds in order to become functional. These compounds are known as prosthetic groups, (also called coenzymes) and are usually vitamins, especially those belonging to the B vitamin group. Some enzymes also require trace amounts of a metal, such as copper, to function. Enzymes, therefore, consist of either pure proteins, proteins with a prosthetic group, or proteins with a prosthetic group plus a metal cation.

Through their action, enzymes convert foods into less complex chemical substances that can be utilized for energy and for the building of cellular protoplasm. Proteins, fats, and carbohydrates are thus broken down to less complex compounds by enzymes in order that they may be utilized by various organisms. More complex carbohydrates are broken down to glucose, a source of ready energy that can be absorbed and eventually converted to carbon dioxide and water or built up into fats that can be stored as a source of reserve energy. When reserve energy is needed, fats are first hydrolyzed (insertion of water to split the molecule) or broken down into glycerine and fatty acids. The fatty acids are then converted to acetates that can be utilized for energy. When the acetates are not completely used, those remaining may be recombined and deposited as fats, an energy reserve.

Proteins are broken down to their primary units (amino acids), in which form they may be incorporated into cellular protoplasm as proteins used for cell repair or for growth. In some instances, the nitrogen portion of the amino acid may be removed and the remaining compound oxidized to provide energy.

As previously stated, enzymes always contain a protein (chain of amino acids) in which the amino acids are combined in a particular sequence, the protein itself having a particular shape or configuration.

There are more than 22 known amino acids. Proteins consist of a large number of amino acids combined in a particular sequence. Also, chains of amino acids are cross-linked one to another and the different proteins form special configurations and shapes. Proteins are also sometimes combined with carbohydrates, lipids, or phospholipids (fatlike compounds containing phosphoric acid as part of the molecule). These are called conjugated proteins. The number and sequence of amino acids in the chain, the shape or relationship of one protein chain with another, and conjugation with carbohydrate or lipid all affect the characteristics (functional properties) and determine the manner in which a protein will react to physical and chemical energy.

Enzymes cause chemical reactions to occur at their fastest rates when the temperature is at some optimum level. Usually, this is in the range of 60°–150°F (15.6°–65.6°C), but some action may occur at temperatures above or below the optimum range. Thus, some enzymes may react slowly at temperatures well below that of the freezing point of water and others at temperatures above 160°F (71.1°C).

Since proteins are changed chemically and physically or are coagulated by high temperatures, especially when moisture is present, enzymes are usually inactivated at temperatures between 160° and 200°F (71.1° and 93.3°C). There are some exceptions to this, however, and at least one enzyme, which splits off fatty acids from fish phospholipids, is known to remain active even after steaming at 212°F (100°C) for 20 min.

Enzymes have an optimum pH at which they cause reactions to occur at the fastest rate. Water solutions having a pH value less then 7 are said to be acidic; those having a pH value greater then 7 are said to be alkaline; and those having a pH value of 7 exactly are said to be neutral. As in the case of temperatures, some action will occur at pHs above or below the optimum, although there are low and high limits beyond which a particular enzyme action cannot take place.

PROTEOLYTIC ENZYMES (PROTEASES)

Enzymes involved in the breakdown or splitting of proteins are called proteolytic enzymes or, more simply, proteases. Proteases comprise two general classes: proteinases and peptidases. Proteinases split the protein molecules into smaller fragments called proteoses and peptones, then into polypeptides and peptides. Peptidases split polypeptides and peptides into amino acids. Because most amino acids in foods are water–soluble, food proteins are essentially liquefied by proteinases and peptidases.

In meat, such as beef, pork, or poultry held in the eviscerated state (intestines and organs removed), the proteases present in the tissues are called cathepsins. The pH of meat tissues is on the alkaline side of the pH optimum for the cathepsins. Also, the temperatures and times under which these products are held prior to utilization are not such that extensive proteolysis can occur. Therefore, while there may be some tenderization of the tissues during holding, which may, in fact, be due to proteolysis, there is not extensive breakdown of the tissues.

In fish, proteolytic enzymes are much more active than in meats. Even when fish is held in the eviscerated state in ice or under refrigeration, there may be sufficient proteolysis to cause softening of the tissues over a period of days. In fish held in the round (uneviscerated), proteolysis is accelerated due to a concentrated source of enzymes present in blind tubules (the pyloric caeca) attached to the intestines. Thus, even though fish in the round are refrigerated, within a few days, sufficient proteolysis may occur to dissolve the tissues of the abdominal wall exposing the entrails. Members of the herring and mackerel families handled in the uneviscerated state are quite subject to this type of enzyme deterioration, especially if they have been feeding when caught. Such fish as flounders and ocean perch, also handled in the uneviscerated state, seem not to be especially subject to this type of deterioration.

Lobsters provide an especially good example of a deteriorative change that may take place through the action of proteolytic enzymes. As long as the lobster is in the live state, autolytic proteolysis does not occur. However, if the lobster dies and then is held for some hours, even under refrigeration and especially at higher temperatures, proteolysis takes place to such an extent that the lower abdominal portion will be partially liquefied. When such a lobster is cooked, the flesh will be soft and crumbly (short-meated) and part of the tail portion will have dissolved, leaving only a part of this section intact. For this reason, lobsters should never be held long after death prior to cooking. The present accepted practice is to cook lobsters from the live state. Other crustaceans (shrimp and crabs) are also subject to enzyme proteolysis, although with shrimp, this usually is not extensive, especially if the head portion (cephalothorax) is removed shortly after the shrimp is caught. The relatively high activity of enzymes in marine species is attributed to the low temperature conditions in the marine environment. That is, in order to make reactions proceed at low temperatures, the activation energy system must be more efficient.

Plants also contain proteolytic enzymes, but these enzymes usually contribute little to deterioration, especially as long as the tissues of fruits and vegetables are not cut or damaged. Some plants provide an excellent source of proteolytic enzymes. Bromelin is found in pineapple juice and is so active that people who handle cut pineapple that has not been heated must wear rubber gloves; otherwise the skin of the fingers will be eroded, which if allowed to proceed may result in the exudation of some blood. Papain is a proteolytic enzyme obtained from the latex of the green papaya fruit. Ficin is a proteolytic enzyme obtained from the latex of certain fig trees. Proteolytic enzymes from plants may be extracted and purified and these enzymes may be employed, for instance, to tenderize meats.

OXIDIZING ENZYMES (OXIDASES)

There are a number of oxidizing enzymes that bring about changes in foods that result in deterioration. In plants, peroxidases, ascorbic acid oxidase, tyrosinase, and polyphenolases may cause undesirable chemical reactions to occur. Peroxidases may oxidize certain phenollike compounds in root vegetables, such as horseradish, causing the prepared product to become darker in color. This does not happen while the tissues are intact but when the vegetable has been cut up or comminuted. Ascorbic acid oxidase, present in certain vegetables, oxidizes ascorbic acid (vitamin C) to a form that is readily further oxidized by atmospheric oxygen. The second oxidation product is not utilized by the human as a vitamin. Therefore, the action of this enzyme may cause loss of the vitamin C content of foods. Peroxidases may also, indirectly, cause a loss of vitamin C in vegetables. In this case, the compounds formed by the action of peroxidase react with vitamin C. Phenolases are present in some fruits and vegetables. These enzymes oxidize some phenollike compounds, also present in plant products, causing brown or dark-colored compounds to be formed when the tissues are cut.

Tyrosinase oxidizes the amino acid tyrosine to form dark-colored compounds. The molecule rearranges and further oxidizes to form a red compound. Polymerization (combination of these compounds) results in the formation of dark-colored melanin compounds.

The enzyme, tyrosinase, which is present in many fruits and vegetables, may cause discoloration of the cut tissue and will also oxidize compounds related to tyrosine. This enzyme is also present in shrimp and some spiny lobsters and may cause a discoloration called black spot. In shrimp, this often occurs as a black stripe on the flesh along the edges of the segments of the tail or as a pronounced band where the shell segments overlap. It is not generally recognized, but tyrosinases are also present in clams. Hence, shucked (deshelled) clams will darken at the surface if oxygen is present and if the enzymes have not been inactivated by heat.

These reactions occur only after the shrimp or clams die. In general, oxidizing enzymes do not cause deteriorative changes in tissues that are intact. In fruits and vegetables, the tissues must be cut or bruised or there must be a breakdown of cells by their enzymes before the action of oxidizing enzymes results in discoloration.

FAT-SPLITTING ENZYMES (LIPASES)

Fats are composed of glycerine (glycerol) and fatty acids. Glycerine is a polyhydric alcohol (3 alcohol groups), and fatty acids are short or long chains of carbon atoms to which hydrogen is attached, either to the fullest possible extent (saturated) or to a lesser extent (unsaturated), the latter resulting in reactive groups in the chain. At one end of the fatty acid chain there is an acid group.

In formation of fats, each 1 of 3 fatty acids combines with 1 of the 3 alcohol groups of glycerine, splitting off water in each case. On the other hand, where water and the enzyme lipase are present, fats are split into their component parts, glycerine and fatty acids.

The fatty acids in most fats that are found in nature consist of a chain of more than 10 carbon atoms, and these fatty acids have no particular flavor or odor. Hence, when lipase acts on most natural fats, no bad odors are generated. However, if fats or oils high in free fatty acid content are used for deep-fat-frying, the oil may smoke during heating, which is undesirable.

$$CH_2OOC(CH_2)_2CH_3$$
$$|$$
$$CHOOC(CH_2)_8CH_3 \xrightarrow[\text{LIPASE}]{\text{WATER}}$$
$$|$$
$$CH_2OOC(CH_2)_{14}CH_3$$

$$CH_2OH$$
$$|$$
$$CHOH \quad + $$
$$|$$
$$CH_2OH$$

$$CH_3(CH_2)_2COOH$$
BUTYRIC ACID (ODOROUS)

$$CH_3(CH_2)_8COOH$$
CAPRIC ACID (SOME ODOR)

$$CH_3(CH_2)_{14}COOH$$
PALMITIC ACID (NO ODOR)

| Fat | Glycerine | Fatty acids |

There are some fats that contain short-chain fatty acids, especially those fats present in the milk of cows or goats. These fats contain butyric (4 carbons), caproic (6 carbons), caprylic (8 carbons), and capric (10 carbons) acids. All these fatty acids have an odor and flavor. Butyric acid, especially, is pungent and considered to be distasteful. When lipase acts on butter, therefore, it splits off butyric acid, which gives the butter a strong, undesirable taste (called rancid). Actually, butter is an emulsion of water in oil and contains about 16% water, the water being present as fine droplets. Butter becomes rancid by the action of lipase produced by bacteria that grow in the water droplets. The lipase acts on the fat surrounding the water droplets. Lipase rancidity in butter, therefore, is really a type of deterioration caused by bacteria.

Enzymes similar to lipase are called phospholipases. Phospholipases split phospholipids. Most phospholipids are similar to fats in that they contain glycerine, two alcohol groups of which are combined with fatty acids. The third alcohol group in this case is combined with a molecule containing phosphoric acid, a short chain of carbons, and a nitrogen group with carbons attached to it. Lecithin is a typical phospholipid. Phospholipase splits off fatty acids from phospholipids. Such action may cause deterioration in foods in that it results in a destabilization of proteins that causes a toughening of the tissues and a loss of succulence (juiciness).

ENZYMES THAT DECOMPOSE CARBOHYDRATES (CARBOHYDRASES)

Fruits contain pectin that supports the particular structure of the product. In processed fruit juices (for instance, tomato or orange juice), if the pectin is broken down, the solids tend to settle to the bottom, leaving a clear serum on top. Pectin consists of a long chain of galacturonic acid molecules with the carboxyl groups partially esterified with methyl alcohol. It has a high water-holding capacity. There are pectic enzymes that will either break down the pectin molecule to smaller units or completely decompose the molecule to its primary unit, galacturonic acid. The emulsifying properties of pectin may be lost, causing settling in fruit juices and softening in fruit. When the pectin in whole fruit breaks down, it may result in deterioration of the fruit due to the action of other enzymes or invasion of the tissues by microorganisms.

In the sugar cane plant, there is an enzyme invertase that breaks down cane sugar (sucrose) having 12 carbon atoms to glucose and fructose, each having 6 carbon atoms. Before sugar cane is harvested, therefore, a part of the plant must be removed to eliminate the source of the enzyme. Were this not done, there would be a loss of sucrose during the processing of the cane. Many other carbohydrases, which break down cellulose or starch or break down more complex sugars to smaller units, exist.

APPLICATIONS

Whereas enzymes may cause a deterioration of foods, they may also be used in the processing of foods to produce particular products or to modify the characteristics of particular products. Proteolytic enzymes obtained from plants may be used for tenderizing meat either by injecting animals with a solution of the enzyme prior to slaughter or by sprinkling the powdered enzyme on meat surfaces and allowing it to react, prior to cooking. In the manufacture of certain kinds of milk powder (e.g., to be used in chocolate), the lipases may be allowed to act on the milk-fat prior to drying to obtain a particular flavor in the finished product. The characteristic flavor of certain cheeses is due to the action of lipases on the milk-fat contained therein. In order to obtain the particular flavor of Roquefort, Gorgonzola, or blue cheese, the milk-fat must first be broken down to fatty acids that can then be oxidized. The lipases that decompose the fats to provide fatty acids are produced by the molds allowed to grow in these cheeses. Enzymes produced by molds then oxidize the specific fatty acids that ultimately result in the unique flavors that characterize Roquefort and other exotic cheeses.

There are may applications of enzyme technology that involve the use of carbohydrate-splitting enzymes. In making malt, barley is germinated to obtain an enzyme that will convert starch to a sugar (maltose), which can be converted by yeasts to ethyl alcohol and carbon dioxide. By this means, various grains can be used as the source of sugar for fermentation. Carbohydrate-splitting enzymes are also used to modify starches used in foods and to modify starches used in sizing and laundering clothes. Invertase (sucrase) is used in the production of chocolate cherries. The cherries are rolled in a mixture of crystalline sucrose and the enzyme before they are enrobed in chocolate. During a short holding period, the enzyme splits the sucrose into a mixture of glucose and fructose, which has a higher water solubility and results in the sweet taste and creamy texture that is characteristic of the product.

There are many other applications of enzyme technology in the food and other industries and it is expected that the number of applications for enzymes will continue to increase. One of the factors that will serve to widen the use of enzyme technology is the development of immobilized enzymes. It has been found that enzymes can be fixed chemically to inert substances, such as glass beads. In this form, they can be packed into a column through which a solution or suspension of the material to be acted on (called the substrate) is allowed to pass. In this manner, the enzyme responsible for the conversion or change in the substrate is not lost or washed out with the substrate. Thus, the enzyme can be used for a number of substrate conversions. Moreover, in this form (immobilized enzyme), the active agent is much less subject to inactivation as, for instance, by high temperature.

9

Chemical Reactions

Foods sometimes deteriorate because of chemical changes not associated with microbial growth or enzyme-induced chemical reactions. Actually, certain components in foods are subject to reactions that involve either a combination with naturally occurring elements (such as oxygen) or with compounds present in the foods themselves.

OXIDATION

One of the changes that occur in foods is the oxidation of fats and oils. Fats and oils are chemically similar and are classified as lipids. Generally, fats are those lipids that are solid at room temperature (e.g., lard, suet), and oils are those lipids that are liquid at room temperature (e.g., olive oil, corn oil). Fats and oils are glycerol esters of fatty acids, such that each molecule of fat or oil contains 3 fatty acids that may be the same as or different from each other. Generally, they are different from each other. The glycerol esters are formed by a condensation reaction that results in the formation of 1 triglyceride molecule and 3 molecules of water.

$$
\begin{array}{c}
\text{CH}_2\text{OH} \\
| \\
\text{CHOH} \\
| \\
\text{CH}_2\text{OH}
\end{array}
\;+\; 3\,\text{RCOOH} \longrightarrow
\begin{array}{c}
\text{CH}_2\text{COOR} \\
| \\
\text{CHCOOR} \\
| \\
\text{CH}_2\text{COOR}
\end{array}
\;+\; 3\text{H}_2\text{O}
$$

Glycerol   Fatty acids   Triglyceride   Water

In the preceding formula, R is the symbol that represents one of many different hydrocarbon chains. Usually, the Rs in the fatty acids will differ from each other, although they could be the same. However, each of the Rs in the triglyceride must correspond to one of the Rs in the fatty acids from which the triglyceride was formed. A hydrocarbon chain simply means that it is made up of a number of carbon atoms bonded together, as a string of beads, with one or two hydrogen atoms linked to each of the carbon atoms. The carbon atoms on each of the 2 ends of the string may sometimes have 3 hydrogen atoms attached to them.

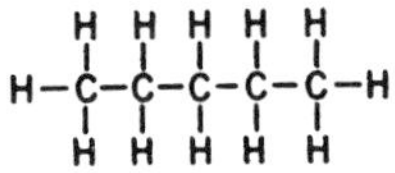

A hydrocarbon chain

Fats in nature usually contain long carbon chains, the carbons of which are mostly saturated with hydrogen with an acid (carboxyl) group at the end (e.g., butyric acid).

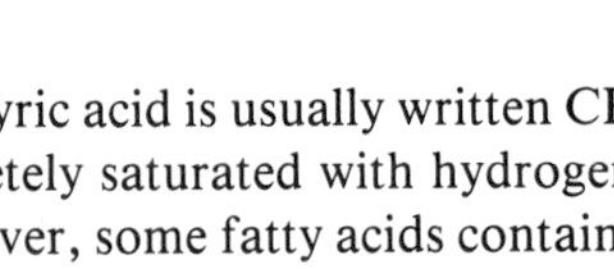

Butyric acid

The formula for butyric acid is usually written $CH_3 \cdot (CH_2)_2 \cdot COOH$.

Fats that are completely saturated with hydrogen atoms are called saturated fatty acids. However, some fatty acids contain 1 or several groups of 2 adjacent carbon atoms in which the carbons are not fully saturated with hydrogen (see the following formula).

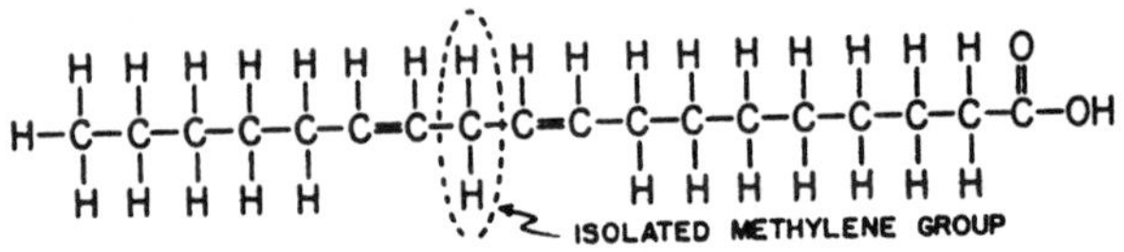

Linoleic acid

As can be seen, there are 2 sites of incomplete saturation shown by the double bonds (note that each of the unsaturated carbons has only 1 hydrogen atom attached to it). Fatty acids having 1 or more sites of incomplete saturation are called unsaturated fatty acids. Unsaturated fatty acids having a given number of carbon atoms have a lower melting temperature than saturated fatty acids having an equivalent number of carbon atoms. Thus, linoleic acid (unsaturated, with 18 carbon atoms) melts at 23°F (-5°C) while stearic acid (saturated, with 18 carbon atoms) melts at 157.3°F (69.6°C). When a lipid is made up of many unsaturated fatty acids, it will be liquid at room temperature. On the other hand, lipids, such as suet or beef fats, containing comparatively few fatty acids with unsaturated groups, are solid at room temperature. Fatty acids that contain none or only 1 unsaturated group are not especially subject to oxidation, but those with more than 1 unsaturated group oxidize readily. However, oxidation proceeds much faster in fatty acids containing 1 or more sites in the carbon chain in which there is first a group of 2 carbons not fully saturated with hydrogen followed by a carbon saturated with hydrogen (an isolated methylene group) followed by another group of 2 carbons not fully saturated with hydrogen. In linoleic acid (see preceding chemical formula), the isolated methylene group is identified by the dotted enclosure. Notice the pair of incompletely saturated carbons on each side of the isolated methylene group. The greater the number of sequences of this particular configuration (arrangement of atoms) in the fatty acid molecule, the faster the rate of oxidation. Thus, when linoleic acid has an isolated methylene group (a sequence of 2 carbons not saturated with hydrogen, 1 carbon saturated with hydrogen, and 2 carbons not saturated with hydrogen), it is said to oxidize 10 times as fast as when it does not have an isolated methylene group.

Oxygen, or a source of it, must, of course, be present for oxidation of fats to take place. However, a large amount of oxygen is not required for this reaction, and in foods, it is very difficult and commercially impractical to package them (under a vacuum or in an inert gas, such as nitrogen) so that sufficient oxygen is absent to prevent changes in fats. The reason for this is that in foods oxygen dissolves to some extent in the water present and also becomes trapped or occluded in the tissues.

Certain sources of energy accelerate the oxidation of fats. One of these is heat, and generally, the higher the temperature at which a fat is held, the faster the rate of oxidation. Light of certain wavelengths, especially wavelengths in the ultraviolet or near ultraviolet regions, accelerates the oxidation of fats. High-energy radiations, such as cathode, beta, and gamma rays, also greatly accelerate the rate at which fats oxidize.

Metals and their compounds accelerate the oxidation of fats. The probable formation of metal soaps with small amounts of free fatty acids present in fats may be the active agents in accelerating oxidation when pure metals are involved. Much less than a part per million to only a few parts per million of metals is required to accelerate the oxidation of fats. It is considered that the following is the order of decreasing activity as pro-oxidants for fats— copper, manganese, iron, nickel, zinc, and aluminum.

When fats oxidize, short-chain carbon compounds containing one or more groups in which 2 adjacent carbons are not saturated with hydrogen are formed. These compounds have odors and flavors that are generally undesirable and unacceptable. This change in fats and in the fats present in foods is called rancidity. (This should be distinguished from hydrolytic rancidity, in which lipase hydrolyzes fat, splitting off short-chain fatty acids, such as butyric acid.) Butyric acid has an undesirable taste and odor.

Oxidative-rancidity odors are generally sharp and acrid and usually may be described as linseed-oil-like, tallowy, fishy, or perfumelike. The more solid fats, as beef and mutton fat, are more apt to be tallowy when rancid, while pork fat, vegetable oils (soybean oil, cottonseed oil, corn oil, etc.) and fish and whale oils usually have the linseed oil flavor and odor when rancid. Under some conditions, vegetable or marine oils may be fishy or have a perfumelike odor when rancid. This appears to be a preliminary stage that eventually develops to the linseed oillike odor and flavor.

Oxidative rancidity may be a cause of deterioration in many forms of fish, meat, and poultry; there are instances in which oxidation of fats may be responsible for undesirable changes in shellfish and even vegetables.

When food products are dried, their fats may soon oxidize, even those that contain small amounts of fat, such as vegetables, shrimp, and some fish, since whatever fat or oil is present is now exposed to oxygen over a large area. The colors of certain vegetables (e.g., carrots), spices (e.g., red pepper and paprika), and crustaceans (e.g., shrimp) are due to chemical compounds known as carotenoids. These compounds contain many groups in which adjacent carbon atoms are not fully saturated with hydrogen. If the small amounts of fat present undergo the first stages of oxidation (peroxide formation), a fading of color may occur in these compounds, as from deep yellow or red to light yellow or the color may be bleached out entirely. Off-flavors and odors may or may not be associated with such changes in these foods, but the color change represents a deterioration of the product.

NONENZYMATIC BROWNING

There are several types of nonenzymatic browning. One type is caused by a chemical reaction known as the *Maillard reaction*. This chemical change is initiated by a combination of an amino acid and a sugar. The amino acid may be present in the food as a separate entity (free amino acid) or it may be an amino acid present in the food as part of a protein. The sugar must be of a reactive type, containing a reactive portion known as a carbonyl group.

$$
\underset{\text{Sugar}}{
\begin{array}{c}
\overset{\displaystyle\overbrace{\text{HC=O}}}{} \\
\text{(HCOH)}_N \\
\mid \\
\text{CH}_2\text{OH}
\end{array}}
\quad + \quad
\underset{\text{+ Amino acid}}{\text{RNH}_2}
\;\rightleftharpoons\;
\underset{\text{Addition compound}}{
\begin{array}{c}
\text{RNH} \\
\mid \\
\text{HCOH} \\
\mid \\
\text{(HCOH)}_N \\
\mid \\
\text{CH}_2\text{OH}
\end{array}}
\;\underset{-\text{H}_2\text{O}}{\rightleftharpoons}\;
\begin{array}{l}
\text{CONTINUING} \\
\text{TO OTHER} \\
\text{REACTIONS}
\end{array}
$$

The carbonyl group in the sugar is identified by the broken-line circle. A carbonyl group also occurs in other chemical compounds, the aldehydes and ketones. Once the reaction is initiated, it proceeds through a long series of chemical changes resulting in complex compounds that are flavorful and brown or black in color, causing changes in the flavor and color of the food.

When sugars are heated at high temperatures, they turn brown and then black. This reaction involves the dehydration or removal of water from the sugar resulting, through a series of reactions, in the formation of furfurals, ring compounds of 4 carbons with 1 to 2 side groups. These ring compounds further combine to form complex chemical compounds that are brown or black in color and that have an odor and flavor entirely different from that of the sugar. This is called caramelization, although the flavor produced may be different from that which we know as caramel candy where the components of milk are involved in the typical flavor of the confectionery.

Caramelization proceeds very fast at high temperatures such as are attained when sugars are heated directly. However, at lower temperatures, as those encountered in the normal handling of many foods (usually above 50°F [10°C]) when the right conditions are present, caramelization will proceed fast enough to cause a deterioration of foods.

A third type of browning may be caused by the oxidation of ascorbic acid (vitamin C). Once oxidized, the same type of compounds may be formed as in the case of caramelization of sugars.

Browning may take place in foods of all moisture contents. Hence, in canning, at least part of the difference in flavor between that of the fresh food and that of the canned product is due to reactions that are manifest by browning, and some types of food cannot be canned successfully because of browning (e.g., scallops and cauliflower). However, browning proceeds fastest in foods of low to medium moisture content. Thus, some dried foods are especially subject to changes caused by nonenzymatic browning.

As has been pointed out, the color difference (and in some cases, flavor) between fresh and heat-processed foods is probably due to browning reactions. The browning reactions can be minimized if canned foods are given a high-temperature–short-time process (HTST process) as compared with regular processing temperatures and times. However, browning reactions may proceed in HTST-processed foods during storage if they are held at temperatures above 50°F (10°C). Apparently, browning occurs slowly, if at all, when the moisture content is less than 2%, and only by freeze-drying can the moisture in foods be reduced to this low level. Therefore, these products are freeze-dried to a low moisture content and packaged so that moisture is not resorbed from the atmosphere. For this reason, fruit juices are generally not dried except by freeze-drying. The moisture content must be held at low level throughout storage if the freeze-dried product is to be stable. Dried egg products, whites, and whole egg mixtures (usually spray dried to a moisture content of about 5%) are quite subject to nonenzymatic browning reactions, resulting in a low acceptance of these products. For some time now, methods have been available to remove the sugar (glucose) from these products prior to drying, resulting in much improved products due to the prevention of adverse nonenzymatic reactions.

Sugar can be removed from foods by subjecting them to fermentation by bacteria or yeast before drying. The microorganisms consume the sugar during the fermentation process, thereby eliminating one of the necessary components required in the Maillard reaction. Another process for preventing the Maillard reaction involves the addition of two enzymes (glucose oxidase and catalase). The oxidase converts glucose to gluconic acid that does not combine with amino groups, but one of the products of the conversion is hydrogen peroxide, an undesirable compound, and the role of the catalase is to break down the peroxide.

While many processed foods may be adversely affected by nonenzymatic browning, there are other foods dependent on this type of reaction for their typical odor, flavor, and color. Maple syrup develops its typical color and flavor because of the Maillard reaction that takes place between sugar and an amino acid normally present in the sap of the maple tree. The typical color and taste of prunes is due to nonenzymatic browning that occurs when prune plums are dried and stored. The flavor and color of coffee are due to nonenzymatic browning that occurs in the components of the coffee beans when they are roasted (comparatively high temperatures are used for roasting). In the cooking of many foods, browning flavors and odors are produced. Roasted, broiled, or fried meats, or broiled or fried fish are examples of this type of change. The flavors and colors produced in the crusts of breads during baking are another example of the importance of the Maillard reaction that results in desirable changes.

THE STRECKER DEGRADATION

The Strecker degradation is a reaction that takes place between an amino acid and certain fragments of sugar or compounds produced by bacteria that contain reactive groups known as dicarbonyls, as follows.

$$R-CH_2-\underset{\underset{NH_2}{|}}{CH}-COOH \ + \ CH_3-\overset{\overset{O}{\|}}{C}-\overset{\overset{O}{\|}}{C}-OH \longrightarrow R-CH_2-\overset{\overset{O}{\|}}{CH} \ + \ CH_3-\underset{\underset{NH_2}{|}}{CH}-COOH \ + \ CO_2$$

Amino acid	+	Pyruvic acid (a dicarbonyl)	→	Aldehyde	+	Amino acid (different from the original amino acid)

The reaction results in the formation of an aldehyde, a different amino acid, and the splitting off of carbon dioxide. The new compound containing the aldehyde group is flavorful, which may or may not be desirable.

The Strecker degradation takes place when milk is heated to high temperatures for long periods or during storage after milk is heated to high temperatures for short periods and then stored at room temperature. This is probably the reason that fluid milk cannot be canned or heat-processed by ordinary methods. If fluid milk is given a high-temperature–short-time type of heating processing (HTST), it will not develop the off-flavor, provided the canned product is stored at temperatures below 50°F (10°C). Canned fluid milk, given a HTST treatment and held at room temperature, soon develops a caramelized flavor. In the manufacture of caramel confectioneries, condensed milk, cream, or some combination of the two, together with corn sugar, cane sugar, or both, are heated to high temperatures. The caramel flavor that develops is probably due to the Strecker degradation. This type of change in foods, therefore, is sometimes desirable and sometimes not desirable.

THE AGGREGATION OF PROTEINS

The aggregation of proteins causes deterioration of some foods. This change results in a bonding of protein chains to form a more closely knit network, and it would appear that in this process some of the water loosely held by the protein is squeezed out, causing drip from frozen foods upon defrosting. Protein aggregation occurs mainly in low-fat fish, such as cod, during frozen storage and is correlated with the liberation of free fatty acids from phospholipids by the phospholipase enzymes in the muscle. Some studies tend to prove that the protein aggregation and toughening that occur in some fish during frozen storage are due to enzymes that cause a breakdown of trimethyl amine oxide (present in the flesh of some fish) to dimethyl amine and formaldehyde.

$$(CH_3)_3 \equiv \overset{+}{N} - \overset{-}{O} \xrightarrow{\text{enzyme}} (CH_3)_2 = NH + H-\overset{\overset{O}{\displaystyle\parallel}}{C}H$$

Trimethyl amine oxide   Dimethyl amine   Formaldehyde

It is well known that formaldehyde causes an aggregation or denaturation of proteins.

It has been theorized that in the presence of the free fatty acids, there is a reaction between free fatty acids and proteins to form a cross-linked network within the muscle, resulting in a close association of protein fibers.

Another theory of what happens during protein aggregation is that the splitting off of fatty acids destabilizes the protein molecules, causing them to form a closely bonded mass, since in normal muscle, the phospholipid itself, from which the fatty acids are split off, is bonded or conjugated with the protein.

Protein aggregation does not take place in high-fat fish, such as salmon. It is theorized that the reason is that the free fatty acids split off by phospholipases dissolve in the fat present in the tissue of high-fat fish, and due to dilution, become unavailable for bonding with the protein. There is also the possibility that the proteins in high-fat species are different from those containing little fat, hence are not destabilized by a splitting of fatty acids from phospholipids. Another possible explanation is the absence of the enzyme that splits trimethyl amine oxide, which is believed to cause toughening in the lean species of fish in which this enzyme has been found.

When protein aggregation occurs in frozen products, the tissues become tough and dry and lose succulence when cooked. This change is temperature-dependent and does not occur to any extent in marine products held at temperatures below $-22°F$ ($-30°C$). At $-40°F$ ($-40°C$), cod held for 1 year may not be distinguished from the fresh product. The reason why the protein aggregation change does not occur at very low temperatures may be that water is not available to provide for the hydrolysis or splitting off of free fatty acids from phospholipids as brought about by the phospholipases, or that enzymes that decompose trimethyl amine oxide are not active.

Part III

Food-Processing Methods

10

Heating

The development of the modern heating process started in France during the first decade of the 1800s by Nicholas Appert who preserved foods in sealed glass jars in boiling water. In 1810, Peter Durand of England developed the metal can that was fabricated and sealed by hand soldering. In 1819, William Underwood of the United States started the first canning factory in Baltimore. But to preserve foods in boiling water took too long, requiring about 6 hours, so salt was added to the water bath, which increased the boiling temperature, thereby shortening the processing time. However, the salt corroded the cans, so the next innovation was to heat in steam under pressure. The higher the pressure, the higher the temperature (see Table 10-1) and the shorter the processing time. These early pressure chambers evolved into the modern retort.

By the early 1900s, the manufacturing and sealing of cans were accomplished by machines. The lid used for the cans contained a rim to which a plastic gasket could be added, and the rim could be sealed tightly by machine by first crimping it over and under the flanged top of the can body and then pressing the two together by a second roller operation. The plastic gasket made the can airtight by filling the tiny voids produced between the rim of the can cover and the flange of the can as they were brought together. This is essentially the method used today for hermetically (airtight) sealed metal containers. Normally, cans are described in terms of the dimensions of the diameter (D) and the height (H) (see Fig. 10-1), and each of the dimensions is given in numbers having 3 digits each. The first digit is in inches (1 in. = 2.54 cm), and the next 2 digits are in 1/16 of an inch (0.16 cm). Thus, when a can is described as a 202 × 214 can, this means that its diameter is 2 2/16 in. (5.40 cm) and its height is 2 14/16 in. (7.30 cm). Not all cans are round,

123

TABLE 10-1.   Boiling Points of Water at 0–20 PSIG
(0–1408 g/CM^2) (at Sea Level)

Pressure (at Sea Level)		Temperature at Which Water Boils	
(psig)	(g/cm^2)	(°F)	(°C)
0	0	212.0	100.0
1	70.4	215.4	101.9
2	140.8	218.5	103.6
3	211.2	221.5	105.3
4	281.6	224.4	106.9
5	352.0	227.1	108.4
6	422.4	229.6	109.8
7	492.8	232.3	111.2
8	563.2	234.7	112.6
9	633.6	237.0	113.8
10	704.0	239.4	115.2
11	774.4	241.5	116.4
12	844.8	243.7	117.6
13	915.2	245.8	118.8
14	985.6	247.8	119.9
15	1056.0	249.8	121.0
16	1126.4	251.6	122.0
17	1196.8	253.4	123.0
18	1267.2	255.4	124.1
19	1337.6	257.0	125.0
20	1408.0	258.8	126.0

however, and, as in the case of sardine cans, 3 dimensions are given: the length, the width, and the height.

Various lacquers have been developed for lining cans, especially for preventing food discoloration that could occur as a result of interactions between the food and the can. Other innovations include quick-opening cans with pull tabs, as are used for soft drinks, sardines, and nuts; cans that are opened with a slotted key that comes with the can, as are used for sardines and cured hams; pressurized cans that use a propellant to dispense whipped cream and cheese spreads; and extruded or drawn cans, as are used for soft drinks, tuna, and sardines. The extruded can has several advantages over the conventional can, a major one being the elimination of the bottom and side seams, which reduces the probability of seam failures, eliminates the use of lead (used in the side seam), and permits more stable stacking on shelves, requiring somewhat less vertical space.

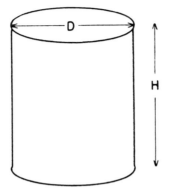

FIGURE 10-1. Diameter (D) and height (H) of a metal container.

PRETREATMENT OF FOODS

It is generally necessary for foods to undergo a treatment prior to the canning process, but these pretreatments differ depending on the foods, and no attempt will be made to cover all of them here. Some pretreatments are applied to many different foods. One of these, usually applied to vegetables, is blanching. Vegetables are first washed, usually in water and detergent, then rinsed. They are then passed over belts, where any remaining foreign matter, such as weeds or stalks, can be removed by hand. Blanching consists of heating in steam (no pressure) or hot water (usually about 210°F [98.9°C]) until the temperature of the food is brought up to about 180°–190°F (82.2°–87.8°C) in all parts (see Fig. 10-2), then cooling in water. Blanching shrinks the product, providing for a better fill of the container and removing gases, thus allowing better vacuum after sealing. The blanching process also destroys enzymes in the food that otherwise might react during the initial heating in the retort and cause discoloration or off-flavors in the product. When very high-temperature, very short-time methods of heat processing are used, enzymes might not be inactivated, which would cause development of off-flavors in the food. However, this can be prevented by blanching. Finally, blanching tends to fix the natural color of vegetables and it provides a clearer brine in the canned products.

VACUUM IN CANS

The Need for Vacuum

Foods are packed under vacuum for several reasons. If canned foods were not under vacuum, the cans would swell should they be stored at higher tem-

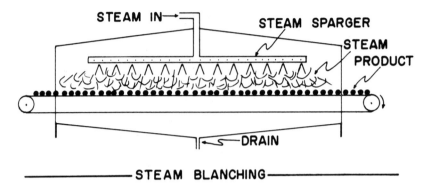

STEAM BLANCHING

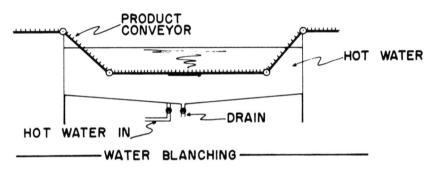

WATER BLANCHING

FIGURE 10-2. Continuous blanching.

peratures or lower pressures than those at which they were packed. Thus, cans packed at sea level at ordinary temperatures would swell due to expansion of gas within the can if the cans were shipped to Denver, Colorado, which because of its high altitude (about 1 mi [1.61 km] above sea level), is under reduced pressure, or if the cans were shipped to tropical areas or held in unusually hot places. When cans are in a swelled state, they are normally suspected of containing food that has spoiled, because when bacteria grow, many of them produce gases. Thus, a perfectly good canned food might be discarded because it could be suspected of being spoiled. Another reason for canning foods under vacuum is to remove oxygen which, of course, is in air. During heat processing, oxygen reacts with the food, causing undesirable changes in color and flavor of the product, as described in Chapter 9.

Finally, if at least some of the air is not removed from the container prior to sealing, then the product may have to be cooled under pressure (usually air pressure). Otherwise, the can will buckle (a permanent distortion along the cover seam), and such cans will be discarded. The reason for the buckling can be explained. During the heating process, the retort is under pressure, for example, 20 psi (1.41 kg/cm²). As the temperature inside the can reaches the high temperature in the retort, moisture in the food or brine vaporizes, exerting pressure against the inside of the can. In addition, the residual air in the can tends to expand as the internal temperature increases, and the expanding air also exerts a pressure against the inside of the can. By the end of the process, the can is under equilibrated pressures from both the inside and the outside (see Fig. 10-3). In this situation, the can is not unduly stressed, because the internal pressure is counterbalanced by the outside pressure and vice versa.

At the end of the process, the external pressure, relative to the can, may be immediately released by shutting off the steam supply to the retort and opening the retort valve to the outside, allowing all its internal steam to escape. However, the internal pressure in the can cannot be released immediately because the can cannot be vented to the outside. Thus, the wall and lids of the can are under internal pressure, causing distortions, possibly even damage, to the seals (formed by the lids and the can body). This problem can be eliminated by replacing the hot steam in the retort with air under pressure. In this way, the heat source is removed without altering the pressure equilibrium. With the removal of the heat source, the contents of the can will cool down, condensing water vapor and cooling the residual air, returning it to its original volume, thus reducing the internal pressure until it no longer pushes against the inside of the can. Removing as much air as possible from the container prior to processing tends to minimize buckling. However, even

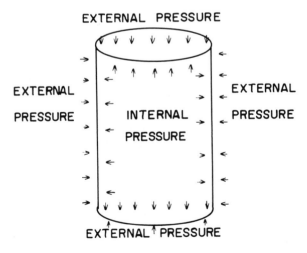

FIGURE 10-3.   Pressure equilibrium during thermal processing.

with vacuum packing, cans of large diameter must be cooled under pressure to prevent distortion of the container.

Some foods, such as whole kernel corn, may be packed under a very high vacuum in order to provide for good heat penetration, when only a small amount of liquid (canner's brine) is used with the foods. When this is done, a special (beaded) can with protruding ridges around the central part of the can body to strengthen the can may have to be used. Otherwise, the container body may panel or become flattened due to the difference in pressure between the inside of the can and atmospheric pressure on the outside.

Obtaining the Vacuum

Vacuum in canned foods may be obtained in several ways. One of the most common methods is to add hot food to the container. In this way, the residual air is removed, resulting in a partial vacuum. A second method is to add cold food to the container and to preheat it by passing it through a steam box uncovered, or only partially sealed, prior to sealing. Using either of these techniques, the heat causes the product and the air in the headspace to expand, pushing air out of the container. In addition, the water vapor in the headspace displaces air, and trapped air in the food is driven out. In this condition, the can is sealed, and when the product is cooled it will be under vacuum, since much of the air has been removed from the container.

A vacuum in canned foods can also be obtained by subjecting the container to a mechanical vacuum just prior to sealing it in the chamber. A good vacuum can be obtained in this manner, but there are some limitations. For instance, if the product is packed in liquid, such as vegetables packed in canner's brine or fruit packed in syrup, when the vacuum is applied, much of the liquid may be flashed out. This is caused by the dissolved and occluded (trapped bubbles) air in the liquid that comes out as a gas when a sudden vacuum of high intensity is applied. The sudden release of air causes some of the liquid to spatter out of the can. To avoid this, liquids must be subjected to vacuum treatment prior to filling into the can in order to remove dissolved and occluded air.

The third type of vacuum used in canning foods is called a steam jet vacuum. Just before the cover is placed on the can to be sealed, a jet of steam is forced over the contents of the can. This does not provide a high vacuum and only removes air from the headspace of the food in the can. It is used mainly for materials packed without liquid.

LIQUIDS IN CANS

Vegetables and fruits are usually packed in liquid. Canner's brine, a weak solution of sugar and salt, is ordinarily used for vegetables, and sugar solutions that may be as concentrated as 55% sugar or as dilute as 25% sugar are used for fruits. These liquids afford some protection against heat damage because they permit convection heating, which occurs at a faster rate than does conduction heating. With solid packs, such as tuna fish, corned beef hash, and even concentrated soups, such as pea or mushroom, heating takes place in the container through conduction. In convection heating (occurs when liquids are present), a hot layer of liquid rises along the sides of the can body (heat rises), travels over the top to the center, and flows down the central axis as more hot liquid moves up the sides. This mixing serves to speed up the transfer of heat. Thus, in Figure 10–4 the heat transfer pattern in convection can be seen to be more widespread.

In the conduction heating of solid packs, heat penetrates from all sides of the container, but since solid foods are poor conductors of heat, heat travels toward the center of the container only relatively slowly.

In convection heating, the slowest heating point in the container is along the central axis ¾ to 1 ½ in. (1.91 to 3.81 cm) from the bottom (can in the upright position). In conduction heating, the slowest heating point in the container is along the central axis at the geometric center of the container.

FILLING THE CANS

Foods must, of course, be filled into cans before the cans can be sealed, and this is usually done by machine. For instance, with peas, a central hopper,

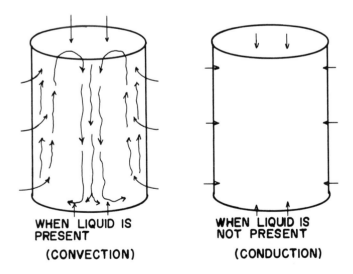

WHEN LIQUID IS
PRESENT
(CONVECTION)

WHEN LIQUID IS
NOT PRESENT
(CONDUCTION)

FIGURE 10-4.   Convection and conduction heating patterns in cans of foods.

which is kept filled with peas, is located above a rotating plate with openings through which the peas can fall. When the plate rotates to the point at which the plate opening is just below the hopper, the opening is just above a bottom container (below the plate), which when filled will hold a certain volume or weight of peas. The peas thus fall down and fill the bottom container that then rotates to a point where the peas are released into a can. With vegetables, after the food is added to the container, canner's brine is added automatically to fill the can, filling all voids and covering the vegetables. This liquid is usually added hot, and since such foods are not packed under vacuum, the hot liquid provides whatever vacuum will be present in the container after processing and cooling. Canner's brine is held in a reservoir on the filling machine and is heated in this reservoir. As will be explained later, the temperature of the brine should be held at 170°F (76.7°C) or higher.

Some products, such as whole tomatoes, must be placed in the can by hand. This is done with the use of a table containing openings along its edges. The peeled tomatoes are placed in the center of the table, and workers seated around the table pull the tomatoes over to the openings and allow them to fall through into a can located below the opening.

Other foods, such as asparagus spears, must be entirely hand-packed. The spears must be arranged within a metal band; the band is pulled tight in order to allow the product to be inserted into the can, which has been laid on its side and is then released once the end of the group of spears has been inserted well within the can opening.

Semiliquid packs that heat by conduction, such as concentrated pea soup or mushroom soup, may be filled hot and can be filled volumetrically by automatic means. Solid packs like tuna fish and corned beef may be filled by hand. A small amount of hot liquid (brine or oil) may be added to provide some vacuum, or the product may be passed through a steam (exhaust) box to be heated and provided with some vacuum before the can is covered and sealed.

SEALING THE CANS

Cans are sealed automatically by machine. In sealing, the cover falls onto the top of the can automatically; the base plate of the sealer (upon which the can rests) raises the can with cover up tightly against the chuck. The edges of the can cover and the flanged body top are subjected to the action of two different rotating rollers. The first roller crimps the cover and body flange so that the edge of the cover is bent around and under the edge of the body flange; the second roller flattens and presses the top seam together so that it forms a tight seal with the help of the plastic gasket located in the outer rim of the cover (see Fig. 10-5).

1. PRIOR TO SEALING

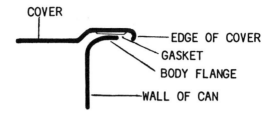

2. AFTER FIRST ROLLER OPERATION

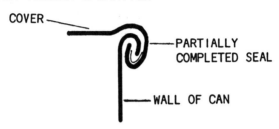

3. AFTER SECOND ROLLER OPERATION

FIGURE 10-5.   Cross-sections of cover and body of can at three stages of sealing.

In the canning operation, it is imperative that the sealing machines provide a tight seal. This can be checked by removing the cover to observe the configurations of the cover hook and body hook (see Fig. 10-6). The dimensions of the seal components may then be measured. It is known that such dimensions should fall within certain limits. Tools for exposing the seam components and special micrometers for measuring their dimensions are available. A simple way to determine that the base plate, first operation (first roller) and second operation (second roller) of the sealing machine have been adjusted properly is to fill a can with boiling water, seal, cool, then measure the vacuum in the can by means of a gauge that reads in inches (1 in.

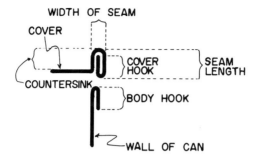

FIGURE 10-6. Components of can seam in exploded view.

= 2.54 cm) of vacuum. The vacuum gauge has a sharp shaft that is pushed through the cover of the can, and a rubber gasket prevents air from entering the can. If a vacuum of 10 in. (25.4 cm) or more is obtained, it can be assumed that the can is effectively sealed.

The sealing operation should be checked at the start of the day's operation and periodically throughout the processing period. The importance of an effective seal cannot be overemphasized due to the unfavorable economic impact that will certainly result from FDA seizures of product and product recalls from the market and/or from lawsuits if food poisonings should occur.

THE HEAT PROCESS

The next operation in food canning is heat processing. Heating times and temperatures for canned foods are based on the destruction of the spores of *Clostridium botulinum,* since this organism has been known to survive an inadequate process and thereafter grow out, producing toxins that can cause sickness and, in some instances, death. To obviate this possibility, a system was set up to ensure the destruction of any spores of *Clostridium botulinum* that might be present in the food.

The first step in developing the new process was to find the most resistant spores of *Clostridium botulinum,* which turned out to be those of certain type A strains. (There are seven known types of *Clostridium botulinum,* each having a number of strains. More about this organism is found in Chap. 6.) The reason that the minimum process was necessarily based on *Clostridium botulinum* is that the toxin produced by the various strains of this particular organism is the most powerful toxin known. In one experiment performed by the authors, the toxin produced by one strain of type B was so powerful that when a bite-size piece of beef containing it was diluted about 10^8

(100,000,000) times, all the mice into which it was injected died. It is considered from these results that if a human had eaten a small amount of that meat, he would surely have died. Next, the heating times at various temperatures (for instance, at 220°, 230°, 240°, and 250°F [104.4°, 110°, 115.6°, and 121.1°C]) that would destroy 60 billion spores of the organism were determined. A curve of thermal death times was then constructed so that the time at any temperature required to destroy 60 billion spores could be obtained from the curve. The curve was generated by plotting the logarithm of the time in minutes (y axis) versus the temperature (°F) (x axis).

Next, thermocouples were placed in cans of food at the slowest heating point (geometric center for conduction heating foods, ¾- 1 ½ in. [1.91-3.81 cm] above the bottom of the center line for convection heating foods), and as the cans were heated in the retort (retort at a particular temperature), the temperature of the slowest heating point in the product was recorded at intervals of every few minutes after the steam was turned on. With the data from these two experiments, thermal death times for spores of *Clostridium botulinum* and temperature of the product at the slowest heating point as it was heated in the retort could be tabulated, as shown in Table 10-2. Thus, the lethality rate could be calculated.

Next, a curve was drawn on rectangular coordinates in which the lethality rate was plotted on the ordinate, y axis, against time of heating in minutes on the abscissa, x axis (see Fig. 10-7). It should be noted that the amount of lethality accumulating before the temperature reached 212°F (100°C) was negligible, since more than 400 min at this temperature are required to destroy 60 billion spores of *Clostridium botulinum*.

Once the curve was drawn, the processing time required to destroy 60 billion spores of *Clostridium botulinum* could be obtained. For instance, if 1 in. (2.54 cm) of distance on the y axis were equivalent to 1/100 of a lethal effect (lethality rate), and 1 in. (2.54 cm) on the x axis were equal to 10 min of time, then 1 in.^{2} (6.45 cm^2) under the curve would provide 1/100 × 10 or 1/10 of a lethal effect, and it would require 10 in.^{2} (64.5 cm^2) under the curve to obtain

TABLE 10-2.   Calculation of Lethality Rates

Time *(t)* After Steam Turned on (min)	Temperature (T) of Slowest Heating Point at Time t (°F)	Thermal Death Time (TDT) of Spores at Temperature T (min)	Lethality Rate (1/TDT)
t_1	T_1	TDT_1	$1/TDT_1$
t_2	T_2	TDT_2	$1/TDT_2$
t_3	T_3	TDT_3	$1/TDT_3$

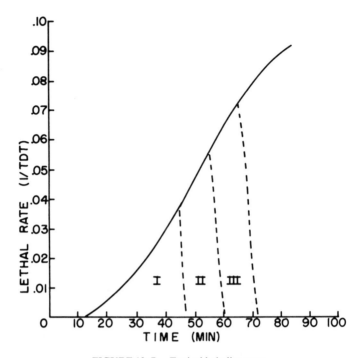

FIGURE 10-7.   Typical lethality curve.

one lethal effect or to destroy 60 billion spores of *Clostridium botulinum.* The time under the curve, after the heat was turned on, corresponding to 10 in.[2] (64.5 cm^2) would then be determined, and this would be the processing time, steam on to steam off. There are other methods for determining the processing time for canned foods, but these need not be discussed here.

   Actually, few canned products are subjected to a heating effect as low as that required to destroy *Clostridium botulinum.* The reason is that there are many bacterial spores that are more heat-resistant than those of *Clostridium botulinum,* and if a minimum botulinum kill were used (heating sufficient to destroy 60 billion spores of *Clostridium botulinum*), the more resistant spores might survive, grow out, and cause spoilage of the food. A minimum *botulinum* kill is equivalent to the heating of all parts of the food (this means the slowest heating part) to the equivalent of 2.5 min at 250°F (121.1°C). Many foods are heated to the equivalent of 7 min at 250°F (121.1°C) at the slowest heating point, indicating that, in practice, the heat process is based on thermophiles that have even higher heat resistances than *C. botulinum.*

THE CONVENTIONAL HEAT-PROCESSING CHAMBER (RETORT)

The ordinary retort (see Fig. 10-8) is the three-crate retort in which one crate of cans is placed on top of another in the retort. When cans are placed in these crates, they may be allowed to fall into the crate haphazardly or they may be placed in the crate on end in an orderly manner. If the latter system is used, perforated metal separators must be placed between the layers of cans. This provides for an adequate circulation of steam around the cans necessary for optimum heat transfer to the product.

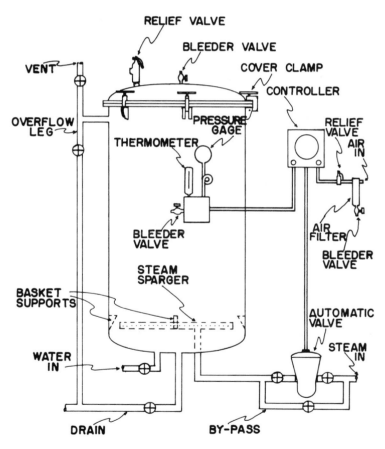

FIGURE 10-8.   Conventional retort.

All retorts should be fitted with automatic steam valves that can be set to allow steam to flow into them to raise the processing temperature only to the desired point. Retorts should also have a temperature sensor (inside of the retort) attached to a recorder on the outside and a chart showing temperature and time of processing for each batch of product. Processing charts should be identified with the code on the cans of each batch and should be kept on file. If the product is to be cooled in the retort after processing, an air pressure system with automatic inlet valve that can be set for a definite air pressure should be a part of the installation. In such installations, there should be an automatic pressure outlet valve attached. Otherwise, when cans with high vacuum are cooled, the outside pressure may become high enough to cause paneling of the cans.

All retorts must be fitted with fast-opening valves to allow venting of the retorts. When the steam is first turned on, the vent valve should be opened wide and left open until the temperature is raised to 220°F (104.4°C). This removes, from the retort, air that would otherwise cause cold spots around some of the cans and thus prevent adequate heating. The reason for this is that air is a poor heat conductor. Also, during retorting, a small bleeder petcock at the top of the retort should be kept in the wide open position. This removes air that may come in with the steam and also provides for good circulation of the steam.

COOLING HEAT-PROCESSED FOODS

Cans of food that have been heat processed may be cooled in the retort by allowing water to flow in after the steam has been turned off, in which case they may be cooled under a pressure of air or steam exerted over the water level in the retort. In other operations, the retort may be blown down and the crates of cans removed and moved slowly through a cooling canal. In either case, the cooling water should be potable (drinkable) and should not have a high bacterial count. The reason for this is that as the vacuum is forming in the can due to the cooling, the gasket in some cans may be soft enough to permit microscopic amounts of the cooling water to be sucked into the cans. If the cooling water is high in bacterial count, enough bacteria, which may cause spoilage or even disease, may thus enter the can and contaminate the product. Thus, it is desirable to chlorinate cooling water so that it contains a residual of 5 ppm available chlorine. This level of chlorine is enough to keep the water relatively free from bacteria.

During cooling, the average temperature of the product in the can should be brought to 95°–110°F (35°–43.3°C) as quickly as possible. The reason for this is twofold. First, if this temperature is maintained, the surface of the can will be warm enough to evaporate moisture remaining from the cold water bath. Should this water not be evaporated, it would cause rusting of the outside of the can, possibly spoiling the label and making the container unsightly, so that it would have to be rejected. Second, if the temperature is not lowered to the above-stated range, it may be sufficiently high to promote the growth of residual thermophilic bacteria (see Chap. 7), which would cause spoilage of the food within the can.

Thermophilic bacteria form spores, and the spores of many types of thermophilic bacteria are unusually heat-resistant. Therefore, in canning operations, an attempt is made to keep as many thermophilic bacteria out of the product as possible. This can be accomplished by preventing the buildup of these bacteria at various points in the canning operation in the plant. The commercial process used today will reduce the number of thermophiles in foods to a minimum so that only a few thermophilic spores will be present in the product. The few remaining spores will cause no problems, provided the product is held at temperatures below 110°F (43.3°C). Therefore, in cooling freshly processed cans, the average product temperature is brought to 110°F (43.3°C) or below since thermophilic bacteria require only a few hours of growth to cause spoilage.

After or before cans are heat-processed, they must be washed to remove grease and food particles that get onto the outside of the can during the various procedures involved in the operation. This is done by passing the can through alkaline or detergent solutions, then through rinse water. If done after heat processing, the temperature of the rinsing solutions should be high enough to provide for evaporation of the water, thus preventing corrosion of the outside of the container.

After cooling, cans of food are usually packed into cases or stored in large masses in a warehouse in conditions in which they cool very slowly to room temperature. To prevent growth of thermophiles in the product prior to canning, canner's brine in the reservoir on the filling machine should be held at 170°F (76.7°C) or higher, a temperature at which no growth could take place.

OTHER METHODS OF HEAT PROCESSING

There are a number of types of processing retorts for canned foods that have come into use in recent years and are quite different from the conventional retort.

Continuous Agitating Retort

In the agitating retort, cans enter the retort continuously on a conveyor through a special inlet that prevents loss of steam. In the retort, the cans are conveyed back and forth for whatever period of time is necessary for sterilization. Also, while being conveyed, they are rotated around their long axes. Except for solid-packed foods, this action causes some agitation of the product within the can, speeding up heat penetration and shortening the processing time. Cans exit from the continuous agitating retort through a special valve and enter the cooling system that is set up much in the manner of the retort except that it is filled with cooling water.

In another type, the agitort, the cans or containers of cans are attached to a wheel that rotates during processing. In this system, the cans are rotated end over end, so the air in the headspace will travel along the sides of the can to mix the food, and back again (see Fig. 10-9). The agitation of the contents hastens heat transfer even in semisolid packs. In this system, the cans are cooled within the agitort. Because the process depends on the rate at which the cans rotate, special equipment has been devised to count the rotations the cans undergo during the process.

The Hydrostatic Cooker

Hydrostatic cookers (see Fig. 10-10) are used in Europe and to some extent in the United States. In this system, there is a central chamber with a narrow entrance on one side and an exit chamber on the other side. The system is partially filled with water, and when steam is turned on in the central chamber, the water is forced up to higher levels in the entrance and exit legs (chambers).

Cans enter through the warm water of the entrance chamber on a conveyor, gradually entering warmer water as they approach the steam chamber. They are conveyed through the steam chamber at temperatures and for times that provide for commercial sterilization of the product. They are then

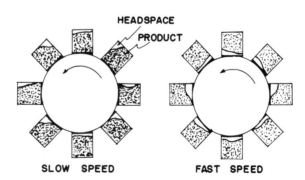

FIGURE 10-9.   Headspace patterns in fast-speed and slow-speed agitorts.

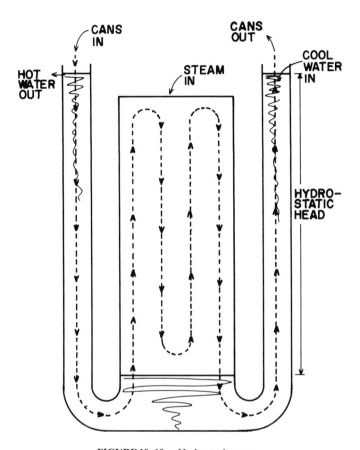

FIGURE 10-10.   Hydrostatic retort.

conveyed out of the steam chamber, first through the warm water and eventually through the cold water of the exit chamber. The cans may be rotated around the long axis as they are carried along. Because the pressure in the hydrostatic cooker depends on the water head (height of water), this type cooker is quite high (about 40 ft [12.2 m]).

The agitort and the hydrostatic cooker are somewhat faster than other heat-processing methods, both because of the agitation that speeds up heat penetration and because in such conditions somewhat higher temperatures (up to 270°F [132.2°C]) may be used without causing excessive heat damage to the product. This allows for the canning of some semiliquid foods, such as mushroom soup or cream-style corn, in large cans. Since the labor involved and the cost of the container per unit weight of food are smaller as the can size is increased, it is economical to can foods in larger containers. This is desirable for institutions feeding large numbers of people, because it costs them less to buy and handle large cans.

HTST Process

There are systems for processing canned foods at high temperatures for short times. These are referred to as HTST processes. In such systems, commercial sterilization is achieved at temperatures of 280°–300°F (137.8°–148.9°C) in 15–45 sec. Large discrete particles cannot be processed by HTST methods because they require some time for heat to penetrate their centers. HTST methods are applied only to liquids, and to foods that have been puréed (mashed bananas, concentrated pea soup, etc.).

Aseptic Fill Method

The aseptic process was deemed by the Institute of Food Technologists to be the most important food science innovation during the 50-year period 1939–1989. In one system, the puréed material or liquid is passed in thin layers through a heating system wherein the temperature of the product is raised quickly. The product is then pumped to a holding chamber where it is held at high temperatures for 10–20 sec, then pumped in thin layers through a cooling system wherein the temperature of the product is lowered quickly. It is next pumped to a filling system where it is forced into presterilized cans, and the cans are sealed with presterilized covers. Such systems must be presterilized with very high temperature gas or steam before the operation is started. Moreover, the filling and sealing of cans must be carried out under high temperatures, provided by steam or hot gas, to prevent the entrance of bacteria. Other systems use flexible pouches or sealed plastic trays.

Cooking Under Pressure

Another HTST method of sterilizing canned foods is carried out in pressure chambers. As the pressure of the air in a chamber is raised above atmospheric pressure, the temperature at which water boils is raised; and if suitable pressures are used, temperatures of 280°F (137.8°C) or higher may be attained. In these conditions, foods that contain discrete particles may be heated in open steam kettles in the pressure chamber for sufficient time to allow sterilization at the center of the food particles, then filled into cans and sealed. The cans are then inverted, allowed to stand for a few minutes, then cooled. It is not necessary to presterilize the cans in this case since the high temperature of the product, when filled, will destroy whatever bacteria may be adhering to the inside. The containers are inverted to ensure contact between the bacteria adhering to the inside of the cover and the very hot product that would, of course, destroy the bacteria. Personnel working in chambers under pressure may need to be pressurized slowly in locks when entering and depressurized slowly in locks when leaving. Otherwise, they may be subject to the bends, a condition caused by nitrogen dissolving in the blood when humans are subjected to high pressures, and coming out as gas bubbles when the pressure is suddenly released. A system employing both cooking under pressure and aseptic filling is now being used to can such products as chicken salad.

The Sous Vide Process

This process, developed in France and used in various European countries, will be given only minor mention here, because it is not approved by the U.S. Food and Drug Administration. By this process, foods are packed in vacuum and heat-processed but not enough to provide for the destruction of botulinum bacteria. The products, reputed to be of superior quality, must be held under refrigeration until prepared for consumption; otherwise surviving bacterial spores can vegetate and produce toxin.

Microwave Processing

Microwave energy, usually generated by a magnetron, occurs as alternating current at either 915 or 2450 megahertz. Both frequencies are authorized by the federal government for use with microwave ovens. Because water molecules are polar (have positive and negative ends), they tend to oscillate as they try to align themselves alternately between the positive and negative charges of the microwave energy. When frozen foods are exposed to microwave energy, the liquid water in them (all frozen foods contain some water in the liquid state) begins to heat due to the friction created by high-speed oscillations of the water molecules. Most of the water in frozen foods is in the ice state and is not affected by the microwave energy, until heat generated by the liquid water molecules is conducted to the ice, melting it, and thereby producing more liquid water to become involved in the heating process.

   The first application of microwave energy in industry occurred during the 1970s when cooperative experiments between the Gloucester Laboratory, a USDC facility, and the Raytheon Co. resulted in the introduction of a continuous microwave tunnel in the seafood industry for thawing or tempering of shrimp and fish blocks. In tempering, the product is not quite thawed yet lends itself to further processing such as cutting and/or coating with a breading.

   Those early experiments also tested the feasibility of using microwave energy for shucking oysters. The innovation soon spread to the meat industry, and now microwave processing is extended to other applications including baking, pasteurization, and sterilization. Because the highest temperature attainable in conventional microwave units is 212°F (100°C), it is necessary to pressurize the processing chamber of the microwave unit in order to achieve the high temperature required to effect sterilization in a reasonable time period.

Containers

Cans. For general commercial applications, the speed with which cans may be handled during the process and the structural protection they lend to the contents may make them still the most desirable overall container for heat-sterilized foods.

Flexible Pouches. Flexible pouches have several advantages over metal and glass containers: (1) Their shape adapts to available space. (2) They are lighter in weight. (3) When empty, they require less space. (4) When filled, their thickness dimension is small, permitting faster processing times and mitigating heat damage to foods. (5) Heat penetration is greater. (6) They are not subject to corrosion or breakage. (7) They are easier to open.

Flexible pouches have a few disadvantages: (1) Pouches cannot be filled as rapidly. (2) They are awkward to handle (e.g., stacking), especially the larger ones. (3) They give no structural support to fragile contents. (4) They are somewhat vulnerable to tearing and cutting.

The materials used in pouches are generally composite laminates and quite strong. They include an outer layer of polyester, which has nearly the tensile strength of steel and resists wear and tear, an inner layer of nylon-11 or polypropylene that resists wear and tear and seals well, and aluminum foil as a middle layer for eliminating light from the contents as well as for making the pouch material impermeable to gases. The layers are bonded together with an adhesive. While flexible pouches can be processed in conventional retorts, special systems have been developed; in most cases, the systems are continuous.

Glass Containers. As a container material, glass has several desirable properties. It permits visibility of the product, imparts no taste, and is noncorrosive. The use of glass containers precedes by centuries the use of metal cans and, of course, flexible pouches. The advances in closures of glass containers are probably more dramatic than the advances in the design of the containers and, in fact, have forced the changes in container design. Cork closures have been perhaps the most important. Cork is light, compressible, hermetically sealable, inexpensive, plentiful, and stable. Corks have long been in use for closing glass bottles, and still are. Ordinary cork closures (stoppers), however, are unable to withstand the buildup of internal pressure, except where the pressure is not too great and when they are used with bottles having small openings, such as in wine and champagne bottles. The diameters of the openings of glass jars used for preserving fruit and vegetables are so large that a fitted cork would be easily pushed out (remember that for any given pressure, the total force increases as the area of the opening of the glass container increases). Even for small openings, it was necessary to develop holddown devices, such as clamps and wire fasteners, when high pressures were expected, as in the bottling of beer. The crimped metal crown with cork liner was an effective closure for beer and soda bottles. However, aluminum screw-caps are now used in nearly all cases.

Variations of screw-top, wide-mouth jars evolved to the modern Mason jar (named after its inventor). Tight-fitting, screw-type closures find a wide variety of uses in modern glass containers for commercially pasteurized and heat-processed foods as well as in home-canning operations. In home-canning, a Putnam-type closure (wire clamp with an eccentric lever that forces a glass lid tightly against a rubber gasket that fits over the lip of the jar) is widely used. The Putnam-type container is quicker to close and to open and generally requires less strength for usage.

However, it was not until more advanced jar closures were developed that canning in glass became significant. These closures include the Phoenix cap, the Sure Seal cap, and the Vacuum Side Seal cap, types found in many tumbler-sized tapered jars like those used for cheese spreads and jellies; and the Amerseal cap, a modified screw-type cap as found in capping jars for apple sauce, jellies, and wide-mouth fruit juice bottles.

Screw-type and pressed/pry-off-type lids and caps are currently in wide-spread use. Also, there is a growing trend to make containers tamperproof or to show when they have undergone tampering.

Microwavable Containers.   The ease and speed (few minutes) with which microwavable entrees can be heated and served will accelerate an already growing demand for them. Not only are microwave ovens available in nearly every home, but they are also available in nearly every workplace where they are used by nearly all employees. Packaging for microwavable meals includes trays made of high-gas-barrier materials such as polypropylene bonded to an ethylene vinyl alcohol polymer that satisfies the criteria for such containers: (1) microwavable, (2) lightweight, (3) unbreakable, (4) easy to open, and (5) reclosable.

CANNING OF ACID FOODS

Acid foods are considered to be those that have a pH of 4.5 or lower. Acid foods that are canned need not be heated at high temperatures to attain commercial sterilization. The reason for this is that bacteria, including those that form heat-resistant spores, are more easily destroyed by heat when present in acid solutions. Moreover, spore-forming bacteria generally will not grow in foods having pH values of 4.5 or less. There are some exceptions to this; for instance, *Bacillus thermoacidurans* may grow in tomato juice (maximum pH 4.5) and cause spoilage.

Acid foods are ordinarily processed by heating the cans in boiling water until all parts of the product have reached 180°–210°F (82.2°–98.9°C), and then are cooled. An exception is tomato juice, which is now often processed by flash heating to 250°F (121.1°C), holding at this temperature for 0.7 min, cooling to 200°–210°F (93.3°–98.9°C), filling into presterilized cans, sealing, and inverting the can so that the sterilizing effect of the heat (200°–210°F [93.3°–98.9°C]) at that pH will act upon the can cover.

Those foods that have a pH of 4.5 or less are apples and apple juice, apricots, blackberries, blueberries, boysenberries, cherries, cherry juice, all citrus fruits and their juices, currants, gooseberries, loganberries, papaya juice, peaches, pears, pickles, pineapple in various forms and pineapple juice, plums, prune juice, raspberries, rhubarb, sauerkraut and sauerkraut juice, strawberries, tomatoes, tomato juice, and youngberries.

WAREHOUSE STORAGE
OF CANNED FOODS

When canned foods have been heat-processed and cooled and the cans have been cleaned and dried, they are either stored in warehouses in bulk until labeled, cased, and shipped out, or they are labeled, cased, and stored in a warehouse until shipped out. Lithographed cans may be used, in which case labeling is not necessary.

Warehouses should be maintained so that the temperature does not rise much above 85°F (29.4°C) or fall below 50°F (10°C). Very high temperatures may promote the growth of thermophilic bacterial spores present in small numbers in the food. Very low temperatures may lower the temperature of the cans to the point that in sudden hot spells the cans will sweat (condense moisture), eventually causing external corrosion of the cans.

11

Drying

The preservation of foods by drying is probably the oldest food preservation process practiced by humans. It is believed that many foods, especially grains and fruits of high sugar content, were preserved by primitive peoples by allowing them to dry in the sun. Spices and fish, cut into thin strips, were also preserved in this manner.

There are a number of different methods of drying foods for preservation. The most important are sun drying, tunnel or cabinet drying, drum drying, spray drying, and freeze-drying.

PRETREATMENT

Foods to be dried must be washed, and some peeled and cut. Others may be precooked. Cut fruits are subject to darkening through enzyme action and must be either blanched or treated with salts or sulfur dioxide. However, if treated with sulfur dioxide, the product must be so labeled, because of known allergenic reactions in some consumers. Certain vegetables may be pretreated in the same manner. Sulfuring may also be required to limit nonenzymatic browning (the Maillard reaction). Browning refers to the development of brown color.

Various dried egg products (egg white, dried egg yolk, and dried whole egg products) are also subject to browning and are susceptible to the development of off-flavors. In this case, the reaction involves a combination of a small amount of glucose, which is naturally present, with the proteins. Because of this, dried egg products, especially egg whites, may be treated with glucose oxidase and catalase. The glucose oxidase converts glucose to gluconic acid (which does not combine with amino groups) and hydrogen perox-

145

ide. The purpose of the catalase is to convert the undesirable peroxide to water and oxygen. The elimination of glucose may also be done by natural fermentation, using microbes. However, this process can be considered unsanitary, and in order to avoid product spoilage and even food poisoning, it is necessary to hold the product at 130°F (54.4°C) for several hours after drying.

Since prunes are naturally coated with a thin layer of wax, drying is greatly speeded up by predipping the fruit in dilute lye solution, then in hot water, prior to drying.

METHODS OF DRYING

Sun Drying

Sun or natural drying is still used in hot climates for the production of dried fruits or nuts. This may be done in direct sunlight or in shaded areas where the drying is accomplished by the hot dry air. It should be apparent that sundried fruit is produced only in areas where the climate provides periods of relatively high temperatures, relatively low humidities, and little or no rainfall. Prunes, grapes, apricots, peaches, and pears are dried in this manner. Some of these fruits are also dried in tunnel or cabinet dehydrators.

In sun drying, small fruits are prepared and spread on trays to dry in the sun for several days, then stacked to complete the drying cycle in shaded areas. Larger fruits, such as apricots, peaches, and pears, are halved and pitted, and apples are peeled, cored, and sliced prior to drying. Such fruits are sulfured to prevent enzymatic browning. Sun drying times vary between 4 and 25 days, depending on the size of the product, the type of pretreatment, and so on. During sun drying, precautions must be taken to prevent contamination from wind-blown dust and dirt. Moisture contents in the sun-dried products vary between 10% and 35% depending on the tendency of the dried product to absorb moisture. After drying, some fruit may require moisture-vapor-proof containers.

Hot-Air Drying

When mechanical dehydrators are used, the product is placed on metal mesh belts in a tunnel, or in a cabinet on trays where controlled, elevated temperatures are used. Heated air is circulated by blowers and the air temperature, relative humidity, and air velocity are controlled. Hot-air driers of this type are classified as parallel flow, counter flow, direct flow, or cross flow, depending on the direction in which the product moves in relation to the direction of flow of the heated air. In bin, loft, and fluidized-bed driers the heated air is blown upward through the product.

The hot air used in tunnel or cabinet driers may or may not be recirculated. If it is recirculated, the relative humidity must be carefully regulated since during each passage over the food, the air takes up moisture, raising its relative humidity.

The air in dehydrators is heated either by steam tubes or coils, or by being mixed directly with the combustion gasses of gas or oil. Electric resistance heaters are used in rare instances. In all cases, except natural draft driers, the hot air or gas is circulated by blowers or fans of different designs and is discharged from the drier through a ventilator that may be equipped with a fan to increase its capacity, thus increasing the amount of air that can be circulated through the drier (Fig. 11-1).

The time required for the drying of a particular product depends on the characteristics of the raw material (moisture content, composition, shape, and size), the temperature and humidity of the air in the drier, the rate of air circulation in the drier, and so forth.

Initially, drying of foods occurs through evaporation of moisture from the food surface. Later, in the drying cycle, drying involves the diffusion of water, water vapor, or both, to the surface of the food.

In the initial stages of drying, air velocities are usually regulated at about 1000 ft/min (304.8 m/min), but in the later stages, the air velocity is usually

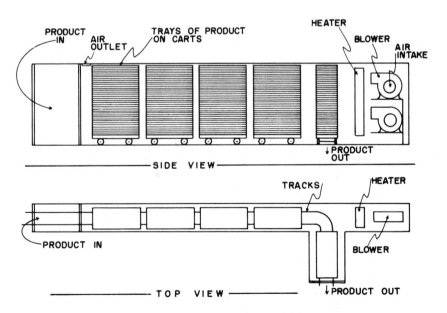

FIGURE 11-1.   Continuous tunnel drier.

lowered to about 500 ft/min (152.4 m/min), since this rate will remove all moisture available at surfaces at this point of the drying cycle. High initial rates of drying are said to prevent adherence of the dried particles to drying trays and belts, thus facilitating unloading. Water-repellent plastics, such as polyethylene or Teflon, may be used for coating trays and belts to prevent sticking of the dried food.

Due to evaporation of moisture, which lowers the temperature, product temperature is below that of the air in the drier during the initial stages of drying and up to a point where approximately one-half of the moisture has been evaporated. The product temperature then starts to rise, and at the end of the drying cycle approaches that of the air.

Foods undergo some form of breakdown, or loss in quality, when they are exposed to heat. The amount of damage they undergo increases as the temperature to which they are exposed increases, and it also increases as the time of exposure is increased. Therefore, it is important to control both time and temperature during the drying cycle. In the beginning of the drying cycle, higher temperatures can be used for two reasons: (1) The amount of surface water in the foods is highest in the beginning of the drying cycle, so most of the energy of the hot air is expended in vaporizing surface water, and (2) the tendency of the food to be heated by the hot air is partially counterbalanced by the cooling effect of the evaporation of the surface water.

In the later stages of drying, the amount of surface water in the product is relatively low; therefore, it is prudent to lower the temperature of the air to a point where the energy is just sufficient to vaporize the surface water. If the air temperature is not lowered, the excess energy will go into raising the temperature of the product, which by this stage is not being cooled sufficiently by evaporative cooling. For the drying of vegetables, the initial temperature of the air is 180°–200°F (82.2°–93.3°C). In the later stages of drying, the temperature is reduced to 130°–160°F (54.4°–71.1°C).

Fluidized-bed Drying

In fluidized-bed drying (a special type of hot-air drying), the product is fed in at one end to lie on a porous plate and is agitated and moved along toward the exit at the other end by hot air that is blown up through the product. The air that has passed through the product, picking up moisture, exits through an outlet at the top of the drier. More about fluidized-bed processing is found in Chapter 13.

Drum Drying

Milk, fruit, vegetable juices, purées, and cereals may be dried with drum driers. These products are allowed to flow onto the surface of two heated stainless steel drums rotating in opposite directions with little clearance between them. The product dries on the drums and is scraped off by stationary blades fixed along the surface of the drum (see Fig. 11-2). Refrigeration may be used to lower the temperature of the dried product quickly. Drum drying can also be carried out under vacuum, in which case the drying is accomplished at lower temperatures and the product is protected from oxidation. In the ordinary drum drying, the process is controlled by varying the moisture content of the raw material (preconcentration), the temperature of drum surfaces, the space between the drums, the speed of rotation of the drums, and the amount of vacuum applied.

Spray Drying

Milk, eggs, soluble or instant coffee, syrups, and other liquid or semiliquid foods are spray-dried (see Fig. 11-3). The liquid material is sprayed into the top of a chamber simultaneously with hot air, which is also blown in at the top. The cool, moist air exits near the bottom, and the dried particles fall to the bottom and are collected by gravity flow, or by the aid of scrapers that may also be used to remove dried material from the walls or bottom. Cyclones (conical-shaped collectors) may be used to collect particles escaping with the exit air.

Particle size is an important factor in spray drying, and the liquid is, therefore, dispersed into the drying chamber through a pressure nozzle or by centrifugal force generated by a disc rotating at high speed. Both methods atom-

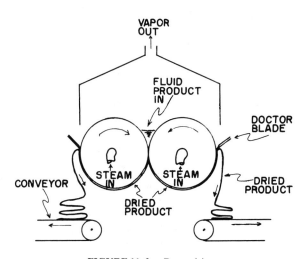

FIGURE 11-2.   Drum drier.

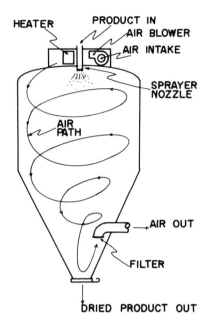

FIGURE 11-3.   Spray drier.

ize the liquid, producing droplets of a size that will be dried by the heated air through which they must fall on their way to the bottom of the drying chamber. The material may be preconcentrated in some instances, or aids, such as gums, pectin, or milk solids, may be added prior to spray drying. In any case, it is necessary to lower the moisture content and temperature of the product to the point where particles will neither stick together nor stick to the wall of the spray drier.

In spray drying, the temperature of the food reaches a maximum of about 165°F (73.9°C) and only remains there for a short period of time. However, in spray drying the moisture content can be lowered only to about 5%. Thus, spray drying does not cause much heat damage to foods, but because of their relatively high moisture contents, spray-dried foods may undergo some spoilage during storage. The shearing action of the atomization step of spray drying may affect the functional characteristics of some proteins, such as those of egg products (whipping qualities, etc.).

Spray drying tends to produce fine powders that neither wet nor disperse readily when reconstituted. The material thus tends to clump and form a mass through which water does not penetrate. In order to avoid this, a process known as agglomeration may be used. In this case, the dried material is slightly rehumidified; for instance, dried milk powder may be heated with steam under controlled conditions that surface-moisten the product. By other methods, the preconcentrated product is injected into the drying chamber with a steam injector. The latter procedure causes the dried product to form in the shape of beads or bubbles, which break into flakes that disperse readily in water. Vacuum puff drying may also be used to produce a product that disperses in water without forming clumps.

Freeze-Drying

The freeze-drying of foods is carried out by first freezing the product and then subjecting it to a very high vacuum wherein temperatures are high enough to assist in the evaporation of moisture but low enough to prevent melting of the ice in the product (see Fig. 11–4). In this method, the water, existing as ice in the food, is evaporated directly as a vapor without passing through the liquid phase (sublimation). The vapor is condensed outside the evaporation chamber. The resulting product has a honeycombed structure containing much surface area, and because it maintains its original shape, its specific gravity is reduced considerably, as is the moisture content.

In freeze-drying, the maximum surface temperatures used depend on the composition of the food. Some foods, such as vegetables and mushrooms, can withstand 180°F (82.2°C); others, such as fatty fish, require temperatures as low as 100°F (37.8°C). The vacuum applied must be very high (less than 0.02 in. [0.05 cm] mercury), and most foods require even higher vacuums for good results.

As in the case of foods dried by other methods, it may be necessary to blanch or to treat the foods prior to freezing them, or to treat them with chemicals to provide a source of sulfurous acid to inactivate or inhibit enzymes. This is especially the case with vegetables (garlic and onions excepted) and mushrooms. Meats are sliced or cut into small enough portions to permit reasonably fast drying. Chicken is usually precooked, boned and diced prior to freezing and drying.

While it has been stated that faster freezing rates with the resulting uniformly distributed small ice crystals are preferable for foods that are to be freeze-dried, some investigators have found that slower rates of freezing result in better rehydration (reabsorption of water) of the dried food, hence better quality. The temperature to which the frozen food is brought prior to the drying process will depend on the product itself and should be low enough to rule out significant amounts of melted material. For most foods this temperature is around −7°F (−21.7°C), but for some fruit juices may be as low as −26° to −30°F (−32.2° to −34.4°C).

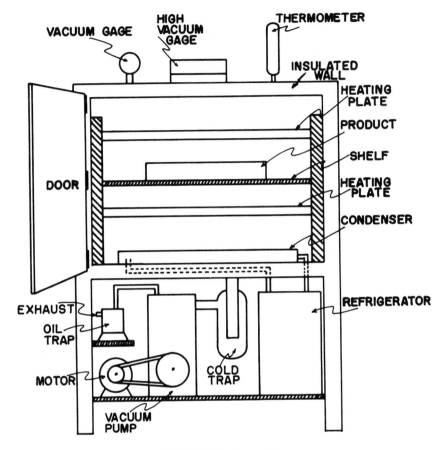

FIGURE 11-4.   Freeze drier.

During freeze-drying, by most commercial methods, the highest food temperature is that of the dried surface layers. The temperature of the ice in the food is determined by the degree of vacuum present in the evaporation chamber. The higher the vacuum, the lower the ice temperature.

Freeze-dried foods are dehydrated to lower moisture contents than those dried by other methods. Usually, the moisture content of the freeze-dried food is below 3%. Since large surface areas are present in freeze-dried foods, it may be necessary to use an inert gas, such as nitrogen, to break the vacuum and so prevent chemical changes, such as oxidation of fats, which may occur shortly after contact with air is made.

Puff Drying

Puff drying may be used for some foods that are temperature-sensitive, such as fruit or vegetable juice concentrates. With this method, the product may be heated in an oven and suddenly subjected to a high vacuum. In other applications, the product is evacuated to remove air, then heated with steam, then puffed by reapplying the vacuum. Puffing may also be attained by raising the temperature of the food under conditions that raise the temperature of the water in the food above $212°F$ ($100°C$) to provide pressure. The product expands or puffs when the external pressure is released. This is done with some cereals, providing a porous, puffed structure.

Microwave Drying

Despite the demonstrated potential for the use of microwave energy for drying foods, there is no sizable application of this process at this time.

RECONSTITUTION OF DRIED FOODS

Dried foods ordinarily must be reconstituted (water must be added back to them) before they can be eaten. During drying and during storage, changes take place in the foods that affect the rate and extent to which water will be taken up by the dried product. Changes in protein and other components cause dried foods to have a somewhat lower rehydrated moisture content than that of the raw material from which the dried product was made. There is also a redistribution of soluble components during rehydration.

It has been observed that some dried foods rehydrate better when the water is held at low temperatures (below $40°F$ [$4.4°C$]). Other foods are said to rehydrate better when the water used is at higher temperatures, with some foods rehydrating satisfactorily in boiling water.

PACKAGING OF DRIED FOODS

In the packaging of dried foods, some products require only minimal specifications (cereals, some vegetables, etc.). Others require packages that are essentially moisture-vapor-proof. Hygroscopic materials, especially some dried fruit juices, which readily take up moisture, must be packaged to prevent moisture from entering.

Freeze-dried foods have a very low moisture content. If their low moisture content is not retained, they lose their desirable characteristics because of nonenzymatic browning (see Chap. 9). Moreover, since the water has been removed, such components as fats are exposed to the oxygen of the air over a large surface area, subjecting them to an accelerated rate of oxidation that eventually leads to rancidification and off-flavor development.

Certain freeze-dried foods, such as fatty meats (especially pork), lobster meat, crab meat, and shrimp, require protection against both oxidation and moisture absorption. They must, therefore, be packaged under vacuum or in an inert atmosphere in packages that are impervious to both moisture and oxygen, such as hermetically sealed metal containers and flexible pouches made of laminated aluminum foil and plastic. Fruit juices, dehydrated whole milk, and certain freeze-dried egg products must also be protected against both oxygen and moisture.

Some products, such as certain freeze-dried vegetables and mushrooms, need only be protected against moisture.

THE EFFECT OF DRYING ON MICROORGANISMS

The main purpose of drying foods is to lower their moisture content to a particular level that will exclude the growth of microorganisms (bacteria, molds, and yeasts). For any given moisture content, one food may support the growth of microorganisms while another will not. Whether or not microorganisms will grow in a dried food depends on the water activity.

The lower the water activity of a food, the less probable that microorganisms will grow. Generally, molds will grow at lower water activities than yeasts and yeasts will grow at lower water activities than bacteria. For this reason, molds are more apt to grow in dried foods than are yeasts or bacteria. In drying foods, therefore, the moisture content is lowered to the point where microorganisms will not grow and it is kept that way through packaging, which excludes moisture.

Water activity can also be lowered by soluble components, such as sugar or salt. Thus, certain syrups and salted, partially dried foods (e.g., fish) are relatively stable as far as the growth of microorganisms is concerned, although there may be conditions in which they become subject to the growth of yeasts or molds.

DETERIORATION IN DRIED FOODS

Oxidative Spoilage of Dried Foods

Regarding the chemical changes that may take place in dried foods, oxidation of fats is one of the chief causes of deterioration. This is especially the case with fish, shrimp, crab meat, lobster, and other seafoods, and also a factor of some concern with meats such as pork. The pigment that provides the red color of cooked crustacean foods may also be changed or entirely bleached through the oxidation. Packaging under vacuum or in an inert atmosphere, such as nitrogen, and in such a manner as to exclude oxygen, may be used to protect dried foods against oxidation of fats. There may be instances in which antioxidants can also be added to the food to inhibit oxidation of fats. Antioxidants are chemicals that tend to interfere with the type of oxidation to which unsaturated (adjacent carbons of the fatty acids not fully taken up with hydrogen atoms) fats are subject. For instance, the tocopherols (vitamin E) are antioxidants.

Very small amounts of chemical antioxidants are required to provide a considerable protection against the oxidation of fats. For instance, only about 0.02% of a chemical antioxidant may be added to fats or oils subject to oxidation. However, antioxidants are fat-soluble and are not generally soluble in water. For many foods, therefore, in which the fat is solid or generally distributed throughout the food, there is no known method of getting antioxidants into the fat itself. Hence, there is no good method of preventing rancidification of the fat of some foods through the use of antioxidants. The packaging of dried products in such a manner as to exclude light is another procedure that may be used to assist in the prevention of fat oxidation since light energy accelerates fat oxidation and rancidification.

Nonenzymatic Browning in Dried Foods

Nonenzymatic browning is another cause of deterioration in dried foods. This may be due to caramelization (a dehydration of sugars) or to the combination of certain sugars and proteins, either process leading eventually to the formation of brown- or black-colored compounds that not only cause off-flavors but also discolor the food. The best protection against such changes is to lower the moisture content to the point where the rate of nonenzymatic browning is greatly reduced. In some foods this may mean lowering the moisture to less than 2%. Sulfurous acid or a source of this compound may also be used to inhibit nonenzymatic browning. Browning may also change proteins, lowering their nutrient quality and affecting their rehydration properties.

Enzymatic Changes in Dried Foods

Enzymatic changes may take place in dried foods during drying, storage, or rehydration. Generally, such changes are prevented by preblanching of the food, or by using sulfurous acid to inhibit enzyme action. Lowering and retaining the moisture content to 2% or less will inhibit enzyme changes during storage, but this process will not prevent such changes from taking place during rehydration of the food.

12

Refrigeration at Temperatures Above Freezing

Unlike drying or freezing, both methods of preserving foods in certain areas of the world for centuries, the refrigeration of foods at temperatures above freezing is of comparatively recent origin, but the history of this method of food processing is well documented. Ice and snow had been used by the Romans and the early French for the preparation of iced drinks, but the application of refrigeration at temperatures above freezing as a means of extending the storage life of foods was started in the United States in the middle 1800s. It is now the most popular method of food preservation, and it is estimated that more than 85% of all of our foods are refrigerated (temperatures above freezing) at one point or another in the chain of food handling from harvesting to consumption.

At the start, ice, harvested from lakes and ponds that had frozen over in the winter, was put in ice-warehouses and used during warm weather to keep foods cool in ice boxes, the forerunners of the modern refrigerator.

The next step was to develop mechanical refrigeration systems that would produce ice to replace natural ice, and, eventually, mechanical refrigeration systems were used to cool rooms, trucks, and boxes where food could be held without the use of ice. The use of ice was at its peak in the United States as late as the early 1930s.

The first household refrigerators, of course, were ice boxes in which ice was placed in a chamber at the top in order to cool a lower chamber where food was kept. Water from melting ice was allowed to run down to a container beneath the ice box and this had to be emptied periodically.

At this point, the refrigeration capacity of ice deserves mention. The cooling capacity of ice is such that if one should supercool 1 lb (0.45 kg) of it to 20°F (-6.7°C), then this ice would have the capacity to lower the temperature of 1 lb (0.45 kg) of food about 6°F (2.83°C) before any of the ice would melt. At that point, the temperature of the ice would have risen to 32°F (0°C). However, when heat is added to ice that is at 32°F (0°C), the ice temperature no longer can be raised. Instead, the ice begins to melt, but the temperature remains at 32°F (0°C). It so happens that when 1 lb (0.45 kg) of ice melts, it lowers the temperature of 24 lb (10.9 kg) of food about 6°F (2.83°C). It can be seen from this that the cooling effect of ice is greatest at the point when it is melting.

Since little was known about the theory and principles of refrigeration in the early days, much research was required to develop effective systems for circulating cold air in cold storage rooms. As a matter of fact, in fishing boats, fish were first refrigerated by a pile of ice in one corner of the pen instead of being applied directly to the fish as it is today.

MECHANICAL REFRIGERATION

While ice is still used for refrigerating fish and some shellfish, and in some cases, fresh produce during shipment and during holding or display at the retail level, most foods are refrigerated by mechanical systems.

A mechanical refrigeration system consists of an insulated area or room (the refrigerator) and a continuous, closed system consisting of a refrigerant, expansion pipes or radiator-type evaporator located in the refrigerator, a pump or compressor, and a condenser (see Fig. 12–1). The compressor and condenser are located outside the refrigerator. The refrigerant, usually ammonia, or one of the freons, flows into the expansion pipes as a liquid. Here, it evaporates to a gas, and in changing from the liquid to the gaseous phase, it absorbs heat. The gas is pulled into the compressor by the suction action of the pump and is then compressed into a smaller volume. The latter action causes the gas to heat up. This heat must be taken out and this is done by passing the condensed gas through a system of pipes or radiators usually cooled by water, sometimes by forced air. Cooling the condensed gas liquefies it, whereupon it is returned to the evaporator in the refrigerator. The conversion of the gas to a liquid also produces heat that is transferred to the water or air of the condenser. Special valves at both ends of the evaporator allow the required flow of liquid refrigerant in, and of gas out, of the expansion system in the refrigerator.

There are a number of ways in which refrigeration may be applied to the insulated area to be cooled. Expansion pipes where the refrigerant is evaporated may be located along the walls of the refrigerator. In this case, natural circulation of air (the cold air being heavier) may be depended on to refrigerate areas within the room away from the expansion pipes, or some type of forced-air circulation may be used. In some instances, radiation-type evapo-

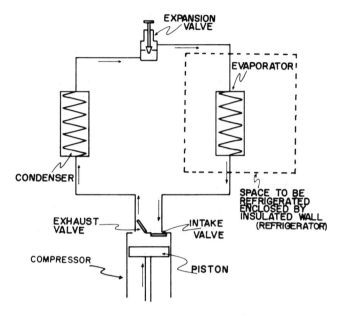

FIGURE 12-1. Principle of mechanical refrigeration.

ration units are used. A fan that blows air through the radiator fins provides circulation of cold air throughout the refrigerator. An indirect method of cooling refrigerators depends on the use of refrigerated brine in an outside container, cooled (usually below the freezing point of water), then sprayed into a chamber within the refrigerator and returned to the outside cooler. The cold brine spray refrigerates and humidifies the air within the chamber and causes it to circulate outside of the chamber throughout the refrigerator. Refrigerated brine circulating through pipes may also be used.

REFRIGERATION PRACTICES

Raw materials, such as fish, meats, poultry, vegetables, and fruits, should be held in a different refrigerator from cooked foods, or the cooked foods should be placed in impervious containers before they are placed in the same refrigerator with the raw foods. This precaution is necessary to prevent bacteria on raw materials from contaminating the cooked foods.

The available refrigeration capacity for all refrigerators used to hold foods at temperatures above freezing should be sufficient to take care of peak loads. That is, when comparatively large amounts of material are to be placed in the refrigerator within a short period of time, the refrigeration capacity must be adequate to cool all parts of all products down to the desired holding temperature within 1-3 hr. Often this is not possible and some alternative must be used. The usual alternative is to precool the product to or near to the desirable holding temperature before it is placed in the refrigerator. The product can be precooled in an insulated area where refrigerated air can be blown through the product, or in a chamber where the product can be placed under vacuum. (The basis of vacuum cooling is accomplished by evaporation of water from the product under low pressure.) Heat exchangers and thin film evaporators may be used for liquid or semiliquid materials.

Products should not be placed in the refrigerator in large bulk form unless they have been precooled. Individual units may be placed on trays and the trays placed on racks to facilitate cooling of the product within the refrigerator. Once cooled, the individual units may be stacked closer together to conserve space. Liquids to be held in large quantities must be precooled before placing in the refrigerator, or they can be poured into small containers to facilitate cooling.

Large commercial refrigerators should not open directly to the outside but rather to an ante room that in turn opens to the outside, to reduce the amount of heat entering the refrigerator from the outside. The doors should be of the swinging, self-closing type.

Fish, meats, and poultry should be held at temperatures above, but as near 32°F (0°C), as possible, to maintain good edible quality and prevent spoilage because of excessive enzyme action or excessive bacterial growth. Since these products generally freeze below 31°F (-0.56°C), a good temperature range for them is 31° to 35°F (-0.56° to 1.67°C). Such a temperature range is attainable in the well-regulated refrigerator.

OTHER REFRIGERATION METHODS

An early development for chilling some foods, especially seafoods, was the use of brine (salt solutions of varying concentrations) as a cold dip or spray. Chilling with brine is faster and more uniform than chilling in ice, and the practice is still used today. Because the temperature of the brine can be reduced to well below freezing (down to -6°F [-21.1°C] when sodium chloride is used and down to -67°F [-55°C] when calcium chloride is used), brines have also been used for freezing and, to a degree, are still used today.

CSW (chilled seawater) is used to chill fish at sea. CSW consists of seawater and a predetermined amount of ice (usually in crushed form) sufficient to cool the catch and to hold it at the temperature of melting ice, which in seawater is somewhat below 32°F (0°C). As with brine, CSW cools more rapidly and more uniformly than does ice alone.

RSW (refrigerated seawater), also used to chill fish at sea, is similar to

CSW except that cooling is accomplished with mechanical refrigeration, which permits control of the RSW temperature. Actually, the salt concentration of RSW can be increased if it is desired to operate at temperatures below the freezing point of seawater.

In dehydrocooling, foods are subjected to evaporative cooling under vacuum. Heat loss is at the rate of 970 Btu/lb water (539 kcal/kg). When dehydration may be a problem, the product may be sprayed with cold water.

13

Freezing

HISTORY OF FREEZING

The preserving of foods by freezing has a history that dates from antiquity, this type of preservation being used by such ethnic groups as Eskimos, and Native Americans of certain cold areas. Fish caught in the winter months in cold climates were frozen and held frozen in the cold ambient air. Red meats were also frozen and held in natural, freezing, ambient conditions.

According to some records, the earliest use of artificial freezing was in the mid-1800s, when fish were frozen in pans surrounded by ice and salt. In the late 1800s, fish, meats, and poultry were frozen by ammonia refrigeration equipment, with fish being the most important in terms of volume. The commercial freezing of fruits and vegetables started in the early 1900s, the former preceding the latter.

By 1990, the U.S. production of frozen foods reached a value of about $30 billion and a volume of about 55 billion lb (about 25 billion kg). See Figure 13-1 for the growth rate curve of the value of frozen foods.

However, so-called "quick freezing" as we know it today was started in the United States in the early 1920s. There is no exact definition for quick freezing, but one definition states that the fall in temperature from 32° to 25°F (0° to −3.9°C) must occur in 30 min or less. Clarence Birdseye is credited with starting the quick freezing of foods, and he must be given credit for promoting the development of frozen foods.

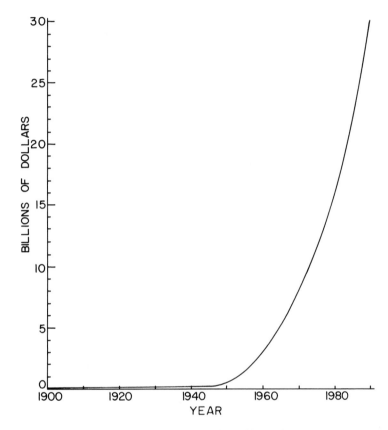

FIGURE 13-1.   U.S. production of frozen foods.

THE PRESERVATIVE EFFECT
OF FREEZING

The spoilage of foods by microbes and by chemical reactions is possible because of a sufficiently high water activity in foods due to their high water content. Foods can be preserved by freezing, because the water activity can be lowered to levels that prevent the functioning of microbes and significantly reduce the rates of chemical reactions. The water in foods does not start to freeze at 32°F (0°C) because of dissolved substances in it. It starts to freeze at a slightly lower temperature. As the temperature is lowered, in the freezing cycle, water molecules in the foods begin to form ice (crystallize), there is a tendency for randomly distributed water to form the orderly network pattern of ice crystals and, as the water freezes, molecular freedom of movement becomes restricted.

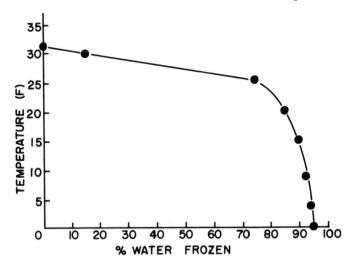

FIGURE 13-2.   Freezing of water in foods at 0° to 32°F (-17.8° to 0°C).

When foods are allowed to freeze slowly, water molecules, even though they are slow moving, have time to migrate to seed-crystals, resulting in the formation of large ice crystals. When foods are made to freeze rapidly, the sluggish water molecules do not have enough time to migrate to ice crystals at any distance and instead are "frozen in their tracks," so to speak, forming relatively small ice crystals made up of local water molecules. In most cases, small ice crystals are more desirable than large ice crystals, and rapid freezing methods are employed.

Even when food is rigid from exposure to temperatures of less than 28°F (−2.2°C), some of the water remains in liquid form, and it is not until the temperature of the food is lowered to about −76°F (−60°C) that all detectable water is converted to ice. Figure 13-2 shows the temperatures at which various percentages of the water are frozen.

FREEZING METHODS

Air-blast Freezing

Air-blast freezing is one of the most commonly used procedures for freezing foods. The foods are packaged and placed on racks, and the racks are wheeled into insulated tunnels (see Fig. 13-3) where air at −20° to −40°F (−28.9° to −40°C) is blown over the product at a speed of 500–1500 ft/min (152.4–457.2 m/min). When the temperature of the product reaches 0°F

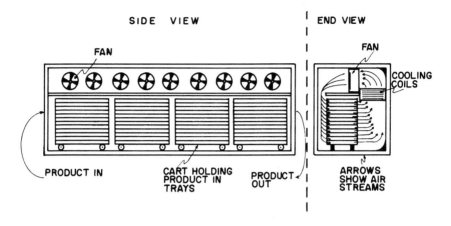

FIGURE 13-3.   Tunnel blast freezer.

($-17.8°C$) in all parts, the packages are put into cases and the cases are placed in storage at $0°F$ ($-17.8°C$) or below. Air-blast freezing may also be applied to packaged products placed on a belt and carried through cold air tunnels.

A modification of air-blast freezing is used to obtain free-flowing frozen products, such as peas. In this case, the product is frozen, prior to packaging, on a belt operating in a refrigerated, insulated tunnel. Air at $-20°F$ ($-28.9°C$) or below is blown over the belt as it moves along. The frozen product empties from the belt into a hopper from which it is promptly removed, then packaged, cased, and stored. One drawback of the cold air-blast method is that moisture is lost to the cold air since the product is not packaged. Peas, for example, lose about 5% moisture when frozen by this method.

High-altitude freezing, a form of blast freezing, appears feasible but has not been tested and will therefore be given only minor mention. By this process, foods are frozen, during transport, in a modified jet aircraft (Boeing 727) at the high altitudes at which these aircraft normally fly, where the ambient temperatures are as low as $-60°F$ ($-51.1°C$).

Fluidized-bed Freezing

The fluidized-bed process was described in Chapter 11 as a means of drying food particles, using hot air as the medium. The same process can be used to freeze foods when cold air is used as the medium. The use of the word *fluidized* derives from the fact that the food particles in air-suspended motion undergo a flow from the starting edge of the bed or perforated plate to the opposite edge where the process ends, thus simulating fluidity. A major advantage of this process is that the food particles are individually quick-frozen (IQF). Even particles that normally tend to agglomerate may be IQF.

Dehydrofreezing

The removal of heat from foods can be accomplished by evaporative cooling, which can be accelerated by subjecting the foods to reduced pressure (as in a vacuum). However, this process entails the loss of water, which can be prevented by spraying the product with cold water.

Plate Freezing

In plate freezing layers of the packaged product are sandwiched between metal plates. The refrigerant is allowed to expand within the plates to provide temperatures of $-28°F$ ($-33.3°C$) or below, and the plates are brought closer together mechanically so that full contact is made with the packaged product. In this manner, the temperature of all parts of the product is brought to $0°F$ ($-17.8°C$) or below within a period of 1.5-4 hr (depending on the thickness of the product). The packages are then removed, put into cases, and stored.

Continuous-operating plate freezers are used in commercial plate freezing. In one such system, the freezer is loaded at the front and unloaded at the rear after completion of the freezing cycle. This is done automatically and continually. In another continuous system, the packages are fed automatically on belts that place them in front of eight levels of refrigerated plates. The packages are forced into the spaces between the plates and the plates closed to provide contact. As freezing proceeds, the packages are advanced so that with each opening of the plates the packages are advanced by one row with a new set of packages entering the front row. By the time the packages reach the far side of the plates, the foods are completely frozen, and they are pushed out of the freezer or unloaded to be cased and stored.

Liquid Freezers

Liquid refrigerants such as liquid nitrogen and liquid freon may be used for the quick freezing of foods. Liquid nitrogen has a temperature of $-320°F$ ($-195.6°C$), and liquid freon has a temperature of $-21°F$ ($-29.4°C$). The individual food portion in this case is placed on a moving stainless steel mesh belt in an insulated tunnel where it is sprayed with liquid refrigerant (Fig. 13-4). Excess refrigerant is recovered, filtered, and recycled. The food leaves the freezer in the frozen state and is thereafter packaged, cased, and stored.

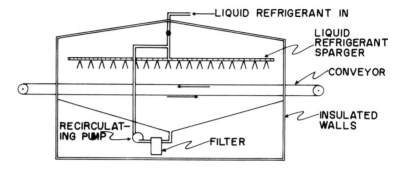

FIGURE 13-4. Continuous liquid-refrigerant freezer.

This method provides very fast freezing and is being used mostly for certain marine products, such as various forms of frozen shrimp.

Slow Freezing

Some foods, such as whole fish and fruit in barrels (used for the manufacture of jams and jellies), are frozen in bulk by placing them in a cold room on racks (individually or in pans) or standing them on cold room floors. The temperature of such rooms may be as low as − 10° to −30°F (−23.3° to −34.4°C), and some air circulation may be used within the storage room. In such instances, freezing proceeds at a slow rate. Fish frozen in this manner are immersed in cold water or sprayed with cold water (in pans) to form a glaze (coating of ice) that helps to protect it against dehydration during frozen storage. The glaze is built up in layers and, during long storage periods, must be replaced as it is lost by sublimation.

GENERAL CONSIDERATIONS
OF FREEZING PRESERVATION OF FOODS

There are three methods of freezing foods: fast freezing, sharp freezing, and slow freezing. There is no good definition for differentiating among the various freezing rates. It is obvious that with some methods, as for food frozen in bulk, the product is frozen slowly.

It is generally agreed that the quality of foods that are frozen quickly is better then the quality of foods that are frozen slowly, and that the lower the temperature to which the food is brought the better the retention of the characteristics of the fresh product. The reasons are that (1) rapid freezing results in the formation of a large number of very small ice crystals that are evenly distributed, and this causes less damage to the tissues of the food; (2) soluble components move about within the food to a lesser degree when the product is quick-frozen since the time required for solidification of the food is shortened; (3) the rates of chemical and biochemical changes are reduced or prevented by decreasing the temperatures rapidly to a certain point.

While the freezing rate is important to the quality of the frozen food it should be noted that the temperature at which a frozen product is held after freezing is more important than the temperature to which it is brought during freezing. It is obvious that if a food is frozen to $0°F$ ($-17.8°C$), then stored at $10°F$ ($-12.2°C$), the same changes will take place and at the same rate as if the food were brought only to $10°F$ ($-12.2°C$) originally. In fact, additional damage is incurred when the product goes initially from $10°$ to $0°F$ ($-12.2°$ to $-17.8°C$) and back to $10°F$ ($-12.2°C$), since any freezing cycle has an adverse effect on the quality of foods. Because frozen foods are stored for much longer periods than those required for freezing, storage changes are of much greater significance to the quality of the product than are the initial changes due to freezing. It has been shown by government research workers that changes causing deterioration of many frozen foods occur approximately twice as fast at $5°F$ ($-15°C$) as at $0°F$ ($-17.8°C$), twice as fast at $10°F$ ($-12.2°C$) as at $5°F$ ($-15°C$), and so on. Actually, frozen storage warehouses usually attempt to maintain temperatures of $0°F$ ($-17.8°C$), an FDA requirement for all foods shipped interstate and a requirement for all food-handling establishments, including restaurants. It should be remembered that the lower the temperature, the longer the shelf-life and the better the quality.

Whereas changes often take place in frozen foods during storage after freezing, the major changes take place during distribution after freezing. Frozen foods may be carried to retail outlets in trucks that are not refrigerated or in which the refrigeration is not adequate to hold the temperature at $0°F$ ($-17.8°C$). Frozen foods may be delivered to the retail outlet and left on the unloading platform at ambient (outside air) temperatures for several hours, sometimes even subjected to the direct rays of the sun. At the retail outlet, products are sometimes placed out of refrigeration, either in an open-top display case above the load line, or out of the case entirely. Open-shelf-type frozen food display cases now used in many retail stores are usually incapable of maintaining temperatures of $0°F$ ($-17.8°C$), especially around the products displayed at the front of the shelf, since refrigerated air is blown from the back of the shelf to the front, and cold air, being heavier than warm air, tends to flow out and down to the floor area in front of the case. As a matter of fact, in stores using this type of display case, the cold air can be felt as one walks through the aisle where such storage cases are located. Since high storage temperatures greatly accelerate deteriorative changes in frozen foods, loss of their quality occurs more often during distribution and display at retail stores than during freezing and subsequent storage in frozen food warehouses.

PREPARATION OF FOODS FOR FREEZING

Many foods preserved by freezing require some type of pretreatment, but only a selection will be described here. Citrus juices are oftentimes concentrated to about one-fifth of their original volumes, then diluted back to one-fourth of the original volumes with fresh juice prior to freezing. This dilution with fresh juice is done to add back flavor components since most of the flavor compounds are removed during vacuum concentration of the juice. When this product is to be reconstituted it requires the addition of water equal to three times its volume.

Except for a few, such as onions, vegetables must be blanched before they are frozen and stored. Vegetables are blanched by heating in steam or hot water (about 210°F [98.9°C]), while being carried along a perforated metal belt or screw conveyor, until the temperature of all parts reaches 185°–200°F (85°–93.3°C) (see Fig. 10-2), then cooling with sprays of water or in water flumes. Vegetables are blanched prior to freezing because enzymes are present, and if not inactivated by the heat, they would cause certain spoilage reactions to take place in the food during frozen storage. These reactions would produce off-flavors (haylike flavors) in the vegetable.

Blanching times vary with the type of food, the type of heat used, (steam or hot water) and the bulk of material being heated. The heating must reach a high enough temperature in the product and remain at that temperature long enough to inactivate the particular enzymes that cause off-flavors. Very high temperatures, used for sterilizing certain types of canned foods, applied for a few seconds, will not destroy all the enzymes; the time is too short. Blanching times used for frozen vegetables may be relatively short (about 1 min in water at 210°–212°F [98.9°–100°C] for peas) or relatively long (about 9 min in steam for corn on the cob).

Besides destroying enzymes that would cause off-flavors and texture changes, blanching has a cleaning effect and destroys contaminating bacteria. Moreover, blanching fixes the color of green vegetables by removing air from beneath surface tissue and possibly affecting the chlorophyll.

PACKAGING

Packaging is an important factor in the freezing of foods. It is not possible to maintain high humidities in frozen storage rooms because moisture present in the atmosphere of freezer storage rooms tends to condense and freeze on the expansion pipes or other apparatus used to cool the room, thereby reducing the cooling efficiency of the system. Packages used for frozen foods, therefore, must be reasonably moisture-vapor-proof. Otherwise, the product will dehydrate, causing undesirable changes in its appearance and accelerating loss in flavor and juiciness. Toughness and other manifestations of deterioration in quality will also be accelerated. Even when food is packaged in vapor-proof material, however, there can be some moisture lost from the food. This may happen when there is too much space within the package not occupied by the food itself. This results in the formation of what is called cavity ice or ice within the package. In such instances, the product, which is warmer than the package, loses water to the cavity space by evaporation, since any water vapor in the cavity space is condensed on the colder package. Under these conditions, there is a transfer of water from the food to the inside of that part of the package surrounding the cavity. Cavity ice formation may cause the same undesirable changes to take place as when moisture is lost to the atmosphere outside the package, although it usually occurs in localized areas.

The frozen-food package should have sufficient mechanical strength; that is, it should have adequate burst strength and tear strength at low temperatures and high wet strength against water exposure.

During freezing, the package will be subjected to stresses due to the expansion of the product. Because of this and possible cavity ice formation, the package should conform closely to the shape of the food. A suitable flexibility is, therefore, a desirable property of the packaging material.

Packages should be liquid-tight since some frozen foods (fruits packed in syrup) may have some free liquid that could leak out, and some are thawed in the package, which could also cause leakage.

Transfer of moisture-vapor through packaging may take place through pores or cracks in the container or by diffusion of moisture through the packaging material. The loss of moisture through seals, and package imperfections such as pores, may account for the greatest loss of moisture from frozen foods.

Tin or aluminum cans, waxed paper tubs or cylindrical containers, rectangular paper cartons treated with special waxes, plastic bags of polyvinylidene chloride or polyethylene, and aluminum foil wraps or aluminum dishes are all used for the packaging of frozen foods. Many of the paper containers are used in combination with cellophane, waxed paper liners, or overwraps.

PROBLEMS WITH FREEZING
OR THAWING OF BULK FOODS

Most of the changes occurring in frozen foods takes place during frozen storage rather than during the freezing process itself. There are some instances, however, when foods are frozen very slowly, during which time undesirable changes occur. When strawberries in sugar are frozen in bulk form in cold rooms, the freezing time is long, and the deterioration during freezing is equivalent to that which would occur in 2 years of storage at 0°F (-17.8°C) after freezing.

The defrosting of bulk-packed foods, fruit in barrels, liquid egg frozen in 30 lb (13.6 kg) tins, and so forth may be responsible for a considerable loss of quality. When frozen, bulk-packed foods are allowed to defrost at room temperature, the outside layers of the food will have been held at room temperature for a long period of time before the inner layers become defrosted. This period of holding at room temperature may result in enzyme changes or in loss of quality due to the growth of microorganisms.

QUALITY CHANGES DURING
FROZEN STORAGE

A number of different changes may take place in frozen foods during storage. These changes may be physical, chemical, enzymatic, and, in rare cases, microbial. Microbial changes occur when refrigeration is inadequate.

Desiccation or drying out is a kind of change that takes place in frozen foods under conditions of poor packaging or varying storage temperatures. Such loss of moisture in poultry occurs first around the area of the feather follicles, causing a speckled or "pock-marked" appearance. Protein and fat changes may also be accelerated when moisture is lost from the surface areas of frozen foods.

Crystallization is a physical change that may occur in some types of frozen foods. Certain types of dairy products, such as ice cream and concentrated milks or creams, sometimes undergo this type of change, which is due to the crystallization of lactose or other sugars that do not readily dissolve upon defrosting, causing an undesirable texture called sandiness. A similar change may occur in some types of sweetened citrus juices during long storage.

Loss of volatile flavor components may occur in some frozen foods, such as fruit, during frozen storage because these compounds boil or evaporate at temperatures that are even lower than the temperature at which the foods are stored. This causes a loss of the typical flavor components of the foods.

The breaking of gels or emulsions during defrosting may take place with some foods. High-moisture fruits, such as tomatoes, the liquid of which is held by pectin gels, are subject to this type of change and have, therefore, not been frozen successfully. Foods packed with a white sauce or gravy are also subject to this type of physical change and it has been found that fluctuation of storage temperatures greatly accelerates the curdling and "weeping" of the gravy or white sauce.

Protein denaturation is a general term for the physicochemical change occurring especially in flesh-type foods during frozen storage. It results in a toughening of the tissues and dryness or loss of succulence. It is considered that this type of change in stored frozen fish is due to enzymes that break off fatty acids from phospholipids in tissues or to enzymes that decompose trimethylamine oxide and produce formaldehyde. The free fatty acids combine with protein chains, which causes them to aggregate or bind themselves into a closer matrix, resulting in the squeezing out of water (drip occurring during defrosting) and a firming or toughening of the tissues. Protein changes of this type occur especially in lean fish but also, to some extent, in poultry and meats. Grinding of tissues of this kind appears to accelerate protein changes during frozen storage.

As might be expected, the oxidation of some of the components of frozen foods is a cause of some of the major changes that may take place during storage. Oxidation of ascorbic acid or vitamin C is a change of this kind. In fruits in which enzymes have not been inactivated by heating, this may be accelerated by enzyme action, but it can also occur through straight atmospheric oxidation. while this change may cause no loss of edible quality, it results in a loss of the nutritional quality of the food.

The fats of foods may oxidize during frozen storage, resulting in a change recognized as rancidity. The fats of meats may undergo this change but fish fats are especially subject to this kind of deterioration since the fatty acids in fish fats contain many adjacent carbons not fully saturated (combined) with hydrogen. They are, thus, very subject to reacting with oxygen, a process that eventually leads to the formation of compounds that cause the off-flavors recognized as rancid flavors. Fatty fish become rancid faster in frozen storage than do lean fish, but even lean fish are subject to rancidification during relatively short periods of frozen storage.

The colors of fruits and vegetables may deteriorate through oxidation during frozen storage, resulting in a less desirable appearance.

Enzymes may cause various changes in foods during frozen storage. It is not possible to freeze and store whole uncooked lobster, since, during storage, enzymes react with the proteins causing the meat to become soft and crumbly after cooking. On the other hand, if whole lobsters are cooked to inactivate the enzymes and then frozen and stored, the oil in the digestive gland (tomalley) oxidizes and becomes rancid causing off-flavors that spread into the meat itself.

In fruits, enzymes, called polyphenolases, accelerate the oxidation of certain chemicals leading to the formation of brown- or black-colored compounds. This is the reaction that one sees when an apple or peach is cut and allowed to stand at room temperature for a short period of time. In preparing apples for freezing, therefore, peeled apple slices are treated with a salt that liberates sulfurous acid (sulfur dioxide) and are held under refrigeration for sufficient time to allow this compound to diffuse into the tissues. The sulfur dioxide inactivates or inhibits the enzymes that promote enzymatic browning. Also, in preparing sliced peaches for freezing, small amounts of ascorbic acid (vitamin C) are added to the syrup since this compound is a reducing agent (counteracts oxidation reactions).

In general, microorganisms will not grow in frozen foods unless they are held at temperatures above 15°F (-9.4°C). At this temperature there may be enough free liquid in the food to allow the growth of some microorganisms, especially molds. However, at such temperatures, quality degradation from other factors occurs at such a rate that the food would soon be spoiled because of other changes not due to the growth of microorganisms.

Frozen foods have not often been involved in the transmission of foodborne disease although, if grossly mishandled, as by defrosting and then holding out of refrigeration for some time, they may constitute a public health hazard.

SHELF-LIFE OF FROZEN FOODS

The storage life of frozen foods, at temperatures that today are considered to be economically practicable, is not without definite limits. Some idea of the length of time that frozen foods may be expected to retain high quality may be obtained from Table 13–1.

THAWING

While freezing is one of the most effective means of preserving foods over long periods, the need to thaw them prior to reprocessing in food plants or for domestic use represents one of the undesirable aspects of freezing preservation. Thawing is time-consuming and, in some cases, is associated with loss of product quality. Evidence shows that it normally takes food longer to thaw than to freeze under similar heat transfer conditions, because the thermal conductivity of ice is four times greater than that of water, and the rate of temperature change in ice proceeds at nine times the rate that it does in water. During freezing, the water at the interface is in the ice form, whereas during thawing, it is in the liquid phase. Another important aspect to thawing is that, unlike the freezing cycle where the interface water freezes first thereby immobilizing surface spoilage bacteria, the interface water is in liq-

TABLE 13-1.   Approximate Time[a] (in months) of High-Quality
Shelf-Life of Some Foods

Product	0°F (-17.8°C)	10°F (-12.2°C)	20°F (-6.7°C)
Orange juice (blanched)	27	4	1
Peaches	12	<2	0.2
Strawberries	12	2.4	10 days
Cauliflower	12	2.4	10 days
Green beans	11–12	3	1
Green peas	11–12	3	1
Spinach	6–7	<3	0.75
Raw chicken	27	15.5	<8
Fried chicken	<3	<1	<0.6
Turkey pies or dinners	<30	9.5	2.25
Beef (raw)	13–14	5	<2
Pork (raw)	10	<4	<1.5
Lean fish (raw)	3	<2.25	<1.5
Fat fish(raw)	2	1.5	0.8

[a]It should be noted that the above storage life times refer to those periods when a quality difference between the frozen and the fresh product can first be detected by an expert panel and do not refer to spoilage or rejection times.

uid form, which provides the spoilage bacteria with good growing conditions for nearly the entire duration of the thawing cycle.

The Educational Foundation of the National Restaurant Association and the FDA recognize three accepted methods for thawing foods:

1. Under refrigeration below 45°F (below 7.2°C).
2. Under running water below 70°F (below 21.1°C).
3. As part of the cooking process. This includes microwave thawing, which should only be used on foods to be prepared for service immediately after thawing.

There is some evidence to indicate that, as far as the quality of the product not associated with bacterial decomposition is concerned, the faster a frozen food is defrosted, the better the result. Foods packaged in small units defrost in a few hours during holding at room temperature and during this time are not subject to an undesirable amount of decomposition due to bacterial growth. However, foods frozen in bulk, such as barrels of fruit, 30-lb (13.6-kg) containers of egg mixtures, fruit, large fish, or blocks of meat used for sausage products, may present a defrosting problem. Because bulk-frozen foods take long to defrost and because it is well known that the rate at which the food defrosts is dependent on the temperature to which it is exposed, there may be a tendency to defrost the food at relatively warm temperatures. When this is done, the outside portion of the food is subject to bacterial decomposition or the growth of yeasts and molds before the inner portions defrost. Some methods of alleviating the problems associated with the defrosting of bulk-frozen foods have been developed.

Refrigerator defrosting (holding at temperatures of 35°–40°F [1.7°– 4.4°C]) is probably the best method of defrosting bulk-frozen foods when no fast method is available. This would apply to large whole fish, fruit in barrels, and apples in 30-lb (13.6-kg) containers, since bacterial or mold growth would be limited under these conditions. However, in industrial processing, where bulk-frozen products are thawed as an intermediate step in the manufacture of the company's line of products, the refrigeration space required may be so large as to discourage this practice.

In defrosting eggs in 30-lb (13.6-kg) containers, it may be possible to use a machine that breaks up or grinds the product into a kind of slush that can be used in that form in preparing baked foods.

Large blocks of meat used for manufacturing sausage products can be ground in the frozen state and used as such, although this may cause problems in further handling of the meat emulsion.

By the use of microwave energy, food can be thawed rapidly and with virtually no quality loss. That is because microwaves, by their unique character, cause a temperature rise throughout the product rather than only on the surface from which the heat must be conducted through the product, as occurs in conventional heating processes. A more detailed description of microwave heating is given in Chapter 10.

Since the heat generated in foods by microwaves is quite rapid (about 10 times more rapid than by baking), when uneven heating in a frozen product does occur, the temperature differences within a food can become great. This, however, happens only under certain conditions, and it can be dealt with quite easily. For this condition, and also when one wants to ensure very uniform temperature control, one solution is to apply the microwave energy in intermittent bursts. By this technique, the absorbed thermal energy generated during a burst of microwaves is allowed to be distributed by conduction during the intervals between the bursts, thereby permitting the temperature of the food to increase more uniformly, albeit more slowly. Developments such as wave guides and turn tables have improved the distribution of microwave energy significantly.

The particular advantage of using microwave energy for thawing foods is that deterioration by microorganisms is not a factor. The feasibility and benefits of microwave thawing of frozen meats and fish have been adequately demonstrated, especially for thawing frozen shrimp blocks.

14

Addition of Chemicals

The practice of preserving food by the addition of chemicals is quite old, and ordinary table salt (sodium chloride) has been used as a preservative for centuries. It might be surprising to think of a naturally occurring substance as a chemical preservative, but it will be seen that many chemical substances used in the preservation of foods occur naturally. When they are used with the proper intent, they can be used to preserve foods that cannot be easily preserved by other means. They should not be used as a substitute for sanitation and proper handling procedures. Sometimes chemicals are used together with other processes, such as holding at refrigerator temperatures above freezing.

To preserve foods, it is necessary either to destroy all of the spoilage microorganisms that contaminate it or to bring about conditions that prevent the microbes from carrying out their ordinary life processes. Although preservation is aimed mainly at microbial spoilage, it must be remembered that there are other types of spoilage factors, such as oxidation.

SODIUM CHLORIDE

When sufficient salt is added to food, it makes water unavailable to microorganisms. Since microorganisms require water to survive, they cannot exist when their water requirement is diminished by the addition of salt. We can reduce the amount of water available to microorganisms by lowering the water activity (a_w). For more on a_w, see Chapter 7. Microorganisms require high levels of a_w. Most bacteria require a minimum a_w level of 0.96, although halophilic bacteria can grow at a a_w of 0.75. Most yeasts grow at a_w levels of 0.90 and above, although a few can grow at a a_w level of 0.81. Molds can

175

grow at lower a_w levels, with some able to grow at a a_w level of 0.62. While salt preserves foods mainly by lowering the a_w, the chloride ion is believed to inhibit bacterial growth, independently.

Some precautions must be observed in the salting preservation of flesh-type foods, such as fish or meats. When these products are salted, several days will be required before enough salt has diffused into all parts of the product to inhibit the growth of microorganisms. If, therefore, precautions are not observed, the growth of spoilage or even disease-causing bacteria may occur is some parts of the food before enough salt has diffused into the product to inhibit growth. The usual procedure is to hold products under refrigeration during salting until there has been an adequate "take-up" of salt throughout the food. Fish and meats should never be held at temperatures above 60°F (15.6°C) during salting. Preferably, holding temperatures during such procedures should be at 40°F (4.4°C) or slightly below.

Salted, undried meats, such as corned beef, should be held at 40°F (4.4°C) or below at all times after curing since there are some microorganisms that may grow in the salt contents present in such products. Chipped beef, which is dried as well as salted, has a low enough moisture content to prevent the growth of all microorganisms and may be held at room temperatures.

Salt cod, which has a moisture content of 40% or higher, should be held at temperatures of 40°F (4.4°C) or slightly below since it is subject to spoilage through bacterial growth. On the other hand, well-dried salt cod and certain types of salted and smoked herring (which have dried during smoking) may be held at room temperatures without spoilage.

ACIDIFICATION

Acidification is a method of food preservation. As has been pointed out, all microorganisms have a pH at which they grow best (see Chap. 7), and a range of pH above or below which they will not grow. Generally, it is not possible to preserve all foods by adding acid to the point where no microorganisms will grow. Most foods would be too acid to be palatable. Enough acid may be used to inhibit the growth of microorganisms provided that such treatment is combined with some other method of preservation. Certain dairy products, such as sour cream, and fermented vegetables, such as sauerkraut, are preserved through lactic acid produced by the growth of bacteria together with the holding of these products at refrigerator temperatures above freezing. When sauerkraut is canned, it is given a heat process sufficient to destroy all spoilage and disease microorganisms.

Pickles are preserved by the addition of some salt, some acid, and a heat process sufficient to raise the temperature of all parts of the food to or near 212°F (100°C).

Pickled herring are preserved by the addition of some salt, some acetic acid (vinegar), and the holding at refrigerator temperatures above freezing. In this case, the nonacid part of the acetic acid molecule has an inhibiting effect on the growth of microorganisms.

FATTY ACIDS

The salts of certain fatty acids have an inhibitory effect on the growth of microorganisms. Thus, sodium diacetate (a mixture of sodium acetate and acetic acid) and sodium or calcium propionate

$$CH_3—CH_2—\overset{\overset{\textstyle O}{\|}}{C}—ONa$$
sodium propionate

are added to bread and other bakery products to prevent mold growth, as well as the development of a slimy condition known as "ropiness," due to the growth of certain aerobic, spore-forming bacteria (see Chap. 7 for definition of spore-forming bacteria). Caprylic acid, $CH_3—CH_2—CH_2—CH_2—CH_2—CH_2—CH_2—COOH$ or its salts or the salts of other fatty acids may be used in cheeses to prevent the growth of mold.

As pointed out previously, it is the nonacid part of the molecule of fatty acids or their salts that inhibits the growth of microorganisms. It is believed that the effect of these compounds is the destruction of the cell membrane of microorganisms.

SULFUR DIOXIDE

Sulfur dioxide (SO_2) is used in some foods to inhibit the growth of microorganisms. Sulfur dioxide may be used as such, or as a source of this compound; for instance, sodium bisulfite ($NaHSO_3$) may be added to foods. Sulfur dioxide inhibits a rather narrow range of microorganisms and is usually applied together with another chemical inhibitor to prevent the growth of undesirable yeasts or bacteria in fruit juices, which are stored prior to fermentation, to produce wine or vinegar.

The inhibiting effect of sulfur dioxide may be due to the prevention of the utilization of certain carbohydrates as a source of energy or to the tying up of certain compounds concerned with the metabolism of some microorganisms.

For many years, sulfiting agents have been classified as GRAS (generally regarded as safe) substances by the FDA for use as food preservatives when used in accordance with GMP (good manufacturing practice). But in 1986, following several deaths from the consumption of fresh fruits or vegetables that had been treated with sulfites, the FDA withdrew the GRAS status of sulfites for this use. It was found that asthmatics react, sometimes severely, when exposed to sulfites. Also, because sulfites have been found to destroy thiamin, these agents may not be used in meats and other foods containing thiamin. Although sulfites may still be used in foods that have not been excluded by the FDA, their presence must be declared on the label when their concentrations exceed 10 ppm (parts per million). It has been calculated that in concentrations of 10 ppm or less, these agents should not cause adverse reactions in humans.

SORBIC ACID

Sorbic acid, $CH_3—CH=CH—CH=CH—COOH$, inhibits the growth of both yeasts and molds. This compound is most effective at pH 5.0 or below. This compound can be metabolized by humans, as are fatty acids, hence is generally recognized as safe. Sorbic acid is used in certain bakery products (not yeast-leavened products, since it inhibits yeast growth), in cheeses, and in some fruit drinks, especially for the purpose of preventing molding. It is believed to inhibit the metabolic enzymes of certain microorganisms required by these species for growth and multiplication.

SODIUM NITRITE

Sodium nitrite, $NaNO_2$, is added to some food products to inhibit bacterial growth and to enhance color. It is added to most cured meats, including hams, bacon, cooked sausage (such as frankfurters, bologna, salami), and to some kinds of corned beef. Nitrite provides for the red or pink color of the cured and cooked sausages and of the other cured products after cooking. The nitrite combines with the red coloring material of meat, the myoglobin, and prevents its oxidation. If the meat were not treated with nitrite, it would discolor during cooking or during storage. When red meat is heated, as in cooking, the color turns from red to gray or brown due to the conversion of myoglobin to the oxidized form, metmyoglobin. Upon extremely long or extremely high heating or upon exposure to light and air (oxygen), even the nitrited myoglobin may be oxidized to metmyoglobin, with the result that the red or pink color is lost.

   In addition to stabilizing the color of cured or cured and cooked meats, the industry claims that nitrite acts as a preservative in that it tends to prevent the growth of spores of *Clostridium botulinum* that may be present. *Clostridium botulinum,* of course, is a disease-causing organism.

Nitrite is also used in some fish products, such as smoked whitefish and chubs, for the specific purpose of preventing the outgrowth of *Clostridium botulinum.*

Sodium or potassium nitrite may not be used in meats or on fish that are to be sold as fresh. In cured products, it is allowed in concentrations not to exceed 0.02% (200 parts of nitrite per million parts of the food). There is some question as to whether or not nitrites should be allowed in foods in any concentration. It has been found that nitrite-cured products, especially those cooked at high temperatures, such as bacon, may develop nitrosamines, compounds formed by the reaction of nitrites with amines, and nitrosamines are known to be extremely carcinogenic or cancer-promoting.

OXIDIZING AGENTS

Oxidizing agents, such as chlorine, iodine, and hydrogen peroxide, are not ordinarily used in foods, but they are used to sanitize food-processing equipment and apparatus and even the walls and floors of areas where foods are processed. Thus, there is no doubt that small residuals, especially of chlorine or iodine, can get into foods.

Hydrogen peroxide may be used to destroy the natural bacterial flora of milk, prior to inoculating with cultures of known bacterial species, for producing specific dairy products. In such cases, all of the residual hydrogen peroxide must be removed by treating with the enzyme catalase (see Chap. 9). This treatment with catalase must be carried out prior to the inoculation of milk with cultures of desirable bacteria; otherwise the hydrogen peroxide will destroy the added bacterial culture, the growth of which is the objective of culturing milk.

Oxidizing agents are believed to destroy and inhibit the growth of microorganisms by destroying certain parts of the enzymes essential to the metabolic processes of these organisms.

BENZOATES

The benzoates and parabenzoates have been used as preservatives mainly in fruit juices, syrups (especially chocolate syrup), candied fruit peel, pie fillings, pickled vegetables, relishes, horseradish, and some cheeses. The probable reason that the benzoates and the related parabenzoates have been allowed as additives to food is that benzoic acid is present in cranberries as a natural component in concentrations that are higher than 0.1%.

Benzoic acid

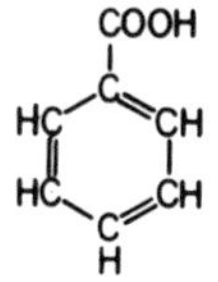

COOH
HC—C—CH
HC—C—CH
H

or its sodium salt is allowed in food in concentrations up to 0.1%. Para-hydroxybenzoic acid

COOH
HC—C—CH
HC—C—CH
C
OH

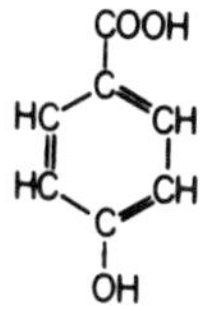

or its esters, for instance, propyl para-hydroxybenzoic acid, may also be used. The benzoates are most effective in acid foods in which the pH is as low as 4.0 or below. The parabenzoates are said to be more effective than the benzoates over a wider range of pH and against wider groups of microorganisms.

Investigations have indicated that benzoates prevent the utilization of energy-rich compounds by microorganisms. It has also been found that when bacteria form spores in the presence of benzoate, the spore may take up water and germinate to the point of bursting and shedding the spore wall, but enlargement and outgrowth into the vegetable cell with subsequent cell division and multiplication does not occur.

ANTIBIOTICS

Antibiotics are compounds produced by one species or strain of microorganisms, but they are effective in preventing the growth of other microorganisms. No detailed discussion of the formulas and chemistry of antibiotics will be given here because of their wide variability and complexity. Antibiotics are used primarily to destroy disease-causing bacteria and to prevent diseases in humans and animals. Antibiotics are not effective against viruses, and, therefore, are useless for treating or preventing viral diseases.

Tetracyclines, especially Aureomycin (chlortetracycline) and Terramycin (oxytetracycline) were once allowed in foods in this country, as preservatives, but they are now banned. Tetracyclines are wide-spectrum antibiotics, that is, they are effective against a wide range of bacterial species. On the other hand, some antibiotics are relatively specific. Penicillin, for instance, is effective against cocci, the spherical-shaped bacteria. Antibiotics were banned in foods because they are not destroyed completely by cooking, and the residuals might permit a buildup of a resistant bacterial flora in humans. When antibiotics are used for medicinal purposes subsequently, nonresistant strains would be eliminated, creating a condition where the resistant strains would have very little competition and would be able to reproduce in abnormally large numbers.

The antibiotics, nisin and tylosin, are polypeptides, which are components of proteins. Nisin is allowed in small concentrations in canned foods in some countries on the basis that it is naturally produced by bacteria. It is used in the manufacture of many dairy products in some countries. Nisin in canned foods is considered to prevent the outgrowth of spoilage bacteria that may survive heat treatments tailored to destroy only disease-causing bacteria.

ANTIOXIDANTS

One of the ways in which food spoils involves the oxidation of fats. When this occurs, foods develop off-flavors, off-odors, and sometimes off-colors. Among the measures taken to prevent oxidative degradation of foods is the addition of certain chemical compounds which, because of their effect, are called antioxidants.

There is a large number of compounds having antioxidant properties but differing in some respects. True, or primary, antioxidants are phenolic in nature (contain a phenol ring

or have similar structures in the molecule), and they may be derived from natural or synthetic sources. Secondary antioxidants normally are acids that include ascorbic, citric, tartaric, and phosphoric acids. Although phenolic antioxidants are effective when used alone, their effect is enhanced synergistically when acid antioxidants are added. Tannins, which are widespread in plants, are natural antioxidants, as are vitamin E, vitamin C, spices, sugar, and others. The use of antioxidants has greatly reduced the problem of rancidity in fats and oils and in foods containing fats and oils or to which fats or oils are added during processing.

OTHER COMPOUNDS

A number of chemical compounds may be used in the solutions with which fruits are washed. The compounds are used mainly on citrus fruit to prevent mold growth, but some may be used in the washing solutions applied to apples, pears, and quinces, as well as to citrus fruits. Included among these compounds are hexamine (hexamethylenetetramine), sodium chlorophenate, 2-4D (dichlorophenoxyacetic acid), 2-4-5T (trichlorophenoxyacetic acid), diphenyl and boric acid. Some of these compounds are applied to oiled papers used for wrapping citrus fruits.

The latter group of compounds is toxic to humans and is generally not allowed in foods. Used on citrus fruits, these compounds are applied to the peel, which is not generally consumed by humans. However, diphenyl is allowed in citron (candied citrus peel), which is eaten by humans, in concentrations up to 100 ppm of the candied peel. This is probably allowed on the basis that citron is eaten only rarely and then in comparatively small amounts.

Diethyl pyrocarbonate is used primarily in fruit juice or fruit drinks to prevent the outgrowth of yeasts which, if present, could cause fermentation. Its effectiveness appears to be limited to situations where the microorganisms are present in low concentrations.

IV

Handling and Processing of Foods

15

Meat

Of the many foods obtained from the land, humans tend to prefer animal foods, mainly beef, pork, poultry, and mutton as well as their by-products (e.g., cheeses, milk, and eggs). The most important source of meat in the United States is cattle. Horses have not been an important source of meat, except during wars when meat shortages have occurred.

A market exists for domestically produced game-type meats. These include buffalo, bear, elk, kangaroo, and rabbit. They are usually expensive and selected mainly as gourmet items. The meat is generally tough and very "gamey." In general, this type of meat is prepared in moist heat.

The proportion of meat-derived foods that humans consume is related to the general affluence of the society in which they live. The reason for this is that the use of animal flesh as food tends to use up a much greater amount of calories, proteins, and other nutrients that might be available directly from plants. It is reported that it takes about 10 lb (4.5 kg) of plant food to produce about 1 lb (0.45 kg) of beef. Thus, in deprived societies, the population is compelled to derive most of its nutrition from plants rather than from animals.

Animal foods offer more than just palatability. Since animals are biologically similar to humans, it should be obvious that animal foods contain many of the nutrients that are required by humans to carry out their own body functions. For example, in most cases, the animals are good sources of the essential amino acids, as well as the vitamins and minerals required by humans.

Meat and meat products include the muscle tissues of cattle, hogs, sheep, and other animals, as well as the organs of these animals. The organs used are the tongue, heart, brain, liver, kidneys, and sometimes the lungs. Some of the by-products derived from the animals that are used in the meat industry include the intestinal walls, used as casings for making different types of sausages. Fat is used for the production of lard and tallow; the tallow is used as a source of raw material for making soap and candles. Other by-products include leather for shoes and a variety of other commodities; wool for textiles; gelatin, which is used in the production of gelatin desserts and other similar food products; blood, which is used in some sausages and in feeds; bone, which is used mainly in fertilizers and feeds; animal scraps from the slaughtering plants, which are used in the manufacture of feeds; and a variety of enzymes and other chemicals used in different industries, especially in the food and pharmaceutical industries.

Except for tongues, head meats are generally used in the production of sausages. Tripe, prepared from the first and second stomachs of cattle, is cooked for about 3 hr and sold as is, or it may be cured. The sweetbreads (pancreas and thymus) are marketed either fresh or frozen. Both gelatin and animal glue are prepared from the collagen derived mainly from the bones and the hide, but also from other parts, such as the sinews, ears, snouts, and trimmings. Oxtails, although quite tough, have a distinctly desirable flavor, and are used in making oxtail soup.

When livestock animals are grown for meat production, the males are castrated. There are two reasons for this. Upon castration, the hormone balance in the animal is affected so there is an increased amount of fat deposited throughout the musculature. Because of this, the meat tends to be more succulent and more tender. The second reason for castration is that the strong odor usually associated with viable males tends to disappear.

As explained in Chapter 26, the tenderness of beef is inversely related to the age of the animal, and marbling, an effect describing a uniform distribution of relatively high amounts of fat in the muscle, is not always a reliable indicator. At this point, it should be noted that with increasing knowledge of the relationship between saturated fat and cholesterol consumption and heart disease, dietary trends have changed, and more people are opting for less fatty foods. As a result, beef and pork producers have changed feed formulas to lower the fat levels in the beef and pork that they produce, and they have asked the USDA to publish the new lower fat and cholesterol values for beef and pork.

Generally, animals are allowed to rest for a period just before slaughter. This is done in order that they not use up all their muscle sugar (glycogen). When the animal is slaughtered with an amount of glycogen in its body, the glycogen is converted under anaerobic conditions to lactic acid. The presence of this acid has a preservative effect on the meat. On the other hand, if the animal is not rested before slaughter and it uses up its glycogen, there will not be enough lactic acid formed to have the preservative effect, and thus the meat will spoil sooner.

After slaughter, the carcass portions are aged in cold rooms at low temperatures just above freezing, usually 35°F (1.7°C). This process may take up to one month, depending on temperature, humidity, and other conditions, but ordinarily, meat is held for about 12 days prior to consumption. The aging is accelerated if the beef is stored at higher temperatures, but the higher temperatures permit the growth of bacteria and surface spoilage to occur. However, since the spoilage is on the surface, this problem can be resolved by storing the meat at the higher temperatures in the presence of ultraviolet light, which has a bactericidal effect.

Sometimes a processor is willing to accept the microbial growth in order to hasten the tenderization. Since the bacteria and mold growth create a certain amount of spoilage on the surface of the meat, the processor must then trim the surface in order to remove the effects of microbial growth and spoilage. The main purpose of aging is, of course, to tenderize the meat. Meat cuts can be tenderized just prior to consumption by the addition of commercially prepared enzymes, which have a proteolytic effect; that is, they tend to break down the proteins. However, this is a slow process if added only to the surface, and it is believed that injection into the meat or into the bloodstream of the living animal just before slaughter is a more effective way of producing tender beef.

When meat is heated in the presence of water, as in boiling or in the making of stew, the connective tissue is changed to a sort of tender gelatin and it becomes more palatable. On the other hand, when the meat is heated without water, such as in an oven in dry heat, the connective tissue tends to become tougher. The amount of connective tissue present in the meat depends on the location of the meat in the animal. The tenderloin, for example, has very little connective tissue, especially in the younger animals.

Although boiling tends to make meat less tough, one of the disadvantages is that taste components are extracted from the meat, and, therefore, boiled meat is less tasty. Of course, the water in which the meat has been boiled acquires the meat flavor components and can be concentrated and sold as a meat extract, which can be used as a base for soups and stews. Also, little browning (which enhances meat flavor) occurs during boiling.

Some points to remember in the cooking of meat are the higher the temperature during cooking, the more the shrinkage; the lower the temperature during cooking, the higher the quality and the more uniformity of doneness throughout the meat. A certain amount of aging is beneficial from a quality standpoint. In fact, some chefs will hold the meat at room temperature for a considerable period before they finally put in into the oven. In the case of roasts, it has been found that an oven temperature of 375°F (190.6°C) should be maximum and 325°F (162.8°C) about minimum.

Of the different types of protein of which meat is composed, the contractile proteins are of some importance. These include myosin, actin, and tropomyosin, plus some other minor ones. When these proteins are extracted from the cells in the meat, either with salt solution or with mechanical agitation, such as chopping or grinding, they form a sticky substance that has binding qualities. When a mass of comminuted meat is heated, the contractile proteins coagulate, and they hold the small pieces of meat together. This is the way that so many formed products, such as sausages and meat loaves, are produced.

Unfrozen meat should be stored in a temperature range of 28° to 38°F (−2.2° to 3.3°C). The relative humidity should be in the range of 85-90%. The high humidity will prevent excessive drying and shrinkage. In addition, high humidity tends to preserve the white color of the fat in the meat. The storage room should have a reasonable circulation of air to ensure more uniform distribution of the humidity and heat removal. Meats stored for long periods are generally frozen and stored at temperatures in the range of − 10° to 0°F (−23.3° to −17.8°C).

Since many diseases can be transmitted from animals to humans, all meats shipped interstate in the Untied States are subject to inspections for wholesomeness under the authority of the Meat Inspection Act. "Wholesome" meat is safe to eat and is without adulteration. In addition to the wholesomeness inspection, meat is graded for quality. Although the lean is more valuable than fat, the best cuts of beef have some fat, and the fat is well distributed, giving the marbling effect cited earlier. The prime grade is of the highest quality, but in general, this is limited in amount and sold only to restaurants, hotels, and the better eating places.

It should be noted that in federally regulated plants, the inspection for wholesomeness is mandatory. The grading of the meat is optional.

BEEF/VEAL

The most important beef animal breeds in the United States are the Angus, Hereford, Galloway, and Shorthorn. Less important are the Santa Gertrudis, the Chambray, a cross between a Charolaise bull (French) and a Brahma cow, and the Brangus, a cross between an Angus bull and a Brahma cow. The latter breeds were developed to produce cattle resistant to screw worm (an insect infesting cattle), Brahma cattle being resistant to this parasite.

Much of the cattle population of the United States is raised on the Western range, which includes the Great Plains, the Rocky Mountains, and the intermountain and Pacific Coast regions. The raising of calves produced in these areas may be finished elsewhere. These feeding areas include the beet pulp feeding area of Colorado, the cottonseed cake section of Texas, the corn belt area (especially Iowa) and certain southern states, especially Florida, and California.

Discarded dairy animals supply a considerable portion of the cattle slaughtered in this country. Veal calves are produced mainly in dairying areas (especially Wisconsin), and slaughter calves (3–12 months old) are also produced in the southwestern areas.

Farmers and ranchers may sell cattle to terminal markets (who sell to various buyers), local markets, auctioneers, or packers. Usually, cattle are shipped by truck to stockyards near or at the point of slaughter.

Steers (males castrated prior to sexual maturity) and heifers (females beyond the veal and calf age that have never calved) make up the major portion of beef animals. Cows (females that have calved), bulls (mature males), and stags (castrated after reaching sexual maturity) make up the remainder of the beef animals.

At the point of sale, cattle may be graded in the live state. Grading is based on conformation (shape, build, and breed of the animal), finish (quantity and distribution of the fat), and quality (quality of the hair and hide, moderate bone mass, etc.)

The term *conformation* is used to describe the structural characteristics of the beef animal. For the best conformation, the animal should be short and compact. A rather blocky, or large-bodied, short-legged appearance is good.

Basically, the best structural characteristics or conformation is valuable to the retail butcher because apparently he is able to make more profitable cuts from the animals having the top conformation, and because there is a relationship between good conformation and good quality.

In the United States and many other countries, animals must be rendered insensible to pain before slaughter (see Fig. 15–1 for general slaughtering scheme). With cattle, this may be done by hitting them on the head with a maul or the bolt from a specially devised gun. Due to religious laws, cattle for kosher meats are slaughtered by first cutting the throat with a special knife, in one motion, severing the jugular vein, and then stunning. In ordinary slaughter, after the animal is stunned, it is shackled at the hind legs and raised from the floor in an upside-down position, after which it is bled by severing its jugular vein.

After bleeding, the head is skinned and severed at the neck. The body is lowered to the floor or to a cradle, the skin is cut ventrally and pulled back from the belly portion, and the lower legs are removed. Hooks are inserted in the cords of the hind leg section, and the body is raised to the half-hoist position. Most of the skin is removed in this position after which the carcass is raised to full hoist and skinning is completed. Also, in this position, the sternum (breastbone) is opened with a saw, the belly is split, the bung and esophagus are tied off, and the viscera are removed. The viscera are inspected by veterinarians, and the carcass is split into halves with a saw. The hide is inspected, salted, and sent to the tannery.

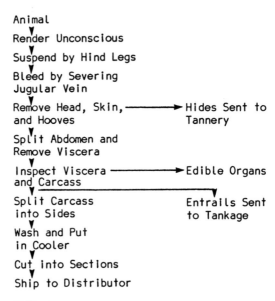

FIGURE 15-1.   General scheme for slaughtering animals.

The split carcass is washed, and, if it is not to be boned out soon after cooling, it is covered with a cloth to shape the surface fat. Sides handled in this manner are sent to a cooler where 24–48 hr will be required to bring the temperature of all parts to about 35°F (1.7°C).

Dressing, including skinning, may be carried out completely while the animal is hanging from a rail. Mechanical instruments, such as hide pullers, may be used to increase the efficiency of rail dressing.

In the past, when slaughtered beef was not to be used in local areas, it was shipped out as sides or, more often, as quarters. Today, a considerable amount of beef is cut into various primal cuts, such as rounds, ribs, and loins (see Fig. 15-2). The various sections, usually without bones, are packaged, usually under vacuum, in a film that is impervious to moisture and oxygen. The packages are boxed and shipped to distributors and retailers. Some retail chains prepare their own primal cuts from sides or quarters, packaging them in film under vacuum and shipping them in master cartons to their retail stores. Since the meat has been boned and trimmed of excess fat, meat department personnel at the stores have little to do but cut the meat into individual portions, package the various cuts, and place them on display. Primal cuts packaged in moisture- and oxygen-impermeable film, under vacuum, and held at temperatures between 32° and 40°F (0° and 4.4°C), are said to have a storage life of at least 21 days.

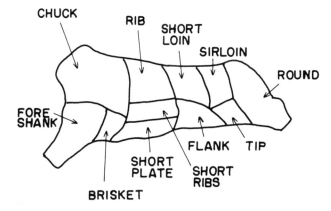

FIGURE 15-2.   Cattle carcass.

Inspectors from the USDA evaluate beef carcasses and specify various grades. These are "prime" (the best beef from steers and heifers), "choice" (the next best from heifers, steers, and young cows), and "select" (the third best). There are grades of lesser quality, but they are generally used for purposes other than as steaks, roasts, and so on.

A veal carcass is shown in Figure 15–3.

PORK

There are many breeds of hogs which, in this country, have become pretty well mixed in recent years in order to produce meat-type animals (more lean and less fat) rather than lard-type animals. Part of the reason for getting away from the high-fat type of hog has been that other oils and fats have

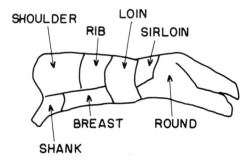

FIGURE 15-3.   Veal carcass.

largely replaced lard, which previously was the chief fat used for cooking. Some breeds of hogs, such as the Poland-China, Berkshire, Chester White, and Hampshire, are not mixed.

The north-central states, especially Iowa, produce most of the hogs raised in the United States. Hog production is said to be increasing in the southern states.

Hogs are fed soybean meal, tankage (heated slaughterhouse wastes), meat scraps, fish meal or milk, or combinations of these as a source of protein. Carbohydrate foods consist mainly of corn, but other grains are used. Minerals may be added as supplements. Antibiotics may be added as feed supplements to lessen disease and to provide for a better utilization of food. In this instance, the antibiotics serve to limit the growth of bacteria in the intestines, which themselves utilize food, thus causing some portion of the feed to be unavailable to the animal. Some vitamins, especially B-12, may be added to hog feed, since they may serve as growth factors.

Slaughter hogs are classified as barrows (males castrated prior to sexual maturity), gilts (young females that have not produced young pigs), sows (mature females that have produced young or that have reached an advanced stage of pregnancy), stags (males castrated after reaching maturity), and boars (uncastrated males).

Hogs are graded according to conformation, finish, and quality as U.S. No. 1, U.S. No. 2, U.S. No. 3, medium, and culls, this grading being listed in the order of desirability.

Prior to slaughter, hogs are rendered insensible by electric stunning or by exposure to an atmosphere of carbon dioxide. The hog is then shackled by the hind legs and raised to a conveyor after which a knife is inserted into the neck to sever the jugular vein. After bleeding for about 6 min, the hog, still on the conveyor, is passed through a water bath (water temperature about 140°F [60°C]) where it is immersed for 5 or 6 min. This facilitates removal of hair in a machine that has mechanically driven beaters. The loose hair is washed away with a water spray.

The carcass is then suspended by the hind legs by inserting the ends of a gambrel under the achilles tendon in each hind leg and attaching the gambrel to a moving conveyor. Remaining hair is scraped or singed off.

During dressing, the head is partially severed, the carcass is opened, and the viscera are removed. The edible organs are inspected by veterinarians and removed to refrigerated areas to be sold later as such or used for further processing. The carcass is then split and removed to the cooler where the temperature of all parts should be brought to 35°F (1.7°C) within a period of 18 to 24 hr.

Hogs are generally not shipped as sides. Usually, they are cut up into hams, loins, shoulders, bellies, and back fat before shipment to distributors or to processing plants that manufacture various pork products. See Figure 15-4 for hog carcass.

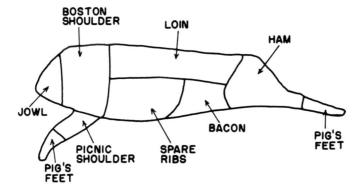

FIGURE 15-4. Hog carcass.

MUTTON/LAMB

The bulk of the sheep produced in the United States is said to be made up of crossbreeds developed for the production of both meat and wool. Pure breeds include Cheviots, Lincolns, Oxfords, Shropshires, Rambouillets, and Merinos.

Sheep are raised on ranges in arid and semiarid regions and on farms. On farms, flocks of sheep are smaller than those raised on ranges. Where conditions allow, lambs may be fattened on the range, but during winter storms, the feed must be supplemented with protein concentrates, corn, hay, barley, and oats.

Fattening of lambs may take place in the corn belt states, especially during the fall and winter months. This may be done in corn fields, stubble fields, or pastures. Some fattening occurs while the animals are confined to barns. Most lamb fattening is carried on from September through May.

Sheep are classified as ewes (females), wethers (males castrated prior to reaching maturity), rams (uncastrated mature males), and lambs about 3–12 months in age that do not show their first permanent teeth. Lambs are identified by the break joint—the temporary cartilage in the leg bone just above the hoof. As the animal grows older, the break joint loses its redness and sawtoothed appearance, and the cartilage is replaced by bone. Spring lambs are those from new crops marketed before July 1 and weighing 70–90 lb (31.8–40.9 kg). As with beef cattle and hogs, grading of slaughter lambs is based on conformation, finish, and quality.

Sheep are sold directly to the ultimate buyer or indirectly through a commission agent. Since most sheep are produced west of the Mississippi and are consumed in the East, they must be transported for comparatively long distances for slaughter. Lambs and sheep are shipped both by truck and by rail, in double-decked cars.

Lambs are slaughtered after stunning by inserting a knife below the jaw to sever the jugular vein while the lamb is shackled by the hind legs to a conveyor. The hind legs are skinned and the joints of the forelegs are broken just above the feet. The whole pelt is then removed after which the carcass is opened and the viscera removed. After removal of the head, the carcass is washed and removed to the cooler. Inspection of the viscera, carcass, and edible organs is done by veterinarians. As in the case of beef and pork, diseased sheep are discarded and used for tankage. In coolers, the temperature of all parts of the carcass should be lowered to 35°F (1.7°C) within 24 hr.

The lamb carcass is not split prior to shipment to the distributor or retailer. Sheep carcasses are classified into two categories—mutton and lamb (the latter is under 12–14 months of age). Lamb and mutton carcasses are graded as prime, choice, good, utility, and cull. A sheep carcass is shown in Figure 15–5.

CURED MEAT PRODUCTS

Much pork and some beef are cured or processed in some manner. (Veal, lamb, and mutton are ordinarily not cured.) During the cutting up of these animals, there are always some portions trimmed off from the carcass. Much of the trimmings from both beef and pork carcasses is used for the production of fresh or cooked sausage. Some of the fat that is trimmed off, especially from beef, is sold as such to be used for rendering. Fat rendered from trimmings of this kind is mostly used for the manufacture of soap. Bones

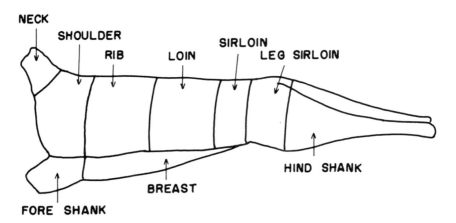

FIGURE 15–5.   Sheep carcass.

may be used for the manufacture of bone meal and, in some instances, for the production of gelatin. Pork skin is used almost entirely for the manufacture of gelatin.

Curing agents for meat products may include only salt (sodium chloride), as in the manufacture of New England-style corned beef. However, more often, curing agents include salt, sodium nitrate, sodium nitrite, and table sugar (sucrose) or glucose. Sometimes reducing agents, such as vitamin C or the related iso-ascorbic acid, are used to facilitate the coloring effect of nitrite, and in many instances, spices, and materials such as monosodium glutamate, are used as flavor enhancers. Nitrite also inhibits the growth of *clostridium botulinum,* a producer of a powerful toxin, and imparts a characteristic flavor.

When freshly cut, the color of meat is purplish red due to its pigment (myoglobin). After cutting the meat, the myoglobin soon becomes loosely bound to oxygen to form oxymyoglobin (bright red), and, if exposed to oxygen for some time, the bond becomes more permanent and the meat takes on a gray or brown color as metmyoglobin is formed. If nitrite is allowed to react with myoglobin, oxymyoglobin, or even metmyoglobin, under good reducing conditions, it replaces the oxygen and forms a compound known as nitrosomyoglobin. When meat containing nitrosomyoglobin is cooked to coagulate the protein, this compound is called nitrosohemochrome. The latter two compounds are pink or red in color, and they are somewhat more permanent than oxymyoglobin and less subject to oxidation to form the brown or gray metmyoglobin.

In the curing of hams, a brine (55–80% saturated with salt, containing 20–50 lb [9.1–22.7 kg] of sugar, about 1.5 lb [0.68 kg] of sodium nitrite, and 1 lb [0.45 kg] of sodium nitrate per 100 gal. [378.5 liters] of pickle) is used. Small amounts of ascorbic acid or iso-ascorbic acid may also be added. Ascorbic acid is added to provide reducing conditions in the meat, which facilitates the formation of nitrosohemochrome. Phosphate (for the retention of water) is allowed in cured meats in amounts not to exceed 0.5%. This pickle is pumped into the ham through the exterior iliac artery. The hams are placed in tierces (casks) and may or may not be covered with pickle. Curing in this manner may require 5–10 days, depending on the size of the product. The curing should be carried out at a temperature of 40°F (4.4°C) or below.

In smoking, moistened hardwood sawdust is usually burned in a mechanically controlled smoke generator (located outside the chamber where the product is hung) for purposes of treating with smoke and heat. Oak and hickory sawdust or logs (logs may be used in a special smoke generator) are mostly used for the production of smoke. The temperature of the smokehouse can be regulated by thermostatically controlled heating units within the smokehouse.

Hams to be canned may be dry rubbed with a mixture of 70–80 lb (31.8–

36.3 kg) salt, 25 lb (11.4 kg) sugar, and 1 lb (0.45 kg) sodium nitrite. In this case, they will be held in the cure mix for about 14 days.

After curing, the hams are washed, hung to dry (with or without covering with a stockingette), then smoked. The time and temperature of smoking must be sufficient to raise the temperature of all parts of the ham to at least 137°F (58.3°C). This is a USDA regulation that has been introduced to make certain that a roundworm, *Trichinella spiralis,* is destroyed. This parasite infests hogs, bears, and certain other animals and may infest the human. Cured hams to be boiled or canned may be smoked, but generally are not. Hams for canning are cured, skinned, boned, and placed in the can (some gelatin and various spices or flavoring agents may be added), and the cans are sealed under a slight vacuum and then heated in an agitated water bath at 165°–180°F (73.9°–82.2°C) until an internal temperature of 150°–165°F (65.6°–73.9°C) is reached. Boiled hams are placed in metal molds before cooking. Neither boiled nor canned hams are commercially sterile and must be refrigerated in order to prevent spoilage.

In preparing bacon, the belly portion of the hog is stitch-pumped with the curing solution. This is done by machines that through needlelike projections inject the curing solution simultaneously and automatically into the meat in a uniform pattern. The amount of pickle used for bacon is 5–10% of the green (uncured) weight. It is composed of a 65–75% saturated salt solution containing 20–100 lb (9.1–45.4 kg) of sugar, 1–1.5 lb (0.45–0.68 kg) of sodium nitrite, and ¾–1 lb (0.34–0.45 kg) of sodium nitrite per 100 gal. (378.5 liters) of pickle. The pumped bellies may be placed in cover pickle (the pickle covers the product) or dry rubbed with curing salts during curing. Curing times are short, and in some cases, the product is smoked almost immediately after pumping with pickle. During smoking (a period of 12–15 hr), the product is heated to an internal temperature of 120°–125°F (48.9°–51.7°C). This is done to develop the red color in the lean portion of the product. If the temperature were raised to 137°F (58.3°C) in all parts, as required for hams, much fat would be rendered out and lost. Apparently, regulatory agencies consider that bacon will be cooked prior to consumption so as to raise the temperature of all parts to 137°F (58.3°C) or higher.

After smoking and cooling, bacon slabs are squared up (uneven ends cut off), the product is sliced by machine, and it is packaged (usually under vacuum) so that a representative portion of the product can be viewed (through the plastic film) without opening the package.

Canadian bacon is prepared in a similar manner to that of regular bacon, except that pork loins, trimmed of fat, are used instead of bellies. Also, curing times are somewhat longer than for regular bacon, and during smoking, the internal temperature must be raised to 137°F (58.3°C) or higher. Pork shoulders and shoulder picnics are cured and smoked much in the same manner as are hams.

Special pork products, such as capocollo, are prepared from boneless pork butts (part of the shoulder). They are dry cured for at least 25 days at temperatures not lower than 36°F (2.2°C). Special spices are used in the curing mixture with table salt, nitrite, and nitrate as the main ingredients (not more than 1 oz [28.3 g] of nitrite for each 100 lb [45.4 kg] of meat). After curing, the product is smoked for not less than 30 hr at a temperature not lower than 80°F (26.7°C), and then held in a drying room for at least 20 days at a temperature not lower than 45°F (7.2°C). These times and temperatures are specified to make certain the *Trichinella spiralis* has been destroyed, since this product is eaten without cooking.

Some beef products are cured, or cured and dried. Among these are corned beef, pastrami, and chipped or dried beef. Corned beef is usually produced from the brisket (lower forward portion of cattle near the foreleg). The fresh briskets are pumped with pickle and placed in cover pickle for 7–14 days at a temperature of 40°F (4.4°C) or below. In most cases, nitrite is used as an ingredient of the pickle, but in New England–style corned beef, only salt is used. In producing pastrami, table salt, nitrite (in limited amounts as stated above), and nitrate, together with spices, are used in curing solutions.

Corned beef and pastrami are often sold as the cured product to be cooked in the home, restaurant, or delicatessen. However, they may be cooked and sold in the sliced (packaged) or unsliced form. Corned beef (containing nitrite) is also canned as corned beef hash, a mixture of cooked corned beef, cooked potatoes, and flavoring agents, such as onions. Some corned beef is cooked and canned as such.

Chipped beef is produced from beef hams or other portions that make up certain parts of the round section of the hind quarter. Usually cutter and canner grade cattle are used for this product. The beef hams are placed in tierces and covered with a pickle of high salt content containing not more (usually less) than 2 lb (907.2 g) of nitrite per 100 gal. (378.5 liters) of pickle. They are held in this manner for 50–65 days at a temperature below 40°F (4.4°C) (but above 34°F [1.1°C]). After curing, the product is hung in a room of low relative humidity and allowed to dry to the point where the salt content is 10–14%. It is then sliced in thin sheets and placed in glass jars that are capped under vacuum. This product is not heat-processed. The high salt content and the nitrite are sufficient to prevent the development of food spoilage or disease-causing bacteria. The vacuum packing is necessary to retain the pink color of chipped beef, and it prevents the development of mold growth.

Regarding the stability of cured meats, it should be pointed out that impurities in the salt used in the curing process may considerably affect the development of rancidity. For example, salt may contain traces of copper, iron, and other metals that are natural catalysts for initiating and accelerating rancidity.

SAUSAGE PRODUCTS

The meat ingredients used in a variety of sausage products may come, in part, from trimmings resulting from the cutting of beef quarters into rounds, loins, and so on, and from the cutting of hogs into loins, hams, and shoulders. However, the chief source of meat for sausage comes from low-grade cattle and hogs. Bull meat is a prime ingredient for certain types of cooked sausage.

Fresh pork sausage is not cooked or smoked. The meat is ground and seasoned (usually only salt, sugar, sage, and pepper are added for seasoning, but ginger may also be used). Some ice, up to 3% by weight based on the meat ingredient, may be added. The product is mixed and stuffed into natural casings. In federally inspected plants, the meat ingredient is limited to contain not more than 50% of fat. The natural casings used for fresh pork sausage are made from the outer covering of the small intestine of sheep. Larger plastic or natural casings may be used for sausage.

Fresh pork sausage should be held at temperatures very near 32°F (0°C) after manufacture, since it is quite subject to bacterial spoilage, to oxidation of the fat (rancidification), and to loss of the typical pink color. Usually, when bacterial spoilage occurs, other types of spoilage do not.

Frankfurters (see Fig. 15-6), the most popular type of sausage, are comminuted, semisolid sausages prepared from one or more kinds of raw skeletal muscle meat (usually pork and beef) or raw skeletal meat and raw or cooked poultry meat (no more than 15% of the total ingredients, excluding water). The product is seasoned, cured, and usually smoked. The seasonings usually include sugar and spices such as pepper, nutmeg or mace, mustard, garlic, and corriander to improve flavor. The curing salts usually contain sodium nitrite and sodium erythorbate (sodium iso-ascorbic acid) to prevent the growth of *Clostridium botulinum* and to develop the color. There have been studies showing that nitrites, in combination with protein and heat, produce carcinogenic nitrosamines. The USDA sets limits on the amount of nitrites, nitrates, or a combination of the two at 200 ppm. This corresponds to about ¼ oz per 100 lb (about 7 g per 45.4 kg) of meat.

Work is being done to develop curing solutions that do not contain nitrites but still destroy *Clostridium botulinum*. One such ingredient is sodium hypophosphite, which closely resembles nitrite in its preservative effect and is a GRAS substance. Approved phosphates may be added for water retention, and products such as dry milk, cereal, and soy flour may be added for a total of 3.5% of the finished product. It may contain meat by-products such as hearts, snouts, and tripe but must be labeled as "frankfurter with by-products" or "frankfurter with variety meats." Water or ice, or both, may be added to facilitate chopping or to dissolve the curing ingredients. If smoking is done, it may be with hard wood smoke or with liquid smoke spray.

Beef, Pork, and/or Chicken
↓
Comminute, Adding Some Ice,
Curing Agents, Spices, Salt,
Fillers, etc.
↓
Remove Trapped Air by
Vacuum
↓
Add Fat and Emulsify
↓
Extrude Emulsion into
Casings
↓
Make Filled Casing
into Links
↓
Temper at Room Temperature
↓
Smoke at 165°F
↓
Cook in Hot Water Sprays
(Water Temperature about
175°F)
↓
Cool

FIGURE 15-6.   Sequence for production of frankfurters.

When the process is complete, the frankfurters may not contain more than 30% fat and not more than a 40% combination of fat and water.

Frankfurters may also be made from a single species and may be labeled "beef frankfurter" or "turkey frankfurter." The poultry franks have grown in popularity because they are often formulated so that there is less fat in the finished product. Some of the beef producers are also making lower-fat varieties. Whatever the case, all ingredients must appear on the label in decreasing order, by weight.

By one method used in the production of frankfurters the meat is passed through a meat grinder and then finely comminuted in a silent cutter (a large metal bowl in which knives rotate at right angles to the plane of the bowl, which also rotates). While in the silent cutter, ice is added to prevent the temperature of the meat from rising above 60°F (15.6°C). It should be noted that the finished product may contain up to 10% added water (federal regulations), the purpose of which is to facilitate cutting and to provide more succulence to the finished product. Curing agents, spices, and fillers (if used) are added while the meat is in the silent cutter. The nitrite is added separately from other additives, because if it is mixed with the other additives before it is added to the frankfurter mix, the preservative effect of the nitrite will be diminished.

When ascorbic or iso-ascorbic acid is used to assist in color development, it is added about 1 min before the end of chopping in the silent cutter. Colloid mills or similar equipment may be used to comminute the meat instead of the silent cutter. From the silent cutter, the meat emulsion is put into metal carts, which may be placed in a vacuum chamber to eliminate trapped air bubbles. The air may also be removed in a mixer under vacuum.

The meat emulsion consists of a continuous phase, which is the water, and a dispersed or discontinuous phase, which is the fat. The fat is dispersed more or less uniformly in the water. The emulsifier, in this case, or the agent that maintains this uniform dispersion of the fat, is actually the fraction of proteins that has been solubilized, especially in the presence of salt. In preparing the emulsion, one must heed the temperature rise during preparation, and the rate at which the fat is added as well as the speed with which the emulsion is mixed. The temperature should not be too high. If it exceeds 68°F (20.0°C), or thereabouts, the emulsion may break down. The optimum rate at which the fat should be added depends a great deal on the rate at which the fat can be emulsified.

If the fat is added more slowly than the emulsification rate, then the mixing time will be unnecessarily extended, creating an increase in temperature and a decrease in the amount of fat that can be emulsified. If the rate at which the fat is added greatly exceeds the rate at which it can be emulsified, then it is quite possible that little or no emulsion will be formed. The viscosity of the mix, the size of the fat droplets, the type of fat, and a considerable number of other factors affect the emulsion characteristics.

The meat emulsion is next placed in a stuffing machine where a powered piston extrudes the product into a stuffing horn and then into artificial (cellophane or other plastic) or natural casing (sheep or other animal intestine). The stuffed casing comes out as a long cylinder, which is then made into link form, generally by machine.

The linked sausage is hung on racks at room temperature (if ascorbic acid has not been added) to provide for the development of color; this is called tempering. The linked frankfurters are then smoked and cooked.

During smoking and heating, the frankfurters are hung in air-conditioned or natural draft smokehouses. During the first phase in the smokehouse, a temperature of 130°-140°F (54.4°-60°C) is used for 10–20 min. Smoke is then introduced, and the temperature is slowly raised to 165°F (73.9°C) and held until the internal temperature of the product reaches 140°-165°F (60°-73.9°C). After smoking, the product is cooked with hot-water (170°-180°F [76.7°-82.2°C]) sprays. This may be done in the smokehouse or in a special chamber known as the Jordan cooker. Immediately after cooking, the internal temperature of frankfurters should never be less than 150°F (65.6°C), and preferably should be at 155°F (68.2°C) or slightly higher. After cooking, the frankfurters are hung in a cooler.

Color is sometimes added to the water used to cook frankfurters, and colored cellulose casings are sometimes used to enhance the appearance of the product. Frankfurters stuffed into natural casings are not skinned after manufacturing, but those stuffed into cellulose casings are removed from the casing before they are sold. The links of sausage are passed through a bath of warm water, then into the skinning machine, where the casing is slit with a blade, then rolled off or blown off.

After skinning, the frankfurters are packaged and immediately returned to the cooler, which should be held at a temperature near 32°F (0°C), until shipped out. Frankfurters, like other perishable foods, eventually spoil when held for long periods at temperatures near but above freezing. When spoiled, frankfurters either become slimy, due to the growth of bacteria or yeasts, or they turn green on parts of the surface. Greening is due to hydrogen peroxide produced by the growth of bacteria of the *Lactobacteriaceae* group. The hydrogen peroxide reacts with the nitrosohemochromagen (color complex of nitrite and myoglobin) and oxidizes it to form a green color.

At times, green rings on the inside of frankfurters, near the surface, may be encountered. This is not due to bacterial growth in the product after manufacturing. It is believed to be due to high bacterial counts in the fresh meat used for producing frankfurters. The bacteria are killed during smoking and cooking, but their end products are not destroyed and cause green rings to form during, or shortly after, manufacturing.

In continuous frankfurter manufacturing, automatic stuffers extrude the emulsion into molds, which pass through an automated tempering, smoking, cooking, and cooling unit. The product is packaged immediately after exit from the processing unit.

Bologna is another type of smoked and cooked sausage. The ingredients and manufacturing procedures for manufacturing bologna are similar to those used in making frankfurters, but the size of the casing, hence the size of the bologna, is much larger in diameter, and the length of the bologna link is proportionately longer than the frankfurter link. When not sufficiently cooked, bologna may develop green cores after processing.

There are many other types of meat sausage produced. Among the smoked, uncooked sausages are country-style pork sausage and country-style sausage that contains beef, as well as pork. These products contain moderate amounts of curing agents. Cooked sausages are made both with and without curing agents added, and are stuffed into natural cellulose or saran casings. In the manufacture of Braunschweiger or liver sausage, pork liver and jowls, with or without beef, are used.

Types of sausage vary, depending on the style of cutting or grinding of the meat, the size and shape of the product, the seasonings used, the degree of smoking, and the cooking procedure. A few of the different types include kielbasy, knockwurst, cooked salami, mettwurst, and Polish sausage.

There are various loaf-type specialty products, such as chicken loaf, luncheon meat, meat loaf, and head cheese, and these may be processed in casings or in metal containers. In the latter instance, they are usually placed in casings after cooking. This type of product may be cooked in hot water or baked in an oven. The products may be deep-fat fried, after baking, in order to brown the surface.

Some types of sausage are deliberately handled to permit a bacterial fermentation to occur in the product during processing. During the bacterial fermentation, lactic acid is produced, lowering the pH of the product to around 5.0. The lactic acid assists in the preservation of the product and contributes to the particular flavor of this type of sausage.

Fermented sausages are either of the semidried or dried type. Most fermented sausages are smoked, and the semidried type is heated to an internal temperature of at least 137°F (58.3°C). Many dried types of fermented sausage are not heated to temperatures above 90°F (32.2°C).

Curing salts are among the ingredients used in the production of fermented sausages, but nitrate sometimes replaces nitrite. During processing, bacteria remove oxygen from the nitrate, reducing it to nitrite. As stated earlier, nitrite provides the typical red or pink color in the meat.

After mixing with the curing agents, the meat for semidried sausage is held in pans for 48–72 hr in a refrigerated room 38°–40°F (3.3°–4.4°C). The meat is then remixed, stuffed into casings, and held at 50°–60°F (10°–15.6°C) for 12–48 hr, then smoked. Smoking is accomplished in stages: first, at a temperature of 80°–90°F (26.7°–32.2°C) for 12–16 hr, then, at 100°F (37.8°C) for 24 hr, and finally, at 137°F (58.3°C) for 4–5 hr. During the processing of semidried sausage, conditions at first favor the growth of bacteria that reduce nitrate to nitrite. This is followed by the growth of lactic acid–producing bacteria. To ensure the type of fermentation desired, it is possible to obtain cultures of appropriate bacteria, which may then be added as an ingredient of the product. Typical semidried sausages are thüringer, cervelat, Lebanon bologna, and pork roll.

Dried sausages, such as Italian salami and pepperoni, are not heated to temperatures above 90°F (32.2°C), but they are stabilized against microbial spoilage because of their low pH (due to the action of lactic acid–producing bacteria), their low moisture content, and their high salt content. Spices and curing salts also contribute to the preservation of the product. Some dried sausages are smoked.

During the manufacture of dried sausage, the meat, curing salts, and spices are mixed, and the mixture is passed through a grinder. The ground product is then placed in pans and held in a room at 38°–40°F (3.3°–4.4°C) for 2–3 days. After being stuffed into casings, the sausage is held on racks in a room at 70°–75°F (21.1°–23.9°C) and at a relative humidity of 75–80% for a period of 2–10 days. Smoked varieties are then smoked at low temperatures (not above 90°F [32.2°C]). Finally, the sausage is dried by hanging in a room at 45°–55°F (7.2°–12.8°C) (relative humidity of 70–72%) where there is an adequate air movement (at least 15 air changes per hour). Drying times vary between 10 and 90 days, and the moisture loss during drying is 20–40% of the weight of the freshly smoked product.

16

Dairy Products

Dairy products are produced from milk. In the United States, essentially all dairy products are produced from cow's milk, although minor quantities of goat's milk products may also be manufactured.

Because milk and milk products have traditionally been priced on their valued component, the fat, standards have been established mainly for this component but include provisions for other components, as well, at both the federal and state levels. The standards for milk and milk products may be found in the Code of Federal Regulations (CFR) Number 21, part 131. This is available from the Office of the Federal Register, National Archives and Records Administration, Washington, D.C.

FLUID MILK

The Holstein breed outnumbers all others used in the United States for the production of milk. Jersey and Guernsey breeds tolerate hot weather better than Holsteins, hence may be the predominant types used for the production of milk in hot-weather areas. Some Ayrshire, and Brown Swiss or Shorthorn breeds are used in certain areas.

Cow's milk contains an average of 3.8% fat (called butterfat), 3.3% protein, 4.8% lactose (a 12-carbon sugar), 0.7% ash (minerals), and 87.4% water. Milk also contains vitamins and other nutrients in small amounts, making it the most complete of foods. The young of mammalians survive on it exclusively. However, components of milk from different species vary, and occasionally the young of one species may be unable to tolerate the milk from another species, mainly because of differences in the lactose contained therein. The fat content of milk from Ayrshire and Brown Swiss, and especially from Guernsey and Jersey breeds, is slightly higher than that from Holstein cows, but the latter breed generally produces much more milk than the others. Most milk is produced on farms that deal primarily with the raising of dairy cattle.

Microorganisms in Milk

As drawn from the cow's udder, milk seldom, if ever, is free from microorganisms; bacteria, molds, and yeasts are usually present in small numbers, among which the bacteria are most significant from the standpoint of quality and the transmission of food-borne disease. The control of microbial activity in milk and milk products, especially the control of bacteria and bacterial growth, is the most important function in the handling and manufacture of dairy products.

Raw milk, when improperly handled, may undergo any of several adverse changes. It may become sour due to the growth of bacteria that produce lactic acid, or it may become foamy due to the growth of gas-producing coliform bacteria or yeasts. Raw milk may also be subject to peptonization (digestion of the casein), the formation of rope (a viscous polymer of sugars), and sweet curdling, when bacterial growth is not controlled.

Dairy herds are tested for tuberculosis and tested for and vaccinated for brucellosis, and most milk is pasteurized to prevent the transmission of a variety of food-borne diseases. However, some pathogens may survive the pasteurization process, possibly because they may be protected by fat in which they may become encapsulated. *Listeria monocytogenes* is one such species (see Chap. 6).

Most, but not all, certified milk is pasteurized. However, certified milk must be produced from herds that have been inspected, tested, and found to be free from disease, and the milk must be drawn and handled under the best conditions of sanitation. There are bacterial standards for certified milk that limit the number and types of bacteria that may be present.

Sources of Bacteria in Milk and Methods
of Limiting Bacterial Contamination

Some bacteria are normally present in the udder of the cow, and these may contribute to the bacterial flora of milk. However, unless the udder is infected, it is not considered to be an important source of such microorganisms. Other sources of microbial contamination of milk are the body of the cow, milking machines and other equipment and utensils, the air in the milking barn, and the hands, nose, and throat of those attending to the milking process. In the handling of milk upon delivery to the processing plant or dairy, further sources of contamination may be encountered.

In order to limit the number of bacteria present in raw milk, certain precautionary procedures are ordinarily applied. The flanks, udder, and teats of the cow should be washed, treated with a sanitizing solution, and dried before milk is drawn. Large dairy farms often have a special wash pen for cows to be milked. Utensils, including the milking machine, should be cleaned and disinfected either with live steam or with a solution of chlorine (about 200 ppm of available chlorine). Bulk milk tanks may be cleaned manually with detergent and water at about 130°F (54.4°C), then sanitized with chlorine solution, or cleaned mechanically with detergent and water at 150°F (65.6°C), and finally sanitized with chlorine solution. Outlet valves and the outside of the tank must be cleaned and sanitized manually. Cleaning in place (CIP) may be used to clean, sanitize, and rinse the milk pipe line, the teat cup assembly, and the bulk milk tank if a vacuum or pressure system is available.

The water supply used on dairy farms should be potable and located so that there is no possibility of contamination with animal or human discharges. Where municipal sewerage systems are not available, human wastes and floor washings from milk handling areas should be disposed of in septic tanks or cesspools. Manure should not be allowed to accumulate near milk handling areas and is best disposed of by spreading in thin layers on pastures.

Flies may be controlled in milk-handling areas, at least to some extent, by flytraps that utilize entrapment liquids, by poisons, such as formaldehyde, or by electric fly killers. The control of other insects, such as cockroaches, may require the use of an approved insecticide.

The walls and floor of the milking area should be kept clean, and the room should be reasonably well ventilated and free from dust. Personnel involved in the handling of milk should not have a history of intestinal disease. Flush toilets, in rooms that do not open directly into the area where cows are milked, should be provided for personnel, and handwashing and sanitizing facilities should be available at or near the area where milk is drawn. The hands of the milker or milking attendant should have been cleaned, sanitized, and dried before milking is started.

Handling of Milk on Farms

Milking is generally carried out by machine rather than by hand. At first, a small amount of milk is drawn and examined for impurities, after which the cups of the milking machine are applied to the teats of the cow. The cups are connected to a hose that leads to a holding container, and milk is collected by suction and a rhythmic squeezing action. After milking, the cups are immersed in a nonirritating bactericidal agent before applying them to the teats of another cow. Milk from the cow passes through the milking machine from which it flows through a glass or stainless steel pipe to a bulk cooling tank cooled by refrigerated water or refrigerant sprayed directly or expanded into a jacket that covers the outside of the tank. During cooling, the milk is slowly agitated mechanically to provide for faster heat transfer. Milk should be cooled to approximately 40°F (4.4°C) within 2 hr after it is drawn, although there is no evidence that microbial growth can occur in fresh drawn milk for the first few hours.

Milk may undergo a number of adverse changes during its handling. If held for any length of time without adequate cooling, it is subject to various types of spoilage due to the growth of microorganisms. In addition, milk may develop various off-flavors due to the feed consumed by the cows, especially when they have fed on wild onions, french weed, or ragweed. Large proportions of beets, beet tops, potatoes, cabbage, or turnips in the fodder provided for cows may also cause the development of off-flavors in the milk. Lipase, an enzyme present in cow's milk, may cause a hydrolysis of fat, splitting off butyric acid, which causes an off-flavor and off-odor. Milk that has been cooled, then warmed to about 85°F (29.4°C), then recooled or homogenized in the unpasteurized state, is subject to this kind of off-flavor development. Off-flavors due to the oxidation of some of its components may occur in milk, especially if traces of copper are present, since copper catalyzes this type of reaction. Milk, therefore, should be kept out of contact with equipment that contains copper.

Transportation of Fluid Milk

Milk is transported from the farm to the receiving station or to the fluid milk processing plant in pickup tankers. Pickup tankers are insulated, stainless steel tanks, usually having a holding capacity of more than 5000 gal. (18,925 liters) on a trailer handled by a motorized vehicle. No refrigeration is provided for pickup tankers, since the insulated container prevents a significant rise in the temperature of the milk during the period required for transportation and delivery to the processing plant. The production of whole milk involves a series of steps, the important ones of which are shown in Figure 16-1.

When receiving the milk, the operator of the tanker first tests the product, which has been stored in bulk tank, for odor and flavor and, if not suitable, the milk is rejected. If acceptable, the volume of the product in the bulk tank is measured with a rod. It is then agitated, after which a sample is taken in a glass or plastic bottle from which the butterfat content will be determined, since the farmer is paid on the basis of butterfat content. A comingled sam-

Raw Milk
▼
Clarify
▼
Adjust Butterfat Content
▼
Fortify with Vitamin D
▼
Pasteurize
▼
Enhance Flavor (Flash Heat
with Injected Steam and
Cool with High Vacuum)
▼
Homogenize
▼
Cool
▼
Pour into Containers

FIGURE 16-1.   Production of whole milk.

ple is also taken to be tested for the presence of antibiotics using the *Bacillus subtilis* test or equivalent as required by the Pasteurized Milk Ordinance of the U.S. Public Health Service. If there is no problem, the samples from the individual farmers will not be tested. If there is a problem, however, each individual farm sample must be tested, and the farmer responsible for the contaminated milk must pay for the entire load. Because of such a severe financial consequence, farmers are very careful not to attempt to sell milk from cows that have been recently treated with antibiotics.

The milk is then pumped from the bulk tank into the tanker through a sanitized plastic hose after which the hose is capped. The final step is to prepare a weight ticket for the farmer and tabulate the weight, temperature, and other data of the product on a record sheet.

Pickup tankers, including auxiliary equipment such as hoses, must be cleaned and sanitized, as are dairy farm milking and milk-holding equipment, after delivery of the product to the processing plant.

Processing of Fluid Milk

Milk, as delivered to the processing plant, is first clarified while cold. Clarification consists of passing the milk through a centrifuge similar to a cream separator but operated at low speed. This treatment is sufficient to separate out dirt and sediment that might be present, depositing them as a layer on the inner surface of the centrifuge bowl. The clarifier is not operated at sufficient speed to separate the cream from the milk. After clarification, the milk is usually pumped into a storage tank equipped with an agitator. While in the storage tank, the milk is sampled, and the butterfat content is determined. It is then standardized by adding enough cream or skim milk (milk from which cream has been removed) to provide the fat content required by state regulations. The milk is then fortified with vitamin D at the rate of 400 USP units per quart (0.95 liter).

The next step in fluid milk processing is to pasteurize it. During pasteurization, milk must be heated in all parts to 145°F (62.8°C) and held at this temperature for 30 min, or it must be quickly heated to 161°F (71.7°C) and held at this temperature for 15 sec, heated to 191°F (88.3°C) and held for 1 sec, or heated to 194°F (90°C) and held for 0.5 sec, then cooled. Pasteurizing at temperatures above 145°F (62.8°C) is called the high-temperature–short-time (HTST) method, and both heating and cooling are carried out over a short period of time. Milk may be pasteurized in insulated vats heated by coils carrying hot water, or in vats heated by hot water sprayed within a jacket surrounding the sides and bottom of the vat. With low-temperature pasteurization, the milk is ordinarily agitated during heating and cooling (see Fig. 16–2). Plate heaters and coolers (see Fig. 16–3) or tubular heaters may be used to pasteurize and cool milk. When tubular heaters are used, the product travels in one direction through an inner tube while the hot water for heating or the refrigerated liquid for cooling passes in the opposite direction through an outer tube surrounding that which carries the product.

Today, milk is usually given what is called a flavor treatment to provide a product that is uniform in odor and taste. During flavor treatment, milk is instantly heated to about 195°F (90.6°C) with live steam (injected directly into the product) after which it is subjected to a vacuum of about 10 in. (25.4 cm) in one chamber and to a vacuum of about 22 in. (55.9 cm) in another chamber. The high vacuum treatment serves to regulate flavor, to cool the milk to about 150°F (65.6°C), and to evaporate water that may have been added through the injection of steam.

While the milk is still hot, it is usually homogenized by passing it through a small orifice that breaks up the fat globules to a small size, preventing the separation of cream from the milk. The milk is then quickly cooled to about 35°F (1.7°C). This is done by the same general procedures used in heating, except that refrigerated water or brine, or directly expanded ammonia is used in the coils, vat jacket, outer tubes of the pasteurizer, or tubes of the plates on the cooling side of the plate pasteurizer. During HTST pasteurization and during flavor treatment and homogenization, milk is passed through the

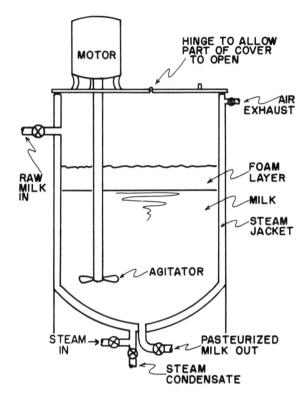

FIGURE 16-2.   Batch pasteurizer.

heating and cooling cycles at such a rapid rate that at no time is it held for long periods at high temperatures.

After processing and cooling, milk is filled mechanically into containers made of waxed or plastic-coated cardboard of different volumes up to 2 qt (1.9 l) and of semirigid plastic containers of 2 qt (1.9 l) or 1 gal (3.8 l), and the containers are sealed. In this state, milk should be held as close to 32°F (0°C) as possible until consumed.

In plants producing fluid milk or milk products, all equipment, including tanks or vats, pasteurizers and coolers, homogenizers, pipe lines, and pumps, should be of sanitary design. There should be no threaded pipes. Joints should be of the clamp type that can be easily disassembled for cleaning and sanitizing. All surfaces contacting milk or milk products should be readily accessible for cleaning and sanitizing regardless of whether they are to be cleaned in place (CIP) or disassembled. The suitability of equipment

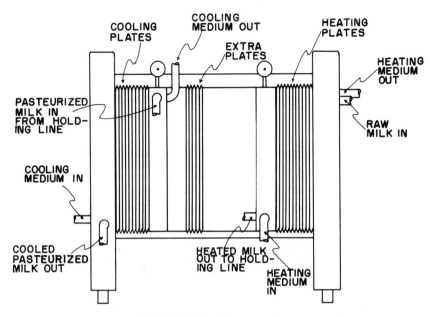

FIGURE 16-3.   Plate pasteurizer.

for cleaning and sanitizing, and the frequency with which this is done, are equally important.

Skim milk (0.5% fat) and low-fat milk (0.5-2.0% fat) are produced from whole milk passed through a centrifuge at high speeds, after the milk has been heated to 90-110°F (32.2-43.3°C), to remove the butterfat as cream. These products are usually fortified with vitamins A and D prior to pasteurizing and cooling. In some cases, sodium caseinate (a derivative of casein, the main protein in milk) is also added. The cream from the centrifuge may be separated as approximately 40% butterfat (heavy cream), 30% butterfat (all purpose cream), or 20% butterfat (light cream). The creams higher in butterfat may also be diluted with skim milk to provide the various fat densities or to produce a product known as half-and-half (about 10.5% butterfat).

Since cream tends to spoil more quickly than milk, during pasteurization it is given a more drastic heat treatment than that given to milk. When batch pasteurization is used, cream is heated to 150°-155°F (65.6°-68.3°C) and held at this temperature for 30 min prior to cooling. When the HTST method is used, cream is heated to 166°-175°F (74.4°-79.4°C) and held at this temperature for 15 sec prior to cooling. Table cream (light cream or half-and-half) is usually homogenized after pasteurization. All cream, after pasteurization, should be quickly cooled to 35°F (1.7°C) and containerized. It should be held at 35°–40°F (1.7°–4.4°C) until consumed or subjected to additional processing.

Chemical, bacteriological, and temperature standards for grade A milk and milk products, as issued by the U.S. Public Health Service, are listed in Table 16–1.

Large quantities of skim of low-fat milk are dried. This may be done by spraying atomized droplets of milk into a chamber through which heated air is circulated (spray drying, see Fig. 11-3) or milk may be dried by allowing it to flow over the surfaces of two heated metal drums that rotate toward each other (drum drying, see Fig. 11-2). With the latter method, the dried milk is scraped from the drums, as they rotate, by metal scraper blades. Dried milk (usually the spray dried type that contains about 5% of moisture) may be rehumidified to slightly higher moisture content after drying. This treatment agglomerates the fine milk particles to form clumps of milk powder, which results in a product that dissolves or disperses in water much more readily than the finely powdered dried milk. It is, therefore, considered to be an instantly soluble product.

Milk is used for the manufacture of a wide variety of popular dairy products, and these are described in the following paragraphs.

TABLE 16–1.   Chemical, Bacteriological, and Temperature Standards for Grade A Milk and Milk Products

Grade A raw milk for pasteurization	Temperature	Cooled to 50°F or less and maintained thereat until processed.
	Bacterial limits	Individual producer milk not to exceed 100,000 per ml prior to commingling with other producer milk.
		Not exceeding 300,000 per ml as commingled milk prior to pasteurization.
	Antibiotics	No detectable zone with the *Bacillus subtilis* method or equivalent.
Grade A pasteurized milk and milk products (except cultured products)	Temperature	Cooled to 45° F or less and maintained thereat.
	Bacterial limits	Milk and milk products—20,000 per ml.
	Coliform limit	Not exceeding 10 per ml.
	Phosphatase	Less than 1mg per ml, by Scharger Rapid Method (or equivalent by other means).
Grade A pasteurized cultured products	Temperature	Same as above.
	Coliform limit	Do.
	Phosphatase	Do.
	Bacterial limits	Exempt.

OTHER DAIRY PRODUCTS

Ice Cream

Regular ice cream may contain about 10% butterfat (added as cream), milk or skimmed milk, sugars (sucrose and/or dextrose), gelatin or vegetable gums (to provide body), eggs, and flavoring such as vanilla, fruit, fruit extracts, fruit juices, cocoa, chocolate, and nuts. Low-fat ice cream may be made by using less butterfat (as cream) and adding more milk solids or sodium caseinate or both. Generally, the butterfat content of ice cream is regulated to a certain minimum by state requirements, and low-fat mixtures must be labeled as something other than ice cream, for example, ice milk.

There are various systems and procedures for the manufacture of ice cream. A typical method is described in Figure 16–4. Liquid ingredients (milk, cream, concentrated skim milk, etc.) are mixed in one tank and liquid sweeteners (sugar, corn syrup) in another tank. The liquids are blended together with the dry ingredients (stabilizers, emulsifiers, whey solids, etc.) and

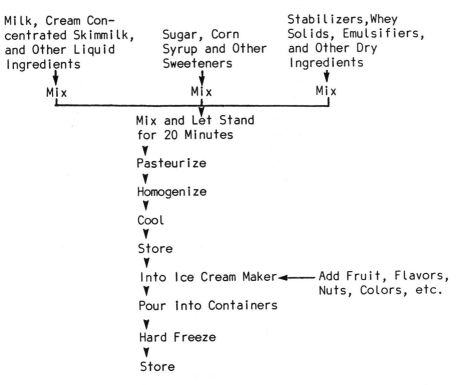

FIGURE 16–4.   Manufacture of ice cream.

allowed to stand ("soak") for about 20 min. The mixture is then pasteurized, homogenized, cooled to about 36°F (2.2°C) while agitating, and pumped to storage tanks. From the storage tanks the mixture is metered into the freezer, and as this is done, measured amounts of flavoring materials, fruit or nuts (when used), and possibly coloring are added. The freezer consists of a tube with walls refrigerated to a temperature of 5° to 15°F (−15° to −9.4°C) and blades that rotate at 175–225 rpm. The blades scrape the inner walls of the tube and incorporate air into the mixture as it is cooled. The blades also cause the product to move through the freezer, and at the time of exit the ice cream is plastic and has a temperature of 22° to 26°F (−5.6° to −3.3°C). In this form it is filled into cardboard or plastic containers. The containers are capped and placed in hardening rooms that usually have a temperature of −20° to −50°F (−28.9° to −45.6°C). Special systems may be used for hardening ice cream. After hardening, ice cream is stored at 0°F (−17.8°C) or below.

Ice cream in the plastic or unfrozen state may be added to small molds carried on a belt through refrigerated brine. A stick is inserted (at the start, if a partially frozen mix is used, or when partially frozen, if the liquid mixture is used), and the product is allowed to freeze and solidify thoroughly. The frozen portions are removed from the molds and dipped in warm, liquid chocolate. The cold ice cream hardens the chocolate, and the product is then wrapped, packaged, and placed in storage at 0°F (−17.8°C) or below. Some plastic ice cream is extruded between sheets of cookielike pastry, prior to wrapping and hardening, to produce ice-cream sandwiches.

Since air is incorporated into ice cream as it is manufactured, the volume of the finished product is much larger than that of the liquid mixture from which it was produced. This increase in volume is called overrun. Overruns for ice cream vary between 60% and 120%, but the weight of the ice cream cannot be less than 4.5 lb per gal (2.04 kg per 3.785 l). The overrun can be calculated as follows:

$$\% \text{ Overrun} = \frac{(100) \times (\text{weight per gallon of mix} - \text{weight per gallon of ice cream})}{\text{weight per gallon of ice cream}}$$

Ice Cream Substitutes, Sherbets, and Ices

A number of ice cream–like products that are either low in cholesterol or calories, or both, have been developed due to the large consumer demand for these products, but they cannot be sold as ice cream because they do not meet the standard for this product. A product called mellorine substitutes butter-fat with vegetable oil, and ice milks and dairy soft serves use only low amounts of butterfat. Frozen yogurt, one of the fastest-growing ice-cream substitutes, has been formulated to taste, feel, and look like ice cream, yet is is much lower in fat, cholesterol, and total calories than ice cream and even ice milks and dairy soft serves. Thus, frozen yogurt is sweeter and less acidic than traditional yogurt, which is described in the next section.

Nondairy frozen desserts include tofu-based products and nonfat soft serve-type products to which are added gums to absorb water and to trap air when mixed. Much work is being done to produce nonfat, low-cholesterol, low-calorie frozen desserts.

Sherbets are fruit or mint-flavored frozen desserts containing some milk solids, as in the case of milk ices. The sugar content of sherbets is somewhat higher than that of ice cream. High overruns in sherbet are not desirable, since this product tends to develop a spongy texture when overruns are higher than 25–40%.

Ices and frozen suckers contain no milk solids. The mixture consists chiefly of a solution of fruit juices and 30–32% sugar. Ices may be frozen in an ice-cream freezer, or the mixture may be added to molds and a stick inserted into the partially frozen material, and then completely frozen as the molds pass through a bath of refrigerated brine.

Cultured Fluid Dairy Products

In the United States, the three most utilized cultured dairy products are yogurt, buttermilk, and sour cream. Yogurt is made from whole milk that has been boiled to increase the solids or from whole milk to which 1–5% of nonfat milk solids have been added. Stabilizers (e.g., gelatin, alginates, gums) are generally added to the milk mixture in producing yogurt. The mixture is either preheated to 150°F (65.5°C), homogenized, then heated to 185°F (85°C) and held at this temperature for 30 min for purposes of pasteurization, or it is heated to 195°F (90.6°C) and held for 25 sec in order to pasteurize it, then homogenized. In either case, the mixture is cooled to about 113°F (45°C), then inoculated with the starter culture.

The starter culture consists of a mixture of *Lactobacillus bulgaricus* and *Streptococcus thermophilus* that has been added to sterile milk and allowed to grow, providing high concentrations of the respective bacteria. The inoculated milk product is then mixed and filled into containers that are sealed and packed in cases. The filled cases are then held at 106°–108°F (41.1°–42.2°C) for a period of 3–4 hr, then placed in a cooler where the product temperature is eventually brought to 40°–45°F (4.4°–7.2°C). The product is then stored at about 35°F (1.7°C). Fruit-flavored yogurt may be prepared by adding a portion of fruit or fruit mixture to the containers before the yogurt is added. (The reader is reminded that frozen yogurt was discussed in the prior section on ice-cream substitutes.)

In the preparation of buttermilk, skim milk is pasteurized either by heating to 185°–190°F (85°–87.8°C) and holding for 30 min, or by heating to 195°F (90.6°C) and holding for 2 min. After pasteurizing, the product is cooled to a temperature of 71°–72°F (21.7°–22.2°C), then inoculated (about 0.5–1.0%) with a culture of *Streptococcus lactis* or *Streptococcus cremoris* (to produce lactic acid) and *Leuconostoc citrovorum* or *Leuconostoc dextranicum* (to produce flavor). The milk is incubated at the stated temperature until the acid content is about 0.8% (pH of 4.5), after which the coagulum is broken by agitation and the product is cooled to 40°–45°F (4.4°–7.2°C). After cooling, the product is allowed to stand for about 2 hr, to remove air that may have been incorporated during agitation, then filled into cartons. Buttermilk should be held at 35°–40°F (1.7°–4.4°C) until consumed. If butter granules are to be included, about 2% of the cultured milk is removed and cream is added to obtain a butterfat content of about 15% in the removed portion (sufficient to produce a butterfat content of 0.75% in the finished buttermilk). This mixture is brought to 65°F (18.3°C) and then churned by circulating through a centrifugal pump. When butter granules are formed, the churned product is cooled and added to the bulk of the cultured skim milk. In order to obtain butterfat granules in buttermilk, melted butter may also be sprayed into the cultured product to provide a butterfat content of about 1%.

Sour cream is prepared from light cream (the fat content must be 16–20% depending on state regulations) to which 8–9% of nonfat milk solids and/or 0.25–0.5% of stabilizers (gelatin, gums, etc.) may have been added. In some cases, small amounts of rennet (a coagulating enzyme) are also added. The cream mixture (without rennet) is first pasteurized by heating to 165°F (73.9°C) and holding for 30 min or by heating to 180°–185°F (82.2°–85°C) and holding for 25 sec. The cream or cream mixture is homogenized before cooling. After cooling to about 72°F (22.2°C), the mixture is cultured with the same bacteria used to produce buttermilk. If rennet is to be used, it is added at the time of culturing. After incubation, to produce an acidity of 0.65 to 0.70% (pH 4.5), the product is cooled to 40°F (4.4°C), filled into cardboard containers, and held at 40°F (4.4°C) for 1 to 2 days to solidify the fat. Sour cream should be held at 35°–40°F (1.7°–4.4°C) until consumed.

Cheeses

There are many types of cheeses of which only those most commonly used in the United States will be described according to their basic steps. It should be kept in mind that technological advances result in automation of some of the steps, often resulting in higher efficiency and sometimes in minor changes from original procedures (e.g., the introduction of ultracentrifugation has decreased the amount of solids normally lost to the whey).

Cottage Cheese.   In the manufacture of cottage cheese, skim milk is pasteurized at 145°F (62.8°C) for 30 min or at 161°F (71.7°C) for 16 sec, cooled to 90°–72°F (32.2°–22.2°C), and inoculated with the starter culture (*Streptococcus lactis* with or without a culture of *Leuconostoc citrovorum*). A small amount of rennet may also be added. The mixture is then stirred for about 10 min and incubated, during which time the curd is set. With the short-set method, the inoculated mixture is allowed to incubate for about 4 hr, whereas the long-set method requires 14–16 hr of incubation (more starter culture and higher incubation temperatures are used in the short-set method than in the long-set method). During the set, an acidity of 0.48% to 0.52% and a pH of 4.6 are reached. After incubation, the curd is cut by passing wire knives through it. To produce small curd cheese, the knives are set to cut the curd in ¼–½ in. (0.6–1.3 cm) squares. For producing large-curd cheese, the knives are set to cut the curd in ½– ¾ in. (1.3–1.9 cm) squares. After cutting, the curd is allowed to stand for 15–20 min and is then cooked. Cooking requires slowly raising the temperature of the water in the jacket of the vat to 120°–125°F (48.9°–51.6°C). After cooking, the curd is pushed to one end of the vat, and the whey is drained off. The curd is then washed by adding cold water over it and allowing it to stand for 10 min; it is then drained. The temperature of the curd is now about 85°F (29.4°C). A second and third washing and draining are used, during which the temperature of the curds is brought to 60°F (15.6°C) and 45°–40°F (7.2°–4.4°C), respectively. The product is drained for 30 min after the last washing. The curd is then salted (0.75% to 1% of salt is sprinkled over it) and mixed, after which cream may be added and mixed in (cream containing 12% to 14% of butterfat is used) to bring the butterfat content of the product to 4%. The cream may be added and mixed in the cheese vat or in a blender. The cheese is then mechanically filled into cardboard or plastic cups, capped and stored under refrigeration. Cottage cheese should be held at 35°–40°F (1.7°–4.4°C) until consumed. Some cottage cheese is pasteurized and cooled after packaging, then refrigerated. Low-fat and unsalted varieties of cottage cheese are also produced.

Cheddar Cheese.   Cheddar cheese (see Fig. 16–5) is made from whole milk. Prior to culturing, the milk may be pasteurized with heat or treated with hydrogen peroxide (to destroy bacteria). If hydrogen peroxide is used, the milk must be treated with the enzyme catalase to decompose residual hydrogen peroxide before the culture is added. Some cheddar cheese is made from raw, unpasteurized or untreated milk. If raw (unpasteurized) milk is

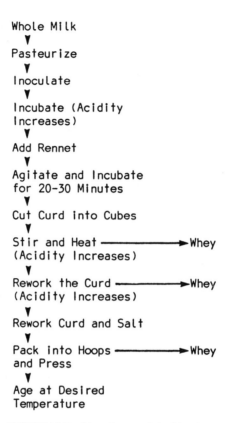

FIGURE 16-5.   Manufacture of cheddar cheese.

used, the cheese must be held for at least 60 days at a temperature of 35°F (1.7°C) or lower prior to sale for consumption. This is required to destroy staphylococci, which, if present, will grow and produce a toxin (should cheese be held at 50°F [10°C] or higher) and to destroy the toxin that might be present due to the growth of these bacteria in the milk used to make the cheese. The toxin causes intestinal disturbances in humans (see Chap. 6).

In the manufacture of cheddar cheese, the temperature of the milk is brought to about 86°F (30°C), after which starter cultures consisting of *Streptococcus lactis* and *Streptococcus cremoris* are added (an amount equivalent to 0.5-1% of the volume of milk). The starter is mixed with the milk and allowed to incubate for 30-60 min. During incubation, and acid content (as lactic acid) of about 0.2% is reached. A coagulating enzyme (rennet[*]) is then added (2 or more parts of enzyme per million parts of milk) and

---

[*]It has been reported that rennet was the first successful agricultural DNA transfer product.

mixed with the milk. In order to set the curd, the mixture is allowed to stand for a period of 20–30 min. The curd is then cut into cubes of about ½– ¾ in. (1.3–1.9 cm). After stirring the cubed product for 10–15 min, the temperature in the jacket of the cheese vat is raised to bring the temperature of the product to 100°–106°F (37.8°–41.1°C) for a period of 30 min. The final cooking temperature is maintained for a period of 35–45 min, during which time the acid content of the mixture increases. After cooking, the curd is cheddared (the whey is drawn off, and the curd is heaped into a mass that mats together and is then cut into slabs piled one upon another).

During cheddaring, acid formation continues as some of the moisture is expelled from the slabs of cheese. When the acid content has reached about 0.5%, the slabs of cheese are milled by machine or cut into portions that are about ⅝ in. (1.6 cm) square and 2 in. (5.1 cm) long. This facilitates salting. Enough salt is then sprinkled over the cheese and mixed with it to provide a salt content of about 1.5% in the finished product. The salted cheese is then placed in hoops or forms that are placed on racks to which pressure is applied. The cover of each hoop fits within the container so that as pressure is applied to the cover it presses the curd, squeezing out the whey. Pressing lasts about 24 hr or more.

After pressing, the cheese is aged. Aging time and temperature vary according to whether mild or sharp cheese is to be produced. Cheddar cheese may be aged for 12–18 months at 32°–34°F (0°–1.1°C), for 8–10 months at 38°–40°F (3.3°–4.4°C), or for 60 days at 38°–40°F (3.3°–4.4°C).

Cheddar cheese is much lower in moisture content than is cottage cheese, which has a moisture content of about 79%. After curing, the moisture content of cheddar cheese must not exceed 39%. Also, the milk solids of cheddar cheese must contain not less than 50% butterfat.

During the aging of different kinds of cheese, various microorganisms (bacteria or molds) grow and produce enzymes that modify the protein to provide the typical texture of the product. Also, microorganisms produce small amounts of chemical compounds from the components of the curd, which provide the typical flavor of the cheese. During the aging of cheddar cheese, the lactic acid streptococci continue to grow for about 2 weeks after which *Lactobacillus* species grow and predominate. Eventually, micrococcal species become established as the predominant members of the bacterial flora.

In the manufacture of some types of cheese, lactic acid, or another suitable acid, may be added to the milk, instead of the cheese being cultured with bacteria, to produce the required acidity (about 0.2% of lactic) to bring the pH to a level suitable for the coagulating action of the enzyme, rennet.

Process Cheese.   Various kinds of process cheese may be manufactured using different types of cheese (cheddar, Swiss, blue, etc.), as the main ingredient. Generally, green (not fully aged) cheese is ground together with some aged cheese. Some water, an emulsifier (disodium phosphate, Na_2HPO_4), salt, and powdered skim milk are added, and the ingredients are heated and mixed, then extruded into molds. The molded (shaped) cheese is wrapped with plastic and sometimes packaged. Oftentimes, sorbic acid in small quantities is included in the ingredients to prevent the growth of molds (fungi). The cheese may or may not be sliced prior to wrapping with plastic. Process cheese may also be filled into glass or plastic containers. Other ingredients of process cheese may include gums (locust bean gum, etc.), pimientos, cream, skim milk cheese, condensed whey, and certified cheese color, the particular ingredients depending on the type of process cheese being manufactured.

Swiss (Emmenthaler) Cheese. The general procedures applied in the making of cheddar cheese are used in the production of all cheeses, but variations in the procedure of manufacture and aging are responsible for the different texture and flavor characteristics of particular types of cheese.

In the manufacture of Swiss cheese, either raw or pasteurized cow's milk may be used. After the milk is warmed to 88°-94°F (31.1°-34.4°C), the starter cultures are added. Starter cultures may include small amounts of *Streptococcus lactis* and/or *Streptococcus cremoris* (when pasteurized milk is used). However, larger amounts of cultures containing *Streptococcus thermophilus, Lactobacillus bulgaricus,* and especially *Propionibacterium shermani* are also added. After about 30 min of holding at the temperature indicated, the cultured milk is coagulated with the enzyme, rennet, and the curd is cut into small kernels, stirred for 20-30 min, then heated. During heating, the temperature is raised to 126°-130°F (52.2°-54.4°C), and the mixture is stirred. Heating is continued until the curd is firm. The cooked curd is then drained and taken up in a cloth, then pressed in hoops or forms of a large enough size to produce wheels of cheese weighing 125-210 lb (56.8-95.3 kg) or blocks weighing 24-90 lb (11.4-40.9 kg). Pressing lasts for a period of 24 hr. The wheels or blocks of cheese are then immersed and held in a salt solution for a period of 1-4 days, then removed and held at 50°-60°F (10°-15.6°C) for 5-10 days. Swiss cheese is aged at 55°-70°F (12.8°-21.1°C) for a period of 3-6 months.

Swiss cheese contains not more than 41% moisture and the solids contain not less than 43% butterfat. During aging, the lactobacilli and/or streptococci convert milk sugar (lactose) to lactic acid and the *Propionibacterium* group converts the lactic acid to propionic acid, acetic acid, carbon dioxide, and water. The propionic acid provides the typical flavor and the carbon dioxide (a gas) forms the holes or "eyes" of the cheese. The "eyes" are usually 0.3-1.0 in. (0.8-2.5 cm) in diameter and about 1-3 in. (2.5-7.6 cm) apart.

Some defects may develop in Swiss cheese. If the growth of the propionibacteria is not at optimum, when unsuitable conditions exist, for example, incorrect aging temperature, or presence of antibiotic in the milk, the bacteria may produce too little or too much carbon dioxide, resulting in "eyes" that are too small or too large, and improperly spaced. The cheese may also be crumbly or not sufficiently elastic if improperly cultured or aged. Bitterness rarely occurs in Swiss cheese, but when this happens, it is believed to be caused by the growth of a penicillin-resistant *Streptococcus* that survives in milk containing a residual of the antibiotic, or by a starter culture that does not produce a sufficient number of peptidases (enzymes) to decompose bitter peptides.

Roquefort, Gorgonzola, and Blue Cheese.   The main difference among these cheeses is that Roquefort is made from sheep's milk while Gorgonzola and blue are made from cow's milk. Also, to be so labeled, Roquefort cheese must be made in France.

Blue cheese may be made from raw, heated, or pasteurized whole milk or from skim milk and cream mixtures, but the butterfat content should be about 3.5%. Raw milk or milk that has been heated at temperatures lower than those used for pasteurization is preferred, since lipase action is required for the ripening of this type of cheese (lipase is an enzyme that splits fats into glycerin and fatty acids) and heating at pasteurization temperatures inactivates lipase. If skim milk and cream are used as the main ingredients, and the cream is too yellow in color, it may be bleached by treating with benzoyl peroxide. If whole milk is used, the temperature is adjusted to 85°F (29.4°C) and the milk is homogenized. If skim milk and cream are used, the cream is homogenized. After homogenization, the temperature of the product is raised to 90°F (32.2°C), a lactic acid starter culture is added, and the product is held at 90°F (32.2°C) for a period of about 1 hr. The enzyme rennet is then added to coagulate the mixture, which is allowed to stand for another 45–60 min. The curd is then cut into 1/2-in. (1.3-cm) cubes, after which it is stirred for 15 min while being held at the incubation temperature. The whey is then drained, and the curd is mixed with about 1% salt, then placed in racks lined with cheesecloth and allowed to drain. After draining, the curd is placed in sterilized hoops, and, as the hoops are filled, the curd is mixed with bread crumbs on which a culture of the mold *Penicillium roqueforti* has been inoculated and allowed to grow.

The hoops containing the curd are held at 65°–68°F (18.3°–20°C) for part of the day, after which the product is placed in a room at 50°–55°F (10°–12.8°C) where salt is applied to the surface of the cheeses daily until the salt content reaches 4–4.5%. The cheeses are then removed to a ripening room where they are held for 2–3 months at 50°–55°F (10°–12.8°C) and a relative humidity of 95%. During ripening, the cheeses are mechanically pierced through the flat surface side with wire needles. The latter procedure permits air to enter the product so that the mold, which requires oxygen, will grow. After curing, the surfaces of the cheeses are scraped, and the cheeses are then cut into small wedges and wrapped in plastic or aluminum foil. Some blue cheese is packaged in plastic cups.

The flavor of blue-type cheeses is due to a blend of fatty acids (butyric, caproic, caprylic, and capric) produced by the action of lipase on butterfat, and methyl ketones, formed from fatty acids, such as caprylic, by oxidative enzymes produced by the mold, *Penicillium roqueforti*. Blue-type cheese should contain 46% moisture, or less, and the milk solids should consist of not less than 50% butterfat.

Camembert Cheese.   Camembert cheese is made from pasteurized cow's milk having a butterfat content of 3.5–3.7%. After pasteurization, the milk is cooled to 85°–86°F (29.4°–30°C) and inoculated with a starter culture of lactic acid–producing streptococci. The milk mixture is then incubated for 1 hr at the stated temperature after which the enzyme rennet is added, and the material is allowed to stand for another hour while the incubation temperature is maintained. The coagulated material is then cut into ¼-in. (0.6-cm) cubes, and the product is stirred until the curd is firm, after which the whey is drained. The drained curd is then filled into small, perforated forms 4.5–5 in. (11.4–12.7 cm) in diameter and 1.0–1.5 in. (2.5–3.8 cm) deep. After draining for 18–24 hr (without pressure), the small cheeses are removed from the forms and salted daily until the salt content is about 2.5%. After salting, the surfaces of the cheeses are inoculated with spores of the mold *Penicillium camemberti*. The mold inoculum is prepared from cultures grown on crackers, and inoculation of the cheeses is carried out by spraying with, or dipping in, a water suspension of the mold culture. The cheeses are ripened or cured over a period of several months in a room held at a temperature of 55°–58°F (12.8°–14.4°C) and a relative humidity of 85–90%.

During ripening, mold grows on the surfaces of Camembert cheese and lactic acid–producing streptococci continue to increase in the product. The enzymes produced by these microorganisms convert much of the milk proteins to water-soluble polypeptides and amino acids. Ammonia may be formed from amino acids during long periods of ripening. The moisture content of Camembert cheese is about 50% and at least 50% of the solids present must be butterfat.

Limburger Cheese.   Limburger cheese is made from raw or pasteurized whole cows' milk. The milk is brought to a temperature of 85°–90°F (29.4°–32.2°C), inoculated with a starter culture of lactic acid–producing streptococci, and held at the stated temperature for a period of 1 hr. The enzyme rennet is then added, and the temperature is maintained while holding the product for an additional hour. The curd is then cut, stirred, and the whey drained off. It is then placed in forms to make individual cheeses, but the hooped cheese is not pressed. The cheeses are salted by rubbing the surfaces with dry salt or by dipping them in a solution of salt, then aged for several months at a temperature of 60°-61°F (15.6°-16.1°C). During aging, a bacterium, *Bacterium linens*, grows in the cheese and produces the particular flavor components of the product. Limburger cheese is highly flavored and is enjoyed by some people but disliked by many. The moisture content of the cured product is about 42%.

Parmesan Cheese.   Parmesan cheese is made from cow's milk that has had part of the butterfat removed. The milk, pasteurized or not, is brought to a temperature of 90°-100°F (32.2°-37.8°C) and inoculated with a starter culture of lactic acid-producing streptococci that grow at comparatively high temperatures. The inoculated product is held at the stated temperature for 1 hr. The enzyme rennet is then added, the temperature being maintained until the mixture has set. The curd is then cut and stirred, after which the whey is drained off. The curd is salted and saffron may be added as a colorant. After salting, it is placed in forms and allowed to drain, without pressing, over a period of at least 1 week. The drained cheeses are aged in a room held at about 50°F (10°C) for a period of 1 year or more. During aging, the cheeses are periodically cleaned and rubbed with oil.

Parmesan cheese is of the hard variety and has a moisture content of about 34%. This type of cheese is ordinarily grated and sprinkled on various types of prepared food.

Mozzarella Cheese.   In the production of this cheese, whole milk is pasteurized and then centrifuged to remove some of the fat. The product is then inoculated with lactic acid and rennin. After some time, the whey separates out and is removed. The remaining curd is processed and then kneaded to develop its elasticity. Salt is then added, and the cheese is cut into loaves or balls and packaged. The cheese may also be packaged as a shredded product.

Ricotta Cheese.   Also called recooked cheese, it is made by high-temperature heating of acidified cheese whey from other production such as cheddar, Swiss, and provolone. To the whey, 10% milk or skim milk may be added. The whey is heated and the coagulated albumin is dipped out and allowed to drain. With its growing popularity, ricotta is often made from whole milk, giving it the characteristic of creamed cottage cheese. The moisture in this cheese usually ranges between 70% and 80%. *Ziger* is the German name for ricotta-type cheese.

Other Cheeses.   There are several hundred types of cheeses. No attempt will be made to discuss them all. Certain cheeses not already discussed will be briefly described.

Brie cheese is a high-moisture-content, highly salted, creamed cottage cheese.

Edam cheese is of the hard variety and is made from whole cow's milk. It is shaped into a round form, and coated with paraffin colored with red dye. The moisture content of this cheese is about 33%.

Muenster cheese is manufactured in much the same way as Limburger cheese. However, it is aged at low temperatures and hence has a mild flavor. The moisture content of Muenster cheese is about 52%.

Neufchatel cheese is a type of creamed cottage cheese that is formed into small molds. The curd is not heated or cooked after cutting. It has a moisture content of about 57%.

Stilton cheese is made from whole cow's milk, with or without the addition of cream. The curd is not pressed but is well drained. During aging, a blue-green mold grows in the product, and the cheese takes on a marbled appearance. It has a final moisture content of about 33%.

BUTTER

Butter is made from cream having a butterfat content of 25–40%. The cream used is ordinarily pasteurized and cooled and may be sweet or unsoured or may be cultured with *Streptococcus diacetyllactis* (a strain of *Streptococcus lactis*) and allowed to ripen at 70°F (21.1°C). Sweet cream, to which a culture of *Streptococcus diacetyllactis* has been added, then held at temperatures below that at which the organism will grow, is sometimes used to produce butter, and a culture of the organism may be added directly to butter, made from uncultured cream. The purpose of adding bacterial cultures to the cream from which butter is made is to produce diacetyl, the main flavor component of butter. Prior to pasteurization, the cream is neutralized with alkali, if necessary, to regulate the acidity to about 0.4%, since excess acidity may hinder the churning process and may also cause the development of off-flavors in the butter during storage. Pasteurization is carried out by heating the cream to 160°–170°F (71.1–76.7°C) and holding at this temperature for 30 min or by quickly heating the cream to 185°F (85°C) and holding at this temperature for 1 min. After pasteurization, the cream is cooled to 40°–50°F (4.4°–10°C) and held at this temperature for several hours prior to churning.

Butter is produced by a continuous churning method. The cream is first concentrated to 80% butterfat by centrifugation, after which it may be further concentrated to more than 90% butterfat. This butterfat is then pasteurized and partially cooled, after which specific amounts of nonfat milk solids and water are added and mixed. The mixture is then solidified under controlled cooling temperatures and extruded into the required shape or form. It is then wrapped with parchment, packaged, cased, and stored, or it may be added to parchment-lined boxes holding 50 lb (22.7 kg) of the product and stored at 35°–40°F (1.7°–4.4°C) to be formed and packaged at some future date. Butter that is to be held for significant periods of time is usually formed, packaged, placed in shipping cases, and stored at 0° to −10°F (−17.8° to −23.3°C). At this temperature, it has an almost indefinite storage life.

Since several species of bacteria may grow in the water present in butter, the product must be handled as a perishable one. The water in butter is present as very small droplets; therefore, this product may be considered a water-in-oil emulsion. While yeasty, tallowy, or otherwise off-flavors are rarely present in butter, the most common type of deterioration is the development of a strong odor and flavor that is wrongly called "rancidity." This type of off-flavor is caused by the growth of certain bacteria in the water droplets present in the product. These bacteria produce the enzyme, lipase, which splits off fatty acids from the butterfat. Butterfat contains short-chain fatty acids, especially butyric acid (CH_3—CH_2—CH_2—$COOH$), that are very potent in odor and flavor and cause the strong off-flavor that may develop.

Salt is added in concentrations of 1–2.5% by weight to much of the butter produced. Since the moisture content of butter is only about 16%, the water phase of the salted product contains about 6–15% of salt. Salt adds flavor to butter, but it is added primarily to inhibit the growth of bacteria that might produce lipase, thus causing off-flavors. Although the addition of salt will not indefinitely prolong the storage life of butter at temperatures above freezing, it will extend it to a significant degree. For this reason, sweet butter, which contains no salt, is more perishable than the salted product when held at 32°F (0°C) and above.

DAIRY PRODUCT SUBSTITUTES

Factors that have favored the growth of dairy substitutes include their relatively low cost, adverse publicity associated with the saturated fat content of butterfat, low-caloric value, and the freedom of substitutes from the strict standards that apply to dairy products. These factors have permitted the formation of a broad spectrum of imitation products, each having a unique identification. Ice-cream substitutes have already been discussed earlier in this chapter. Oleomargarine, the butter substitute, is discussed in Chapter 24.

Filled Milks

Filled milks are products that resemble whole milk but they contain no fat that is derived from milk. They contain vegetable fats combined with nonfat milk solids or with a mixture of nonfat milk solids and nonfat solids, derived from sources other than milk.

Imitation Milks

These products resemble whole milk but contain no actual milk ingredients. They generally contain water, vegetable fats, corn sugar, starch, vegetable protein, sodium caseinate, vitamins, minerals, and stabilizers, such as gums or alginates. Imitation milks usually do not taste like whole milk and often require the addition of flavorings.

Both imitation and filled milks are used as a basis for the formulation of synthetic and semisynthetic flavored milk drinks, ice cream and other frozen desserts, butter, cream cheese, coffee cream, whipped cream, and other imitation dairy products. All these products are processed, stored, and distributed in a manner similar to that of the dairy products that they resemble.

WHEY

Whey is the fluid by-product of cheese manufacture. It is produced in far greater volume than cheese, the ratio of whey to cheese being about 10:1. For numerous reasons, whey is underutilized, and not more than half of the U.S. production is used. The rest, amounting to billions of pounds (billions of kilograms) represents a waste disposal problem. Considering the growing rate of cheese production and the ever-tightening constraints on the disposal of processing plant effluents, the problem of what to do with whey is one of major proportions. Whey comprises about 5% lactose, 2% other milk components, and 93% water.

The utilization of whey is impeded mainly by the fact that its major solids component, lactose, is not easily digested by a large part of the world's population, is not fermented by many microorganisms, and is only about one-third as sweet as sucrose. Therefore, to obtain a particular sweetness, it is required in larger amounts than other sugars. Whey can be made sweeter by hydrolyzing the lactose with lactase producing glucose and galactose.

$$C_{12}H_{22}O_{11} \xrightarrow[+H_2O]{Lactase} C_6H_{12}O_6 + C_6H_{12}O_6$$

Lactose   Glucose   Galactose

Glucose and galactose are sweeter than lactose; therefore, the resultant whey is a more effective sweetener. With hydrolysis of the lactose, the resulting sugars are metabolizable by that segment of the population that cannot tolerate lactose in its diet. Of the few microorganisms that can ferment lactose, *Kluyveromyces fragilis* has been reported to be the most efficient. Many typical fermentation organisms are unable to ferment lactose.

Glucose is readily utilized by fermenting organisms (such as *Saccharomyces cerevisiae*). Since only the glucose is readily fermentable, in the production of alcoholic beverages from whey, it is necessary to add sugar even when the lactose has been hydrolyzed (galactose is not readily fermented). If the lactose has not been hydrolyzed, the sugar requirement is even higher. A factor hindering the use of whey for the production of certain beverages is its protein, which tends to produce an undesirable cloud.

Attempts to find uses for whey have produced numerous practical applications. It has been used in the manufacture of liquid breakfasts, snack drinks, alcoholic drinks, imitation milks, soft drinks, baked goods, lactic acid, vinegar, ice cream, sherbet, ice pops, fudge, candy caramel, and other confections. One of its functions in many applications is as a substitute for nonfat dry milk. Whey can be used to produce a sweet syrup that, while not economically competitive with corn syrup, has potential value because of its properties as a humectant and a texture enhancer. Current investigations indicate that whey may be used in the production of wine.

17

Poultry and Eggs

In the United States, most poultry used for food are chicken and turkey. Some ducks and geese are consumed, but they are relatively insignificant as food sources. The rise in poultry consumption in the United States is mainly due to its low production costs and its dietary health benefits. Its low production costs result largely from the high feed-conversion ratio for growing poultry. For every pound of feed, the yield in poultry is about 0.56 lb (0.25 kg), a much greater yield than can be obtained in the production of beef, pork, or mutton. The health benefits of poultry are due to the low-fat and low-cholesterol contents of its lean portions, which are about 3.6% fat, of which about one-third is saturated and about one-fourth is polyunsaturated.

In comparison, lean beef has about 10.2% fat, of which about one-third is saturated and about one twenty-fifth is polyunsaturated. A comparison of the fat amounts and fat compositions given above easily reveals the significantly lower cholesterol content in poultry as compared to beef. The low cost of poultry and, especially, the public's perception of its health benefits accounts for the increased use of poultry in the production of a hamburgerlike product and in the production of all-poultry frankfurters. Poultry is also allowed in the production of conventional frankfurters in amounts of up to 15% (see Chap. 15), and poultry is also being used in the production of a bologna-type product and could conceivably be used in other cold-cut products. In all cases where poultry is used, either wholly or partially, the fat and cholesterol contents of these products are significantly lower than in their beef counterparts.

Today's modern technology, by manipulating genetics, allows poultry grown for meat purposes to grow rapidly, to be disease-resistant and to have good meat qualities including a tender texture, good flavor, and a light color.

228

Chickens having white feathers are preferred over other types, because there are no dark pin feathers, which, if not removed, detract from the appearance. Also, the skin of white-feathered birds is much lighter and, therefore, more desirable.

POULTRY

Present poultry breeds have been developed from wild birds, jungle fowl of Southeast Asia, and wild turkey of North America. Capons, roasters, and broilers are mostly mixed breeds or hybrids.

Chicken

Male parents are usually selected from silver or dominant white Cornish varieties, because they develop meaty breasts and legs. Female parents are usually selected from Cornish strains with white plumage.

For meat production, almost all flocks are started from 1-day-old chicks, and, ordinarily, "straight-run chicks" (about half male, half female) are used. Broiler flocks of this type are usually raised in a housing system that provides 0.5 ft^2 (464.5 cm^2) per bird until they are 2 weeks old and 1.0 ft^2 (929 cm^2) per bird between 2 and 10 weeks old. At the end of 10 weeks, they will be removed for slaughter. For capons and roasters that are 10–20 weeks old, 2–3 ft^2 (1858–2787 cm^2) of floor space per bird is used. Older birds (fowl) require 4–5 ft^2 (0.36–0.46 m^2) per bird. Commercial growers commonly raise at least four flocks of broilers per year.

In raising birds for meat, the floor and walls of the chicken houses (brooders) must be cleaned and disinfected. Fresh litter (usually shavings) is then put down on the floors. The day-old chicks, which may have been debeaked to prevent cannibalism, are introduced. Lights are kept on continually, and the temperature of the brooders is brought to 95°F (35°C) in cold weather or 90°F (32.2°C) in hot weather. The temperature of the brooders is lowered 5°F (2.8°C) weekly until 75°F (23.9°C) is reached, and it is held there until the birds are well feathered, in winter for 8 weeks and in late spring and summer for 4–6 weeks.

Troughs or hanging feeders may be used to hold food for meat-type birds, and hoppers for grit and calcium supplement may be used. Feeders, which must be adequate in size and number, may be filled automatically. Water troughs or hanging waterers may be used (16 ft [4.88 m] of watering space per 200 birds at 75°F [23.9°C], 20 ft [6.1 m] per 200 birds when the temperature goes above 80°F [26.7°C]). Feeders and waterers should be kept clean, and waterers should refill automatically.

Food for meat-type birds, a complex mixture, is obtained from feed companies that are expert in formulating such rations. Recommended starter feeds contain corn, fish meal, poultry by-product meal, corn gluten meal, soybean meal, alfalfa meal, dried distiller's solubles, small amounts of calcium and phosphorus salts, iodized salt, and A, D, E, K, and several B vitamins. Trace amounts of antibiotics are usually added to feeds to prevent diseases. Among the above ingredients, corn and soybean meals constitute the major portion of the starter feeds. Finishing feeds, which may also include dried whey and steamed bone meal, are used for birds from 6 weeks old to marketing sizes. Capons and roasters are fed increasing amounts of corn after 12–15 weeks of age.

Predators, such as rats and mice, must be kept out of poultry houses. Floors, litter, walls, roosts, and even the birds themselves may have to be treated with malathion insecticide to get rid of mites, lice, or ticks.

Birds grown for meat are the same age, and once marketing size is reached, they are placed in cages and removed from the growing house. They are slaughtered and processed elsewhere. Prior to installing new flocks, the house is cleaned and disinfected. In order for a growing operation to be economical, the number of birds in roaster and capon flocks must be no less than 2000, and in broiler flocks, no less than 6000.

Some poultry processing plants are small, but the trend is to process poultry in plants capable of handling at least 10,000 birds per hour. These plants are usually divided into at least two rooms that separate bleeding, scalding, and defeathering from the eviscerating and chilling operations (see Fig. 17-1).

The birds are not fed for about 12 hr before they are to be slaughtered in order that their crops will be empty. This is important because it makes the operation much cleaner. The birds, shackled by their feet, are carried in the upside down position by conveyors from one operation to another. After shackling, they are slaughtered by slitting one or both of the jugular veins in the neck. An electrified knife or a stationary electric stunner may be used to render them unconscious prior to bleeding. Rendering birds unconscious prevents broken wings and bruising due to the flopping around during bleeding. After their jugular veins are severed, they are allowed to bleed from one to several minutes. Still attached to the conveyor, they next pass through the scalding tank, containing water at 135°–140°F (57.2°–60°C) for larger birds or 122°–128°F (50°-53.3°C) for broilers. Immersion times vary with the size of birds, but several minutes in the scalding tank are required even for broilers. If scalding time or temperature is too high, the skin may be damaged.

Automatic picking machines are used to remove the feathers from poultry. In some systems, the birds are beaten by flexible rubber fingers as they pass through the machine. In other systems, they are dropped into baskets where feathers are removed by flexible rubber fingers rotating on a central shaft.

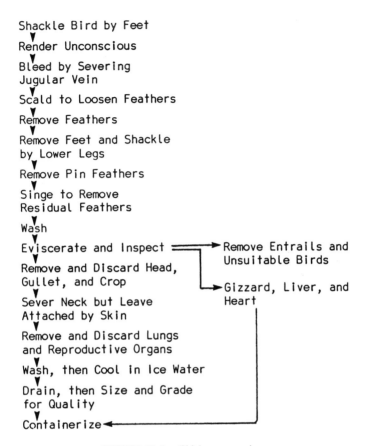

FIGURE 17-1.   Chicken processing.

After the birds are defeathered, their feet are cut off, and they are rehung on the moving shackles by the lower legs. They then pass along a line where workers remove pin feathers by hand with the aid of a knife. Then they pass through a gas flame for singeing residual pin feathers. They are washed externally by water sprays as they pass along the conveyor.

Evisceration is usually carried out as the birds pass along the conveyor. The oil gland* may be cut out before or after evisceration. A circular cut is made around the vent and the intestine is then pulled out a few inches. Another cut is then made through the abdominal wall from the vent toward the

---

*Oil gland: A gland that secretes oil, especially the one at the rump of a bird from which it takes oil for preening its feathers.

breastbone for broilers. For larger specimens a horizontal cut is made. The gizzard, liver, heart, and intestines are pulled out and allowed to hang so that they may be examined by a government inspector (a veterinarian) for signs of disease. Diseased birds are removed and destroyed. Gizzards that pass inspection are opened, emptied, peeled, and washed, and then packaged together with the livers and hearts, either for insertion within the bird or for holding separately. Intestines are not used.

The heads, gullets, and crops are removed and discarded, and the neck may be cut off and allowed to hang by the skin. Suction tubes are used to remove lungs and traces of reproductive organs or these are scraped out by hand. Both the interior and exterior of the bird are thoroughly washed. The neck and neck skin are placed in the body cavity.

The birds are next cooled, either in an air-agitated ice-water slush in tanks, in continuous ice-water chillers, or in moving refrigerated air. During chilling, the temperature of the birds, which may be 80°–95°F (26.7°–35°C), is lowered to 35°F (1.7°C), and they lose some residual blood and pick up a few percent of moisture from the chilled water. After chilling, they are drained, sized according to weight, and graded for quality. Grading is based on conformation, fleshing, covering with fat, the presence of pin feathers, torn skin, bruises, and so on.

Graded birds are packed in wooden or waxed-fiber-board boxes. They should be surrounded with crushed ice and held at temperatures below 40°F (4.4°C). When the product is held at 28°F (−2.2°C), a significant extension in the shelf-life may be realized.

Some poultry is bagged or wrapped with plastic and frozen, either by cold-air blast, by contact with refrigerated plates, by immersion in liquid nitrogen at −320°F (−195.6°C), or by spraying with liquid freon-12 (−21.7°F [−29.7°C]).

Chickens are classified, according to age and condition, as broilers or fryers, roasters, capons (males castrated prior to maturity), stags (young uncastrated males), hens, or stewing chickens or fowl (hens older than 20 weeks), and cocks or old roosters. Poultry may also be classified for quality as grade A, B, or C.

Some chicken products are battered and breaded, deep-fat fried, and frozen. The high-quality storage life of uncooked chicken at 0°F (−17.8°C) is more than 2 years if adequately packaged, while the high-quality storage life of fried chicken is less than 3 months at this temperature.

Some chicken is also precooked, deboned, and heat-processed in glass jars or cans. Some deboned poultry is used as an ingredient of canned soups.

Chicken is also precooked, deboned, cut into cubes or small portions, frozen, and then freeze-dried. This product is used as an ingredient of dried soups.

The edible portion of chicken is about 54%. This includes about 39% meat and about 15% skin and parts of the viscera that are also edible. The protein content of the chicken is about 20%, the fat content is about 14%, the ash is about 1%, and the remaining 65% is water.

Turkey

Turkey is the second most important poultry in the United States. In recent years, there has been a movement to develop strains that produce more meat, especially breast meat. This development has mostly been limited to white- and bronze-feathered birds.

Turkey raising requires the same basic conditions as does chicken raising. For birds that are 1–3 weeks old, 1 ft^2 (0.09 m^2) of floor space is required. Birds that are 4–8 weeks of age require 1.5 ft^2 (0.14 m^2) per bird, and birds that are 8–15 weeks old require 2 ft^2 (0.18 m^2) per bird. Turkeys are vaccinated to prevent erysipelas, salmonellosis, and other diseases.

In growing turkeys, a serious disease called blackhead has been known to break out. It was eventually learned that the disease was caused by a bacterial infection carried by chickens, and it was soon realized that if turkey flocks were going to be kept healthy, they would have to be kept away from chickens or from places where chickens had been, since the bacteria were found in heavy concentrations in chicken droppings and in areas that had been contaminated by chicken droppings.

Turkeys require a higher protein and vitamin content in their food than chickens, although, as with chickens, the protein content of the food is gradually reduced as the birds mature. Turkeys may be marketed as broilers 12–15 weeks old or as mature roasting birds 20–26 weeks of age.

Turkeys are slaughtered, defeathered, eviscerated, and further processed in much the same manner as chickens, except for some differences. Longer bleeding times are required for turkeys. They must also be scalded for longer times and at higher temperatures to facilitate the removal of feathers. With turkeys, the tendons in the legs are pulled out after defeathering and removing the feet. Further processing is essentially the same as for chickens. During cooling, turkeys pick up 4.5–8% water, the smaller birds absorbing the highest proportional amounts. Grading of turkeys is based on the same characteristics as those for chickens, and they may be graded for quality as A, B, or C.

Larger percentages of turkeys are frozen and sold to the consumer in the frozen state than is the case with chickens. However, a less proportional amount of turkey meat than chicken meat is canned or dried. Some turkey is frozen, to be used later as an ingredient of pies or dinners. While the meat appears to be quite stable at 0°F ($-$17.8°C) as an ingredient of pies, the meat alone is somewhat less stable than chicken meat in frozen storage.

Ducks and Geese

Ducks and geese are both raised for human consumption, although the amount of the consumption of these species is insignificant in comparison to that of chickens and turkeys. Ducks and geese, for human consumption, have been developed from wild species. Their production and processing are similar to those of chickens.

EGGS

Except for some variations due to breeds, and sometimes even individual hens, the chemical composition of eggs is fairly constant. Of the total weight of the egg, the shell is about 10.25%, the white is about 59.50%, and the yolk is about 30.25%. The shell, largely calcium carbonate, has an outer coating (the cuticle) that protects the pores of the main part of the shell, as long as it remains intact. Inside the shell there are two membranes, the one next to the shell being thicker and tougher than the one covering the contents of the egg.

The white of the egg is about 10.5% protein, about 88% water, less than 1% ash. Small amounts of fat, sugar, carbon dioxide, and other constituents are present. The white is in two distinct parts: the thick, jellylike part that surrounds the yolk, and a less viscous "thin white" that spreads out when the egg is broken out of its shell. However, the thick white will also spread if it is cut, since its inner part is of thin consistency.

The yolk is about 15.5% protein, about 49.5% water, about 33.5% fat, about 1% ash. Small quantities of numerous other constituents, including vitamins, are also present. It is surrounded by the vitellin membrane, which when ruptured or cut, causes the yolk to spread when the egg is broken out of the shell. The yolk is much more complex chemically than the white, and accounts for the major nutritional composition of the egg, one of the most complete foods available to humans.

The egg contains a small air pocket that develops after the egg is laid when it starts to cool from the body temperature of the hen, contracting the contents of the egg and pulling the inner membrane in with the egg contents. Since the eggshell is actually porous, the space formed by the contraction of the contents is soon filled by air that can be taken in through the shell.

The raising of chickens for the production of eggs has similar requirements to those of raising chickens for meat, but there are some differences. The chief breeds used for egg production are white leghorns that lay white-shelled eggs and New Hampshires, Plymouth Rocks, and Rhode Island Reds that lay brown eggs. Some cross breeds are used.

In egg-laying flocks, only one age of bird is used, ordinarily. Chicks are usually received at an age of 1 day, although they may be obtained as starter birds at an age of 6–8 weeks. For an egg-producing operation to be economically feasible, the minimum number of egg-laying birds required is at least 2500.

Space requirements for egg-laying birds are similar to those for meat-type birds. An inside temperature in the range 45°–80°F (7.2°–26.7°C) is considered satisfactory for egg-laying flocks. Floors and walls should be easy to clean. Feeders and waterers should be provided, as in the case of meat-type birds.

Laying nests may be constructed of metal or wood. Roll-away floors with egg trays are desirable, since this type of nest minimizes the number of dirty eggs. With this arrangement, once the egg has been laid and the hen leaves the nest, the egg rolls away from the area where it is laid to a collecting area, where it will not be dirtied by droppings. One nest for each four birds is considered adequate. An individual nest should be about 10–12 in. (25.4–30.5 cm) wide, 12–14 in. (30.5–35.6 cm) high, and 12 in. (30.5 cm) deep. To keep the nest clean, a perch is provided below the entrance of the nest.

Roosts (8–10 in. [20.3–25.4 cm] of space per bird) are 13–15 in. (33–38.1 cm) apart above dropping pits. Such pits should be cleaned periodically and should be constructed to facilitate cleaning.

The recommended food requirements for laying birds seem to be somewhat less complex than for meat-type birds, although the vitamin requirements are somewhat more complex. Antibiotics are included, and ground limestones or ground oyster shells are added as a source of necessary egg-shell ingredients. Feed requirements amount to 85–115 lb (38.6–52.2 kg) per bird per year depending on bird size.

Poultrymen located near cities may sell eggs directly to consumers via home deliveries, or they may sell to produce dealers, cooperatives, shippers, or hucksters.

In smaller operations, eggs should be collected from laying houses at least three times daily in cool weather and four or five times daily in hot weather. They should be gathered in plastic or rubber-coated mesh baskets. Nests and baskets should be kept clean, since the interior of dirty eggs soon becomes contaminated and subject to spoilage. The larger egg producers cage the hens over conveyor belts, and eggs are collected continuously. After collecting, eggs should be placed in storage at 40–45°F (4.4–7.2°C) and a relative humidity of 70%. No other materials, including other foods, should be stored in egg storage rooms, because pungent odors are readily absorbed by eggs.

Dirty eggs can be cleaned by buffing or washing, but unless done under rigidly controlled conditions, the interior may become contaminated with bacteria during cleaning. It is desirable, therefore, to emphasize production of clean eggs.

The egg shell presents a barrier to the entrance of microorganisms, but there are pores in the shell large enough to allow the entrance of bacteria and even molds. The number of pores that are found in the shell vary in the range 100–200 per cm^2. When just laid, the pores of the shell are sealed by a thin layer of protein, the cuticle. If buffed or washed, this protein coat is removed; during washing under improperly controlled conditions, contaminated water may enter the egg.

The logical reason for the porosity of the shell is to allow for the flow of gases in and out to the developing embryo in case the egg has been fertilized. The inner membranes also tend to prevent the entrance of microorganisms. In egg white, there is an enzyme (lysozyme) that tends to lyse or disintegrate some bacteria. There is also a substance in raw eggs, avidin, that ties up biotin, a required factor for the growth of some microorganisms. Finally, there is a material in fresh white that binds with iron, making it unavailable to several species of *Pseudomonas* bacteria that are responsible for more than 80% of the egg spoilage.

The cuticle may be lost not only by washing; it can also be dissolved by droppings. In any case, about 3 weeks after the egg is laid, the cuticle becomes brittle and particles chip off. Some bacteria are not affected by lysozyme and require little or no biotin. As they are held in storage, enzymes within the eggs cause chemical changes that deteriorate the iron-binding properties of the egg white. The defense mechanism against spoilage is, therefore, eventually lost, so that if microorganisms penetrate the shell, spoilage will occur. One of the most satisfactory treatments has been the application of mineral oil, which has increased the shelf-life of the egg by reducing the contamination by bacteria and molds through the shell pores.

After the eggs are cooled, they should be packed in clean, odorless containers (usually holding 30 dozen) held at 45–50°F (7.2–10°C) prior to shipment. They should be packed with their large ends up to prevent the air pocket from migrating upward into the yolk, which would increase the chances of spoilage due to airborne bacteria. All eggs should be candled (examined while in the shell under proper lighting) before selling to consumers. This should be done on the farm if they are sold directly to the consumer or by the distributor or retailer when marketed through retail channels. Candling is done to cull out specimens with such defects as blood spots, blood rings, meat spots, and germ spots (in fertile eggs).

Eggs are classified according to size as jumbo (30 oz [851 g] per dozen), extra large (27 oz [766 g] per dozen), large (24 oz [680 g] per dozen), medium

(21 oz [595 g] per dozen), small (18 oz [510 g] per dozen), and peewee (15 oz [425 g] per dozen).

Eggs may be graded according to the interior quality and the condition and appearance of the shell (see Fig. 17–2). For grade AA, the shell must be clean and unbroken, and when broken out of the shell, the egg must cover a comparatively small area, the white must be thick and stand high, and the yolk must be firm and stand high. For grade A, the shell must be clean and unbroken, the broken-out egg must cover a comparatively moderate area, the white must be reasonably thick and stand fairly high, and the yolk must be firm and high. For grade B, the shell must be clean and unbroken, the broken-out egg covering a wide area with only a small amount of white that can be considered thick, and the yolk somewhat flattened, covering a comparatively large area. Dirty or broken eggs may not be graded.

Processing of Eggs

Almost all eggs used in bakeries have been preserved either by freezing or by drying. The eggs should first be candled to eliminate rots, blood rings, and so on, and then washed before they are broken out. At one time, eggs were broken out by hand. Today, this is done almost entirely by machine. Machines

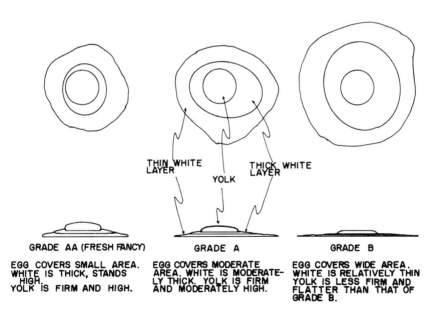

THIN WHITE LAYER   THICK WHITE LAYER   YOLK

| GRADE AA (FRESH FANCY) | GRADE A | GRADE B |

EGG COVERS SMALL AREA. WHITE IS THICK, STANDS HIGH. YOLK IS FIRM AND HIGH.

EGG COVERS MODERATE AREA. WHITE IS MODERATELY THICK. YOLK IS FIRM AND MODERATELY HIGH.

EGG COVERS WIDE AREA. WHITE IS RELATIVELY THIN YOLK IS LESS FIRM AND FLATTER THAN THAT OF GRADE B.

FIGURE 17-2.   U.S. grades for eggs (broken out).

break the egg out into cups, which may or may not also separate whites from yolks, depending on whether the process is to produce whites, yolks, or whole egg magma (mixed white and yolk). While the separation of the egg is such that the white can be separated so that it is free of yolk, the yolk cannot be separated so that it is entirely free of the white. In fact, standards or definitions concerning yolk allow as much as 20% white, which is impossible to remove in the separation. As the eggs in cups are carried along by an endless conveyor, they are examined by inspectors. If a particular cup contains a bad specimen, the cup with the egg is removed and replaced with a clean, chemically sanitized cup. The egg from the removed cup is then discarded and the cup is washed and sanitized by rinsing in a chemical solution (usually 50 ppm or more of chlorine). As the conveyor moves along, the contents of each cup are emptied into one container when eggs are to be kept whole, or the whites and yolks are emptied into separate containers when separation is desired.

Egg products produced in the United States must now be pasteurized prior to freezing or drying, in order to destroy *Salmonella* bacteria, since in the past the disease salmonellosis has been traced to contaminated eggs. After screening to remove chalaza and shell fragments, eggs are pasteurized by passing them through a plate-type heat exchanger. The product is heated to 140°-145°F (60°-62.8°C) and held at this temperature for 1-4 min prior to cooling. Cooling may be carried out in tanks provided with cooling coils and paddles that agitate the product to facilitate cooling, or in thin-film heat exchangers.

After cooling to 40°F (4.4°C), the pasteurized eggs may be placed in metal cans holding about 30 lb (13.6 kg) of product. The filled cans are then placed in a cold room at 0° to −20°F (−17.8° to −28.9°C) until the product is frozen, after which it will be held at 0°F (−17.8°C) or lower until shipped out to the distributor or to the point of utilization.

Frozen whole egg magma and frozen yolks are subject to deterioration during frozen storage. Ingredients in the yolk tend to form a gummy mass during frozen storage. In order to prevent this, 5-7.5% salt or glycerin or 5-10% sugar may be added and mixed with the product.

Whites, yolks, or whole egg magma may be spray-dried by being forced through a nozzle (to form droplets) into a chamber of heated air where most of the moisture is removed from the droplets to the heated air, which is vented to the outside. The dried product falls to the bottom of the drier and is collected. Spray-dried eggs have a moisture content of about 5%. This moisture content is not sufficiently low to prevent nonenzymatic browning during storage. Nonenzymatic browning involves sugars; thus, it can be prevented by removing sugars from eggs when they are allowed to undergo a natural fermentation at 70°F (21.1°C) over a period of several days. This is done when bacteria are allowed to grow and ferment out the sugar. While this method is effective in removing sugars, it is considered to be unsanitary, since disease bacteria may also grow during fermentation.

Sugars may be removed from egg products by adding yeasts, which utilize sugars, and holding the product at temperatures and for periods that will allow for an adequate growth of these microorganisms. The use of yeasts to ferment sugars, however, may produce undesirable flavors in egg products.

A mixture of two enzymes, glucose oxidase and catalase, may be used to remove sugars from eggs. By this method, the sugar (glucose) is oxidized to gluconic acid and hydrogen peroxide by glucose oxidase, and the hydrogen peroxide, which is undesirable, is decomposed to water and oxygen by catalase (see Chap. 9). The enzyme method is probably the most satisfactory means of removing sugar from egg products. Treatment of these products to remove sugar must be carried out prior to drying.

The heating encountered during the pasteurization treatment and the physical forces encountered during spray drying have some effect on the functional characteristics (whipping quality, etc.) of egg products, especially those made from whites. Therefore, in some countries, egg white is allowed to undergo a natural fermentation and is then dried in cabinets on trays. In such instances, to eliminate disease-causing bacteria that may be present (since the product was not pasteurized prior to drying), the dried product is held at 130°F (54.4°C) or at higher temperatures for several days. This heat treatment after drying is said to destroy disease-causing bacteria.

Egg Consumption

Because eggs are among the most complete foods available to humans and have been relatively inexpensive, their consumption rate in the United States has been high. However, warnings by the American Heart Association over the past two decades that eggs are high in cholesterol and should not be consumed at rates exceeding three per week, followed by the emergence on the market of no-cholesterol egg substitutes that are just as nutritious as eggs, brought a downward trend in egg consumption. Then, using newer methods of analysis, egg producers and the U.S. Department of Agriculture showed that the cholesterol content of eggs is lower than originally reported. This caused the experts to revise their recommendation from three eggs per week to four eggs per week. This revision, together with conflicting reports regarding the roles of cholesterol and saturated fatty acids in promoting cardiovascular disease, have apparently stopped the downward trend in the rate of egg consumption.

18

Fish and Shellfish

Although the word *fish* is used to classify one type of food much the same as meat, poultry, and cheese, varieties of fish are much greater in number than those of other foods. In the United States alone, at least 50 species of fish and shellfish are used as food for humans. Considering that the variations among aquatic species are relatively greater than those among species of meat animals, we can appreciate the magnitude of the time, space, and effort required to give even minimum coverage to fish as food.

Of the flesh foods eaten by humans, fish have the highest feed-conversion ratio. Every 1 lb of feed yields about 0.67 lb (0.30 kg) of fish. Fish also require much less space than other animals (e.g., catfish space requirements are about 2500 lb per acre [2750 kg per ha]; silo systems can reportedly produce about 1 million lb of fish per acre [1.1 million kg per ha]). These facts suggest that fish for human use will eventually be produced largely by fish farming. It may be that the situation is beginning to change. Methods of culturing oysters, clams, mussels, abalone, shrimp, crawfish, crabs, northern lobsters, salmon, catfish, carp, buffalofish, milkfish, tilapia, shad, striped bass, trout, mullet, and plaice are being investigated in various countries. In some countries, several freshwater species (catfish, carp, trout, and tilapia) have been raised as a commercial enterprise for some years and milkfish have been raised (from the captured young fish) for many years in the Philippines. Oysters are now grown commercially in some areas, and the raising of shrimp in Japan is already commercialized.

As the availability of other animal protein decreases, a situation now existing even in affluent countries, it may be that greater efforts will be applied to the culturing of marine and freshwater species of fish and shellfish, and eventually these species may play a much more important part as a worldwide supply of animal protein.

Fish flesh is readily digested, and it is subjected to highly active bacterial enzymes. Therefore, fish tends to deteriorate rapidly and cannot be held at temperatures above freezing for long periods. A simple principle that applies to all fresh food, and especially to fish, is the 3/H rule: *Handle the product under strict sanitary conditions* (to keep the microbial contamination at a minimum). *Handle the product at a cool temperature* (microbes multiply rapidly and spoilage reactions proceed rapidly at warm temperatures but both proceed slowly at cool temperatures). *Handle the product quickly* (fish deteriorate as a function of time as well as temperature). To give some idea of the importance of temperature, fresh caught fish will generally last about 12 days if held in ice (temperature at about 32°F or 0°C) whereas they will last only about 4 days at 46°F (7.8°C), a temperature sometimes found in domestic refrigerators. There are at least three reasons why fish spoil so rapidly at refrigerator temperatures. Primarily, because they are readily digestible; second, because the muscle glycogen is nearly depleted during harvesting, leaving little to be converted to acid, which would act as a preservative; finally, because the bacteria found on fish are psychrophiles—that is, they can grow well at low temperatures, and their enzymes are functional at low temperatures. Even among psychrophiles there is a range of optimum growth temperatures for different species, and it is known that some of the psychrophilic bacteria found naturally on fish grow at such low temperatures that they are not reliably detected by standard bacteriological plating techniques.

FISHING METHODS AND EQUIPMENT

Hook and Line Gear

Hand Lines. The hand line (see Fig. 18-1) is one of the simpler types of equipment used to catch fish. It has a baited hook attached to the end of a line and a weight or "sinker" fixed to the line in a position above or below the hook. The hook is barbed so that, once caught, the fish cannot escape. The sinker must be heavy enough to keep the line more or less vertical in the water. The line is let down to or near the bottom, and when the fish bites at the bait and becomes hooked it is pulled into the boat and removed from the hook. Some ground fish are caught in limited quantities with hand lines.

Pole Lines. At one time, pole lines were used extensively to catch tuna and may still be used to a limited extent for this purpose. Pole lines have a nylon hoop attached to a short bamboo pole. A heavy line is fastened to the hoop. The line is short and is fixed to a wire leader at the end of which a barbless hook and feathered "jig" is secured. The hook is thrown into the water; the

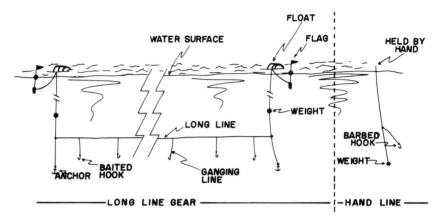

FIGURE 18-1.   Line fishing.

jig attracts the fish, which tries to take it, becomes hooked in the process, and is then swung out of the water and over the deck. Since the hook is barbless, the fish falls off the hook and onto the deck and the hook and jig are returned to the water. For this type of operation, fishermen stand on a platform over the side of the boat in a position just above the water.

Long Lines.   Long lines (see Fig. 18-1) are used to catch halibut and, in some instances, cod and haddock. The long line has a comparatively heavy central line to which short lines or "gangings" are attached at right angles to the main line and at distances of every few feet (1 ft is about 30.5 cm). A barbed hook, which is baited, is fastened to the end of each ganging. An anchored line carrying a float and flag is fixed to each end of the central line, the anchor holding the gear on the bottom and the flag, which rests above the water surface, serving to indicate the position of the gear. In setting the long line, the float and anchor at one end are thrown overboard, and the central line, with gangings and baited hooks, is run out and allowed to sink to the bottom. The anchor and float at the other end of the line are then thrown overboard. After the set has been allowed to lie for a period of several hours, the float and anchor at one end are taken in, and the line is pulled into the boat with (for halibut) or without the aid of a rotating block or cylinder. As the fish reach the boat they are flung onto the deck, or removed from the hook by hand with or without the aid of a "gaff" (large unbarbed hook with a short handle). As the line, with fish removed, is brought into the boat, it is coiled into tubs so that the hooks can be baited without difficulty. Long lines may be set over a distance of one mile (1 mi is about 1.6 km) or more.

Trot Lines.   Trot lines are sometimes used to catch the blue crab. They are similar to long lines, consisting of a central line, with gangings, attached at both ends to an anchor and a float. They differ from long lines in that the ends of the gangings are baited but contain no hook. As the line lies on the bottom, the crab grabs the ganging with its biting claw to feed on the bait and hangs on even if pulled out of the water. The trot line is allowed to lie on the bottom for a period of time, then pulled into the boat through a metal ring beneath which a small net is positioned. As the crab hits the ring, it releases its hold on the ganging and falls into the net from which it is transferred to the boat.

Troll Lines.   Troll lines (see Fig. 18-2) are used to catch certain species of salmon and may be used occasionally to catch other fish found near the ocean surface. The lines are strung from poles or masts. The terminal end of each line contains a hook that may be baited but usually has a metal "spoon" attached to the line and to the hook by swivels. As the boat moves along, the spoon rotates and flashes in the water, attracting the fish, which bite at it and become hooked. A mechanical attachment to the line may be used to pull the hooked fish automatically to the side of the boat.

Nets

Gill Nets.   Gill nets (see Fig. 18-3) are used to catch salmon and shad and sometimes to catch herring, mackerel, cod, and haddock. Gill nets are constructed of twine, the mesh size of which is large enough to allow the fish (of a particular species) to swim through until the thickest part of its body

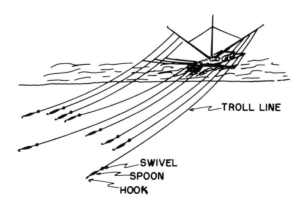

FIGURE 18-2   Troll line fishing.

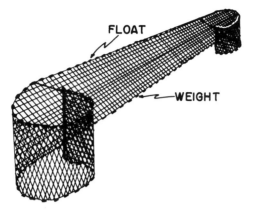

FIGURE 18–3.   Drift gill net.

stops it from swimming further. When the fish tries to back out of the mesh, it is prevented from doing so by its gill covers, which must be opened in order for the fish to pump water through the gills for the purpose of obtaining oxygen. Drift nets have floats that keep the top of the net at the surface of the water and weights or sinkers attached to the bottom that keep the net extended vertically in the water. In fishing, the net is let out to extend at right angles from the boat, which is allowed to drift. Eventually the net is removed from the water, and the fish are taken from the net. Anchored gill nets may be used to catch some types of fish.

Otter Trawls.   Otter trawls (see Fig. 18-4) are used to catch cod, haddock, flounder, and other bottom fish. The otter trawl is a large, cone-shaped net that is towed behind the fishing boat along or just over the bottom. The mouth of the net is fitted with floats at the top and weights at the bottom that serve to keep it open vertically. Attached to the towing lines, near each side of the mouth of the net, are "doors" or large rectangular wooden frames that keep the mouth of the net open in the horizontal direction. The far end (cod end) of the otter trawl has a mesh small enough to retain fish of edible size but large enough to allow very small fish to escape. After the net has been towed for some time, it is pulled up to the boat and the "cod end" is tied off with a strap. This portion of the net is then hoisted out of the water to a position over the deck, and the bottom end is opened by a line attached to a special closing mechanism, which allows the fish to fall onto the deck of the boat.

Purse Seines.   More fish are caught with purse seines (see Fig. 18-5) than by any other method. The purse seine is a long, deep, fine-meshed net that

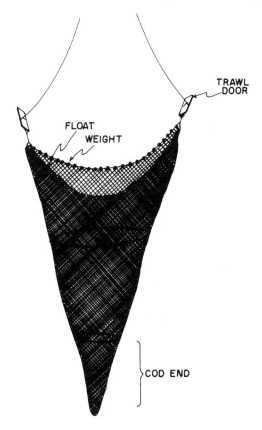

FIGURE 18-4. Otter trawl.

has floats at the top and weights at the bottom to keep the net, when let out, in a vertical position in the water. Along the bottom and ends (vertically), rings are attached through which lines are run to allow for closing the bottom of the net when a school of fish has been surrounded. Purse seines are used to catch fish that swim together in large groups (schools) near the surface of the water. Menhaden, tuna, salmon, herring, mackerel, and other fish are caught with purse seines. When a "school" of fish is sighted, one end of the net is attached to a small power boat that encircles the fish, paying out the net as it goes, after which the purse lines are drawn, closing the bottom of the net. Portions of the net are then brought aboard the fishing vessel with a power block, concentrating the fish in the "bunt," a portion of the net that is constructed of stronger twine. Once in the bunt, the fish are pumped into the vessel or a carrier boat with a large suction hose attached to a centrifugal pump. The fish may also be removed manually with a "brail," a large dip net

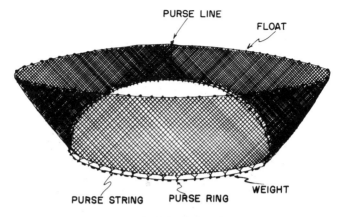

FIGURE 18–5.   Purse seine.

attached to a boom that can be guided by a long handle. A release mechanism attached to a line allows the opening of the bottom of the brail to discharge the fish and provides for closing it once the fish have been emptied from the net.

Traps.   Pound traps (see Fig. 18–6) are used less frequently than formerly to catch fish but are still sometimes used to catch salmon, herring, mackerel, and other species. Pound traps are constructed of twine and have a small mesh size. They differ somewhat in construction, but a typical configuration is a leader, running outward from shore to a V-shaped section called the heart (there may be another V-shaped section farther from shore called the

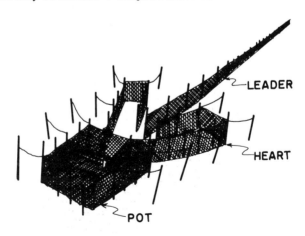

FIGURE 18–6.   Single-heart pound net.

inner heart); the outer heart (or inner heart when used) is connected to a rectangular section, called the pot, by a narrow, funnellike entrance. This may have a rectangular section (the spiller) connected to it by a funnellike entrance. The pot, or spiller when used, is located farthest from shore. The netting of the leader, outer heart, and inner heart, when used, extends from the water surface to the bottom. The netting of the pot and spiller, if used, extends from the surface to the bottom, and the bottom is enclosed with netting. The various parts of the pound trap are attached by ropes to poles anchored to the bottom or driven into the bottom mud.

In operation of the pound trap, fish swimming near the surface contact the leader and follow it into the heart section and thence into the pot and into the spiller, when used. The fish are removed from the pot or spiller with a powered brail with or without concentrating the fish in a section of the netting by loosing the rope fastenings and pulling part of the netting into or under the boat.

Pots

Pots (see Fig. 18-7) are used mainly for catching crabs, lobsters, and, in some instances, certain freshwater fish. Lobsters are caught with pots that are constructed from wooden laths spaced about 1 in. (2.54 cm) apart or from wire mesh covered with plastic. The pot usually has several chambers

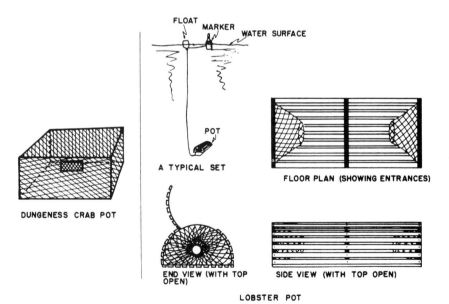

FIGURE 18-7.   Entrapment devices.

and is weighted at the bottom to keep it upright on the bottom. The bottom of the pot is flat while the body is semicircular in shape. Entrances to the pot are provided by circular openings attached to the frame with netting. In fishing, the pot is baited with fish portions in a mesh container fixed to a spindle. The pot is lowered to the bottom, attached to a rope that has a buoy or float at the upper end that rests on the water surface. After a period of 24 hr or more, the pot is raised from the bottom (usually with the aid of a rotating power block), the lobsters are removed, and the pot is rebaited and again lowered to the bottom. Pots may be operated singly or strung out in succession, one attached to another with rope.

Crabs are caught with circular- or rectangular-shaped pots constructed from wire mesh attached to a metal frame. The wire may or may not be covered with plastic. Circular pots used to catch blue crabs are about 42 in. (107 cm) in diameter and 14 in. (35.6 cm) deep. Rectangular pots used for this purpose are about 30 in. (76 cm) square and 14 in. (35.6 cm) in depth. The circular pot has two entrances, and the rectangular type has four entrances. This type of gear is weighted or anchored to the bottom to keep it upright, and a line is connected to the pot and to a buoy or float that lies on the water surface. Crab pots are baited with shucked clams or dead fish and are pulled up to remove crabs 8 to 24 hr after setting. The pot is then rebaited and again lowered to the bottom.

Pots are used on the West Coast of North America to catch the Dungeness, the snow and the King crabs. Except for its larger size, this gear is of similar construction to that used to catch the blue crab, and it is used in a similar manner as that used for blue crabs. Circular pots are used for deepwater fishing and rectangular pots for shallow-water fishing for Dungeness crabs. King and snow crabs are caught with rectangular pots that are about 7 ft (about 2 m) square and 2.5 ft (76.2 cm) deep.

Dredges

Dredges (see Fig. 18–8) are used to harvest scallops, surf clams, hard-shell clams, soft-shell clams, and oysters. Scallops, oysters, and hard-shell clams may be harvested with dredges constructed with a metal-mesh bag positioned behind a toothed metal bar. The dredge is dragged along the bottom, the bar penetrating the bottom mud far enough to remove hard-shell clams and other shellfish and depositing them in the metal-mesh bag. After dragging for a period of time, the dredge is brought to the deck of the boat and emptied onto a platform where the shellfish can be separated from the detritus.

Suction dredges, using a water-jet vacuum to remove shellfish and deposit them onto conveyors that carry them to the deck of the boat, may be used to harvest oysters. Water-jet dredges, with or without an escalator, may be used

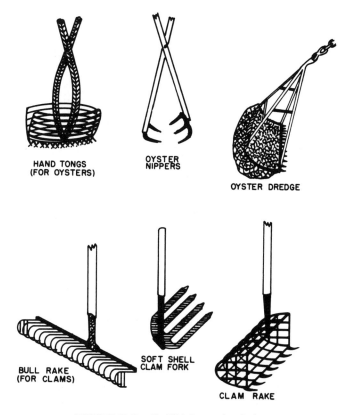

FIGURE 18-8.   Shellfish harvesting devices.

to harvest hard-shell clams. Hydraulic (water-jet) dredges, together with escalators, are used to harvest surf clams and to obtain soft-shell clams from the Chesapeake Bay area.

Tongs, Rakes, and Forks

These implements (see Fig. 18-8) are used to harvest oysters, hard-shell clams, and soft-shell clams. Tongs have a two-sided chamber constructed of metal strips approximately 1 in. (2.54 cm) apart. The bottom part of each half-chamber is fronted by a toothed metal bar. The half-chambers can be made to open or close like the blades of a scissor by means of two long wooden handles connected to a pivot. In fishing, the tongs are lowered to the bottom in the open position, then closed, scraping up whatever is in the path of the closing tongs. They are then raised to the boat where the shellfish are removed and the detritus discarded. Tongs are used in comparatively shallow water.

Rakes are sometimes used in shallow water to harvest oysters, hard-shell clams, or bay scallops. The rake has a basketlike chamber constructed of metal strips or metal wire fronted by a toothed-metal bar. The basket is attached to a long, wooden handle. In fishing, the rake is lowered to and pulled over the bottom as the operator walks from one end of a small boat to the other. In shallow water, the rake is simply reached out as far as possible and pulled toward the operator. After raising the rake to the boat, the shellfish are removed and the waste is discarded.

In some areas, soft-shell clams are harvested with the clam hoe or fork. This is a short-handled, four-tined fork. The tines are flat and fastened to the handle at an angle of about 60 degrees. An area where clam holes are present is selected and the fork is inserted into the mud and pulled up to remove the clam with the mud while preventing breakage of the clam or clams. The clams are removed from the mud by hand and placed in a pail or other similar small tote-type container.

IMPORTANT FAMILIES OF FISH AND SHELLFISH

The Herring Family (*Clupeidae*)

Among the various categories of fish used by humans for food, one of the most important is the family *Clupeidae* comprising pelagic species that travel in groups or schools near the ocean surface.

Sea Herring.   In the United States sea herring (see Fig. 18–9) are found in ocean waters from Alaska to the state of Washington on the West Coast, and from Labrador to Cape Hatteras on the East Coast. Sea herring are plankton feeders, eating the various microscopic plants and animals (diatoms, larvae of various shellfish, etc.) when very young and, as adults, eating small

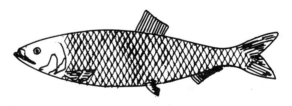

FIGURE 18–9.   Herring (*Clupea harengus*).

shrimp, small fish, and so on. When unmolested, the sea herring may live to an age of 20 years or more.

Most sea herring are caught with purse seines, but some are caught with pound traps or weirs (similar to pound traps but constructed with poles and brush). Gill nets are sometimes used to catch these fish.

The larger fish may be used for export, as there is a foreign market for this species where it is used for human food. The smaller herring, which are canned as sardines, must be held in the purse seine (sometimes for longer than 24 hr) until the stomach is free from feed. This is done to prevent enzyme action, which would reduce the quality of the fish. Fish from the nets are loaded on the boat with a large vacuum pump and are salted. More salt is added at the processing plant after the fish are beheaded and eviscerated. The small herring are then preheated, placed in small rectangular cans, and subjected to steam for 18–20 min. The liquid in the cans is drained and replaced with vegetable oil, tomato sauce, or mustard sauce; and the cans are sealed, heat-processed, and cooled. This product is shelf-stable.

The larger herring are also canned whole but in larger oval cans, usually in tomato sauce. Some large herring are cut transversely into bite-sized pieces and packed in small cans in tomato sauce. This product is also shelf-stable.

Some herring are pickled (salt, vinegar, sugar, and spices) and packed in glass jars. Sour cream, onions, or other flavoring ingredients may be added before sealing the jars. Other pickled products include rollmops (pickled herring strips wrapped around a piece of pickle or onion) and kippered herring (salted and lightly smoked). These products must be refrigerated. Some herring are highly salted and heavily smoked, and this product is shelf-stable. Large quantities of scales from the skins of herrings are recovered and used for the manufacture of pearl essence.

In Alaska, and to some extent in eastern United States, the roe (eggs) is taken from herring approaching the spawning stage, salted in containers and sold at high prices to certain Asian countries.

Large quantities of sea herring harvested in some countries are converted into fish meal, which is used as a protein supplement for cattle and poultry as a portion of the feed. When used for this purpose, the fish are sometimes brought to port in unrefrigerated vessels, although some vessels, especially those operating in southern waters, are refrigerated. At the processing plant, the fish is first cooked in live steam in a continuous cooker, then pressed in a screw-type continuous press. The press cake is dried with hot gases from oil-produced flames in a rotary drier, to a moisture content of 5–8%. The liquid from the pressed product is not discarded. It is first centrifuged to remove oil, which is collected and sold for industrial uses. The remaining liquid (stickwater), which contains proteins, peptides, and amino acids, is then vacuum concentrated to a solids content of 50% and acidified to prevent spoilage. This product may be sold as a protein supplement or it may be added back to the presscake before the latter is dried.

Shad

Shad are anadromous fish (ascend rivers to spawn) that spend the greatest part of their lives in ocean waters as far as 50 mi (80.5 km) from shore. Shad are plankton eaters and are said not to eat fish. They range from the Gulf of St. Lawrence to Florida on the East Coast, but are caught in significant numbers only from New York southward. They were brought, some years ago, to the Pacific waters, and some are now caught in California. Shad are caught in rivers and their estuaries with drift gill nets. Aboard the boats, they are neither eviscerated nor iced, since they are brought to shore shortly after removal from the water.

Shad are used almost entirely as the fresh product, with only small amounts being frozen. They contain many small bones, but can be filleted to eliminate most of them from the flesh. The roe (unfertilized eggs), which prior to spawning is held together by a thin membrane, is highly prized. It is sold fresh, or packaged in moisture vapor-proof material and frozen to be sold to the restaurant trade and, in this state, may be stored at 0°F (-17.8°C) for 6 to 8 months. Longer storage under these conditions usually results in a rancid product due to oxidation of the fats contained therein.

Menhaden

Four species of menhaden, sometimes called "pogy," "bunker," or "moss-bunker," are found in the Western Atlantic. They range from Nova Scotia to Brazil. Menhaden feed on microscopic plants and animals. They are caught with purse seines when schooling near the surface of the water and removed to the hold of the power boat or carrier vessel. Aboard the boat, they may be held without refrigeration, in which case they will be brought to port within a period of 24 hr after catching. Boats that keep these fish in refrigerated holds may remain at sea for several days prior to landing the catch.

Menhaden are not used for human food. They are processed to produce fish meal and oil in the manner described for herring. In the United States, larger quantities of menhaden are caught (several hundred thousand metric tons) than that of any other fish or shellfish.

The Anchovy

The anchovy (family *Engraulidae*) is a small herringlike fish found off the coasts of California and Mexico. It is caught in purse seines, and at one time was used as line bait for tuna fishing and later mostly in the production of fish meal and fish oil. However, a growing amount is used for human consumption in appetizers, garnishes, sauces, relishes, and especially in toppings for pizzas. It is packed in 2-oz (56-g) tins in oil for domestic use and in large tins for industrial use.

Other *Clupeidae*

Pilchards are members of the herring family, and at one time were plentiful off the coast of California, where they were caught with purse seines. They were used for canning as sardines and also to produce fish meal and oil. Due to scarcity, fishing for this species has been discontinued in California, but pilchards are caught and canned by the South Africans.

THE COD FAMILY (*GADIDAE*)

The cod family (see Fig. 18–10) includes the cod, haddock, pollock, cusk, and several species of hake. The members of this family vary greatly in size. The cod may reach a length of 6 ft (1.8 m) and a weight of 200 lb (91 kg) and averages 10–12 lb (4.5–5.5 kg). The haddock may reach 3 ft (91.5 cm) in length and 24 lb (10.9 kg) in weight, but the average is much smaller than this. The pollock reaches a maximum of 3.5 ft (1.1 m) and a weight of 25 lb (11.4 kg). The cusk and the hakes are smaller than those listed above.

The Cod

Cod (see Fig. 18–10) are found on both sides of the Atlantic and are most plentiful around Norway, Iceland, Newfoundland, Nova Scotia, and on Georges Bank off Cape Cod. In the Western Atlantic, they range from Greenland to North Carolina. Molluscs (clams, oysters, scallops, etc.) are

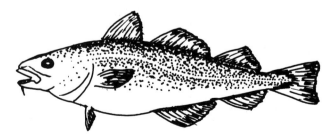

FIGURE 18–10.   Cod (*Gadus morhua*).

said to make up an important part of the diet of the cod, but cod also eat small fish.

By far the largest quantities of cod are caught with otter trawls in waters ranging from 300 to 1500 ft (91 to 457 m) in depth. Small quantities of this species are caught with long lines, hand lines, or gill nets. When caught with otter trawls, the fish are gutted and washed on the deck of the boat. During summer months, the gills must be removed, but the head is left intact. The fish are stored in boxes or pens, in either case layered with ice.

At the processing plant, the fish are washed and filleted, skinless. The fillets are then candled (observed over a bright light) to locate and remove parasites. Fillets to be sold as fresh are precooled, placed in metal tins of 10, 20, or 30 lb (4.5, 9.1, or 13.6 kg), and the tins are refrigerated (mechanically or in ice) until they reach their destination. Some fillets are precooled, packed in small trays, overwrapped with a transparent plastic, and shipped to their destination in insulated containers.

Fillets that are to be frozen for the retail trade are packed in 1-lb (454-g) waxed cartons with or without being first wrapped in moisture vaporproof plastic. The fillets may have been passed through a weak brine (10–45% saturated salt solution) prior to packaging. For purposes of freezing, retail-sized cartons of fillets may be placed on trays, the trays placed on racks, and the racks wheeled into a blast freezer where very cold air is blown over the product, or the cartons may be plate frozen by being placed on trays in contact with refrigerated plates at $-28°F$ ($-33.3°C$). Some cod fillets are frozen, usually in a plate freezer, and then cut into fish sticks or fish portions that are then breaded in a batter of flour, dried milk solids, egg solids, spices, and flavoring. The product is then packaged in retail-sized units and held frozen until sold to consumers.

Although salted cod was once the major export commodity of the United States, only very little cod is now salted in this country. To produce salted cod, the fish are beheaded and split longitudinally; the backbone and the abdominal cavity lining are removed, washed, and layer-salted in closed casks (brine salting), in open tubs, or simply in open piles on a low platform (dry salting). Most of the salted cod is produced by dry salting that is done to produce either a lightly salted product or a heavily salted product. The lightly salted product requires only days to complete, has a relatively low salt content (less than 10%), has better organoleptic properties than the heavily salted one, but it is not shelf-stable. The heavily salted product requires weeks to complete, has a high salt content (about 30%), and is shelf-stable.

Fish cakes are prepared from salt cod by first cooking and freshening the fish to remove most of the salt, then mixing it with mashed cooked potatoes and small portions of oil, onions, and pepper. A proportion of about 40% shredded cooked fish and 60% cooked potatoes is used. This product may be canned without forming or it may be formed into small cakes, deep-fat fried to brown the surface, and frozen, or sold in the refrigerated state. Some manufacturers of fish cakes are using fish sawdust, from fish stick processing, and broken fish sticks as the fish component in fish cakes.

Haddock

The haddock is the second most important member of the cod family. Haddock are found on both sides of the Atlantic from Norway to New Jersey but are most plentiful in waters off Nova Scotia and Cape Cod (Georges Bank). The mature fish feed on crustaceans (crabs, shrimp, etc.), molluscs (clams, etc.), and on small fish. In recent years, the stocks of haddock have been greatly depleted due to overfishing.

Haddock are usually caught in areas where the depth of water is 150–360 ft (45.7–109.7 m). They are caught, handled aboard the boat, and processed to produce fillets, fish blocks, and fish sticks in the same manner as that described for cod. Haddock are not salted and dried. Some haddock are lightly salted and lightly smoked, without heat, to produce a product called "finnan haddie."

Pollock

Pollock are found on both sides of the Atlantic from Norway to the Chesapeake Bay but are most plentiful in waters off Nova Scotia, Cape Cod (Georges Bank), and in the Gulf of Maine. Pollock eat shrimp, crabs and other crustaceans, and small fish. They do not eat bivalve molluscs.

Pollock are caught in waters at levels between the surface and a depth of 450 ft (137 m). They are caught, handled aboard the boat, and processed in much the same manner as that described for cod. Small quantities of pollock are salted and dried.

Hakes

There are several species of hakes, the most important of which is the silver hake or whiting. The whiting is most abundant in waters off Nova Scotia. It is caught and handled in much the same manner as are cod. Some whiting are headed, gutted, washed, and frozen in blocks without further cutting, for utilization as food.

With all members of the cod family, small fish, species not especially prized as food (red hake, etc.), and fish frames (the portion remaining after the fillet has been cut away) may be passed through mechanical meat/bone separators (machines that separate the flesh portion from bones and skin).

This provides a significant yield of edible, ground fish flesh (resembling hamburger in texture) that may be used to produce frozen fish blocks to be further processed into fish portions, fish sticks, and so on. Handled in conventional fashion, such products are not stable in frozen storage since the fat oxidizes and becomes rancid, and the tissues get tough at a faster rate than that of the corresponding fillets held under the same conditions. The faster oxidation of fats is probably due to a greater exposure to oxygen because of the great increase in surface area. The increased rate of toughening may be due to a wider distribution of the enzyme that decomposes trimethylamine oxide to form dimethyl amine and formaldehyde. The latter compound is known to denature proteins. The spoilage reactions may be slowed considerably by storing at lower temperatures, e.g., $-20°F$ or $-28.9°C$. Rancidity can be prevented altogether by protecting the product with a wrapper of gas-impermeable plastic film, for example, polyester, PVC, Nylon 11, aluminum laminate.

THE MACKEREL FAMILY (*SCOMBRIDAE*)

One of the most important segments of the seafood industry in the United States is that which processes fishes of the mackerel family including the various tuna, the Atlantic mackerel, the jack mackerel, and the Spanish mackerel.

Tuna (see Fig. 18–11) are torpedo-shaped fish tapering to a pointed nose and a slender caudal peduncle (the portion near the tail). The more important species of tuna include the bluefin, the yellowfin, the skipjack, the yellowfin, and the albacore. Although some of these species can grow to a relatively large size (e.g., the bluefin can attain a weight of 1000 lb (454 kg), the average size caught is about 30 lb (13.6 kg); the smaller species average less. Mackerel are much smaller than tuna, but they are similarly shaped.

FIGURE 18-11.   Bluefin tuna (*Thunnus thynnus*).

Tuna

The yellowfin tuna is found on the West Coast from Southern California to Southern Chile. Bluefin tuna range from Nova Scotia to Brazil on the East Coast and from Southern California to Northern Mexico on the West Coast. The skipjack is found in the Pacific Ocean from Southern California to Central and South America. The albacore ranges from Puget Sound (state of Washington) to lower California. The yellowtail is found in Pacific waters from Southern California to the coast of Mexico. Several other species of tuna are found elsewhere, especially in the Eastern Pacific Ocean.

At one time, fishing for tuna was carried out exclusively with pole lines. Today, tuna are mainly caught with purse seines which, due to the size of the fish, are made with heavy twine. Some tuna may still be taken with pole lines and some will troll lines.

Most tuna fishing boats make trips lasting for several months, and for this reason, the fish are frozen aboard the boat. In freezing, the whole fish are cooled in a large well with refrigerated seawater (RSW) circulated through it at 28°F (-2.2°C). Once the fish are cooled, the RSW is pumped out of the well, and it is replaced with refrigerated brine at 10°F (-12.2°C) or lower. When the fish are frozen, the brine is pumped out of the well, and the fish are kept frozen by circulating mechanically refrigerated air.

At the processing plant, the fish are thawed in holding rooms at ambient temperature or in tanks with running water. When thawed, the fish are eviscerated and washed. They are then cooked in steam, under pressure, then cooled. When cooled, the heads and skins are removed. The fish are then cut longitudinally after which all bones and the dark meat are removed. The white meat is then shaped, mechanically, into a cylinder, fed to cans, and cut to length. To pack chunk-style tuna, pieces are filled into cans with an adjustable filler. Vegetable oil or a broth containing hydrolyzed vegetable protein in water is metered into the cans, which are then heated in steam, sealed, heat-processed, cooled, labeled, and stored.

Mackerel

Atlantic mackerel are found from the Gulf of St. Lawrence to Cape Hatteras in America, and from Norway to Spain in the Eastern Atlantic. Spanish mackerel range from Maine to Brazil in the Western Atlantic but are mostly caught in waters off the Carolinas and southward of these waters. The jack mackerel ranges from British Columbia to Mexico in the Pacific Ocean.

Mackerel may be taken in pound traps or with gill nets, but by far the greatest quantities are taken with purse seines. If the boat is to remain out of port after the fish are caught, they are held in ice in the round, uneviscerated state. Atlantic and Spanish mackerel are sold to retailers as the fresh product, either as fillets or as the round uncut fish. Some are frozen by placing the round fish in pans and holding at 0°F (−17.8°C), or below in rooms with or without circulating air. The fish, frozen as a block, are sprayed with water for purposes of glazing to prevent dehydration and held in the frozen state until defrosted for sale to restaurants or retail outlets.

Jack mackerel are canned in 1-lb (454-g) tall containers. The fish first pass on a conveyor belt under circular knives that cut off the heads and tails and also cut the fish to can-size lengths. The entrails are then removed, after which the fish are washed and flumed to a container feeding the packing table, where they are filled into cans by hand. The open cans are then heated in a steam box to raise the product temperature to 145°F (62.8°C), after which they are inverted to drain off liquid formed during heating. Oil, brine, tomato sauce, or mustard sauce is then added to cover the fish, and the cans are then sealed and heat processed.

THE SALMON FAMILY (*SALMONIDAE*)

A number of commercially important species of the salmon family are found throughout the world. In the United States, the red, sockeye or blueback, the spring, king or chinook, the silversides or coho, the pink or humpback, the chum or dog salmon are of chief importance. The steelhead trout, which behaves like a salmon, is caught in some volume. All the above-named fish are caught on the West Coast. Only small numbers of Atlantic salmon are caught on the American side of the Atlantic.

Salmon (see Fig. 18–12) have a deep body and a rounded belly. All have a wide, slightly lunate tail. Salmon eat small crustaceans and small fish when young and larger members of these groups as they become older. The Pacific salmon and steelhead trout are anadromous, ascending rivers sometimes more than 1000 mi (1609 km) to lay their eggs in the same rivers or streams in which they were hatched. These fish die soon after spawning.

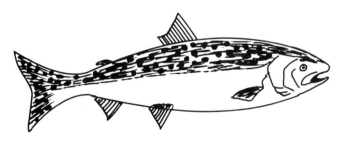

FIGURE 18–12.   Pink salmon (*Oncorhynchus gorbuscha*).

West Coast salmon are caught, in greatest quantities, with purse seines in ocean waters near the coast. Purse seines cannot be operated in rivers or their estuaries, but significant quantities of salmon are caught in estuaries with drift nets. Coho and spring salmon may be caught with troll lines.

By far the greatest quantities canned are West Coast salmon. The fish are first conveyed to a machine, the "iron chink," which removes the head, tail, fins, and viscera. They are next trimmed to remove extraneous material left by the iron chink, after which they are washed. The fish next pass under rotary blades on a slotted conveyor where they are cut into can-sized lengths. The cut salmon pieces then pass on to a volumetric filling machine where salt is added to the can (about 1.25% by weight), and the cans are filled with fish. After filling, the covers are clinched on the cans, which are then sealed under vacuum, or they may be sealed without first clinching, a steam jet being used to remove air from the headspace in the can. After sealing, the cans are washed, heat-processed to provide commercial sterility, then cooled in the retort. The cans are then labeled, if not lithographed, packed in cases, and stored in a warehouse until shipped out. Heat-processing times and temperatures are applied according to the weight of the product in the can.

Some coho and spring salmon are sold fresh as steaks; some are frozen, but they must be protected from becoming rancid by sealing in gas-impermeable containers. Spring salmon are sometimes preserved by salting. The fish are split, trimmed, washed, covered with salt, and packed in casks, after which the casks are filled with saturated salt solution and held at 35°–40°F (1.7°–4.4°C) for 30 days. This product is usually shipped to processors who smoke the fish. In smoking, the salted fish is first soaked in water to remove salt, then smoked at temperatures below 90°F (32.2°C) or hot-smoked at a temperature of about 175°F (79.4°C).

THE FLATFISH FAMILY
(PLEURONECTIDAE)

Many species of flatfish are utilized as food. On the East Coast of the United States, the halibut, the turbot, the sand dab, the fluke, the yellowtail flounder, the blackback flounder, the lemon sole, the plaice, and other species are edible types. On the West Coast, the halibut, petrale sole, English sole, rex flounder, arrow tooth flounder or turbot, Dover sole, starry flounder, rock sole, and other types are caught as edible fish. All the above are flounder; none are true sole. In shape, flounder are flat, comparatively thin fish (see Fig. 18–13).

In the larval stage, the eyes of flounder are on either side of the head, as in other fish. Eventually, one eye migrates to the other side of the head, and the fish becomes reoriented so that the side having the eyes is uppermost. The

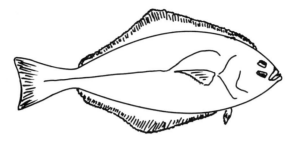

FIGURE 18-13.   California halibut (*Paralichthys californicus*).

fish swim or lie on the bottom with the eyed side uppermost. In some species, the left eye migrates to the right side, and in others, the right eye migrates to the left side.

Flatfish vary in size. While halibut can grow to a very large size, the average weight of those caught today is about 40 lb (18.2 kg); the average size of turbot is about 7 lb (3.2 kg); plaice are about 10 lb (4.54 kg); other species are smaller.

On the East Coast, halibut are found from the Grand Banks (off Newfoundland) to the Gulf of St. Lawrence, and south to New York waters. The turbot is found on the Grand Banks and in Nova Scotian waters. Various other flounders are found from the Gulf of St. Lawrence to South Carolina. The yellowtail is taken only on Georges Bank. West Coast flounder are taken from waters that extend from California to North Alaska. The most important West Coast species, the halibut, is caught mostly in waters that extend from Northern British Columbia to Northwest Alaska.

Flounder are found in waters that vary in depth from less than 50 ft (15 m) to more than 1200 ft (366 m). Halibut, lemon sole, and turbot are mostly found in deep water. The mature flounders feed on crabs, shrimp, worms, squid, and other molluscs but halibut, turbot, and dab are mostly fish eaters.

Small flounder are caught with otter trawls. Aboard fishing boats, they are held in pens or boxes in ice, as are cod, but these fish are not eviscerated prior to icing. On the West Coast, halibut are caught with long lines. The fish are eviscerated, the gills are removed, and they are placed in hold pens in ice much in the same manner as described for cod, but in this case, the "poke" (belly cavity) is also filled with ice.

Small flounders, to be sold either fresh or frozen, are handled, packed, and distributed similarly to cod fillets, described above.

Halibut are handled in the fresh or frozen state. As the fresh product, the fish are beheaded, washed, and packed in ice in boxes. Then they are shipped from the West Coast to the Middle West or the East Coast under refrigeration. If the fish are small, they may be sold by distributors to retailers as received. If the fish are large, they may be sold to retailers as portions. Frozen halibut are beheaded, washed, and placed on racks in freezer rooms at 0°F (-17.8°C) or below. When frozen, the fish are glazed by dipping in water, and then stored at 0°F (-17.8°C) or below until shipped to distributors in the frozen state. Small halibut, after freezing, may be sawed into steaks, trimmed, and packaged in moisture/vapor-proof plastic film as 12-, 14-, or 16-oz (340-, 397-, or 454-g) portions.

OTHER FISH

Many species of fish have not been mentioned in this chapter. Some of these are bluefish, butterfish, croaker, red and black drum, eels, groupers, mullet, ocean perch (fairly important fish of small size, caught with otter trawls, handled aboard boats in the iced uneviscerated state, and processed as fresh or frozen fillets), pompano, rockfish, sablefish, sea trout, red and other snappers, spot, striped bass, swordfish and other marine species, as well as freshwater fish, such as buffalofish, carp, catfish, chubs, cisco, trout, and whitefish.

Today, there is a considerable fish farming industry in the United States in which catfish and trout are grown in freshwater ponds. In many countries, carp and tilapia are grown in freshwater ponds and harvested as food for humans.

BIVALVE MOLLUSCS
(CLASS *PELYCOPODA*)

There are other molluscs, besides bivalves, which are used in various countries as food for humans; squid is among them. In the United States, the molluscs chiefly used for food are oysters, a number of clam varieties, and scallops. Bivalves have a calcareous shell that varies in thickness and outer smoothness and is lined with a smooth enamel inside.

Some bivalves are either male or female throughout their life span; others change sex from male, in early stages, to female in later years. When spawning occurs, millions of eggs and sperm are shed into surrounding waters where fertilization takes place.

Oysters

There are five species of oysters in the United States, three on the East Coast, and two on the West Coast, one of which was introduced from Japan. About two weeks after the eggs hatch, the free-swimming larvae attach and cement themselves to a hard surface (rock or shell) on the bottom. To provide for this attachment, oyster growers throw materials, such as the shells of quahogs (the cultch), into the water where spawning takes place. Some time after the set (attachment), the small bivalves may be removed to areas where tidal conditions provide a better supply of food. This also allows more room for growth.

Since oysters and other bivalves may be eaten raw or without sufficient cooking to destroy any disease-causing bacteria that might be present, and since they are grown near the shore, often near highly populated areas, great care must be taken to make sure that bivalve growing areas are not polluted with even traces of human excrement. Control of bivalve harvesting areas is supervised by a division of the Food and Drug Administration but must be effected by state authorities. This control consists of tests for disease-indicator bacteria on shellfish growing waters and on shellfish meats, sanitary surveys to determine that traces of sewage are not reaching the growing areas, and the licensing of shellfish dealers who must record the areas from which the bivalves were taken, from whom they were purchased, and to whom they were sold. Some bivalves may be taken from areas that do not meet the absolute specifications for approved areas but that are not grossly polluted, provided they are depurated in bacteriologically clean waters, either in the ocean or in tanks, under supervision by the state (held in clean waters for periods long enough to allow them to purify themselves or eliminate pathogenic bacteria by siphoning clean water).

Oysters are harvested with rakes, tongs, dredges, or with water-jet vacuum dredges. Oysters and other bivalves, except scallops, are able to live out of water at suitable temperatures for some time, since they can obtain oxygen from that which is dissolved in the water retained within the shell in contact with the gills. Aboard boats, oysters and clams must be held under sanitary conditions away from the bilges. The boat used to harvest bivalves should be outfitted with a chemical toilet so that growing areas will not be polluted with human discharges.

At the processing plant, oysters to be marketed in the shell are washed in seawater, which may be chlorinated, packed in sacks or barrels, cooled, and shipped to restaurants. They should be held at temperatures between 32°F and 40°F (0°C and 4.4°C). Most oysters are shucked (meats removed from the shell) by hand with the aid of a knife. The meats are washed or agitated in fresh potable water by air blown into the wash tank, graded for size, and packed in glass or metal containers. The filled containers are cooled and shipped to market in crushed ice (temperature of the product is about 33°–34°F or 0.6°–1.1°C).

Some shucked oysters held in metal containers are frozen in moving air at

$-5°F$ ($-20.6°C$) and stored at $0°F$ ($-17.8°C$) or below until shipped to market. Oysters may also be breaded, packed in waxed paperboard cartons holding 10–14 oz (284–397 g) of product, frozen between refrigerated plates or in cold air, and stored at $0°F$ ($-17.8°C$) until shipped to market.

Oysters are eaten raw from the half shell, or in stews (lightly heated in milk with some butter) or breaded and deep-fat fried.

The Hard-shell Clam

The hard-shell clam is similar to the oyster in its internal structure. The shell is rounded, symmetrical, and relatively smooth on the outside, coming to a gradual peak near the hinge. The shell is quite hard and thick. Once the larvae have developed into clams that are ⅛–¼ in. (0.3–0.6 cm) in diameter, they burrow into the mud and remain just below the surface of the ocean bottom. The hard-shell clam is found from the Maine coast to the Gulf of Mexico, but is most abundant off the Atlantic Coast from southern Massachusetts up to and including Virginia.

Hard-shell clams may be harvested by hand (feeling for them with the hands or feet and removing them by hand). They may also be removed from shallow water with clam rakes. The largest quantities of this clam are harvested with scratch rakes, with tongs similar to those used to remove oysters, or with dredges. Dredges are used in comparatively deep water and may be of the basket or water-jet type. Aboard boats, hard-shell clams should be handled in the manner described for oysters.

In preparing them for market, hard-shell clams are washed with seawater, graded for size, and cooled. Some clams may be taken from semipolluted waters, provided they are depurated.

In the shell, hard-shell clams are marketed according to size. The different sizes are "chowders" (large size), which are used to prepare chowders, fritters, or stuffed clams; "cherrystones" (medium size), which are used for baking; and "littlenecks" (small size), which are used as steamed clams or for eating raw on the half shell. Hard-shell clams are neither canned nor frozen in significant quantities.

Hard-shell clams may be cultured. In such instances, the bottom is first prepared by removing thick grass, stones, and other debris. Predators, such as starfish, cockles, conchs, and welks, are removed by raking and by towing floor mops over the bottom (to entangle starfish). The young clams, raised in tanks, are then spread over the area by scattering them from the side of a boat, using a shovel. Once seeded, the area is left undisturbed to permit the clams to grow to harvesting size. Predators may be removed from time to time. After seeding, the area may seed itself naturally.

The Soft-shell Clam

The soft-shell clam is found in the Western Atlantic as far north as the Arctic regions and as far south as Virginia, being most plentiful off the coasts of New England, New Jersey, and Virginia. In New England, soft-shell clams are harvested when the tide is low by digging into the mud with the short handled clam hoe and removing them by hand.

In the Chesapeake Bay area, clams are harvested from boats using water-jet dredges and an escalator. They are placed in bags or baskets and brought to the processing plant, where they are washed with seawater and sorted according to size. Specimens 3 in. (7.6 cm) in length or less are usually cooked by steaming. The larger-sized clams are removed from the shell by hand and placed in metal containers, after which the containers are refrigerated by being surrounded with crushed ice. In this form, they are shipped to restaurants to be served as a breaded, deep fat-fried product. Soft-shell clams may be removed from restricted areas and depurated.

Surf Clams

The surf clam or "skimmer" is large, reaching a length of 8 in. (20.3 cm). It is found just below the surface of sandy bottoms in waters 30 to 100 ft (9 to 30 m) deep off Atlantic Coast states from Massachusetts to and including Virginia. Most of the harvesting of this species is done off New Jersey with water-jet dredges having V-shaped scoops. Aboard the boats, the clams are placed in baskets or jute bags and brought to the processing plant without refrigeration.

Surf clams are used primarily for canning. The viscera are not utilized as food. At the canning plant, the clams are washed, then steamed lightly to cook the meat partially and so the shell will open. The meat is then removed by hand, the nectar (liquid left in the shell) being saved. The lower part of the neck (syphon), the mantle, the adductor muscle, and the foot (muscular portion that allows the clam to anchor itself in the mud) are then removed with scissors and diced into pieces about ⅜ in. (1 cm) wide. The diced portions are then filled into cans together with some hot nectar and salt, after which the cans are sealed and heat processed.

Other Clams

Other species of clams used as human food include the butter clam and pismo clam harvested off the West Coast and the ocean quahog harvested off the East Coast. The latter is not as large, nor as much in demand, as the surf clam, but it is used to help fill the demand for surf clam, which exceeds its supply.

Mussels that resemble soft-shell clams, except for the color of the shell and other minor differences, are used to some extent to help fill the demand for soft-shell clams, of which there is an insufficient supply.

It should be noted that all clams and mussels which feed mainly on algae, may at times become toxic to humans (shellfish poisoning). This happens when bivalves feed on certain algae (dinoflagellates) containing substances that are toxic to humans but not to molluscs. Public health officials periodically test bivalves for toxin and close the shellfish beds when there is danger of shellfish poisoning outbreaks.

Scallops

There are several types of scallops, of which the sea scallop and the bay scallop are best known. The internal anatomy of the scallop is similar to that of the oyster, but the adductor muscle, the only part of the scallop that is eaten, is much larger than those of oysters and clams. Once beyond the larval stage, the scallop may attach itself temporarily to some object, but the adult scallop is quite mobile. By closing the opened shell with its adductor muscle, thus forcing water through two holes in the top shell, the scallop becomes jet propelled. These bivalves cannot be held out of water in the live state, as can clams and oysters, since the water drains from the shell, which cannot be tightly closed.

The bay scallop is generally circular in shape with a grooved upper and lower shell and a rectangular projection at the back near the ligament (the bay scallop is the logo that can be seen in any Shell Gasoline sign). The bay scallop reaches several inches (1 in. = 2.54 cm) in diameter, and the adductor muscle may be as large as 1 in. (2.54 cm) in diameter. Bay scallops are harvested with basket rakes in shallow water and with dredges in deeper water.

The sea scallop is much larger than the bay type. It may reach a size of 8 in. (20.3 cm) in diameter, and the adductor muscle may be as large as 3 in. (7.6 cm) or more in diameter. Unlike the bay scallop, the shell of the sea scallop is not grooved. Sea scallops are found in ocean waters 60 ft (18.3 m) or more in depth. While this bivalve ranges from Labrador to New Jersey, it is most plentiful on Georges Bank off Cape Cod. Sea scallops are harvested with dredges. Aboard the boat, the "eyes" or adductor muscles are removed from the bivalves with the aid of a knife, placed in muslin bags, and iced and brought this way to port. The remaining portions are discarded at sea.

Sea scallops are sold in the fresh or frozen form. If frozen for purposes of selling after defrosting, they are placed in freezer rooms in muslin bags and held until shipped to retailers. Some sea scallops are breaded and may be deep-fat-fried prior to packaging and freezing. At 0°F (− 17.8°C), the storage life of scallops is longer than one year.

Other species of scallops include the calico scallop, found off the coast of Florida, and bay-type scallops, found off the coasts of Alaska and Australia and in the Irish sea.

CRUSTACEANS (CLASS *DECAPODA*)

Several types of crustaceans are used as food for humans, most of which are prized as delicacies. Included among these are shrimp (several species); lobsters (American, European, and Norwegian species); crabs (several species); and crayfish (several marine species and the freshwater species). Although the shells of crustacea vary in color, they all turn pink when cooked.

Crustaceans have a hardened external skeleton made up of a calcified polymer of glucosamine (a 6-carbon sugar containing an amine [NH_2] group) called chitin.

The external anatomy of crustaceans consists of the mouth parts, the eyes, the antennae (varying greatly in size) the body or cephalothorax to which five pairs of legs are attached, and the abdomen or tail consisting of a number of jointed segments adjoined to the body. In some crustaceans, the first pair of legs is chelate or enlarged and developed into biting and crushing appendages called "claws." The end section of the tail has several parts, including the fan-shaped telson. In some species, the tail may be contracted or flexed to provide for movement in the water. On the underside of the tail there are a number of attachments called pleopods or "swimmerets," which for certain species are the main appendages providing for movement in the water. some crustaceans will shed an injured claw, then generate and grow a new one.

Crustaceans grow by shedding the old shell (moulting) to become soft-shelled for a short period (the new larger shell soon becomes hard) and filling up the new larger shell, which allows more room for growth; moulting occurs most frequently in the early years of growth. Mating takes place when the female is in the soft-shell stage. The fertilized eggs are attached to the swimmerets, are eventually hatched, and after several larvae stages, the small crustaceans sink to the bottom and assume the general habits of the adult.

Lobsters

Lobsters have either a well-developed first pair of walking legs or biting claws. The European lobster is found around certain parts of the British Isles and mainland Europe. The Norwegian lobster is found mainly around the coast of Norway and the west coast of Sweden. The American lobster ranges from Labrador to the coast of North Carolina in an area that extends seaward for a distance of 50 mi (80 km). However, there are deep-sea lobsters found more than 200 mi. (322 km) from the coast. The depth of water where lobsters are taken is usually 30–150 ft (9–46 m), but deep-sea lobsters live at depths up to 1200 ft (366 m). The American lobster is most abundant off the coasts of Maine and the maritime provinces of Canada. The average American lobster caught measures 9–10 in. (23–25 cm), weighs 1–2 lb (454–908 g), and is 4–7 years old. However, deep-sea lobsters are larger, and specimens weighing more than 40 lb (18 kg) have been caught that are believed to be more than 50 years of age. The food of lobsters includes fish, clams, and other molluscs.

Lobsters are caught in pots (see fig. 18–7) and are held in the live state aboard boats without refrigeration, since they are brought to port shortly after harvesting. Lobsters may be held in the live state, out of water at low temperatures above freezing, for more than one week, if given sufficient air space, since they are able to obtain oxygen from what dissolves in the water on their gills (the gills must be kept moist). They may also be held in the live state for a month or more in ocean pounds, which allow the free flow of water, or in tanks in which seawater is filtered, aerated, and circulated. When held in tanks, the biting claws may be immobilized by the insertion of a wooden plug into the flesh above the thumb or by an elastic band encircling the thumb and claw.

Lobsters are sold mostly to restaurants or to the consumer, in the live state. Lobsters should be cooked from the live state or killed and cooked immediately. The reason for this is that lobsters have a very active proteolytic enzyme system that soon digests part of the tissue of the dead lobster, partially liquefying the meat or causing it to become soft and crumbly (a condition known as "short meated"). Some cooked lobster meat is sold as the canned or frozen product but does not make up a significant part of the catch. The storage life of frozen lobster meat at 0°F (-17.8°C) is at least 8 months. Whole lobsters in the raw, cooked, or partially cooked state cannot be frozen successfully, since when frozen in the cooked state, the tomalley becomes rancid and affects the flavor of the meat, and, when frozen in the raw or partially cooked state, the flesh undergoes proteolysis.

Shrimp

There are numerous species of shrimp used as food for humans. The edible types vary in size from very small, about 2 in. (approximately 5 cm), to more than 10 in. (25 cm). The larger shrimp are called prawns. The overall size of Gulf shrimp as caught is 7–8 in. (17–20 cm). Most shrimp caught by U.S. fishermen are taken from the Gulf of Mexico, and these consist of three main types: white, brown, and pink. Some shrimp are taken from Atlantic waters off the Carolinas, Georgia, and Florida, and some are taken off Alaska, Maine, and Massachusetts. Shrimp are imported from Mexico, India, Panama, Venezuela, Brazil, Guiana, Ecuador, Nicaragua, Colombia, El Salvador, Honduras, Thailand, Surinam, Malaysia, and other countries.

Shrimp are caught with otter trawls that are somewhat modified from those used to catch cod and haddock. In some instances, two boats may be used to tow the trawl attached to an outrigger. Aboard the boat, all but the tails of the shrimps are discarded. The tails are washed and stored in boxes or pens in ice.

At the processing plant, the shrimps may be peeled and deveined (removal of intestinal tract), and they are washed. In some cases, shrimps are dipped in a solution of sodium tripolyphosphate to prevent softening of the texture and loss of water during storage. However, if excess amounts of this salt are absorbed, the cooked product will appear and have the texture of raw shrimp.

Shrimps may be frozen in a plate freezer where boxes of the product are frozen into shrimp blocks or the shrimps may be frozen individually using a liquid freezant (e.g., liquid nitrogen). Prior to freezing, some shrimps are butterflied (split longitudinally), and some may be cooked. Some frozen shrimp may be tempered (partially thawed) in order to coat them with a breading, and then they are refrozen.

Raw shrimp in the shell, when protected against dehydration, have a high-quality storage life of at least 2 years at 0°F (-17.8°C) or below. Cooked shrimp, especially those cooked in hot oil, have a storage life of 3–5 months at 0°F (-17.8°C). Uncooked shrimp, prepared and frozen in the butterfly form, are also subject to storage changes, since there is so much space in the package that is not occupied by the product; thus, dehydration occurs through a continuing two-step process: (1) Moisture from the product vaporizes and fills the voids and (2) moisture from the voids condenses on the inner surface of those parts of the package that are adjacent to the voids.

Frozen shrimp imported from other countries must be defrosted before they can be processed. This may be done by tempering the product at about 40°F (4.4°C) for 24 hr, then completing defrosting by holding the unpackaged shrimp in running water. A more sanitary defrosting method employing microwave heating is now available and, in some cases, already in use.

Considerable quantities of shrimp are canned. For this purpose, they may be delivered to the cannery with the heads on. The shrimp are first washed and separated from the ice. The tails are then removed from the heads, usually by machine. The shell is then removed and the vein taken out by machine. Individual specimens are then inspected, and broken and decomposed shrimp are discarded. The product is then blanched or heated in boiling saturated salt solution (25%) for a period of 45 sec to 3 min. After blanching, the shrimp are graded for size and filled by machine into one of several can sizes. Hot, dilute salt solution is added to the product in the cans, and the cans are sealed immediately. Heat processing to provide commercial sterility is carried out at 250°F (121.1°C) for various times depending on the size of the container.

In the Pacific Northwest and Alaska, very small shrimp may be canned without deveining. Shorter blanching times are used for this product and small amounts of citric acid are added to the brine used to cover the shrimp. The brine is added cold, and the cans are vacuum-sealed prior to the heat processing.

Crabs

Crabs have the general anatomy of other crustaceans, but the body is oval-shaped or disclike instead of cylindrical, as in lobsters, shrimp, and crawfish. Also, the abdomen (tail) is comparatively small, flattened, and permanently flexed under the body. Several species of crab are used as food by humans.

Blue Crab.   The blue crab is found from Nova Scotia to Mexico, including the Gulf of Mexico, and is especially abundant in the Chesapeake Bay region. It is commercially important only south of New Jersey. The semioval body of the blue crab has spiked peaks near the back end. The first walking legs are well developed into biting claws and the last pair of legs (called back fins) is flattened and used to propel the crab in the water. When fully grown, these crustaceans measure 7 in (18 cm) or more across the body. Crabs are caught with crab pots or traps or with trot lines.

Blue crabs are brought to the processing plant in the live state. They are then cooked in live steam or boiling seawater, or in steam at 240°F (115.6°C) for 10 min, or in steam at 250°F (121.1°C) for 8–10 min. After cooling, the back shell, viscera, claws, and legs are removed; then the meat may be removed from the shell with the aid of a small, sharp knife. In hand picking, the body meat adjoining the back fin is separated from the finer body meat, since it is considered to be of better quality and of higher value. Certain machines are now available for removing crab meat from the shell. This may be done by impact, or a roller process may be applied to the cooked or partially cooked debacked body, legs, and claws. Somewhat better yields of meat are obtained by machine picking and much less labor is required to do the job, but machine picking does not provide for the separation of back fin lump meat from the other body meat, unless it is done by hand before the crabs are machine-processed.

After the meat has been picked, it is packed in metal cans that are then closed and heated in boiling water until an internal temperature (at the center) of 185°F (85°C) is reached. This temperature is maintained for one minute. The product is then cooled and held at 33°–38°F (0.6°–3.3°C) prior to distribution.

Blue crab meat is neither frozen nor heat-processed to provide commercial sterility, since either treatment results in a product of poor quality. If blue crabs, when caught, are nearing the molting stage, they may be held in seawater pounds, until they shed their shells. They are then soft-shell crabs, and they are sold in the live state at a premium price, since soft-shell crabs are considered to be a delicacy. High mortality rates are usually encountered during the holding of crabs for molting.

Dungeness Crab.   The Dungeness crab is found from the Alaskan peninsula to Southern California but is most abundant in the area between San Francisco and Southeast Alaska. It may attain a size of 9 in. (23 cm) across the back. It has well-developed biting claws.

Dungeness crabs are caught in water 12–120 ft (3.7–36.6 m) deep. The circular pot is used in deep water, the rectangular pot in shallow water. Ring nets may also be used. Dungeness crabs are brought to port in the live state aboard the boat, held in wells of seawater, and may thereafter be held in tanks of seawater until sold to restaurants in the live state.

In processing, to obtain meat from Dungeness crabs, the back shell of the live crab is first removed, the viscera and gills are then torn away, and the body is broken in half with the legs attached. The sections are then cooked in boiling seawater for 10–12 min; then the meat is removed by hand by shaking or by impacting against a metal container, or it may be removed by running the body and legs between mechanized rollers. Pieces of shell may then be separated by floating the meat in a salt solution of the appropriate specific gravity for the meat to float and the shell to sink. Fresh meat is packed in cans, the cans are sealed, and the product is held at 32°–40°F (0°–4.4°C) for purposes of distribution.

Some whole or eviscerated Dungeness crab is frozen in brine at 5° to 0°F (−15° to −17.8°C), packaged or glazed, and stored at 0°F (−17.8°C) for distribution in the frozen state. A larger amount of this type of crab meat is packed in hermetically sealed cans and frozen in moving air at 0° to −10°F (−17.8° to −23°C). This type of crab meat is not especially stable in frozen storage but may be held for as long as 6 months at −10°F (−23°C) with fairly good results.

Dungeness crab meat is also canned and heat-processed. The meat is packed in cans holding 6.5 oz (185 g) of product. A weak solution of salt and citric acid (pH 6.6–6.8) is then added, covering the meat to prevent discoloration. The cans are then sealed and heat-processed at 240°F (115.6°C) for 60 min, then cooled in the retort. The quality of this product is inferior to that of the fresh meat.

King Crab. This species is not a true crab but is similar to crabs in structure and habits. It is much larger than other crabs, attaining a spread of about 5 ft (1.5 m) and a weight of about 24 lb (10.9 kg).

King crabs are caught off central Alaska to the Aleutian Islands and off the islands of northern Japan. They are harvested with large rectangular pots. Aboard boats, the crabs are held in the live state in wells of circulating seawater.

King crab meat is either canned or frozen. In canning, the whole crab is cooked in boiling water, after which the meat is squeezed out between rubber rollers. The meat is then washed, packed in cans in a weak brine, and the cans are sealed, heat-processed, cooled, and stored. The meat may be frozen in large blocks for the restaurant trade. The legs and claws are also frozen for retail outlets and restaurants.

If properly packaged, and frozen to a temperature of 0°F (-17.8°C) or below and held at this temperature, King crab meat has a high-quality storage life of at least 12 months. Lower storage temperatures provide for an even longer storage life.

Snow or Tanner Crab. This species is relatively large, reaching a size of 5–6 in. (12.7–15.2 cm) across the back and 2.5 ft (76.2 cm) between the tips of the outstretched legs. The snow crab is taken in deep water off central and western Alaska and in the Bering Sea and some is taken off Nova Scotia and Newfoundland. It is caught in large, baited pots, as is the King crab.

Snow crabs are handled and processed in much the same manner as are King crabs, but most of the meat is canned and heat-processed. The meat of the snow crab is inferior to that of the King crab.

Red Crab. The red crab is found from Nova Scotia to South America but is taken almost entirely in deep waters off southern New England. Red crab meat is removed mechanically from the debacked, partially cooked specimens with machinery employing the roller process. Red crab meat is sold mostly as the fresh refrigerated product but some is sold as frozen.

Jonah Crab. The Jonah crab is found in waters from Nova Scotia to North Carolina and is caught in lobster pots. The meat of this crab is difficult to remove from the shell, and the product is sold mostly as cooked-refrigerated or frozen whole crabs or claws.

Marine Crayfish. The crayfish or spiny lobster has become a popular food in the United States. There are a number of different species of marine crayfish ranging from Florida and the Gulf of Mexico to Central and South America. They are also found off Australia, New Zealand, South Africa, and other countries. These species have the general anatomies of lobsters, but the first pair of walking legs is not developed into biting claws.

Since only the tail portion is eaten, this is removed from the live specimen, packaged, with shell on, in moisture-vapor-proof material, and frozen, for sale to restaurants or for the retail trade.

Freshwater Crayfish.   Freshwater crayfish are grown in ponds. Although they have the general anatomy of the true lobster, with well-developed biting claws, they are much smaller, the maximum weight being about 8 oz (227 g). There is presently a small industry in which the small crayfish are placed in rice fields after the rice has been harvested. Here, they eat the rice roots and also serve to fertilize the fields. By planting time, the fields can be drained and the crayfish harvested. Generally, these specimens are handled in the fresh, refrigerated state and are only processed by cooking.

19

Cereal Grains

Of all the plants on which humans have depended for food, those that produce the cereal grains are by far the most important, as they have been since earliest recorded time. Cereal grains are the seeds of cultivated grasses that include wheat, corn, oats, barley, rye, rice, sorghum, and millet. There are a number of reasons why cereals have been so important in our diet. They can be grown in a variety of areas, some even in adverse soil and climatic conditions. They give high yields per acre (0.4 ha) as compared to most other crops, and, once harvested, their excellent storage stability combined with their high nutritional value makes them the most desirable of foods for holding in reserve. They are easy to package and transport and they can be used to produce a large variety of highly desirable foods both for humans and animals, as well as beverages for human consumption.

Cereal grains are the most important source of the world's total food. Rice alone is reported to supply the major part of the diet for more than one-half of the world's population. Cereal grains are the staple food of the peoples of developing countries, providing them with about 75% of their total caloric intake and about 67% of their total protein intake. The grains are eaten in many ways, sometimes as a paste or other preparation of the seeds, more often milled and further processed into flour, starch, oil, bran, syrup, sugar, dried breakfast forms, and so forth. They are also used to feed the animals that provide us with meat, eggs, milk, butter, cheese, and a host of other foods.

All cereal grains comprise three parts: the bran (a layered protective outer coat), the germ (the embryonic part of the plant), and the endosperm (the large starchy part, containing some protein). Except for two amino acids, lysine and tryptophan, most cereals contain the essential amino acids re-

273

quired by humans, as well as vitamins and minerals. When they are consumed with other foods that can supplement the nutritional elements that are low in cereals, the minimum dietary requirements may be met or nearly met. Research in cereal genetics may be expected to produce hybrid cereals that will be complete or nearly complete foods, containing more of the nutritional elements required by humans. A composite proximate analysis of cereal grains indicates that they have a protein content of about 11%, fat about 3%, moisture about 12%, carbohydrate about 68%, and fiber about 6%.

On a world basis, rice is the most important cereal, being produced for human food in the largest amount, while in the United States, corn is produced in the largest amount, although it is used for animal food and other products, as well as for human food. The grain grown in the largest quantity for human food use in the United States is wheat.

For most food uses of cereals, the bran and the germ are removed: the bran, because it is indigestible by humans and because of its adverse effect on the appearance and on some functional properties of flour, and the germ, because of its high oil content, which may subsequently become rancid. The germ is used to produce oil (e.g., corn oil). The bran goes mainly to feed animals. However, with dietary guidelines recommending more fiber, a growing amount of bran is being used in the production of breakfast cereals, bakery products, and other human foods.

The first ready-to-eat cereals were produced just before the turn of the twentieth century, with flaked and puffed cereals following within a decade. Ready-to-eat cereals, made from the endosperm of wheat, corn, rice, and oats, are convenient, nutritious (despite adverse reports to the contrary), and they come in a very large variety of forms, textures, and tastes. The processing of cereals into breakfast commodities was started in the United States and is still largely carried out in the United States, with considerable quantities being exported throughout the world. The most popular of the breakfast cereals are those that are ready to eat. These are formed or puffed and oven-baked.

In the United States, grain is usually sold by the growers to operators of storage elevators, near the farms, where the grain is cleaned and stored. It is then sold directly to processors or to operators of storage elevators (near processors). They may sell directly to the processors or to their brokers.

A brief description of the handling, processing, and use of the more important cereal grains in the United States is found in the following paragraphs.

WHEAT

Whole wheat, consisting of about 13% protein, can contribute considerably to the diet. The flour, made from the whole wheat, is higher in biological value than white flour (made from the endosperm only). Table 19-1 gives some examples of the higher nutritional value of whole wheat flour over white flour.

Wheat is perhaps the most popular cereal grain for the production of bread, and cakes and other pastries. Wheat produces a white flour. In addition, the unique properties of wheat protein alone can produce bread doughs of the strength and elasticity required to produce low density bread and pastries of desirable texture and flavor.

There are many varieties of wheat. They may be classified as hard red winter wheats, hard spring wheats, soft red winter wheats, white wheats, and durum wheats. Winter wheats are planted in the fall and harvested in the late spring or early summer. Spring wheats are planted in the spring and harvested in the late summer. Hard wheats are higher in protein content and produce more elastic doughs than soft wheats. Therefore, hard wheats are used for breads, and soft wheats are used for cakes. Durum wheats are most used for alimentary pastes (spaghetti, macaroni, etc.) and for the thickening of canned soups.

Wheat is harvested by combines that cut the stalk, remove and collect the seed, and either return the straw to the soil, to be plowed under with the stubble and thus provide humus, or compress and bale it for future use as litter, ensilage, and so on.

Wheat may be bagged in jute sacks and stored in warehouses, or it may be stored in bulk in elevators. The latter method provides the best protection against rodent and insect infestation. The moisture content of bulk-stored wheat should not be higher than 14.5% and that of sack-stored wheat not higher than 16%. Otherwise, microorganisms may grow and cause heating and spoilage. When it is necessary to lower the moisture content of wheat, it may be dried in bins by blowing hot air (not higher in temperature than 175°F (79.4°C) across the bins.

TABLE 19-1.   Comparison of Some Nutrients in Whole Wheat and White Flours

Nutrient	Whole Wheat Flour[a]	White Flour[a]
Protein	13%	11%
Thiamin	2.3 mg/lb	0.3 mg/lb
Riboflavin	0.6 mg/lb	0.2 mg/lb
Niacin	26.0 mg/lb	3.5 mg/lb
Pyridoxine	2.0 mg/lb	1.0 mg/lb

[a]1 lb = 454 g

In preparing wheat for milling, it is blown into hopper scales that record the quantity of uncleaned wheat. Some of the coarser impurities are removed by this process. The grain then passes over a series of coarse and fine sieves that further remove contaminating materials, including chaff and straw. Still in the dry state, stones may be removed by passing wheat over short openings that allow the heavier stones to fall out of the mass and be trapped. The wheat is next passed over discs or cylinders containing indented surfaces that remove seeds short or longer than wheat, following a pass through a magnetic separator to remove any metals present. The next cleaning process is dry scouring to remove adhering dirt. The wheat is then washed in water, a process that both removes dirt and adds 2–3% water to the grain. The added water is necessary to provide desirable conditions for milling. A stone trap is included in the washer. Excess water is removed by centrifugation (rotating at high speed). A second wet cleaning with a light brushing action is ordinarily used, followed by aspiration (blowing air through the grain), which is the final cleaning operation. The grain is then carried into a bin from which it is fed to the milling operation. This bin is located on the top floor of the flour mill, the grain having been elevated to this position during the various cleaning operations.

In milling, grain is fed automatically through scale hoppers that regulate the flow of the seeds at rates corresponding to those of the following operations: Milling may be carried out by passing the grain through a series of corrugated rolls rotating toward each other, which remove chunks of the endosperm from the bran. After each passage through the break rolls, the material is sifted through cloth, or wire sieves, and separated according to particle size. The various streams of different-sized flour particles are finally blended to provide the different grades of flour. The more finely ground flour is nearer to white but less nutritious than the coarser ground flour. This results from the more effective removal of bran and germ from finely ground flour. Impact milling is now used in some operations. With this method, the seed is broken open by impact in a machine called an Entoleter, first developed to control insect infestation. Flour particles of different sizes are separated by air classification or by centrifugation.

High-protein flour is desirable for some types of baked products, flour of moderate protein content for others, and high-starch low-protein content flour is desirable for still other baked goods. The smaller flour particles are higher in proteins; the larger flour particles are higher in starch. Through air classification in a turbomill it is possible to separate flour particles into various sizes, which can be blended to provide whatever protein or starch content is required by the baker or other users of flour. Turbomilling, developed in the late 1950s, is considered to be a significant milling innovation, because only through this process is the variety of flour blends for different products possible.

In the United States, wheat flour is enriched with the mineral, iron (as a salt). Enrichment with calcium salts is optional for some types of flour but mandatory for enriched, self-rising flour. Wheat flour is also enriched by the addition of small amounts of the vitamins thiamin, riboflavin, and niacin.

Wheat flour is used to make leavened products, such as bread, cakes, pastries, and doughnuts, and unleavened products, such as alimentary pastes (macaroni, spaghetti, noodles, etc.). Cake mixes are also prepared with flour, and flour is used for thickening canned and homemade stews, soups, gravies, and white sauces.

Various breakfast cereal products are made from wheat. Generally, in these products, the wheat is precooked and passed through heated rolls to form flakes. It may also be shredded, or it may be heated to above the boiling point of water under pressure, with puffed wheat formed when the pressure is released. Wheat bran may also be produced as flakes. High-protein cereals may be produced from wheat together with added wheat starch, sugar, malt, minerals (such as phosphates), vitamins, and other ingredients. Some wheat flakes are coated with very thin layers of sugar.

CORN

Many types of corn are grown in the United States. Sweet corn is produced as a vegetable and eaten fresh, canned, or frozen. Popcorn is also used as a food. However, the type of corn most utilized in the United States and considered as a grain rather than a vegetable is field corn. There are a number of varieties of corn usually classified as starchy or waxy, depending on the characteristics of the carbohydrate present. The development of hybrid strains has improved the yields of field corn, which is lower in protein than wheat, and, like all vegetable proteins, including wheat, corn is deficient in some amino acids and so does not provide a complete protein for humans. Corn is especially deficient in the amino acid, lysine, but a variety of high-lysine corn has been developed that may eventually have a great impact on human nutrition in some parts of the world.

Ears of field corn are harvested by a machine that strips the matured ears from the stalks. If harvested in wet weather, corn may have to be dried before it is stored. Usually, it is allowed to dry on the stalk in the field, is harvested, and stored in small roofed bins or silos with metal or wire mesh walls. Much of the corn storage is done on the farm, since most of the corn crop is used as feed for animals. Stalks and leaves may be harvested, chopped, and placed in piles or in silos to form ensilage for animal feed. Stalks and leaves may also be chopped and returned to the soil for humus.

Corn milled for flour (corn meal) is cleaned, as is wheat, then moistened to a water content of 21%. The germ is removed mechanically. The endosperm is then dried to a moisture content of 15%, passed through crushing rolls, and sifted to remove the bran. With the use of sieves, milled corn is separated into grits (largest-sized particles) and meals and flours (smallest-sized particles).

Most of the corn crop is used for animal feed, but considerable amounts are used to produce cornstarch, corn syrup, and the various sugar derivatives. In producing cornstarch, the corn is cleaned, then placed in vats, where it is steeped in warm water (slightly acidified with sulfur dioxide to prevent fermentation) for about 40 hr. If not previously degerminated, the steeped kernels are passed through mills that separate the germ and loosen the hull. The mass is then passed through tanks of water where the germs (being lighter) float and are skimmed off. The remaining endosperm, containing starch, corn gluten, and hulls, is then finely ground in steel mills. The finely ground material is then passed through sifters to remove hulls, the starch and gluten passing through. The starch is separated from the gluten by centrifugation. The starch particles, being heavier, are separated at the outer region of the centrifuge, the lighter gluten migrating to the center. Starch may be produced from potatoes, rice, tapioca, or wheat by methods similar to that described for corn, except that with potatoes and tapioca it is not necessary to degerm the product.

Starch may be modified chemically to provide properties suitable for various manufactured products. Starch is used as a filler in pies. It is used in biscuits and crackers and as a filler or carrier in baking powder. Starch is used as a thickener in canned cream-style corn, in canned soups, and in canned baby foods. Starch is also used in many types of candies and as an ingredient of the white sauce contained in some frozen foods. Some desserts, such as instant puddings, are largely composed of modified starches, and starch is used for sizing several types of cloth and textiles, and in leather, adhesives, pharmaceuticals, paper, and tobacco. Various types of sweeteners are made from cornstarch, since starch consists of a long straight or branched chain of glucose molecules that may be broken down to short chains of glucose molecules (dextrins), to maltose (two molecules of glucose), or to glucose (dextrose).

Corn syrup is produced by heating starch in water acidified with hydrochloric acid. The hydrolysis, in this case, is only partially completed so that the mixture contains some glucose, some maltose, and some longer chains of glucose. The hydrolysis may be carried out by first heating with acid followed by treating with an enzyme that hydrolyzes starch. The latter method produces a syrup higher in maltose than does the straight-acid hydrolysis method. After hydrolysis, the syrup is neutralized by adding sodium carbonate, filtered, and concentrated to 60% solids, again filtered through bone charcoal, then passed through resins (ion exchange) that take out the salt (sodium chloride formed from the acid and sodium carbonate). The corn syrup may be spray- or drum-dried to about 3% moisture to obtain corn syrup solids, or a more completely hydrolyzed syrup after purification may be concentrated, seeded with fine corn sugar crystals, and crystallized to produce crude corn sugar. Dextrose or corn sugar can be produced in a similar manner from a completely hydrolyzed starch. This product is centrifuged, washed, and dried, the liquor from the centrifuge (first liquor and washings) being concentrated and recrystallized. Corn syrup, corn sugar, and high-fructose corn syrup (see Chap. 5) are used in bakery products, pharmaceuticals, carbonated beverages, confectioneries, ice cream, jams and jellies, meat products, and dessert powders. The cruder, less refined products are used in tanning, for brewing, to produce vinegar, to produce caramel coloring, and in tobacco.

Corn is also used to produce popcorn. The variety used is a specific one. When the dried kernels are heated, internal moisture creates a vapor pressure due to the rise in temperature, and when the pressure is sufficient, the hard outer shell is burst and the pressurized grain is expanded. Essentially, popcorn is a puffed cereal.

OATS

Oats, one of the popular nutritious present-day cereals, was once regarded as useful for feeding only cattle. Oats can grow in colder and wetter climates than can wheat. Oats are harvested much in the same manner as is wheat. The moisture content at the time of harvest should not be higher than 13%.

Milling of oat kernels requires that they first be washed and cleaned and then dried in a rotary kiln or pan drier to a moisture content of about 12%. They are then hulled by impact, the seeds being thrown from a rotating disc against a rubber ring that splits off the hull and leaves the groat mostly intact. After the hulls are removed by passing the product through sieves, the groats are steam heated and passed between rollers to produce rolled oats, or, they are cut into pieces about one-third of the original size and then steamed and rolled to produce quick-cooking rolled oats. Small amounts of oatmeal may be produced by grinding the steamed groats. Steaming facilitates cooking and inactivates enzymes which, if not inactivated, may cause bitter flavors to develop. Oat flour may be produced for use as an ingredient of bread or a thickener for soups. If made from unheated groats, there may be a problem with the development of rancidity.

BARLEY

Barley products do not bake as well as wheat products; thus, barley, containing little or no gluten, is not as popular as wheat when there is an option. However, barley has the advantage of growing in climates too cold and in soils too poor to grow wheat, and, in addition to being a hardy grain, its growth requires a shorter time than does that of wheat.

Some barley is produced in the United States. Spring and winter varieties are planted as in the case of wheat. In the United States, barley is used as feed for cattle and poultry, for the production of malt used in brewing, and as an ingredient of soups. Small amounts of barley flour are also produced.

For producing malt, the grain is soaked in water for several days or until the moisture content reaches approximately 50%. It is then removed from the steep tank and placed in containers where air at $65°-70°F$ ($18.3°-21.1°C$) can be drawn through it over a period of approximately 1 week. This allows the barley to germinate or sprout. The sprouted barley is then kiln dried over a period of 24 hr. Drying is begun at a low temperature that is gradually raised as drying proceeds. The purpose of malting barley is to produce enzymes that will hydrolyze starch to maltose, a sugar that can be utilized by yeasts to produce ethyl alcohol and carbon dioxide. Nondiastatic malt (will not hydrolyze starch) may be produced for its flavor components. Therefore, in drying the sprouted barley, the temperature must not be raised to the point where the starch-splitting enzymes, produced during sprouting, will be inactivated. It would appear, however, that temperatures are raised to the point where some of the sugars present in the sprouted barley are caramelized, hence the dark brown color of malt. Malt is used in the brewing industry for converting the starches present in rye, rice, corn, or other grains to maltose, which can be utilized by yeasts. It is also used in bread baking for much the same reason, although in this case, the purpose is to have the yeast produce carbon dioxide for reasons of leavening (raising the dough), the alcohol produced being largely dissipated during the heating involved in baking.

RYE

Rye, like oats, can grow in colder, wetter climates than can wheat. It is botanically similar to wheat, and also in appearance.

As in the case of wheat, there are winter and spring varieties of rye. In the United States, rye is used for the production of bread and crackerlike bakery products. It is also used as an ingredient of animal feeds and as the source of carbohydrates in the production of rye whiskey.

Rye flour is produced much in the same manner as wheat flour, although it is more difficult to separate the bran from the endosperm; hence much of the rye flour produced contains some of the bran.

In using rye for baking bread, some wheat protein (gluten) must be used as an ingredient, since the protein in rye is not suitable, by itself, to form and retain the structure of the loaf of bread. Rye is richer in lysine than is wheat.

RICE

Rice is a much more important grain even than wheat, as far as worldwide direct utilization by humans is concerned. By far the greatest consumption of rice is in Asia.

In the United States, rice is grown in Louisiana, Texas, Arkansas, Mississippi, and California. Rice is harvested in much the same manner as wheat. Its varieties are classified by the shape of the grain as round, medium, or long. About 60% of the rice kernel constitutes the rice ordinarily obtained by the consumer, the remainder consisting of hulls, bran, polishings, and broken kernels. Mechanical driers are used to reduce the moisture content of rice to about 14%, at which level it can be stored without becoming spoiled by the growth of microorganisms.

Prior to milling, rice is ordinarily steeped in warm water (parboiling), then dried to a moisture content that will facilitate milling. This process loosens the hull and carries some of the soluble vitamins and minerals into the kernel. Parboiled rice is often referred to as converted rice. Once the rice has been dried after steeping, the hulls and bran are removed. In rice milling, the grains are not crushed as in wheat. Instead, they are abraded so that only the surface (hull) portion is removed in shelling machines (also called hulling machines) between abrasive discs or rubber belts. The kernels are then polished. Hulls, bran, and broken kernels are screened out, the broken kernels being separated from the hulls and bran. The more effective the polishing, the whiter and less nutritious the rice.

Some quick-cooking rice is produced by precooking the kernels and redrying. This process provides for the preparation of rice for human consumption by merely bringing the water used for rehydration to the boiling point and allowing the mixture to stand for short periods.

Some puffed rice cereal is produced by heating the rice to a temperature above the boiling point of water in closed containers and suddenly releasing the pressure, which causes the kernel to increase in size, as the water vaporizes, allowing it to escape from the interior to the outside.

About one-third of the rice produced in the United States is used by the brewing industry. This consists mostly of broken kernels, but some whole grain rice is also used for this purpose.

A small amount of rice flour is produced, and most of this is used by those who are allergic to wheat flour. Rice flour may be used, too, for the preparation of white sauces, especially for prepared frozen-food products, since certain types of rice flour produce sauces that do not curdle and weep (separation of liquid from the sauce) when frozen and defrosted.

Rice kernels may be enriched, as is wheat flour, by mixing with a powder containing vitamins and minerals. This powder sticks to the surface of the kernels. The enrichment materials may then be coated with a waterproof, edible film to protect them from being washed off.

The protein of rice is comparable to that of wheat in composition, although rice is lower in total protein than wheat. Neither of these grains contains a complete protein, that is, the proteins do not contain sufficient amounts of certain amino acids to provide for the requirements of the human, although the biological value of rice protein is reportedly superior to that of wheat protein.

OTHER CEREAL GRAINS

Sorghum

Sorghums, comprising four general classes (sweet sorghum, broom corn, grass sorghum, and grain sorghum), are grown in southern sections of the Great Plains and in parts of the Southwest. Some varieties of the grain sorghum class yield glutinous starch, similar to that of corn. During World War II, sorghum was used as a substitute for tapioca, because the importation of tapioca was impeded by the war situation. The deterrent to the use of grain sorghum for the production of starch is the pigmentation of the grain's pericarp, which complicates the production of a white starch. However, enough progress has been made in the development of desirable sorghums to warrant the consideration of sorghum for the production of starch in the future.

Buckwheat

Buckwheat is not a true cereal grain. All the cereal grains belong to the botanical family *Gramineae,* whereas buckwheat belongs to the family *Polygonaceae.* However, from a use standpoint, it is considered to be a cereal food. While it is a minor crop in the United States, only the Soviet Union and France produce more buckwheat than the United States. It is grown mainly in New York, Pennsylvania, Michigan, Maine, and Ohio. Of the few varieties used, the Silverhull is used mainly for producing flour because of the higher yield of the endosperm. Buckwheat is dried to about 12% moisture, cleaned, graded by size, and milled similarly to wheat. Most of the flour is used for making pancakes.

Cottonseeds, Soybeans, and Peanuts

Although cottonseeds come from plants of the family *Malvaceae,* and soybeans and peanuts from plants belonging to the family *Leguminosae,* it should be mentioned that they have been used to produce edible flours. However, these starting materials must be heated to lower their moisture contents and to inactivate their enzymes in order to stabilize them during storage. The heating also improves the flavor of all three sources. A very important function in the heating of cottonseeds is to destroy gossypol ($C_{30}H_{30}O_8$), a toxic compound that is decomposed by heat. Neither of these products is important as a substitute for the true cereals for producing flour; however, for use under conditions that might limit availability of the true cereals, the demonstrated potential of these alternative sources makes them worth investigating.

Millet

Millet is used for food in Asia and, to some extent, in Europe. In many parts of Europe, it is used for hay, as it is used in the United States. Some varieties are used as food seeds for caged birds and poultry.

Triticale

Triticale, a hybrid of wheat and rye, first produced in the late 1800s, combines the high total protein content of wheat with the high lysine content of rye. It is also more adaptable to unfavorable growth conditions and seems to resist wheat rust (a disease caused by molds). The improvement of this hybrid is continuing and can lead to more beneficial genetic changes. This cereal is now being grown on more than 1,000,000 acres (404,000 ha) in 52 different countries.

20

Bakery Products

Bakery products include those leavened (raised) by the carbon dioxide produced by the growth of yeasts (i.e., breads, rolls, etc.), items leavened by carbon dioxide produced chemically through the use of baking powder (including cakes, doughnuts, biscuits, etc.), items leavened by the incorporation of air (i.e., batter-whipped breads, angel food cake, etc.), and unleavened products (crackers, pie crusts, etc.).

Bread and other baked food products (cakes, cookies, rolls, pies, doughnuts, etc.) are important items belonging to the class of foods that is sold in ready-to-serve form. Some of these products are partially baked and require a final baking prior to serving. Growing amounts of baked goods are handled and sold in the frozen form, especially since the quality of baked goods is exceedingly well preserved by freezing. Some baked items, such as cookies and biscuits, are canned, and these products, which must be held under refrigeration until used, need to be baked before serving. The dry ingredients used for some baked goods, especially cakes, are premixed industrially and sold as prepared mixes, and while the user must add the fluid ingredients and bake the product, it is still a convenient system for the consumer. In self-rising flours, chemical leavening agents are added directly to the flour. Some of these premixes are formulated for baking in a microwave oven. These have the advantage of producing cakes in significantly shorter times than are required in conventional baking ovens.

Generally, the high quality of bread and other baked goods goes into a rapid decline soon after the products are removed from the oven. Freezing them is the only method now known to preserve them effectively for long periods.

284

BREAD

Bread is the oldest and most important baked product. It has been made from many of the grains, including wheat, corn, rye, rice, barley, oats, and even buckwheat. The development of its popularity has been due to a number of factors, but an important one is that grains of one type or another have been grown in nearly all the inhabited parts of the world. The composition of the ingredients of a loaf of white bread is approximately 57% flour, 36% water, 1.6% sugar, 1.6% fat or shortening, 1% milk powder, 1% salt, 0.8% yeast, 0.8% malt, and 0.2% mineral salts. The flour used for making bread is usually of the hard wheat type, which is higher in protein than that from soft wheat types. The reason for this is that in yeast leavened products, the gluten (protein) in the unbaked loaf must be sufficient in quantity and of adequate elasticity to form a stretched mass that will entrap bubbles of carbon dioxide. This increases the volume and forms the structure of the loaf. It also allows retention of the structure until sufficient heating has occurred. When, due to heating which coagulates the gluten, a more rigid structure has been formed, the structure of the loaf of bread is fixed.

Maturing or oxidizing agents and bleaching agents are usually added to flour at the flour mill. Included in these are benzoyl peroxide, chlorine dioxide, and potassium bromate. Benzoyl peroxide bleaches the flour, which, without treatment, tends to have a yellowish color. Chlorine dioxide has a bleaching effect, and it has a "maturing" effect on the protein (improves the elasticity of the gluten). Potassium bromate is a maturing agent.

When the ash or mineral content of flour is high, its color is generally darker. This is due to the fact that the minerals in wheat are concentrated in the bran and adjacent layers. Even though the bran is removed, the adjacent layers are retained and because of their high mineral content they impart a darker color to the flour.

Flour millers are able to supply bakers with flour, which has essentially the same protein content from delivery to delivery, as specified by the baker, by blending a variety of flours that have been classified according to protein composition. Also, there are several kinds of equipment, such as the farinograph and the extensograph, that are used to determine the characteristics of different flours by measuring the physical properties of the doughs made from the flours.

Water is a chief ingredient of the dough in baking. The amount of water added is such that the finished loaf cannot contain more than 38% water, according to federal regulation. If the water available to a bakery is hard (contains minerals), the amount of yeast food (mineral salts) to be added may be modified. Also, during the mixing of the dough, a certain amount of heat is generated because of friction encountered during the forcing of the mixing bars through the dough, and from the motor that runs the mixing apparatus, as well. If the temperature rises above a certain point (82°–85°F [27.8°–29.4°C]), the yeast may be destroyed and the gluten and starch of the dough adversely affected. Therefore, the water must be cooled prior to adding it to the ingredients in the mixer, or part of the water must be added as ice, which melts during the mixing and controls the temperature.

Sugar (cane or beet sugar) in small amounts is used in baking bread, since it serves to supply a source of readily utilizable carbohydrate to the yeasts and hence provides for a suitable fermentation that produces carbon dioxide to raise the dough.

Some fat or shortening is added to bread mixtures. Ordinarily, this is a solid fat (an oil that has been made into a solid material through hydrogenation). This facilitates mixing, tenderizes the crumb of the loaf, and prevents staling of the bread. Today, as a rule, small amounts of monoglycerides are also added, since they are more active antistaling agents than fats. A monoglyceride consists of glycerine with which a fatty acid has been combined with only one of the three alcohol groups, the other two alcohol groups remaining as such.

Milk powder is usually added to bread dough, since it has a desirable effect on the texture of the crumb (inside the loaf) of the finished bread. The yeast used in bread baking is *Saccharomyces cerevisiae*. This may be used as a dried material or as a moist compressed cake containing 70% water (the latter type must be held under refrigeration prior to use). Either type of yeast must be suspended in warm water prior to adding to the material in the mixer, in order to obtain an even distribution throughout the dough. A freeze-dried, vacuum-packed yeast is also available. This product has a number of advantages over the other two types. It contains a higher proportion of viable yeast cells; therefore, theoretically, it is required in lesser amounts. It does not need to be suspended in water; therefore, it may be added with the dry ingredients. Because it is freeze-dried and vacuum-packed, it requires no refrigeration, and, theoretically, has a longer shelf-life.

Small amounts of salt (sodium chloride) are used in making bread, since it is desirable for the flavor of the finished loaf and trace amounts may be utilized by the yeast during its growth. During mixing, proofing, and the early part of baking, the yeasts grow and produce ethyl alcohol and carbon dioxide. The latter, a gas, causes the dough to rise, and provides for the volume of the loaf. Leavening action may result to a degree by the vaporization of water in the dough when the temperature of the mass is raised sufficiently in the oven. The increase in loaf volume is also believed to be effected in the presence of shortening, which can entrap air during mixing and release it when the air expands during baking. The ethyl alcohol is largely dissipated during baking, although residual amounts of alcohol, esters, and other components may remain and contribute to the flavor of the loaf.

The malt used in bread making is usually of the diastatic type (contains active enzymes that will convert starch to maltose or glucose). As proofing continues, the small amount of sugar present in flour, and the sugar that has been added to the dough mixture, may become mostly used up by the yeast. Therefore, to continue the yeast growth, the action of the malt enzymes on starch may provide a source of sugars during the latter stages of proofing and the early stages of baking. Since a small amount of sugar is essential to the browning of the crust of the loaf of bread, the malt may also be important in that it provides the sugar in the development of crust color.

The mineral salts added to dough mixtures are called yeast foods. Yeasts require small amounts of nitrogen-containing and phosphorus-containing salts for growth and the production of carbon dioxide. For this reason, small quantities of ammonium salts and phosphates are added to the ingredients of the dough.

In addition to the above components, many special types of bread are produced that contain one or more additional ingredients (i.e., butter, extra milk powder, buttermilk or dried buttermilk solids, dried vegetable powders, honey, etc.).

There are two general methods of handling dough in baking bread: the straight dough method and the sponge method. With either process, flour (stored in bulk in bins), water fat (usually melted), suspended yeast, and milk powder are weighed and added to the mixer automatically.

In the straight dough method (see Fig. 20-1), all the ingredients are added to the mixer and the material is mixed first at low speed (about 35 rpm), then at high speed (about 70 rpm). The mixed dough is then placed in large metal containers or troughs and held in an insulated room at about 80°F (26.7°C) and in an atmosphere of high humidity to allow fermentation. During fermentation, the mass of dough is kneaded several times to allow the escape of some carbon dioxide, which is produced continually during fermentation. In addition, working of the dough in this manner assists in stretching and conditioning the gluten, which is the important ingredient responsible for the formation and retention of the structure of the loaf.

In the sponge dough method, 50–75% of the flour, enough water for a moderately stiff dough, all the yeast, the malt, and the yeast foods are added to the mixer and combined. This sponge is fermented for 3–4 hr, then returned to the mixer and combined with the remainder of the flour and water, the shortening, the sugar, the milk powder, and the salt. The sponge method of baking bread produces a crumb of finer texture and with smaller gas holes than that obtained when the straight dough method of bread baking is used.

After fermentation, or after fermentation and mixing, the dough is divided into pieces that will eventually make up the finished loaf. This is done by a machine that measures the dough by volume and cuts off pieces of the desired size. When cut, the dough has an irregular shape with cut ends

Hard Wheat Flour, Water, Yeast
Sugar, Shortening, Monoglyceride,
Milk Powder, Salt, Malt, Mineral
Salts
▼
Mix
▼
Ferment at 80°F and High
Relative Humidity
▼
Divide into Loaf Size Portions
▼
Dust with Flour and Round
▼
Proof at 80°F and 76% Relative
Humidity
▼
Mold into Final Shape
▼
Put into Bake Pans
▼
Bake in Oven with Increasing
Temperature
▼
Cool
▼
Slice
▼
Package

FIGURE 20-1.   Manufacture of bread (straight dough method).

through which the leavening gas can escape. It is immediately dusted with flour and rounded. This is done by machine. Rounding dries the surface with flour and closes up the cut ends, thus preventing the escape of gas. The rounded dough is then carried on a belt to a proofer, where it is emptied onto another belt and held at 80°F (26.7°C) and 76% RH for a period during which the dough relaxes and increases in volume as more carbon dioxide is produced. The pieces of dough are then molded and shaped by machine. In this process, the floured dough is rolled out into a sheet curled into a loose cylinder, again rolled and the ends sealed. In some operations, two cylinders of dough are twisted together in the molding operation. The cylinders of dough then fall into pans conveyed to the oven for baking. During the first stages in the oven, the dough continues to ferment and increase in volume. As the dough passes through the oven, the temperature is increased, further expanding the dough (increase in volume of the gas due to temperature), and eventually, the gluten in set by the heat, the starch first gelatinized and then set by the heat, and some water and ethanol are evaporated. Eventually, the outer layers of the dough become browned to form the crust. Browning is probably due to both the reaction between proteins and sugars, and caramelization of sugars (see Chap. 9). After baking, the loaves of bread are cooled as they are carried through air-conditioned tunnels. The loaves are cut into slices by machine, and the sliced loaves are packaged automatically by bread-wrapping machines.

Bread and other baked goods are subject to spoilage by molds. Therefore, small amounts of mold inhibitors, such as sodium or calcium propionate, are used and allowed at levels of 0.32 parts per 100 parts of flour (0.32%) in white bread and 0.38% in whole wheat products. Since water and other ingredients are used in bread, the actual concentration of these inhibitors in the finished loaf is much lower than in the flour. Mold inhibitors not only delay the growth of molds in bread, but they also inhibit the growth of certain bacteria that produce a slime in the crumb of the loaf, a condition known as "ropiness."

In today's continuous batter-whipped process of making bread (a third method), a liquid mixture of water, sugar, yeast, milk powder, salt, and yeast food, small amounts of flour, and some vitamins is fermented for 2–3 hr. It is then cooled prior to mixing with liquid shortening and the bulk of the flour. The mixture is then agitated at high speed in a developer, which incorporates air. The dough is then extruded directly into baking pans which, after a short proofing period at 80°F (26.7°C), are conveyed directly to the baking oven. Automation in bread manufacture has led to higher production volumes, lowered production costs, shorter production time, and better control over the properties of the finished product, making it easy to produce large volumes of uniform bread that can meet whatever specifications are desired. Bread made by the continuous process is finer in texture, but it is questionable that much flavor is developed in processes of this type.

Standards for bread and flour, shipped in interstate commerce and labeled "enriched," were initiated by the federal government in 1952. These standards require the enrichment of bread with thiamin (vitamin B-1), riboflavin (vitamin B-2), niacin (a member of the complex of B vitamins, also called nicotinic acid), and iron. Calcium and vitamin D may be added as enrichment agents at the option of the producer.

CAKES AND COOKIES

Leavening in cakes and cookies is produced chemically, and there is no yeast fermentation. The chemicals used to produce carbon dioxide are sodium bicarbonate (the source of carbon dioxide) and sources of acid to react with the bicarbonate, such as potassium hydrogen tartrate (cream of tartar), sodium hydrogen pyrophosphate, calcium hydrogen phosphate, and alum (sodium aluminum sulfate). The desirable chemical leavener produces small bubbles of gas at a constant rate consistent with the period involved in mixing and baking to temperatures that set the structure of the cake. Cookies are formed with dies or by extrusion, and, in many instances, the process is quite complex, since the dough may have to be extruded around a central component of fig paste or other type of filling.

Many prepared mixes are also produced, some of which may be used by bakers, although many are used by the home baker. Soft wheat flour or flour of low or moderate protein content is used for cakes. In premixes, the flour, egg powder, shortening, fruit or flavoring components, and leavening agents are combined in the dry state, although, when mixed, the shortening is in the melted or liquid state, and emulsifiers, such as monoglycerides, which improve air incorporation during mixing, may be used. Much of the successful preparation of cake mixes depends on the kind and quantity of chemical leaveners used. Angel cakes contain egg white and are leavened by the incorporation of air into the mixture. During baking, the air in the cake expands and acts as the leavening agent.

DOUGHNUTS

The ingredients for dough used in the manufacture of doughnuts are similar to those of cake, especially pound cake, except that some doughnuts are leavened with the use of yeast. After mixing, the dough is extruded, cut into doughnut form, and cooked in hot oil (370°–380°F [187.8°–193.3°C]). Fat absorption is reported to be about 15%. Fat absorption may be higher when processing parameters (e.g., temperature of the dough) are not controlled, resulting in greasy doughnuts. When fat absorption is insufficient, the keeping quality of the doughnuts is diminished. When doughnuts are to be sugared, the temperature and relative humidity must be controlled (70°–75°F [21.1°–23.9°C] and 85%, respectively) for optimum sugar pickup. Generally, doughnuts are prepared from materials already premixed elsewhere, and seldom do the manufacturers of doughnuts mix their own formula.

CRACKERS

Crackers are unleavened or only slightly leavened. The flour used for these products consists of wheat flour, although some rye flour is often used. For producing crackers, flour, liquid shortening, salt, and small amounts of a chemical leavening agent, with or without sugar, or a flavoring agent, such as onion powder, are mixed into a dough. The dough is then extruded into the desirable shape and baked without proofing. Milk powder, whey powder, and emulsifiers, such as monoglycerides, may be used with some combination of the ingredients listed.

PIE CRUSTS

Pie crusts, which are also unleavened bakery products, can be made from all-purpose flour, but highest-quality pie crusts are obtained from unbleached soft wheat pastry flour of low-protein content. When the protein content is too high, the desirable flakiness characteristic is minimized, and, to compensate, a larger amount of shortening has to be used. The shortening (see Chap. 26) should be a solid or hydrogenated one (e.g., lard or hydrogenated vegetable fat), and it should be medium firm. Milk powder or milk may be used in small quantities to enhance color. Eggs have the same effect. Salt and sugar may be added. The composition of a high-quality pie crust is approximately 47.5% flour, 1.0% salt, 3.3% nonfat milk powder, 2.0% glucose (dextrose, a 6-carbon sugar), 32.4% shortenings, and 13.8% water. To ensure a high-quality crust, all ingredients should be mixed at a temperature of 60°–65°F (15.6°–18.3°C), and the ingredients combined with a minimum of mixing and handling.

21

Vegetables

Vegetables are plant foods that include various edible parts such as leaves, shoots, roots, tubers, flowers, and stems. They normally do not include fruit, which is the subject of the next chapter. However, tomatoes and olives, which are technically fruit, are included in this chapter, because their culinary role is related more to vegetables than to fruit, for example, a garden salad almost always includes tomatoes and sometimes olives, but it never includes any of the other fruit. Consistent with this, fruit salads never contain tomatoes or olives. Vegetables belong to an important class of foods that supply us with many nutritive requirements, including proteins, starches, fats, minerals, sugars, and vitamins. Vegetables also supply bulk to the diet, as well as a large variety of flavors and odors that provide the knowledgeable chef with a repertoire of culinary tricks. On a world basis, vegetables make up a considerable part of the human diet, with the largest proportion of the total vegetable crop being consumed in the fresh state (not preserved). In the United States, however, the proportion of processed vegetables consumed may be quite high. In the fresh state, vegetables continue to carry on life processes, and they are susceptible to various forms of deterioration, hence requiring sanitary handling under controlled temperatures.

The detention of vegetables after harvesting is detrimental to their quality. They undergo microbial spoilage, they lose water, in many cases they lose sugar, and they give up considerable energy in the form of heat (value reported is more than 100,000 Btu per ton per day [27,784 Cal (kg)/MT/day]). Of course, by the heat they produce, vegetables hasten their own deterioration by microbial action accelerated as the temperature is increased (within limits). Enzymic deterioration, especially at sites where bruises occur, is also accelerated by higher temperatures (again within limits).

Various procedures are involved in the production, preservation, and distribution of vegetables. The seeds may have to be treated, the soil has to be fertilized, the crops have to be sprayed or dusted with insecticides and/or fungicides, and the crops have to be harvested and subjected to one of the various methods of preservation. The finished product is then distributed to the retailer or held in a temperature-controlled warehouse until it is distributed. Vegetables are sold at retail as fresh produce, as canned and heat processed, as frozen, and occasionally as dried products.

Seeds are treated with fungicides or insecticides to prevent loss or decay to either insects or fungus prior to germination and growth of the plant. Bean and pea seeds may also be inoculated with bacterial cultures that take nitrogen from the air and make it available to the plant, which requires the nitrogen for growth.

Various fertilizers may be applied to the soil prior to planting. Generally, fertilizers consist of some combination of nitrogen compounds (ammonium salts, nitrates, or urea), phosphates, and potassium compounds. These chemicals, required for plant growth, are apt to be deficient in the soil. Soil is frequently treated with calcium-containing compounds to neutralize its acidity and provide a pH suitable for plant growth. Liquefied fish wastes are also sometimes used as fertilizers, and chemical fertilizers are sometimes applied in liquid form.

Vegetable crops may be produced by the organization that will eventually handle and process them, or often the processor will contract farmers to grow the crops. Large processors have a field department that employs a number of horticulturists. The field department supplies the seed, specifies the kind and extent of fertilization and soil treatment required, and supplies the ingredients. Soil fertilization and treatment, and planting are done by the farmer. Weeding may be done by actual removal of weeds or by chemical treatment, and the latter may be done by the farmer or the processor. Spraying or dusting with insecticides or fungicides may be done by the farmer or the processor. Personnel from the processor's field department decide when the crop is at the right maturity for harvesting and arrange for harvesting of the crop. If the crop cannot be handled quickly enough, the vegetables may pass their optimum maturity, resulting in a loss of product quality.

The heat unit system can be applied as the harvesting criterion for crops for which the required heat units for optimum maturity are known (e.g., beans, corn, peas). Heat units may be expressed as °F-days or °F-hr (°C-days or °C-hr). Heat units are those days or hr above the minimum growing temperature multiplied by the degrees that the ambient temperature exceeds the minimum growing temperature. For example, if the minimum growing temperature for a given vegetable is 40°F (4.4°C), and during a 2-day period the ambient temperature averages 60°F (15.6°C), then the number of heat units accumulated during the 2-day period can be calculated as

$$(60° \text{ F} - 40°\text{F}) \times (2 \text{ days}) = 40°\text{F-days} \ (22.2°\text{C-days})$$

or

$$(60°\text{F} - 40°\text{F}) \times (48 \text{ hr}) = 960 \text{ °F-hr} \ (533.8 \text{ °C-hr})$$

All vegetables sealed in cans or glass jars must be heat-processed (for typical production sequence see Fig. 21-1) (usually at 240° or 250°F [115.6° or 121.1°C] and sometimes at higher temperatures) to make them commercially sterile. Commercially sterile means that all disease bacteria have been killed, and all bacteria and bacterial spores, which might grow out and cause spoilage under the conditions in which the product will be handled after processing, have been destroyed. The time during which a heat-preserved vegetable must be processed to attain commercial sterility depends on the size of the container, the temperature at which the product is processed, the type of container (glass, metal or plastic), whether or not the product is agitated during heating, whether the vegetable product heats by convection or conduction, and other factors.

When a vegetable or vegetable product is preserved by freezing, it should be brought to a temperature of 0°F ($-17.8°\text{C}$) or below in all parts and held at this temperature or below until sold to the consumer. Vegetables are packaged and frozen on moving chain mesh belts in cold-air tunnels. Packages or vegetables are sometimes placed on trays, the trays placed on racks, and the

FIGURE 21-1.   Production of canned vegetables.

product frozen as the racks are moved through cold-air tunnels. In other instances, vegetables are packaged, the packages placed on trays, and the trays placed between refrigerated metal plates for purposes of freezing the product. Some vegetables are loose-frozen on chain mesh belts in cold-air tunnels prior to packaging. Following are descriptions of planting, harvesting, processing, and general handling of the more important vegetables used in the United States.

ASPARAGUS

Asparagus may be planted from the seed or as roots. If planted from the seed, 700–1000 days will be required before the first harvest. If planted as roots, a crop may be obtained the first year, depending on the age of the roots. Asparagus is cut when the stalks are about 8 in (20.3 cm) long. Asparagus must be handled quickly as it soon becomes tough and loses its sweetness. Some asparagus is sold as the fresh product, and some is sold as frozen or heat-processed.

For freezing, asparagus stalks are cut first at the butt ends, which are discarded, then for length, about 5 in (12.7 cm). The spears and remaining cut portions are then washed (separately), blanched, and cooled. Spears and cut portions are packaged separately and frozen in a plate freezer or blast freezer.

For canning, asparagus spears are handled as above, except that they are cut longer and they are not blanched; otherwise it would be difficult to insert them into a container. If glass jars are used, a small amount of stannous chloride ($SnCl_2$) is added to the brine to prevent fading of the color. When tin-lined cans are used, the addition of $SnCl_2$ is not necessary, since $SnCl_2$ will be formed during the heat processing. The heat process is aided by the convection heating effect of the brine, provided the containers are kept in the upright position.

GREEN AND WAX BEANS

Green and wax beans are planted from seed in the spring or when temperatures will allow. A period of 50–70 days is required from planting to harvesting. Upon harvesting, beans should be cooled to 40°F (4.4°C) and held at that temperature until sold as the fresh product, or until processed.

At the processing plant, beans are sorted for size, washed, and their ends are snipped off mechanically. They are then cut transversally or longitudinally (French-cut) and blanched. Some beans are frozen individually and packed in plastic pouches alone or as a component of mixed vegetables, or they may be first packaged and then frozen in a blast freezer. Some beans are canned in brine and heat-processed.

LIMA BEANS

There are two types of lima beans, baby limas and the Fordhook-type limas. Lima beans are planted as seed. A period of 70–90 days is required between planting and harvest. Pods and beans are separated by a machine just after harvesting. The pods may be returned to the soil or ensilaged for cattle feed, and the beans are taken to the plant where they are washed, blanched, cooled, and graded. They are then washed and inspected for foreign materials and then frozen individually and packaged in plastic pouches.

Some baby lima beans are canned, and they are handled in much the same manner as the frozen product except that they may or may not be passed through the quality grader. The beans are automatically metered into cans filled with hot, weak, salt solution. The cans are sealed and heat-processed. Some lima beans to be canned are allowed to mature and dry out on the vine before harvesting. In such cases, the beans must be soaked in water for purposes of rehydrating prior to further processing.

BEETS

Beets require 50–70 days from planting to harvesting. They are harvested by machine and brought to the processing plant in hoppers or trucks. Generally, they are not cooled prior to processing. Beets are canned but are not frozen. At the canning plant, the tops are cut off by machine, after which the roots are held for several days to allow the skin to wilt, thereby loosening it. The beets are then graded for size by machine. After sizing, the beets are washed with sprays of water or in a soaking tank, and are then peeled. Beets are peeled by steaming at 220°F (104.4°C) for about 20 min, after which the skin is removed. The peeled beets are then trimmed. Small beets are canned whole while the larger beets are sliced prior to filling into cans. The cans, to which beets have been added to a point about 3/8 in. (0.956 cm) from the tops, are then filled with a weak salt solution. The cans are then sealed and heat-processed.

Beets sold in the fresh state are washed, but usually not topped. They should be cooled to 32°–35°F (0°–1.7°C) and held in this manner until sold to the consumer. In this condition, they have a storage life of 10–14 days. When topped and cooled to 32°F (0°C) they may be held for 3–5 months.

BROCCOLI

Broccoli requires 60–70 days from planting before it can be harvested, after which the broccoli must be cooled to, and held at, 35°–40°F (1.7°–4.4°C) until sold as fresh or processed. Cooling can be done by subjecting the product to cold-air blasts or by dehydrocooling (see Chap. 12). Most broccoli is sold as fresh, but some is frozen. Broccoli to be sold fresh is inspected to remove blossomed and insect-infested heads, washed, then bound at the stalks in small retail-sized bunches. The frozen product is prepared by splitting the heads to a smaller diameter and conveying to a station where they pass under a rotary cutter that trims the stalks to a length of 5 in. (12.7 cm). After washing, the trimmed stalks are blanched in free-flowing steam for 2.5–7 min (usually 3–5 min). The blanched product is cooled in water, then packaged and frozen.

BRUSSELS SPROUTS

This vegetable is handled mainly as the fresh or frozen product, and only very little is canned. A period of 90–100 days is required from planting to harvesting. Brussels sprouts are harvested by hand and brought to the processing plant in crates. At the plant, the stalks are removed with a rotary trimmer, after which the heads are passed through a dry rotary rod deleafer and are washed by spraying with water. Brussels sprouts to be handled as fresh are weighed into small, retail-sized baskets and placed under refrigeration at 35°–40°F (1.7°–4.4°C) until sold to the consumer. In this condition, they have a storage life of 3–4 wks. The precooling may be similar to that of broccoli. If they are to be frozen, brussels sprouts are blanched in free-flowing steam for 3–9 min (usually 5–6 min), then cooled. The product is then packaged and frozen.

CABBAGE

Little cabbage is canned and none frozen as such. Most of it is handled in the fresh state or processed to produce sauerkraut. Cabbage requires 60–100 days from planting to harvesting. Cabbages are harvested by hand and placed on a mechanical conveyor belt that loads them into hoppers or trucks. Cabbage is washed, trimmed of loose leaves by hand, and precooled, as is broccoli. This vegetable should be held at 32°–35°F (0°–1.7°C) until sold to the consumer. In this condition, it may be held for 3–4 months.

Cabbage to be used for the manufacture of sauerkraut may be held out of refrigeration until the outer leaves wilt, which facilitates cutting and shredding. The cabbages are then cored with a power-driven cylindrical cutter. After coring, the outer coarse and green leaves are removed with a knife. The trimmed and cored heads are then washed with sprays of water. The washed cabbages are then sliced or shredded by machine into strips that have a width of about 1/32 in. (0.08 cm). The cabbage is salted during or after shredding and then placed in large vats (about 12 ft [3.7 m] in diameter and about 8 ft [2.4 m] deep). It may be salted as it is placed in the vats, by alternating layers of shredded cabbage with salt. The amount of salt added is 2–3% of the total weight. In this condition, the cabbage is then allowed to ferment for 40–90 days, depending on ambient temperatures. During fermentation, bacteria grow and produce lactic acid. At the completion of fermentation, the lactic acid content should not be less than 1.5%.

Most sauerkraut produced today is canned. It may or may not be heated to about 110°F (43.3°C) before it is filled into the cans. In any case, after it has been added to the can, a weak salt solution at 165°F (73.9°C) or higher is added to complete the filling of the can. After adding the brine, the lactic acid content of the mixture should not be less than 1%. The cans are then sealed and heat-processed. Due to the low pH of this product (below 4.0), sauerkraut can be rendered commercially sterile by heating it in boiling water to the point where the temperature of all parts reaches 200°–210°F (93.3°–98.9°C). It may be heat-processed at higher temperatures.

CARROTS

Carrots require 70–85 days from planting to harvesting. At the processing plant, carrots to be sold as fresh are cut from their stems, washed, cooled to about 35° F (1.7°C), weighed, and packed in plastic pouches. The product should be held at 35°F (1.7°C) until sold. Some carrots are processed. Those to be frozen are steamed and sprayed with water to remove the skins. They are then trimmed and inspected. Next, they are diced, blanched in steam, cooled, and then frozen in a blast freezer and packaged as such or as a component of mixed vegetables.

Carrots for canning may be peeled by water sprays after steaming or by immersion in a lye solution. In the latter case, the trimmed and sized carrots are passed through a hot solution of sodium hydroxide (1–3% NaOH) at 200°–212°F (93.3°–100°C) for 18–25 sec. They are then washed in water sprays. Since the larger sizes are packed as the sliced or diced product and only the very small specimens canned as whole carrots, size grading of this product is done prior to peeling. carrots are blanched in free-flowing steam for 5–15 min, then cooled, the blanching time depending on the size of the product. Whole small carrots and diced carrots are filled into cans or glass jars to which is added canner's brine (4% sugar and 1.5% salt). The brine may be heated prior to adding. Cold brine may be added instead, but in this case, the open containers must be heated in steam. In either case, the containers are then sealed and heat-processed.

CAULIFLOWER

Cauliflower is not often canned since it becomes mushy and discolors during heat processing. It is handled mostly as the fresh product, although it may be preserved by freezing. A period of 55–60 days is required from planting to harvesting.

Cauliflower is harvested by hand and brought to the processing plant in baskets or crates. If it is to be handled as a fresh or frozen product, it should soon be cooled to 31° to 34°F (−0.6° to 1.1°C) and held in this state until further processed or sold to the consumer. Handled as the fresh product, the outer leaves are first trimmed off. The heads are then washed in a soaker-spray combination washer. The vegetable is then packed in crates and pre-cooled in cold air or by a vacuum system. Cauliflower has a short storage life (2–4 weeks) and, handled in the fresh state, should be held at 31° to 34°F (−0.6° to 1.1°C) until sold to the consumer. When it is to be frozen, the leaves and base of the stem are cut off with a knife, the core is removed, and the head is broken and cut into individual flowerettes or curds. The curds are then passed through a cylindrical rod cleaner that eliminates loose leaves, small pieces, and so on, and flumed to a washer where they are subjected to heavy sprays of water. After washing, the curds are blanched in free-flowing steam for 3–10 min (usually 4–5 min) and then cooled, packaged, and frozen.

CELERY

Celery is handled almost entirely as a fresh product, since it softens during canning or freezing. Some of it is dried for adding to dried prepared products such as dried soups. Celery requires 112–125 days from planting to maturity.

Celery is harvested, placed in crates, and brought to the processing plant. At the plant, the heads are washed in a combination spray-soaker-type washer, the outer leaves are trimmed off by hand, and the product is re-packed into crates and promptly cooled to 31° to 34°F (−0.6° to 1.1°C). At this temperature, it may have a storage life of 2–3 months. Precooling may be done with refrigerated air or by a vacuum system. Celery should be held at 31° to 34°F (−0.6° to 1.1°C) until sold to the consumer.

SWEET CORN

Sweet corn is handled as fresh, frozen, or canned on the cob, or as canned or frozen kernels. It may also be canned as a mixture of partially macerated corn kernels, starch, and sugar. Corn requires 60–85 days from planting to harvesting. Corn is harvested, mechanically, with or without husks, after which it should be cooled immediately to 32°–34°F (0°–1.1°C), or its quality will deteriorate rapidly. It should be held at that temperature until it is sold as fresh or is processed.

Corn to be canned on the cob is cut at the base, husked, and washed. The ears are then cut to can-sized lengths (from the point) and placed in the can.

A hot, weak, salt and sugar solution is then added to cover the ears, and the cans are sealed and heat-processed.

Corn to be frozen on the cob is handled in the same manner as canned cob corn as far as husking and cleaning are concerned. It is then blanched in free-flowing steam for about 9 min and cooled in water. The blanched and cooled corn may be frozen prior to, or after, packaging.

Corn, canned or frozen as kernels, is handled like corn on the cob as far as husking and washing are concerned. To cut the kernels from the cob, the ears are passed through a machine in which knives, which encircle the cob, follow the shape of the cob so that the cut is made only to a depth sufficient to remove most of the kernels. The cut kernels are passed through strainers made of parallel wires that are set wide apart, in order to remove strands of silk that may be present. The kernels may also be floated in water to remove detritus.

Canned, whole corn kernels are packed in two ways. The kernels may be added to the can and entirely covered with a hot, weak solution of salt and sugar, after which the can is sealed, or the kernels may be added to the can, after which only a small amount of weak solution of salt and sugar is added. In the former case, the product heats by convection, currents of hot brine moving up along the wall of the can, across the top, and down the central axis. In the latter case, the can is sealed under a very high vacuum drawn on the can by mechanical means during sealing.

The high-vacuum product heats both through steam, generated from the small amount of liquid present in the container (the vacuum allowing the steam to spread through the product), and through conduction. The advantage of the latter process is that soluble solids are not, to any extent, leached out from the kernels into the brine. The more mature ears of corn are used for cream-style canned corn, which is a mixture of corn kernels, sugar, water, starch, and salt. The mixture is prepared and cooked to 190°F (87.8°C) prior to filling into the cans. The cans are sealed and heat-processed. Cream-style corn takes longer to process than do the whole corn kernels, because heat transfer through it is by conduction only. A small amount of hominy is canned.

Corn kernels to be frozen are blanched in free-flowing steam for 2–4 min on a wire mesh belt, then cooled with water sprays. During cooling, some sugar and starch present in the kernels are leached out, resulting in some loss of quality. Whole corn kernels to be frozen are filled into plastic pouches or cartons that are then overwrapped.

CUCUMBERS

Cucumbers are used as the fresh product or to make pickles or relishes. A period of 55–60 days is required from planting to harvesting. Cucumbers, grown for the fresh market, are of a variety that produces relatively large specimens. Varieties, grown for processing, include relatively large cucumbers used for the production of relish and medium- and small-sized specimens for pickling.

At the processing plant, cucumbers to be used as fresh produce are washed, and may be covered with a thin layer of wax and polished by machine. They should be promptly cooled to 45°–50°F (7.2°–10°C) and held at this temperature until sold to the consumer. In this condition, they have a high-quality storage life of 10–14 days. At temperatures lower than 45°F (7.2°C), they may develop pitting or dark-colored, watery areas.

Pickles are manufactured as sweet, sour, dill, kosher-dill, and so forth. In the manufacture of pickles, small- or medium-sized cucumbers are submerged in a solution of 10% salt (sodium chloride) and allowed to ferment. During fermentation, which takes several weeks, the sugar in the cucumbers is gradually utilized by bacteria, and salt penetrates the cucumber. The salt in the brine is increased to 15%. (Dill-type pickles are fermented in a less concentrated salt solution.) After fermenting, the cucumbers are soaked in warm water, then packed in glass jars with some combination of vinegar, sugar, spices, and garlic. Pickles in jars should be pasteurized in hot water by bringing their temperature up to 160°–180°F(71.1°–82.2°C). Some cucumbers are sliced vertically or horizontally prior to packing them. Sliced pickles are covered with a weak solution of salt, vinegar, and spices, with or without sugar, and heat-processed as indicated.

Relishes may be made from fermented cucumbers that are freshened, chopped, and mixed with vinegar and spices. Since they are used with other foods, some type of gum, such as locust bean gum, may be added to relishes for liquid retention.

LETTUCE

Lettuce is used entirely as a fresh product, since when heated or frozen, the leaves wilt. This is unacceptable, because lettuce is expected to be crisp and firm when eaten. There are a number of varieties of lettuce—the open head or loose leaf, the romaine, the iceberg, and others. Iceberg lettuce, used in this country, requires a period of 75–80 days from planting to maturity. At the processing plant, lettuces are trimmed, washed and placed in crates; the crates are placed in refrigerated freight cars or trucks. The cars or trucks are then moved into large metal chambers. The chambers are closed and subjected to vacuum, which accelerates the evaporation of moisture from the lettuce, lowering the temperature of the product to about 33°F (0.56°C) through evaporative cooling. During shipment and until sold to the consumer, lettuce should be held at 32°–34°F (0°–1.1°C). At this temperature, it has a storage life of 2–3 weeks.

MUSHROOMS

Mushrooms are sold fresh and canned, and a small amount is frozen as an ingredient of various cooked foods. There are a number of types of edible mushrooms, but the variety commonly used for food is the champignon. Mushrooms are grown in darkened humid rooms (e.g., cellars) in a mixture of horse manure, straw, and loam that has been composted. The period from planting to harvesting is 50–85 days. Harvesting may continue for about 2 ½ months. High humidity and a temperature of about 70°F (21.1°C) are required for growing. Mushrooms to be sold as fresh are cooled to 32°–34°F (0°–1.1°C). Fresh mushrooms have a high-quality storage life of about 5 days at 32°F (0°C), 2 days at 40°F (4.4°C), and 1 day at 50°F (10°C). The freshly handled product is usually sold within 48 hr after harvesting.

Mushrooms to be canned (some mushrooms may be sliced) are soaked in a tank of water for 10–15 min and washed with sprays of water. They are then blanched in water at 175°–180°F (79.4°–82.2°C) for 8–10 min in order to shrink the product, which allows proper fill of the container, and to prevent excessive darkening. The blanched and cooled mushrooms are placed in cans and covered with a hot solution of 1.5% salt and 0.2% citric acid. The acid is used to prevent excessive darkening. In some instances, the solution is not preheated, in which case, open cans are heated in steam until the product reaches a temperature of 150°F (65.6°C). After sealing the cans, the product is heat-processed. The growth medium for mushrooms may contain the organism that causes botulism. Therefore, great care should be taken to make sure that, during heat processing, all the product in the container is subjected to that degree of heat necessary to provide at least a minimum botulinum kill (the equivalent of heating all parts to 250°F [121.1°C] for a period of 2.5 min). Many wild varieties are poisonous, so only commercial varieties should be consumed.

OLIVES

Olive trees are started in nurseries as rooted cuttings and allowed to grow for several years before being set out in orchards. The desired varieties are grafted onto the seedling stock as 2- or 3-year stock. Trees are pruned and thinned yearly, and bear fruit after about 5 years. The trees may bear fruit for many years. Olives are used for the production of olive oil (described in Chap. 24), or they may be canned as black or as green or as green stuffed olives. The latter are usually packed in glass jars. The fruit is harvested when still green, just before turning pink. Large and unblemished olives are used for canning as black or green olives. Small and blemished fruit are used for oil or for chopped olives. Olives must be treated with lye solution (sodium hydroxide) to destroy or decrease the content of a bitter substance.

In the production of black olives, the sized, washed, and inspected fruit is placed in tanks and covered with a 1–1.5% lye (sodium hydroxide) solution at 60°F (15.6°C) for 4–8 hr, the mixture being stirred occasionally. The lye solution is then drained off, and the fruit is exposed to air for 3–6 hr with occasional stirring, to oxidize and set the color (to black). The fruit is then covered with water, agitated by compressed air, and held for 3–4 days. It is next drained and again treated with a 0.5–0.75% lye solution for 3–5 hr, then drained and washed once more. Black olives may or may not be pitted prior to canning. The prepared olives are sized, inspected, placed in cans volumetrically, and covered with a boiling 2.5–3% salt solution. The cans are then sealed and processed at high temperatures.

Green olives are placed in a brine (sodium chloride) solution (2.5–5%), the salt content being increased daily until it reaches 7.5–10%. The fruit is held in this manner for 30–45 days, during which time it undergoes a fermentation, due to the growth of lactic acid bacteria. After washing without agitation in tanks of water for several days, the fruit is treated with lye solution, as in the case of black olives, then rewashed. The fruit is inspected, graded for size, pitted or not pitted, and canned as in the manner of black olives. Olives in large containers (no. 10 cans) must be exhausted (heated) to bring the temperature in all parts to 180°F (82.8°C) prior to sealing the cans, then heat-processed at high temperatures. Green olives may be pitted and stuffed with pimientos or nuts prior to canning. In some instances, olives (usually pitted) preserved in a 10% brine (or higher concentrations) are shipped in barrels to repackers who freshen the pickled product, stuff the individual fruit with pimientos or nuts, and repack it in glass jars. The fruit is then covered with a hot 2.5–3% brine, the jars sealed, and the product heat-processed at high temperatures.

ONIONS

Onions are utilized mostly as the fresh product, but some are dried and small quantities are canned, pickled, or frozen. Onions require 100–110 days from planting to harvest. Onions may be harvested by mechanical diggers and placed in bags, baskets, or lug boxes that are brought to the processing plant on trucks. At the processing plant, onions are topped (stems are removed), dry cleaned, and placed in mesh sacks or bags holding 50 lb (22.5 kg) of product if they are to be stored. Stored onions should be held at 32°–35°F (0°–1.7°C) and at low relative humidity (no ice). Higher temperatures promote sprouting and high humidities promote decay. When distributed to the consumer, they are weighed into mesh sacks in quantities of 2 or 3 lb (0.9 or 1.4 kg).

Some onions, especially small ones, are canned. The onions to be canned are topped, dry cleaned, and peeled in a flame peeler. The heat from open flames loosens the skin, which may then be removed with sprays of water. After washing, the onions are trimmed and inspected. They are then filled into cans volumetrically and covered with hot canner's brine (weak solution of sugar and salt). The cans are then sealed, and the product is heat-processed. Frozen onions are used primarily with other vegetables. They are precooked in steam before freezing because they are used as a cooked vegetable. Onions are loose frozen on chain mesh belts in a cold-air tunnel, then stored in metal containers prior to mixing with other frozen vegetables, such as peas. Freezing and storage requirements are the same as for other vegetables. Some onions are dried, usually in the form of minced onions. They are topped, peeled, washed, and inspected in the usual manner, then diced by machine. The raw, diced product is then dried to a moisture content of about 5% on metal mesh belts, where temperature and humidity can be controlled. They are then packaged, usually in glass containers.

PEANUTS

Peanuts are legumes, and botanically classified as vegetables. They require more than 100 days from planting to maturity, producing a low-growing, vinelike plant, the pods (shells) containing the nuts that are formed underground. The shoots bearing the pods are first formed on the plant above the ground but eventually insert themselves into the soil. Peanuts are harvested by pulling the vines and arranging them in rows to dry for several days. During this drying, the moisture content of the nuts is reduced from about 50 to about 25%. The nuts, in the shell, are then removed from the vines by machine and are further dried to prevent subsequent spoilage. This is usually done in bins through which warm ais is blown, the peanuts being piled in the bins to depths of 5–6 ft (1.5–1.8m). The air used for drying should not exceed 10°–15°F (5.56°–8.34°C) above ambient (outside) temperatures. Dried to a moisture content of 5–8%, peanuts have an almost indefinite storage life at 48°–50°F (8.9–10°C).

Peanuts in the shell may be roasted in hot air to a moisture content of about 4%. The temperatures used are sufficiently high to eliminate the raw beanlike flavor of the uncooked nut. The nuts may be removed from the pods by machine after which the thin skins covering each nut may be removed by machine, if desired. In general, peanuts with or without skins, which are to be sold in the shelled state, are cooked in hot vegetable oil at 300°-380°F (148.9°-193.3°C) until slightly browned or until the moisture content has been lowered to about 2%; then they are salted. Some peanuts are dry-roasted (without using oil for blanching or cooking).

Peanut butter is prepared by grinding the nuts to a fine consistency, mixing with about 3% salt (sodium chloride) and small quantities of emulsifiers, such as monoglycerides. The emulsifiers are used to prevent separation of peanut oil from the other components. In preparing peanut butter, the nuts are first blanched or fried in oil, to develop color and flavor, and to lower the moisture content to about 2%. Some types of peanut butter are prepared this way, but with chunks of broken blanched peanuts mixed with the ground nuts to provide the chunky texture.

Peanut oil may be obtained from peanuts by first subjecting the nuts to pressure, the nuts being enclosed by pressing cloths, then further extracting the cake with hydrocarbon solvents. The presscake is generally used as cattle fodder.

GREEN PEAS

Green peas are mostly canned or frozen. Only small quantities are sold in the pod as fresh. A period of 55–75 days is required from planting to harvesting. Past the optimum maturity, peas have a lower quality. Peas are harvested by machinery that removes the peas from their pods. The pods and vines are cut and returned to the soil or ensilaged for cattle feed. The peas should be cooled, usually in cold water, within 3–4 hr, because they soon undergo spoilage.

At the processing plant, peas to be canned are size graded, tested for tenderness (with a tenderometer), washed and blanched, cooled, inspected, and filled into cans with a hot, weak solution of salt and sugar. The cans are then sealed and heat-processed.

Peas to be frozen are handled in much the same manner as those that are canned, except that different varieties are used for freezing. Due to the fact that off-flavors are more easily detected in frozen peas, they should be processed within 4 hr after vining, even when ambient (outside) temperatures are not higher than 70°F (21.1°C). At higher ambient temperatures, off-flavors develop in shorter periods. After blanching, the peas are cooled and graded. Only immature peas are used for freezing, the more mature ones being diverted to the canning process. The peas are then washed, inspected, and filled into cartons and frozen in a blast freezer, or they may be frozen individually and then packed in plastic pouches as such or as a component of mixed vegetables.

POTATOES

White potatoes, of which there are many varieties, are used mainly as a fresh product. Some are dried, frozen, or canned. Other varieties are best suited to use as boiled or mashed potatoes. Some varieties make a superior baked product, while still others have good all-purpose qualities. Potato plants are grown from sprouted potatoes that have been cut so that each piece includes a sprout and some of the tissue. A period of 60–70 days is required from planting to harvesting.

Potatoes are dug by machine and trucked in bulk or in barrels to the processing plant. At the processing plant, potatoes to be sold as fresh are passed through a dry reel to remove soil. They are then washed, dried, and packed in paper or plastic bags of 5- or 10-lb (2.37–or 4.5-kg) capacity. White potatoes, held at temperatures above 50°F (10°C), lose sweetness as their sugar is converted to starch. At 40°F (4.4°C) or below they become sweeter, as their starch is converted to sugar. For ordinary purposes, when sold in the fresh state, high sugar content is not desirable. Also, if potatoes are to be canned as such or used as a component of corned beef hash or fish cakes, high sugar content is not desirable, since during heat processing, off-flavors and off-colors may develop as a result of nonenzymatic browning. On the other hand, if potatoes are to be processed as a frozen product, such as french fried or hash-browned, the sugar content should be high enough to provide some color without prolonged heating. The sugar content in potatoes that are used in large quantities for the manufacture of potato chips must be controlled. If the sugar content is too low, the desirable light brown color will not be attained during frying. If the sugar content is too high, the potato chips will burn or become black during drying.

Because of these changes in sugar content, white potatoes may have to be conditioned or held at a particular temperature for 1–3 weeks prior to processing. Potatoes handled as fresh may be held for 2–4 months at 40°F (4.4°C) without sprouting. Generally, they are held at 40°–45°F (4.4°–7.1°C) prior to shipment, since during transportation and subsequent handling, they will be held at higher temperatures that will cause the conversion of sugar to starch.

Frozen white potatoes are processed as french fried, baked stuffed, hash-browned, or as some other prepared product. Frozen french fried potatoes are prepared from the fresh product. The potatoes are either washed, peeled in lye, and washed in a neutralizing weak acid solution, or they are heated in steam at 80 psig (5.6 kg/cm^2) for about 10 sec and subjected to water sprays to remove the peel. They are then inspected to remove eyes, after which they are treated in a weak solution of citric acid and sodium bisulfite. This treatment prevents discoloration (browning) due to enzyme action. It should be noted, however, that the use of sulfites in foods is under scrutiny because of adverse reactions that sulfites cause in asthmatics, and this has resulted in FDA restrictions and even bans on the use of these preservatives (see Chap. 14).

The potatoes are then cut into strips. If the potatoes have not been conditioned by holding at the temperature that regulates the sugar content to the desirable concentration, they may have to be blanched in water at about 180°F (82.2°C) for sufficient time to remove excess sugars or, if the sugar content is too low, they may be heated in weak sugar (glucose) solutions. Blanching or precooking is done in water or free-flowing steam for about 2–4 min, after which the potatoes are drained, then cooked for short periods in hot vegetable oil at 350°–375°F (176.7°–190.6°C). Deep-fat frying is done for only sufficient time to give the french fried potatoes a light brown color. After cooling, the potatoes are frozen.

Baked frozen potatoes are baked whole with the skin on. They are then cooled and cut in half lengthwise. The inner material is removed, leaving two half shells of the skin and outer layers of the potato. The inner material is then mashed and mixed with cooked onions, margarine, and various flavoring materials. The half shells are then filled with the prepared mashed product, placed in cartons, and frozen.

Hash-browned potatoes are prepared in the manner of french fried potatoes except that they are frenched to a smaller size and cooked in oil for somewhat longer periods to provide a darker color. Hash-browned potatoes are packaged and frozen.

Some small-sized potatoes are canned. These potatoes are peeled by heating in a lye solution followed by washing in a weak acid solution. The peeled potatoes are then filled into cans, covered with a 1–2% salt solution, and the cans are then exhausted in free-flowing steam, sealed, and heat-processed.

Potatoes preserved by drying are mostly used as mashed potatoes by rehydrating them just prior to use. Some dried potatoes are produced as specialty products, such as scalloped potatoes.

Potatoes may contain toxic glycoalkaloid compounds. One of these is solanine, which appears as a green discoloration that may also involve the tissue below the skin. In such cases, the skin and tissue, so affected, should be removed. With the popularization of potato skins as entrees, the possible presence of these compounds should be considered. Some of the side effects noted from these compounds are headache, nausea, and diarrhea.

SWEETPOTATOES

There are several varieties of sweetpotatoes, most of which are sold in the fresh state, small quantities being either canned or frozen. A period of 70–90 days is required from planting to harvesting. Sweetpotatoes to be handled in the fresh state are dry cleaned to remove soil, washed, placed in bags holding 25 lb (11.3 kg) or more, and cooled. Since sweetpotatoes have a relatively slow respiration rate, they can be brought to storage temperature over a period of several days. Fresh sweetpotatoes should be held at 50°–55°F (10°–12.8°C) at which temperature they have a storage life of 4–6 months. Sweetpotatoes to be canned or frozen are dry cleaned, washed, and then peeled in steam or in a hot lye solution, as are white potatoes. However, prior to peeling, they may be graded for size.

Canned sweetpotatoes may be handled as a solid pack or as individual potatoes packed in canner's brine (2–4% sugar and 1–2% salt). Solid packs are prepared by cooking the potatoes, mashing by passing them through a pulper, then filling the product into cans. The filled cans are then heated in free-flowing steam so that all parts of the product have a minimum temperature of 160°–180°F (71.1°–82.2°C). The cans are then sealed and heat-processed. Sweetpotatoes may also be precooked and canned whole. In this case, they are covered with canner's brine and the open cans are heated in free-flowing steam until the internal temperature of the potatoes reaches 160°–180°F (71.1°–82.2°C). The cans are then sealed, and the product is heat-processed. Sweetpotatoes to be preserved by freezing are peeled as is the canned product. They are then precooked in steam at 240°F (115.6°C) for 5–25 min, depending on the mass of the product, and then cooled. The cooled potatoes are then treated with citric acid (about 0.3%), then passed through a pulper. The pulped or mashed product is filled into cartons volumetrically, the cartons sealed with or without overwrap, and the product is frozen.

SOYBEANS

Soybeans are legumes planted from seed and require 100–130 days from planting to harvesting. At the end of that period, the leaves are dry, and the moisture content of the beans is about 9–10%. In the United States, soybeans are grown mainly in the north central states, especially in Illinois. They are also grown in Arkansas and in the Mississippi delta. The plants are reaped mechanically by a combine that cuts and gathers the plant and threshes the beans from the pod. The beans are collected in trucks and brought to processing plants in bulk. Soybeans are generally not eaten either in the fresh state or as a canned or frozen product, but rather as processed products.

Soybeans contain about 20% oil and 40% protein in the freshly harvested state. The oil from the ground beans is usually extracted by pressing or by extraction with solvents, after cracking the beans to loosen the hulls, which are then removed with suction. Much of the oil obtained from soybeans is used for the manufacture of margarine. Soybeans contain an antigrowth factor and this must be destroyed by heating before the press cake can be used for animal feed or human consumption. Much of the press cake from which the oil has been extracted is used for animal feed supplements.

Soybean protein may be used after grinding the beans, extracting various proportions of the oil, and adding some lecithin as an emulsifier. In such form, it may be used as an extender in sausage products, in blended foods, in baby foods, and in pet foods. The defatted soybean, extruded after heating, may be extracted with water, aqueous alcohol, or dilute acid to dissolve and remove carbohydrates and other ingredients, resulting in a product of higher protein content (about 66–70%). As such, this material may be used in processed meat products, baked goods, and breakfast cereals.

A high-protein soy concentrate (about 90–97% protein) may be obtained by extracting soyflakes (oil removed) with water in which the pH is controlled to optimize the removal of carbohydrates and other materials. This product is used in sausages and canned meats, in coffee whiteners, in whipped toppings, in frozen desserts, and in cheese spreads. Thermoplastic extrusion of fat-extracted soybean flour together with water (flavoring and coloring ingredients may be used) produces a product containing 50–53% protein. This is used as an extender for meat products, such as hamburgers. A soybean base is made from soybean flour by first extracting carbohydrates with aqueous alcohol and dilute acid, dissolving the remaining material in an alkaline solution, and precipitating it in a coagulating bath. This material (about 90% protein) is fibrous, and when mixed with fats, flavoring, and coloring, and then texturized, can be made to simulate cooked beef, chicken, bacon, crab meat, scallops, nuts, fruits, and vegetables.

In some Asian countries, soybean milk is prepared by soaking the diced beans for a few hours in water, mashing the beans, and boiling in water for 30 min (3 parts of water to 1 part of mash), then straining out the solid particles. This soybean milk may be made from whole or defatted beans. The milk may be used as such, or it may be treated, while hot, with calcium or magnesium salts, with rennet (an enzyme), or with lactic acid to precipitate a curd that is then drained and pressed. The curd is eaten in different forms.

It should be noted that soybean protein is not a complete protein as far as human requirements are concerned, being deficient in the amino acids, methionine and tryptophan. It is however, high in lysine, an amino acid deficient in many vegetable proteins. When soybean protein is used as an extender with animal proteins, the resulting mixture is generally adequate in protein requirements.

SPINACH

There are a number of varieties of spinach that may be harvested in the late spring or late fall. Periods of 35–50 days are required from planting to harvesting. Mechanical cutters and loaders are used to harvest spinach, which is brought to the processing plant in bulk. At the processing plant, the spinach leaves are trimmed and inspected to remove dead leaves, passed through a dry reel to remove detritus, then washed in a soaker-type water tank in which the product is subjected to heavy sprays of water. Handled in the fresh state, spinach is usually packed in plastic bags. Spinach deteriorates rapidly and should be quickly cooled to 32°–33°F (0°–0.56°C) and held at this temperature until sold to the consumer. Spinach to be canned may be handled as whole or as chopped spinach (the latter type is cut or chopped by machine prior to blanching). It must be blanched in order to fill the cans with the desired amount of product. Blanching is carried out in free-flowing steam or in water at 180°–185°F (82.8°–85°C) for about 4 min. After blanching, the spinach is subjected to the pressure of a metal roller as it is carried on a conveyor belt to squeeze out some of the water picked up during blanching. The hot spinach is placed in cans and covered with a 2–3% salt solution at 190°–200°F (87.8°–93.3°C). The open cans are then heated in steam until all parts have a minimum temperature of 180°F (82.2°C) (about 10 min). Next, the cans are sealed and heat-processed. Spinach to be frozen is steam blanched for 2–4 min and then cooled in a tank of water equipped with water sprays. It is then subjected to the pressure of a metal roller to squeeze out some of the water picked up during blanching and cooling. The cooled product is filled into plastic pouches or cartons, with or without overwrap, and frozen.

SQUASH

There are a number of types of squash or pumpkins. Summer and zucchini types require 50–60 days from planting to harvesting. Hubbard-type squash (commonly called pumpkins) and others require 90–100 days from planting to maturity. At the processing plant, the summer-type is washed and may be packaged in units of 2–4 small specimens in trays overwrapped with plastic. The larger winter-type varieties are usually washed, drained, then handled in the unwrapped state as individual specimens. Summer-type squash has a storage life of 1–2 weeks at 40°F (4.4°C) and should be rapidly cooled to, and held at, this temperature until sold to the consumer. On the other hand, the other varieties are more resistant to deterioration. At 50°F (10°C) hard-shell Hubbard-type squash may be held for 6 months or longer, acorn squash for 5–8 weeks, and butternut squash for 2–3 months. These types, therefore, do not require quick cooling.

Only the hard-shell or Hubbard-type squash is canned and then only as pie filling. It is washed, cut into chunks by machine, and then cooked in free-flowing steam for 25–30 min. It is then passed through a pulper that macerates the product and removes the outer shell. About 0.5% of salt is then added and mixed. Spices such as cinnamon, ginger, and mace may be added and mixed with the product. Some molasses may also be added. The hot pumpkin mixture is added to cans volumetrically, and the cans are sealed and heat-processed.

Hubbard-type squash to be frozen is handled much the same way as canned squash, except that it is prepared as a vegetable product rather than as a pie filling. Generally, therefore, the frozen product has only salt added. It is also cooled after cooking and before filling into packages volumetrically to be frozen. Summer-type squash to be frozen is washed, mechanically cut into slices ½ in. (1.3 cm) thick, blanched for 3.5 min in water at 210°F (98.9°C), cooled, packaged, and frozen.

TOMATOES

Tomatoes are handled as the fresh product, as well as processed products such as canned whole tomatoes, tomato juice, tomato puree, tomato paste, ketchup, and chili sauce. Tomatoes are frozen only as an ingredient of prepared products such as pizza or cooked lasagna. Tomatoes require 70–85 days from planting to harvesting. Usually, the seeds are planted in soil enclosed by glass or hot frames, and when the plants have reached a height of about 6 in. (15.3 cm) they are transplanted to the growing area. Tomatoes are handled in the fresh state mostly as the mature partially ripened product and sometimes, as the firm ripe tomato.

At the processing plant the tomatoes are washed and sorted. Green specimens are separated from the firm ripe type, and diseased specimens are discarded. Mature partially ripened tomatoes are packaged in cardboard, cellophane-topped cartons. They should be cooled to 55°–60°F (12.8°–15.6°C) and held at this temperature until sold to the consumer. In this condition, they have a storage life of 2–3 weeks. Firm ripe tomatoes generally are held at 45°–50°F (7.2°–10°C), at which temperature they have a storage life of about 5 days. At 32°F (0°C) tomatoes may have a shelf-life of about 2 weeks. However, at this temperature, they are subject to chilling injury and may lose quality. Tomatoes to be canned should be in the firm ripe condition. They are washed and inspected, with green and rotten specimens culled out and mold and rot trimmed out from infected but otherwise good specimens. Trimming is very important since enforcement authorities have methods of detecting mold and rot in finished tomato preparations and can condemn tomato products on this basis.

After trimming, the tomatoes are cored, that is, the pistil and stamen section is cut out. Tomatoes to be canned as whole are scalded with sprays of hot water and cooled with sprays of cold water, which facilitates peeling off the skin. Some varieties have a skin which does not require peeling. The whole peeled tomatoes are then placed in cans after which a brine (2% sugar and 1% salt) is added to cover the tomatoes. In some instances 1% salt and juice from whole tomatoes or from peels and cores are added to fill the cans. The open cans are then heated in water at 175°–180°F (79.4°–82.2°C) until all parts of the product have reached 145°–150°F (62.8°–65.6°C). The cans are then sealed and heated until all parts of the product reach a temperature of 180°–200°F (82.2°–93.3°C) to provide commercial sterility. It should be noted that this process is based on the fact that tomatoes are classified as having a high acid content, which they normally do. However, as tomatoes are allowed to ripen their acidity tends to decrease. In some low-acid varieties, if ripening is allowed to proceed too far, the acidity may be lowered to levels that would make it dangerous to heat process them by the process described above. This has importance where the canning of tomatoes does not include a check of the pH, as in home canning. For this reason, the addition of lemon juice is often recommended in home canning procedures.

For the production of tomato juice, cored and quartered tomatoes are heated in steam (hot break method) to inactivate pectinases, which would otherwise destroy pectin, causing a separation of solids from the juice, and to eliminate oxygen, which would otherwise destroy vitamin C. The juice is then filled into cans and heat-processed. There are alternative methods for producing tomato juice, but a superior process is to flash heat juice in a heat exchanger to 250°F (121.1°C), hold at this temperature for 0.7 min, cool to 200°–210°F (93.2°–98.9°C), fill into presterilized cans, and seal and invert the cans to sterilize the covers, holding in this manner for several minutes before cooling. In order to increase the acidity slightly and add nutrients to the juice, small amounts of citric acid and vitamin C may be added.

Tomato puree and tomato paste are prepared by vacuum concentrating tomato juice. Tomato puree must contain at least 8.37% tomato solids, tomato paste must contain at least 22% tomato solids, and heavy tomato paste must contain at least 33% tomato solids. Salt may be added to these products and baking soda (sodium bicarbonate) may be added to heavy tomato paste to neutralize some of the acid. Generally, these products are added to the container at a temperature near 180°–200°F (82.2°–93.3°C). The containers are then sealed and inverted, allowed to stand for several minutes, and cooled. Due to the low pH (high acidity) of concentrated tomato products, additional heating is not required to attain commercial sterility.

Tomato ketchup or catsup is made by concentrating tomato juice, adding sugar and salt and then a vinegar (10% acetic acid) extract of spices (headless cloves, black pepper, red pepper, cinnamon, mace, onions, garlic, etc.). The finished product should have a salt content of 3% and a total solids content of about 30%. This product is bottled hot and capped under vacuum to eliminate air. Removal of air prevents darkening from tannins extracted from the spice mixture. Tannins turn dark in the presence of oxygen. Further heating to attain commercial sterility is not required.

Chili sauce is made from vacuum-concentrated, finely chopped, peeled, cored tomatoes to which a vinegar extract of spices and red peppers has been added, together with onions and garlic. This product is bottled and handled much in the same manner as ketchup.

Tomato soup, Italian tomato sauce, with or without meat, and other tomato products are canned and bottled to some extent. These products may require various heat treatments to attain commercial sterility, depending on the pH (acidity) of the finished product.

TURNIPS

Turnips require 60–100 days from planting to maturity. Essentially all turnips are handled in the fresh state. At the processing plant, they are dry cleaned, washed, dried, covered with a thin layer of wax, and machine polished. Turnips may be held for 4–5 months at 32°F (0°C), so they may be slowly cooled to 32°–35°F (0°–1.7°C) and held at that temperature until shipped out in large bags or crates. Turnips are sold as unpackaged, individual vegetables. They should be held at 32°–35°F (0°–1.7°C) until sold to the consumer.

22

Fruits

Fruits are botanically classified as those plant parts that house seeds; in other words, they are mature plant ovaries. Fruit includes tomatoes and a few others that are considered as vegetables in the supermarket. Since the popular definition of fruit applies only to what is naturally sweet and what is normally used in desserts, it is understandable that, for example, tomatoes and olives are treated as vegetables.

Berries belong to a class of fruit that are usually small and very delicate. On the other hand, melons as a class are usually large, often with a tough, and sometimes thick, outer skin. Fruits are vulnerable to a variety of diseases and infestations and, therefore, require spraying with protective chemicals during the growing season.

Fruit is often picked prior to maturity, and allowed to ripen in the distribution chain, reaching the consumer when about ready to eat. Fruit is considered to be ripe when it reaches the optimum succulence and texture and there is a desirable balance between sugars and acidity, as well as the subtle elements that contribute to aroma. Fruit that goes past its optimum ripeness enters senescence, a stage of overripeness and breakdown. In this stage, the texture loses its firmness, succulence is diminished, and sugars, acids, and aroma elements generally all decline in concentration. Some fruit, like the banana, has an early senescence, and deterioration, once begun, is rapid. On the other hand, some fruit, like apples, resists the onset of senescence as well as its progression. The onset of senescence can be controlled by keeping the fruit at the lowest temperature that it can tolerate and by increasing the amount of atmospheric carbon dioxide to a controlled level. Too much carbon dioxide can be harmful.

All fruit preserved by canning should be heat-processed to attain commercial sterility. Whereas vegetables and certain other foods require the application of high temperatures (240°F, 250°F [115.6°C, 121.1°C] or higher) for significant lengths of time to attain commercial sterility, most fruit is sufficiently acid (pH usually below 4.5) that commercial sterility can be attained by heating the containers in boiling water to the point where all parts of the product reach a temperature of 180°–200°F (82.2°–93.3°C).

All fruit preserved by freezing should be brought to a temperature of 0°F (−17.8°C) or below during freezing and thereafter held at 0°F (−17.8°C) or below until sold to the consumer. Fruit may be packed in retail-sized containers and frozen in one of three ways: (1) The containers are placed on trays, the trays are placed on racks and frozen as the racks are moved through a tunnel in which blasts of cold air are circulated; (2) the cartons are placed on chain mesh belts that move slowly through a tunnel in which blasts of cold air are circulated; or (3) the cartons are placed on trays, the filled trays are placed between refrigerated metal plates, and the product is frozen with the containers in contact with the cold plates. Therefore, except on those cases where the method of freezing is different from those indicated in the foregoing, no description of freezing methods will be given.

There is a large variety of fruit used in the United States with varying degrees of popularity. Following are descriptions of planting, harvesting, processing, and general handling of the more important fruits.

BLACKBERRIES

Blackberries grow on 2-yr-old brambles or canes. The fruit is used as fresh, in baked products, and for the manufacture of jam and jelly.

At the processing plant, the fruit is washed, inspected (to remove leaves, twigs, etc.), and cooled to 32°F (0°C). The fruit is held at this temperature until sold as fresh in retail-sized baskets overwrapped with clear plastic or until it is processed.

For freezing, the fruit is individually frozen in a cold-air tunnel and packed in large metal cans with cap-type covers and held frozen. When the berries are to be used for producing jam and jelly, sugar is added to the cans so that the ratio of fruit to sugar is 5:1.

For producing jam, frozen fruit from cans is defrosted and the sequence in Figure 22–1 is followed. The amount of sugar added results in a fruit-to-sugar ratio of 1:1. The pectin must be dispersed in the water before added to the mix. Water evaporated during the heating results in a soluble solids content of 68%. Blackberry jelly is produced by a similar process except that only clear juice is used, the amount of pectin is doubled, the soluble solids content is 65%, and the pH is adjusted to 2.9–3.2. Some blackberries are

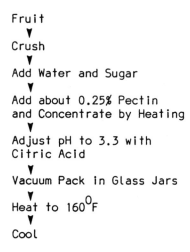

Fruit
▼
Crush
▼
Add Water and Sugar
▼
Add about 0.25% Pectin
and Concentrate by Heating
▼
Adjust pH to 3.3 with
Citric Acid
▼
Vacuum Pack in Glass Jars
▼
Heat to 160°F
▼
Cool

FIGURE 22–1.   Manufacture of fruit jam.

canned and heat-processed in water or light syrup for use as pie filling or in syrup for use in other desserts.

BLUEBERRIES

Blueberries are harvested from both wild plants and cultivated varieties. In the United States, blueberry cultivation is mainly in New Jersey, Michigan, and North Carolina. Blueberry bushes require an acid soil and yield fruit the first year after planting or the first year after the plants have established growth. There are many varieties of both high-and low-bush blueberries. The fruit of the blueberry ripens 50–65 days after the blooms occur. At the processing plant, the freshly harvested berries are passed through a fanning mill where small twigs and leaves are separated by air. They are then graded for size, washed in a flotation-type washer, and passed over an inspection belt where green or partially ripe specimens are picked out by hand. Blueberries handled as the fresh product are usually hand-poured into small baskets, holding 1 pt or 1 qt (473 ml or 946 ml). The baskets are then overwrapped with cellophane, and the product is held at refrigerator temperatures above freezing. Fresh blueberries should be cooled to 32°–35°F (0°–1.7°C) and held at this temperature until sold to the consumer. In this condition, they have a storage life of 4–8 weeks.

Blueberries to be canned, mainly used for pie fillings, are cleaned and inspected, placed in cans, and the cans are then filled with water or with a 10–

30% sugar solution. The open cans are then exhausted or heated in free-flowing steam for 10 min, and finally sealed and heated for short periods in boiling water.

Frozen blueberries are generally used in the production of pie filling, pastries, and jam. Some are packed in retail-sized plastic pouches and sold as such at retail. The usual procedure is to freeze the cleaned and inspected berries on trays that are placed on racks and moved through a cold-air tunnel. The frozen berries are then run through a machine that breaks up clusters of the frozen fruit and the frozen product is packed volumetrically into metal cans holding about 20 lb (9.1 kg) of berries. The cans are closed with slip covers and placed in frozen storage. Some frozen berries may be mixed with dry sugar (4 parts berries to 1 part sugar) or with 50% sugar solution, placed in large metal slip cover containers, and frozen in bulk in cold-air rooms.

CRANBERRIES

In the United States, commercial cranberry production is carried out mostly in Massachusetts, Wisconsin, New Jersey, Washington, and Oregon. There are a number of commercial varieties of cranberries grown in swamp lands or under similar conditions. A period of about 4 years is required from planting to the first harvesting period. Since the blossoms develop in the spring and are susceptible to frost damage, and the plants are susceptible to freezing damage, bogs where the berries are grown may have to be flooded with water, as a protection against cold damage. Diesel oil or chemicals may be used to control weeds and moss in cranberry bogs. For harvesting cranberries, the bogs may be flooded with water to float the berries, which can then be shaken off by machine and collected from the water. In other instances, the bogs are not flooded; the berries are stripped from the vines mechanically and collected on catching frames.

At the processing plant, cranberries are cleaned in fanning mills, then dropped some distance to eliminate soft or rotten specimens (the defective berries do not bounce, those suitable for food bounce up over a barrier), then washed, first in acid or alkaline solutions to remove spray residues, then in water. Destemming is carried out in a rotating vegetable peeler fitted with a smooth bottom plate. Cranberries handled as fresh are packed in paper-lined wooden boxes, and the product is slowly cooled to 36°–40°F (2.2°–4.4°C). Cranberries should be held at 36°–40°F (2.2°–4.4°C) until sold to the consumer. At this temperature, cranberries have a storage life of several months. Cranberries may be held frozen prior to the manufacture of jelly or sauce. They are placed in large metal containers, frozen in bulk in cold-air rooms, and held in this condition until defrosted for purposes of preparing cooked products.

Large amounts of cranberries are used to produce cranberry jelly and cranberry sauce, both retailed as canned products. In the manufacture of cranberry sauce, water, about twice as much sugar as fruit, and about 0.3% of dispersed pectin are mixed together. The mixture is then cooked and evaporated in an open steam kettle to a soluble solids content of 65%. Citric acid solution is then added to bring the pH to 3.0–3.4. In manufacturing cranberry jelly, the clear juice, from the boiled fruit that has been passed through a pulper, is mixed with sugar, about 0.35% of dispersed pectin is added, and no water is used. The mixture is heated briefly to bring the soluble solids content to 65%, and citric acid solution is added to regulate the pH to 3.0–3.2. Both cranberry sauce and cranberry jelly are preserved by heat processing. If the product is heated to about 190°F (87.8°C) prior to filling into containers, further heating is not necessary to attain commercial sterility after sealing the containers. If packed at lower temperatures, the containers should be sealed and heated in a water bath or with sprays of water at 185°–200°F (85°–93.3°C) for 6–10 min prior to cooling.

Large quantities of cranberries are frozen for later processing into sauce, jelly, and juice. Frozen cranberries maintain good quality and have a relatively long shelf-life.

Cranberry juice cocktail is produced from the thawed cranberries. The juice is diluted with an equal volume of water, and sugar is added to bring the specific gravity up to 15°Brix. The juice is then clarified and filtered. The juice is then heated to 185°F (85°C) to inactivate enzymes. The hot juice is then filled into bottles or cans (must be lined with fruit lacquer), and the containers are sealed and laid on their sides to cool.

GRAPES

In the United States, grapes are grown mainly in California, New York, Pennsylvania, Michigan, and Ohio. Washington, Missouri, and Arkansas also produce some grapes. There are many varieties of grapes, but three are predominant in this country. Grapes are utilized to produce unfermented grape juice, vinegar, wine, raisins, jams and jellies, and as the fresh product for the table. Grapes are planted as vines or cuttings from older plants. The cuttings produce arms bearing fruit, the greatest yields coming after 3 yr of growth. Properly pruned and cared for, vines produce fruit for many years.

Grapes to be shipped as fresh are packed in wooden crates, then precooled to about 40°F (4.4°C) in railroad cars or refrigerated rooms. Generally, the grapes will be fumigated with sulfur dioxide prior to or during cooling to prevent mold growth. Grapes that are to be stored for future shipment should be packed in crates, precooled to 36°–40°F (2.2°–4.4°C), placed in refrigerated storage (29° to 32°F [−1.67° to 0.°C]), and fumigated with sulfur dioxide. they should be held in this manner until shipped. Periodic refumigation with sulfur dioxide may be required to prevent spoilage by molds. Under these conditions, grapes have a storage life of 1–7 months depending mainly on the variety. See Chapter 14 regarding the use of sulfite.

The Concord variety is chiefly used for the manufacture of grape juice. The grapes are washed in acid or alkaline solutions, then in water to remove spray residues, then destemmed and crushed by mechanical means. The crushed grapes are heated to about 180°F (82.2°C) to extract pigment from the skins, after which the heated material is subjected to mechanical pressure while enclosed in cotton press cloths. The juice is then filtered, pasteurized by heating to 170°F (76.7°C), and stored in bulk in covered tanks at about 40°F (4.4°C). This provides for the separation of tartaric acid salts (cream of tartar or potassium hydrogen tartrate). The juice is then syphoned off from the tartrate and treated with enzymes, which break down pectins, or with casein for purposes of clarification. It is then filtered and bottled. The bottles are capped and then pasteurized by heating in water at 170°F (76.7°C) for 30 min.

To produce grape juice concentrate, grape juice is subjected to heat and evaporation until concentrated. Volatile components can be recovered from the process, and they can be added back to the concentrate. The concentrated juice may be frozen in retail-sized containers, or it may be shipped in large tanks to food processors for remanufacturing purposes.

Considerable quantities of wine are manufactured in the United States. The European varieties of grapes are mainly used for making wine. The various procedures used in the production of wines will not be described, but the pressed juice, usually after treatment with sulfur dioxide or compounds that liberate sulfur dioxide (to destroy undesirable types of yeast), is allowed to ferment by natural yeasts surviving the sulfur dioxide treatment. During fermentation, sugars are converted to ethyl alcohol until a level of 12–14% alcohol is reached. Brandies may be made by distilling wine containing ethyl alcohol, and these may be used as such for fortifying wines to obtain a higher alcohol content.

In the manufacture of wine vinegar, fermented grape juice (containing alcohol) is allowed to drip over wood shavings in an enclosed cylindrical container. The shavings have been previously soaked in a high-quality vinegar. Air may be introduced into the generator under pressure. Bacteria of the *Acetobacter* group present (from the vinegar) on the shavings convert the ethyl alcohol in the wine to acetic acid.

$$\underset{\text{Ethyl alcohol}}{CH_3CH_2OH} + \underset{\text{Oxygen}}{O_2} \xrightarrow{\text{bacteria}} \underset{\text{Acetic acid}}{CH_3COOH} + \underset{\text{Water}}{H_2O}$$

The effluent from the vinegar generator may be collected and recycled to obtain a complete conversion of the ethyl alcohol. The finished vinegar may be stored for several months at 40°–50°F (4.4°–10°C), then filtered, bottled, and pasteurized.

Raisins are produced from grapes by sun drying and artificial drying. In sun drying, the grapes are picked as bunches and placed in a single layer on wooden trays between the rows of grape vines. The trays are tilted to face the sun. After they are partially dried, the grape bunches are turned and allowed to dry to the point where no juice can be pressed out. The trays are then stacked, and the air drying is continued in the shade until a moisture content of about 17% is reached. After drying, the raisins are placed in sweat boxes to equilibrate, or to even out, the moisture that is present, and then they are packed in retail size containers or in larger containers to be sold to the bakery trade.

In artificial drying, grapes are first dipped in 0.25–1% lye (sodium hydroxide) solution at 200°–212°F (93.3°–100°C) for 2–5 sec to remove a natural wax that impedes drying and to check or crack the skin of the grape to facilitate drying. They are then washed, placed on trays, and treated with sulfur dioxide to prevent enzymatic and nonenzymatic browning during drying. Hence, instead of having the dark brown color of raisins that would normally be expected, the raisins will be of a light yellow color when dried. It should be noted, however, that the use of sulfites in foods are under strict regulations (see Chap. 14). Raisins are dried at temperatures not exceeding 165°F (73.9°C) and at a low relative humidity (about 25%). After the moisture content has been lowered to about 16–18%, the raisins are packaged in containers of various sizes to be sold at retail or for use by the food industry.

Although the freezing of grapes is not of industrial significance, some grapes are frozen, chiefly for use in the production of fruit cocktail. Muscat, Thompson seedless, and Ribier varieties are best for freezing. The grapes are precooled, washed, destemmed, sorted, and packed into 30-lb (13.6-kg) containers, using 18 lb (8.2 kg) of grapes and 12 lb (5.4 kg) of 55°Brix syrup, and then they are frozen.

Some grapes, for example, the Concord variety, are used for producing jelly and jam, with jelly making up the larger part. In jelly making, sugar and about 0.25–0.3% of dispersed pectin are mixed with the clarified grape juice, and the mixture is concentrated in open kettles to a soluble solids content of about 65%. Citric acid solution is added to adjust the pH to 3.0–3.2. The product is then poured into glass jars, vacuum capped, and sprayed with hot water to bring the temperature of all parts to about 160°F (71.1°C), after which the product is cooled.

RASPBERRIES

There are many varieties of raspberries that are either red, black, or purple in color. The purple varieties have been produced by cross breeding the red and black varieties. Raspberries grow on canes the second year after planting, and since the canes produce fruit only once, they must be pruned each year. Raspberries are grown over most parts of the United States, but they are sensitive to both extreme heat and extreme cold. Therefore, in certain areas, the plants may need some type of protection from extremes of weather. Because of their delicate structure, raspberries must be handled carefully during their harvest and processing. They are generally harvested into shallow trays, to prevent crushing, in which they are transported to the plant.

At the processing plant, the fruit is washed with gentle sprays of water and drained on a metal mesh belt. If the product is to be handled in the fresh state, it is placed in small, retail-sized baskets usually with a cellophane overwrap and quickly cooled to 31° to 32°F (−0.56° to 0°C). In this condition, the fruit has a storage life of only 5–7 days.

Some raspberries are frozen for the bakery trade and many for the manufacture of raspberry jam and jelly. To prepare them for freezing, the washed and drained berries may be placed in wooden barrels without sugar, then placed in a room at 0°F (−17.8°C) or below and allowed to freeze slowly. Usually, however, they are mixed with sugar (three parts fruit to one part sugar) then packed in slip cover cans of 50-lb (22.7-kg) capacity. The covered fruit is allowed to freeze in cold rooms at 0°F (−17.8°C) or below. In the manufacture of jam, the defrosted fruit is passed through a pulper that allows essentially all the berries with the seeds to pass through the strainer. Sugar and water are then added, the amount of sugar depending on whether the frozen product was packed with or without sugar. About 0.1–0.15% dispersed pectin is then added and the product is heated in open kettles to concentrate it to a soluble solids content of about 68%. Citric acid solution is then added to adjust the pH to 3.3, and the fruit is packed in glass jars and vacuum capped. The jars of product are then heated to bring the temperature of all parts to about 160°F (71.1°C), after which the product is cooled. Few raspberries are canned.

STRAWBERRIES

Different varieties of strawberries are grown in many areas of the United States, harvested in the winter and spring in southern states and in late spring and summer in northern states. Strawberries require fertile soil, hence soil treatment with fertilizers is usually required. Strawberries are planted as 1-year-old plants that produce the next year. The strawberry plant is a perennial that, if properly cared for, will produce for several years.

For handling in the fresh state, they are usually picked with the calyx or cap intact, since this enhances the keeping quality of the fruit. For processing, the berries are picked without the cap. The berries are placed in baskets of 1-lb (454-g) capacity, and the baskets are placed in crates for transportation to the processing plant. At the processing plant, the berries are washed, inspected on belts to remove green and rotten specimens, then repacked in baskets and crates for shipment as the fresh product. They are then cooled to 31° to 32°F (−0.56° to 0°C) and should be held at this temperature until sold to the consumer. In this condition, they have a storage life of about 10 days. In some cases, strawberries for the fresh trade are precooled in refrigerated water.

Large amounts of strawberries are frozen to be sold to the consumer as such or to be used for the manufacture of jams and jellies or for use in the bakery trade. Few strawberries are canned. Frozen strawberries for retail are sliced, mixed with sugar (four parts fruit to one part sugar), and packed in 12-oz or 1-lb (341-g or 454-g) cardboard, metal end, packages. Some strawberries are frozen individually (whole) on wire mesh belts and packaged in cartons, the cartons overwrapped and placed in shipping cases for holding in frozen storage.

Strawberries used for the manufacture of other foods are usually frozen whole, in wooden barrels, mixed with sugar. A proportion of fruit to sugar of 3:1 or 2:1 may be used. The barrels of fruit are placed in cold rooms at −10°F (−23.3°C) or below. In order to mix the sugar with the fruit, the barrels are rocked during filling and rolled periodically during the several days required for freezing. The frozen fruit is sometimes stored at 10°F (−12.2°C). Strawberry and sugar mixtures may also be packed in slip cover cans holding 30 lb (13.6 kg) of product.

In the manufacture of strawberry jam, water is added to the defrosted fruit mixture, as well as more sugar, the amount of sugar depending on how much sugar was added to the frozen product. About 0.25–0.3% of dispersed pectin is added, and the product is heated in open kettles to a soluble solids content of 65%. The pH is then adjusted to 3.3 with citric acid solution, and the preserve is packed in glass jars and vacuum capped. The sealed jars are then heated to a temperature of about 160°F (71.1°C) (all parts), then cooled. Strawberry jelly is manufactured in a similar manner to that of strawberry jam, except that the fruit is first put through a finisher, after which the juice is clarified or filtered. In manufacturing strawberry jelly, about 0.3–0.35% dispersed pectin is used, and the pH is regulated to 3.0–3.2.

APPLES

In this country, apples are grown in practically every state. They are grown commercially in 35 states with the heaviest production taking place in Washington, New York, Virginia, Michigan, California, and Pennsylvania. There are hundreds of varieties of apples that may be grown on trees produced from seedlings that were grown in nurseries, or from grafts on existing apple trees. The fruit is developed on spurs formed by branchlets of three or more years of growth, the tree yielding fruit for many years thereafter. Fertilization of the soil and periodic pruning and thinning of apple trees are considered necessary for good apple crops.

Apples are used as the fresh fruit, and apples not suitable for fresh fruit are used for the production of juice, cider, sauce, vinegar, jam, jelly, pie filling, and as an ingredient in a variety of baked goods. Pectin is extracted from the peels and cores.

After harvesting, the fruit are washed in dilute HC1 or NaOH solutions to remove spray residues and are rinsed. Apples are cooled to, and stored at, 32°F (0°C) until shipped. Increased storage life is attained by reducing the amount of oxygen and increasing the amount of carbon dioxide in the atmosphere around the apples.

For the production of apple juice, see Figure 22-2. Some juice is not processed beyond the pressing stage and is sold as such or as unpreserved cider.

When vinegar is produced from apple cider, the juice in tanks is seeded with cultures of yeast and allowed to ferment for up to several weeks, depending on ambient temperatures. The fermented juice, containing ethyl al-

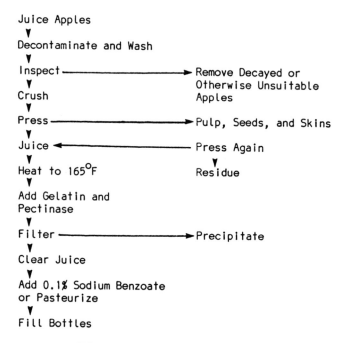

FIGURE 22-2.   Manufacture of apple juice.

cohol, is then mixed with some vinegar and allowed to drip over wood shavings that have been soaked in high-quality vinegar and enclosed in a wooden cylinder (closed but not airtight). Bacteria on the wood shavings convert the ethyl alcohol to acetic acid. This is described above in the production of vinegar from wine. The effluent from the generator may be run through a second time. When the alcohol has been converted to acetic acid, the vinegar is filtered (if necessary), filled into bottles, and the bottles are capped and heated in water until a temperature (in all parts) of about 165°F (73.9°C) is reached.

For the production of apple slices, apples are size-graded peeled, cored, sliced, and immersed in a 3% salt solution. Just before filling into cans, the slices are rinsed to remove salt. They are then filled into cans with 40% sugar solution. The cans are then heat-exhausted, sealed, and heat-processed.

For the production of frozen apple slices, there are a number of procedures, but, basically, the slices are immersed in brine, subjected to vacuum (to remove air), reimmersed in brine, washed, and packed with sugar in a ratio of 4 fruit to 1 sugar. The product is then frozen. One method differs in that a bisulfite dip is included to prevent nonenzymatic browning.

Some apples are dried, although the volume of this type of product has decreased in recent years. For drying, the peeled, cored, and sliced apples are first treated in a weak solution of citric acid and a bisulfite dip. The bisulfite provides sulfur dioxide that inhibits enzymatic browning. The sulfured slices should be held in refrigerated storage for at least 24 hr to allow the sulfur dioxide to penetrate the apple slices. The apple slices are eventually spread on the slatted floors of natural draft, loft-type kilns. In the kilns, heated air rises through the apple slices and removes moisture. After the moisture content has reached about 10%, the apples are packaged in moistureproof containers to be used in the bakery trade.

For the production of apple sauce, peeled and cored apples are sliced, cooked in steam, pulped, and heated to 190°F (87.8°C) with added sugar. The sauce is filled into glass jars that are then sealed and heated to 200°F (93.3°C), then cooled.

Pectin or pectin solutions may be manufactured or obtained from dried apple peels and cores. Fruit contains pectin substances in a form that is not water dispersable, and in this form, cannot be used for the manufacture of jams, jelly, and other foods. The pectin substances in fruits are in the form of protopectin, a more complex, longer chain of the carbohydrate, galacturonic acid (a 6-carbon compound). To obtain pectin that is dispersable in water, the dried apple substances are heated in boiling water for about 40 min. The heat, together with the acid present in the fruit, hydrolyzes the protopectin to pectin, a substance that contains fewer galacturonic acid units than does protopectin. In the presence of large proportions of sugar (about

65% soluble solids) and acid, to provide a pH around 3.0, pectin will form a gel like that which provides the semisolid form for jams and jellies. After extracting the pectin from apple peels and cores, the solution is separated, and the residue is pressed between cloths to obtain more of the extract. The extract is then filtered, bottled, and pasteurized as a pectin solution to be used as such, or it may be spray dried to a moisture content of about 5% and handled in this form. When used, the dried material (pectin) must be dispersed by fast agitation in water, or mixed with granulated sugar to disperse in water, before adding as an ingredient of foods. If added to foods as such, pectin forms lumps that become caked with gelatinous material on the outside, preventing the pectin from dispersing.

Low methoxy pectin may be produced from pectin by treating solutions of this material with an enzyme (pectin methyl esterase). This treatment removes methyl groups from the ester group of the galacturonic acid unit. Low methoxy pectin has the property of forming gels in the presence of comparatively low concentrations of soluble solids (sugar) and at comparatively high pH (as high as pH 6.5), provided that a source of calcium is present. Low methoxy pectin solutions are dried in the usual manner. Low methoxy pectin (less than 50% methoxylated) permits the production of low-calorie jams and jellies, because of the lowered sugar requirement for obtaining the gel.

Some apple jelly is produced. While the unclarified juice is high in pectin, after clarifying, most of the pectin has been removed; therefore, sugar, some water, and about 0.4% pectin are added and mixed. The mixture is then concentrated, by heating in open kettles, to a soluble solids content of about 65%. Citric acid solution is added to regulate the pH to 3.0–3.2, and the jelly is placed in glass jars, capped, pasteurized, and cooled in the usual manner.

APRICOTS

In the United States, apricots are grown mainly in California, Washington, and Utah. Only two or three varieties are grown commercially. Apricots are budded or grafted on seedling stocks of apricot, plum, or peach trees that are 1 year old. The spurs rarely produce well for more than 3 years, so pruning and renewal are required.

Some apricots are distributed as the fresh product, but the bulk of apricots are preserved mainly by drying for use in the bakery trade or in the home. Some apricots are frozen, and some are canned as the halved fruit. Some are also canned as pie filling, baby food, nectar, and jam.

To prepare the fruit for use as a fresh product, it is washed in dilute acid or alkaline solutions to remove spray residues, then in water. It is then packed in shallow boxes and cooled to 31° to 34°F (−0.56° to 1.1°C). The fresh fruit should be held at 31° to 32°F (−0.56° to 0°C) until sold to the consumer. In this condition, it has a storage life of about 1–2 weeks.

In the drying of apricots, the washed fruit is halved and pitted (without peeling) by machine. It is then subjected to a sulfite treatment to inhibit both enzymatic and nonenzymatic browning. It should be noted, however, that the use of sulfites is closely regulated (see Chap. 14). The fruit is then dried to a moisture content of 26–30%. It is then packaged in retail-sized containers or in larger ones for wholesale distribution for industrial use.

Frozen apricots are usually packed as the halved fruit in syrup, but may be packed with sugar. The washed and pitted fruit may or may not be peeled by spraying the halves (cup down) with a hot, weak solution of sodium hydroxide, then washing with dilute citric or hydrochloric acid solution prior to preparing for freezing. Eventually, the fruit is mixed with a 40% syrup containing 0.1% ascorbic acid (to prevent browning) in proportions of 1 part fruit to 1 part syrup. It is then placed in slip cover cans holding 30 lb (13.6 kg) of product and frozen in cold rooms at −10°F (−23.3°C) or below. Some frozen apricots are mixed with granulated sugar containing ascorbic acid. Other packs of apricots are prepared from blanched apricots (the heat treatment destroying enzymes that might cause discoloration). Still others are prepared from fruit that has been treated to inhibit enzyme action by immersing for 3–4 min in solutions of 0.4–0.5% sulfur dioxide. The sugared, blanched, or sulfured fruit is frozen in slip cover cans holding 30 lb (13.6 kg) of product.

For canning, apricots are washed, graded, halved, and pitted (but not peeled). The fruit is then filled into cans to which syrup is added. The cans are then exhausted, sealed, and heat-processed. for pie fillings, no syrup is added to the cans. For baby food, the fruit is pureed, after removing pits, and fibers are removed. Sugar and tapioca are added to the jars, which are then heat-processed. For producing nectar, the puréed fruit is sweetened with sugar syrup and adjusted for acidity with citric acid before filling into cans. For producing jams, the fruit is ground and mixed with sugar, water, and 0.35–0.42% dispersed pectin. The mixture is then heated in open kettles to provide a soluble solids content of about 65%. Citric acid solution is then added to regulate the pH to 3.3, after which the mixture is bottled, capped, and pasteurized.

BANANAS

Bananas are not grown commercially in the continental United States, but some are grown in Hawaii and shipped to the mainland. In the western hemisphere, the chief production of bananas occurs in Mexico and the Central American countries, in Cuba, Jamaica, Haiti, the Dominican Republican,

Honduras, Colombia, and Brazil. Bananas are also grown in some Asian and Middle Eastern countries.

Banana trees are started from young plants that bud from the underground stem or bulb of older plants. The trees bear mature fruit 13–15 months after planting, depending on climate, and each plant requires an area of 100–400 ft^2 (9.3–37.2m^2), depending on soil and water conditions. The trees develop flowering stalks with male and female flowers, and the female flower eventually becomes the fingers (single bananas) of the hand. Only one stem (bunch) of bananas is produced per tree.

The banana stem or bunch contains 6–14 hands (clusters of single bananas on the stem) and weighs 30–130 lb (13.6–59 kg). The stem is harvested when the single bananas are mature but green. The tree is then cut down. Bananas are handled mainly as the fresh fruit and shipped from the growing area while still green. At one time, bananas were shipped as bunches, on the stem, but today, they are handled mostly as hands or groups of single bananas, cut from the stem and packed in plastic-lined boxes. They may be treated with fumigants prior to boxing and should be precooled to 57°–62°F (13.9°–16.7°C). Bananas are subject to a chilling injury if held below 55°F (12.8°C); low temperatures kill certain surface cells and prevent normal ripening. Nor should bananas be held for extended periods at temperatures above 70°F (21.1°C); they must, therefore, be shipped under controlled temperatures. Bananas are ripened at 58–64°F (14.4–17.8°C), but the process can be accelerated by subjecting the fruit to ethylene gas.

While bananas are handled mostly in the fresh state, some are peeled, puréed, and canned for the bakery and soda fountain trade. In such cases, the puréed banana pulp is quickly heated to about 280°F (137.8°C) in a heat exchanger, held at this temperature for a few seconds, cooled in a heat exchanger, filled into sterile, large-sized cans and sealed under aseptic conditions. In such an operation, all parts of the process must be accomplished so that the cooling, filling, and sealing operations are done with the equipment presterilized and the containers sterilized just prior to filling. The cans must also be sealed under high temperature steam or inert gas. Essentially no bananas are frozen and only a very small amount is dried.

CHERRIES

Cherries are grown in essentially all states of this country, but commercial production is limited to about 12 states—Michigan, New York, Wisconsin, and Pennsylvania being the chief producing areas. There are many varieties of cherries that come under two general types: sweet and sour. Sweet cherries are used chiefly for sale in the fresh condition and for the production of maraschino cherries. About equal amounts of sour cherries are canned and frozen. Cherry trees, set out as 1- or 2-year-old stock, bear fruit the year after planting. They should be pruned yearly.

Sweet cherries to be shipped as fresh, or manufactured as some types of maraschino cherries, are picked with stem on, when bright red or black in color. Sour cherries are picked without the stem when deep red. Cherries are brought to the processing plant in lug boxes. At the processing plant, sweet cherries are washed in dilute acid or alkali solution to remove spray residues, then in clear water. Fresh cherries should be cooled to 31° to 33° F ($-0.56°$ to 0.56°C) and held at this temperature until sold to the consumer. Under such conditions, sweet cherries have a storage life of 10–14 days.

Maraschino cherries are produced with or without stems. The fruit is graded for size, then washed and inspected to remove defective specimens. The cherries are next pitted by machine (the stem left on for some types of product). Then the cherries are placed in barrels, covered with a 2% sodium chloride solution containing 0.6% sulfur dioxide (as such or as a bisulfite salt) and about 0.36–0.48% calcium carbonate, after which the barrels are covered. The sulfur dioxide bleaches out the color of the fruit and the calcium in the calcium carbonate tends to firm it. It should be noted that the use of sulfites is now strictly regulated (see Chap. 14). The barrels of fruit are then placed in cold storage (above freezing temperature) and rolled several times daily over a period of about 60 days. After curing, the cherries are leached in running water to remove sulfur dioxide, then cooked in several changes of boiling water. They are then held in a coloring solution for several days. The cherries are then removed from the colorant and covered with a 0.5% solution of citric acid to set the color. After holding for several days, the acid solution is poured off, and the fruit is packed in jars and covered with a hot, 12–20% sugar solution, after which the jars are capped. The bottled cherries are pasteurized in water at 170° or 180°F (76.7° or 82.2°C) to bring the temperature of all parts to about 165°F (73.9°C). Some maraschino cherries are packed in barrels and covered with a 12–20% sugar solution containing 0.1% sodium benzoate for purposes of preservation. Some maraschino cherries with syrup, in barrels, may be heated to about 165°F (73.9°C) in all parts by coils of metal, through which steam is allowed to flow, prior to heading the barrels.

In the canning of cherries, the fruit is washed and inspected, green and decayed specimens being floated out in water or removed by hand from an inspection belt. The cherries are then sized to facilitate pitting, pitted by machine and, if stems are present, the stems are pulled out by machine prior to pitting. Cherries are added to the can after which the cans are filled with water or syrup. If syrup is used, it may vary in concentration from 10–40%. The open cans are then exhausted or heated in free-flowing steam or water at about 200°–210°F (93.3°–98.9°C) for 10–20 min to remove air, after which they are sealed and heat-processed.

In the freezing of cherries, the fruit is soaked in cold water and, if over-ripe, some calcium chloride is added to the water to firm the fruit. It is then graded for size automatically and passed over inspection belts where green and rotten specimens are picked out. After the pits are removed by machine, the cherries are packed in 30- or 50-lb (13.6- or 22.7-kg) slip cover cans or in 50-gal. (189.3-liter) barrels as a mixture of 3 parts fruit to 1 part sugar. The closed cans or headed barrels are placed in a blast freezer or in a freezer room respectively, and the product is frozen.

GRAPEFRUIT

Essentially, all the grapefruit grown in this country is produced in Florida, Texas, Arizona, and California. There are a number of varieties of grapefruit. The trees are planted from nursery stock, and the tree blossoms and fruit must be protected against freezing temperatures. Grapefruit trees require some pruning. Grapefruit is harvested when the fruit has a soluble solids content of 6.5 parts to 1 part acid. The soluble solids are mainly sugar, and the acid is calculated as citric.

At the processing plant, the fruit is inspected to remove undesirable specimens and materials. The fruit is then washed in detergent and one or more microbial inhibitors, dried, waxed, and polished. It is then size-graded and boxed. If it is not fully colored, it is held at 65°–70°F (18.3°–21.1°C) in a weak ethylene atmosphere. When ready for shipment, the fruit is cooled to 50°F (10°C) and held at that temperature until sold.

Some grapefruit is canned as segments. The washed and graded fruit is immersed in boiling water for 4–6 min to loosen the skin. The skin is then scored and removed. This leaves some of the white portion (the albedo) on the fruit. To remove the albedo, the fruit is immersed or sprayed for 25–35 sec with a 2–5% solution of sodium hydroxide at 170°–180°F (76.7°–82.2°C), then washed in cold water. The segments of peeled grapefruit are then separated. After separating, the segments of fruit are added to cans, covered with a 35–65% sugar solution, and the open cans are heated in water at 175°F (79.4°C) for 15–18 min. The cans are then sealed and heated in water at 180°F (82.2°C) for periods depending on the size of the container.

Some grapefruit segments are used in the production of fruit salad. For the production of grapefruit juice, grapefruits are washed, cut into halves, and the juice is extracted. The juice is strained, deaerated, flash pasteurized, and cooled to about 176°F (80°C). At that temperature, the juice is filled into cans or bottles with or without a sweetener. The containers are then sealed and inverted. After 3–4 min, the cans are cooled until the temperature of the juice is lowered to about 100°F (38°C).

Most of the pectin produced in this country is manufactured from grapefruit peel, the albedo of which contains a large amount of pectic substances. In the manufacture of pectin from citrus fruits, peel from the decontaminated and washed fruit is first treated with hydrocarbon solvents to remove the flavedo (the colored portion), then ground, and heated in water to which some hydrochloric or citric acid has been added. After heating, the water extract is filtered and spray dried. Low methoxy pectin may be prepared from the extract by treating with the enzyme, pectin methyl esterase, and then spray drying.

LEMONS

Lemon trees may be grown from nursery root stock, but mostly the fruit is grown on grafts made on stock of the sour orange. Once established, the trees may bear fruit for many years. Since the trees, and particularly the fruit, are damaged by freezing temperatures, they may have to be protected in cold weather. Lemons are produced in this country mainly in California and Arizona. They are harvested when the skin is green or silver in color and ripened to a yellow color in bins, the air of which contains some ethylene. Most lemons are marketed in the fresh state, and as such are handled in much the same manner as are grapefruit. Cooled to about 32°F (0°C) and held at this temperature, fresh lemons have a storage life of 1–4 months.

Some lemon juice is prepared and frozen as a lemonade concentrate. The fruit is washed, sized, and inspected, after which the juice is extracted and screened. Sugar is added to provide a soluble solids-to-acid ratio of 14:1–18:1. The mixture is then evaporated at low temperatures under vacuum to provide a 5:1 concentrate. The screened pulp (which contains some liquid) is then added to the concentrate to provide 2.4–4% pulp, by volume. The concentrated mixture is frozen to a slush having a temperature of 25°F (−3.9°C) in a refrigerated heat exchanger. The slush is filled into cans, the cans sealed and conveyed through a cold-air tunnel until the product is cooled to a temperature of −18°F (−27°C) or lower.

Some lemon juice is evaporated to a concentration of about 2:1 and packaged in glass or plastic containers with 0.1% sodium benzoate. Pulp and sugar are not added to this product, which requires no refrigeration. Pectin is manufactured from lemon peel as in the case of grapefruit.

MELONS

Melons belong, as do squash, to the cucumber family. There are two general types, the *cucumis* species, which includes muskmelon, cantaloupe, and honeydew melons, and the *citrullus* species, including the watermelon and the Chinese watermelon. There are numerous varieties of melon. Although they may be grown in almost any of the 50 states, except possibly Alaska, *cucumis* species require warm weather for good growth and 75–130 days from planting to harvesting; therefore, most are grown commercially in the southern states. The *citrullus* species are grown in the South, but can also be grown in those northern states where 130–140 days of growing weather prevail. In warmer climates, about 85 days are required from planting to maturity.

Melons are planted as seed but may be started in greenhouses or hot frames and set out as plants. Melons do not improve in flavor after harvesting, hence, are picked when fully ripe. Care must be taken to prevent bruising during harvesting and handling. Melons are mostly handled as the fresh product.

At the packing plant, melons are washed, drained, dried, and shipped to retail markets in wooden crates.

Melons are not preserved by drying. Some melons are frozen as melon balls. In preparation for freezing, the melons are halved, the seeds are removed, and the melon meat is removed in ball-shaped pieces. The melon balls are washed with sprays of water, drained, and filled into liquid-tight cartons and covered with syrup (25–30% sugar), and the cartons are sealed. This product is frozen and stored at $0°F$ ($-17.8°C$) or below until shipped to the retailer. Frozen melons should be held at $0°F$ ($-17.8°C$) or below until sold to the consumer. Some melons are used in the production of fresh fruit salad.

ORANGES

The orange is utilized as a food to a greater extent than any other citrus fruit. The trees are set out from nursery stock and must be protected from freezing weather. As with other citrus trees, some pruning has to be done each year. The five states that produce oranges commercially are Florida, California, Arizona, Texas, and Louisiana, with Florida being, by far, the greatest producer. About three-quarters of all oranges, in this country, are used for the production of frozen juice concentrate and for the so-called "fresh" orange juice. Fresh oranges are picked and handled much in the same manner as are grapefruit. When picked, the solids to acid ratio should be 12:1–18:1. Oranges may be dyed by immersing in a solution of certified food dye at $120°F$ ($48.9°C$) for about 3 min prior to waxing, polishing, and cooling, since the color of the skin is often green when the fruit is picked. Some oranges are cooled to $32°–40°F$ ($0°–4.4°C$) and others to $40°–44°F$ ($4.4°–6.7°C$), depending on variety. They should be held at these temperatures until sold to the consumer. Under these conditions, they have a storage life of 1–3 months, depending on variety.

Much orange juice is frozen in a sequence as shown in Figure 22-3. The

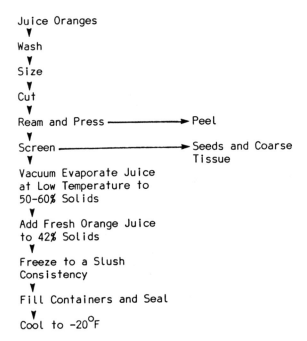

FIGURE 22-3.   Manufacture of concentrated orange juice.

addition of orange juice is to add back flavor, which is lost during the vacuum step.

Orange juice may be frozen in slabs and eventually defrosted and shipped as a slush to be pasteurized and sold as the single strength product. Some orange juice is canned. The juice, filtered from pulp, is heated to 180°–200°F (82.2°–93.3°C), added to the can at this temperature and the cans are sealed, inverted, and air-cooled.

Some orange juice is canned, requiring no refrigeration from a public health standpoint. The process involves the extraction of orange juice from the fresh fruit and collecting it in tanks where it is adjusted for acidity and soluble solids content. The juice is then pasteurized to destroy microorganisms and to inactivate enzymes and it is filled into cans while hot. It is then rapidly cooled to 100°F (37.8°C). Although the product is microbiologically stable at room temperature, there are slight reductions in the nutritional and organoleptic qualities of the product during extended storage. These losses can be prevented by storing at lower temperatures—the lower the better. Pectin and low methoxy pectin may be manufactured from orange peel, as in the case of grapefruit.

PEACHES

Peaches are grown commercially in about 35 states in this country, California producing by far the largest amount. There are a number of varieties classified as clingstone or freestone varieties. The flesh of clingstone varieties, used primarily for canning, adheres tightly to the pit. In freestone varieties, used both as fresh and for canning, the flesh is easily separated from the pit. Peach trees, not long lived, are set out from nursery stock and produce significant quantities of fruit for 7–16 years. Yearly pruning and thinning of peach trees is practiced. Peaches are harvested or picked when in the firm, ripe condition, but before they become soft. The fruit is picked into buckets or bags that are emptied into lug boxes for transportation to processing plants.

At the processing plant, peaches to be handled as fresh are washed in dilute acid or alkaline solutions to remove spray residues, then rinsed in water and allowed to drain and dry. Decayed specimens are removed as the fruit passes over an inspection belt, and the unblemished fruit is packed in boxes. The fruit is air-cooled to 31° to 32°F ($-0.56°$ to 0°C) and should be held at this temperature until sold to the consumer. Handled in this manner, the fresh fruit has a storage life of 2–4 weeks.

Peaches to be canned are inspected to remove decayed and unripe specimens, graded for size, then passed through a machine that cuts each fruit in half and removes the pit. The peach halves, pit cup down, are then immersed in, or sprayed with, a hot lye solution (usually a solution of 6–8% sodium hydroxide at about 140°F [60°C]) for 45–60 sec. The peach halves are then discharged into a shaker-washer where they are subjected to heavy sprays of water that remove the loosened skin and residual alkali. Clingstone peaches are usually canned as halves, while freestone types are canned as slices; therefore the latter types will be sliced before placing in cans. Peaches may be peeled by immersing in alkaline solutions and then subjected to water sprays prior to halving and pitting, or they may be halved and pitted and then subjected to free-flowing steam for 1.25 min. They are then sprayed with water to remove the peel. The halves or slices are placed in cans, and the cans are filled with syrup, having a sugar content of 20–55%. The open cans containing the product are then exhausted by heating in free-flowing steam or water at 180°–200°F (82.2°–93.3°C) for 10 min. Finally, the cans are sealed and heat-processed, with or without agitation, in water at 212°F (100°C).

To produce frozen peaches, the fruits are pitted, peeled, and rinsed first in cool water and then in 2% citric acid. The peaches are then sliced and the slices are filled into containers to which is added 40°Brix syrup containing 0.1% ascorbic acid, and the product is then frozen.

Peaches to be dried, usually the freestone varieties, are washed to remove spray residues, inspected, halved and pitted, placed on wire mesh trays, and treated with sulfur dioxide to prevent discoloration. They are then dried to a moisture content of 26-30%. See Chapter 14 regarding the use of sulfite. Peaches may be puréed to produce a peach base for drinks or to produce peach nectar. To produce purée, peaches are prepared as above, then pulped and reduced to a purée. The purée is mixed with 0.14% ascorbic acid and pasteurized. It may then be filled, while still hot, into containers that are then exhausted, sealed, and quickly cooled, producing a shelf-stable product. The pasteurized purée may also be cooled quickly, filled into sterile containers, and distributed as a refrigerated product. To produce peach nectar, unpasteurized purée is mixed with sucrose syrup, and a small amount of citric acid may be added to adjust acidity. It is then deaerated, flash pasteurized, and filled into cans and sealed. The cans are then inverted for a few minutes, then cooled immediately, until the product temperature is lowered to about 100°F (37.8°C).

PEARS

There are many varieties of pears. The trees are set out as 1-year-old stock, and once they start to bear fruit, they may continue to do so for many years. Ordinarily, the trees are lightly pruned each year. Pears are grown in essentially all states of this country, but California, Oregon, and Washington account for the bulk of the commercial production. The Bartlett pear is the most important variety, both for consumption as fresh and for preservation by canning. Pears do not ripen successfully on the tree and are harvested while still green. They are transported to processing plants in lug boxes or pallet bins, the latter holding about 1000 lb (453.6 kg) of fruit.

At the processing plant, pears are washed in weak acid or alkaline solutions to remove spray residues. They are then washed in water, drained, and inspected to remove defective specimens. They are also usually graded for size, especially if they are to be canned, before placing in storage. Pears to be sold as fresh are cooled to 30° to 31°F ($-1.1°$ to $-0.56°C$) and, stored at this temperature, pears have a storage life of 2-7 months, depending on variety. The storage life of pears may be extended by about 3 months by regulating the oxygen content of the storage atmosphere to 2.5% and the carbon dioxide content to 5%. Pears that are overripe when picked are subject to scald and core breakdown during storage. Pears to be used as fresh fruit are ripened at 60°-70°F (15.6°-21.1°C) prior to or during shipment. After they are ripened, they should be held at 32°-35°F (0°-1.7°C) until processed or sold to the consumer.

Pears to be canned are handled in much the same manner as the fresh product, until removed from storage for processing. The pears may be peeled by machine or by immersion in dilute lye (sodium hydroxide) solutions (about 5%) at about 140°F (60°C) for 40–60 sec, then washed with heavy sprays of water. They are then split in half lengthwise, and the core is removed by machine. The pear halves are placed in cans and covered with a 10–40% sugar syrup, depending on the type of pack. The filled, open cans are then heat-exhausted in water at 175°F (79.4°C) for 10–12 min, after which they are sealed. They are then heat-processed for 10–35 min in boiling water, the time depending on the size of the container.

Pear purée is produced from deaerated pear pulp. Essence, recovered from the process, is added back to the purée, then pasteurized and filled into sterile cans that are then cooled. Pears are not preserved by freezing, commercially, and only a small amount is dried, to about 24% moisture.

PINEAPPLES

Pineapples grow on plants developed from crowns (top leafy portion of the fruit) or from slips and shoots of the plant. The fruit matures in about 1.5 years, but in climates where pineapple is harvested for purposes of canning, planting times are staggered such that some fruit reaches maturity and is harvested each month of the year.

There are two main varieties of pineapple. The red Spanish variety is grown mainly in Florida and the West Indies, as well as some other countries, and is used in the United States as the fresh product. The smooth cayenne variety is grown mainly in Mexico and Hawaii. The red Spanish variety, when ripe, is more acid and contains less sugar than does the smooth cayenne type. When ready for harvesting for purposes of canning, the smooth cayenne variety has about 0.5–0.6% acid (calculated as citric acid) and 10–12% sugar. The fruit is broken from the stalk. If the fruit is to be handled as fresh, it is placed in crates or trucks for transportation to the processing plant. If the fruit is to be canned, the crowns are broken off prior to placing in trucks or in crates and trucks.

Pineapples to be used as fresh may be harvested in the mature-green or ripe condition. They are packed in crates and air-cooled to 45°–55°F (7.2°– 12.8°C). In this condition, the mature-green fruit has a storage life of 3–4 weeks, while the ripe fruit has a storage life of 2–4 weeks. Spoilage of fresh fruit is usually caused by fermentation due to the growth of yeasts or molds.

Pineapple is canned in slices, chunks, crushed, or as pineapple juice. In canning, the fruit is first graded by machine for size. It is cut by machines (Ginaca machines) that cut off the top and bottom, remove a cylindrical section within the peel, and remove the cylindrical section of core from the center. The cut portions are then hand trimmed with knives by workers wearing rubber gloves. Rubber gloves are required since raw pineapple contains a very active proteolytic enzyme that will attack and erode the skin of hands coming in contact with the juice of the fruit. The fruit is next sliced, placed in cans, and covered with a 30%-50% sugar syrup or with pineapple juice containing added sugar. The filled open cans are heat-exhausted in water at 170°F (76.7°C) for 5-12 min, then sealed. Alternately, the syrup is subjected to vacuum and added to the fruit in machines in which the fruit has been subjected to vacuum. In such cases, the cans are sealed under vacuum. The sealed cans are heat-processed in boiling water, in open cookers that agitate the cans, for a period of 30-35 min. Pineapple pieces cut from whole slices, or crushed pineapple obtained from broken slices and from the flesh adhering to the shell remaining after the cylinder of fruit is cut out, may be canned in the same manner. In preparing crushed pineapple, sufficient sugar is mixed with the fruit to provide a total sugar content of 20-24%. The mixture is then cooked in open steam kettles for 10-11 min and filled into cans volumetrically while hot. The cans are sealed and heat-processed in boiling water and then cooled.

Pineapple juice may be obtained from the cylinders of fruit that were cut out by machines by grating and pressing them between cotton press cloths. Pineapple juice may also be prepared from the pressed grated pulp, obtained from the shell left after the cylinder of fruit has been cut out. Pineapples for juice should be harvested in the soft ripe stage in order to obtain the best flavored juice. After pressing, the juice is filtered to remove coarse particles. Next, it is heated to 180°-185°F (82.2°-85°C) in heat exchangers and filled into cans at this temperature. The cans are sealed, inverted, held in this manner for 20 min, then cooled. Some pineapple is also canned as crushed pineapple. Some pineapple is frozen, mostly for the bakery trade, and some pineapple is preserved by drying (15-20% moisture).

PLUMS

Plum trees are set out when they are 1 year old and bear fruit the next year. There are many varieties of plums grown in many areas of the United States. The prune plum, used for the production of dried prunes, is grown mainly in California. Purple plum types, used for canning, are grown mainly in Oregon and Washington.

At the processing plant, plums are washed in dilute acid or alkaline solutions to remove spray residues, then rinsed with water. They are next inspected to remove defective specimens, and graded for size. Those to be sold as fresh are packed in boxes and air cooled to 31° to 32°F (−0.56° to 0°C). In this condition, they have a storage life of 2-4 weeks. Plums to be canned are cleaned, inspected, and graded. Then they are placed in cans by hand and covered with a 25–30% sugar syrup. The filled, open cans are then heat exhausted in water at 180°–190°F (82.2°–87.8°C) for 12–15 min, after which the cans are sealed and heated in boiling water for 20–25 min, depending on the size of the container.

For the production of dried prunes, plums are washed, dipped in boiling lye solution (0.25–1.0% sodium hydroxide) for 5–30 sec, and washed. (The lye treatment enhances drying by its action on the skin of the fruit.) The plums are then dried to a moisture content of 22–25%.

Dried prunes may be canned in a syrup of 20°Brix with 0.4% citric acid, or they may be canned without added fluid (dry-packed). Prunes may also be packaged and distributed as such.

A significant quantity of prune juice is produced. Prunes are steamed 8–10 min to soften them and to inactivate enzymes. They are then reduced to a purée during which time they are pitted. The purée is then cooled to about 120°F (49°C). The purée is filtered and the juice obtained is adjusted to about 22.5°Brix, pasteurized, filled into bottles or cans that are then placed on their sides to sterilize the tops, and cooled. Plums are not commercially frozen.

FRUIT MIXTURES

A sizable quantity of fruit is consumed in such fruit mixtures as fruit cocktail and fruit salads. Canned fruit cocktail generally comprises a mixture of diced pears, peaches, pineapples, whole, small seedless grapes, and halved maraschino cherries in syrup. Fruit salads have a varied composition. Some fruit salads, canned in glass, may consist of bite-sized chunks of pineapple, cantaloupe, honeydew, red melon, and grapefruit, and whole seedless grapes in a light syrup or plain water. Some fruit salads may consist of small chunks of pears, peaches, and pineapple, halved apricots, and whole seedless grapes heat-processed in syrup in cans or jars.

23

Sugar

Sugar, the common name for sucrose (also saccharose), is extracted and refined from sugar cane and sugar beets. There are many substances chemically classified as sugars, and when these are referred to, they are always used with a qualifier such as in milk sugar (lactose), corn sugar (dextrose), and malt sugar (maltose). When the word *sugar* is used without a qualifier, it generally refers to the common sweetener (sucrose). Other sugars have varying degrees of sweetness relative to sucrose, and some sugars differ from sucrose in that they lend varying degrees of bitterness whereas sucrose imparts only a sweet taste. Other important sources of sucrose include palm and maple trees and fruits. Chemically, and in every other way, cane sugar and beet sugar are the same. In addition to providing energy for the body and sweetness to foods, sugar performs numerous other roles in the food industry. It is used in baked products where it contributes to the desirable texture of baked goods, and it stabilizes the foam of beaten egg whites. When it caramelizes, it imparts a unique but desirable color and flavor to surfaces of pastries and cakes. It is used in ice creams and dairy products, in beverages, in the home, in institutions and in restaurants for foods and beverages, in canned and frozen fruits, in canned vegetables, in jams and jellies, and in other types of food. Sugar is also used in some nonfood products. Sucrose is the most important of three naturally occurring disaccharides. It has the formula $C_{12}H_{22}O_{11}$. It may be hydrolyzed, yielding glucose and fructose (levulose), both 6-carbon sugars.

$$C_{12}H_{22}O_{11} + H_2O \rightarrow C_6H_{12}O_6 + C_6H_{12}O_6$$

Sucrose   Glucose   Fructose

SUGAR FROM CANE

Sugar cane is a giant grass belonging to the genus *Saccharum*. While nearly all sugar canes are of the same species, differences in growing condition (climate, etc.) affect the characteristics of the juices. For example, the sugar content of the juices from sugar canes grown in the tropics is higher than in sugar canes grown in cooler climates. In the United States, sugar cane is grown primarily in Louisiana, and some is grown in Florida and Hawaii. Cuba, Puerto Rico, the Virgin Islands, the Philippines, and other countries also produce sugar cane. Sugar cane is grown by planting cuttings from the stalk, each containing a bud. The length of time that the cane is allowed to grow before harvesting varies in different countries and may be from 7 months to 2 years. The yield of sugar from cane juice is about 14–17%. Sugar cane is harvested by cutting the stalks just above the ground. At this time, the tops of the stalks are cut off, because they contain high concentrations of an enzyme that hydrolyzes and greatly reduces the yield of cane sugar. Also at the time of harvesting, the leaves are stripped from the canes, although they may be burned off prior to harvesting. Parts of the sugar cane other than the tops contain some of the enzyme that converts sucrose, and so the cane must be processed shortly after harvesting in order to obtain maximum yields.

At plants producing raw sugar (see Fig. 23–1), the cane first passes through shredders and then through 3–7 roller mills that press out the juice. After the first pressing, the bagasse (the pressed cane) may be mixed with hot water or dilute hot cane juice and again pressed to extract more sugar. Following the final pressing, the bagasse is usually brought directly to the boilers, where it is used as fuel. The wet bagasse is reported to have about one-fourth the fuel value of ordinary fuel oil. However, bagasse is a woodlike fiber, and it also is used to manufacture wallboard. It has been the object of study for use in other applications.

The juice, which is dark green in color, has a pH of about 5.2. After extraction, the cane juice is strained to remove pieces of stalk and other detritus, and a mixture of lime and water (source of calcium hydroxide, $Ca(OH)_2$) is added to raise the pH. The juice is heated to precipitate and remove impurities. The limed mixture is then held in tanks, where the lime-impurities mixture is allowed to settle out, and the clear juice is separated from the sediment. The clear juice is then heated (at temperatures below the boiling point of water) under vacuum to evaporate water and concentrate the sugar to the point where there is a mixture of sugar crystals and molasses. More syrup may be added to the evaporation pans as the syrup is concentrated.

The mixture (called massecuite) is centrifuged to obtain the brown unpurified sugar. The liquid centrifuged from the sugar crystals still contains

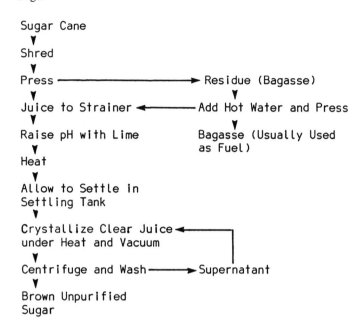

FIGURE 23-1.   Production of raw sugar from sugar cane.

dissolved sugar and is returned to the evaporation pans. When the molasses from the centrifuge treatment reaches a low enough concentration of sugar that removal of sucrose is uneconomical, it is called blackstrap. This is not discarded, but is not returned to the evaporation pans. Generally, blackstrap is sold to the fermentation industries for the production of rum. Sugar may be purified or refined at the plant that manufactures the raw sugar, but usually the raw sugar is packed in jute bags and shipped to sugar refineries. Higher grades of molasses for domestic use may be made from juice obtained from cane that is not pressurized sufficiently to extract all the liquid. The molasses is heated to 160°F (71.1°C) and canned or bottled hot. The containers are sealed, heated in water at 185°–200°F (85°–93.3°C) for 10 min, and immediately cooled.

Raw sugar, as delivered to the refinery, contains 97–98% sucrose. The first step in refining (see Fig. 23-2) consists of mixing the raw sugar with a hot saturated sugar syrup. This softens the film of impurities that envelop the sugar crystals. This mixture is then centrifuged, and during centrifugation, the sugar crystals are sprayed with water to remove some of the impurities. The washed sugar crystals are then dissolved in hot water, treated with lime to bring the pH to 7.3–7.6, and the temperature is raised to 180°F (82.2°C).

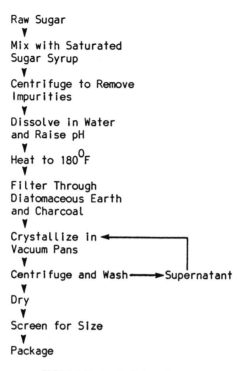

Raw Sugar
↓
Mix with Saturated
Sugar Syrup
↓
Centrifuge to Remove
Impurities
↓
Dissolve in Water
and Raise pH
↓
Heat to 180^0F
↓
Filter Through
Diatomaceous Earth
and Charcoal
↓
Crystallize in ←———————————┐
Vacuum Pans   │
↓   │
Centrifuge and Wash——→Supernatant
↓
Dry
↓
Screen for Size
↓
Package

FIGURE 23–2.   Refining of sugar.

The hot mixture is then filtered through diatomaceous earth or paper pulp. The coloring material in the sugar solution is removed by filtering the hot liquid through bone charcoal, after which the sugar is crystallized out in vacuum pans and centrifuged to separate it from the liquid. During centrifugation, the crystals are washed with water. They are then dried, screened for crystal size, and packaged. The finished dried sugar, which has an indefinite shelf-life, is made available in different grades. Large grained sugar is used for the manufacture of candy and other prepared sweet products. Ordinary table sugar is made up of fine-sized grains. Ultrafine sugar grains (for confectioner's sugar) are produced by grinding the crystals in pulverizing hammer mills. To prevent caking in confectioner's sugar, about 3% cornstarch is used. There are other intermediate grades. Sugar is also prepared as cubes or tablets by forming a mixture of sugar crystals and white sugar syrup under pressure, followed by drying. A variety of "soft sugars," ranging in colors from white through various shades of brown, are produced. These sugars are allowed to retain some of the molasses, which provides their unique flavor.

Invert sugar is made by heating sucrose in the presence of an enzyme (invertase) and some acid, whereupon it combines chemically with approximately $5\frac{1}{4}\%$ of its weight of water. The temperature must not be high enough to inactivate the enzyme.

$$C_{12}H_{22}O_{11} + H_2O \xrightarrow[\text{Enzyme}]{\text{Invertase}} C_6H_{12}O_6 + C_6H_{12}O_6$$

Sucrose Water Dextrose Levulose or Fructose

The dextrose is not as sweet as sucrose but the levulose is sweeter than sucrose with the result that the final syrup, invert sugar, is slightly sweeter than the syrups having the same concentration of sucrose. Invert sugar has special uses in the food industry. Mixtures of invert sugar and sugar are more soluble than sugar alone. In a proportion of 1:1, a mixture of invert sugar and sugar is more soluble than any other combination of their mixtures.

It should be noted that raw sugar contains thermophilic bacteria (spore-forming bacteria that grow at high temperatures—as high as 170°F [76.7°C]). If such bacteria are allowed to grow to high concentrations, they may serve as a source of contamination for such products as canned foods to which sugar is added. The spores of thermophilic bacteria are very difficult to destroy by heat, and canned foods can undergo some deterioration during heat processing. For this reason, during the various filtrations in which sugar solutions are held at high temperatures for comparatively long periods, they should be held at temperatures high enough to prevent the growth of thermophilic bacteria (about 185°F [85°C]).

BEET SUGAR

The sugar beet (*Beta vulgaris*) stores its sugar in the root, unlike the sugar cane, which stores its sugar in the stalk. Another difference between cane sugar production and beet sugar production is that the latter is a continuous operation and does not produce the intermediate raw sugar. Whereas sugar beets contain 16–20% of sugar as sucrose, the yield of sugar per acre (0.4 ha) is considerably less than that obtained from sugar cane, due to the quantity of beets or cane harvested per acre. Sugar beets are planted as seed and require 70 days or more from planting to harvesting. Since the plants are subject to bacterial or mold infection and to infestation with aphids, maggots, and other insects, the plants may need spraying during the growing season. In the United States, beets for sugar are grown mainly in Colorado, California, Michigan, Utah, Idaho, Nebraska, and Montana. Sugar beets are harvested and topped mechanically and brought to the processing plant in bulk by freight cars or trucks. They may be stored outside the processing plant in large piles until treated to extract sugar.

In extracting sugar from beets, the beets are first thoroughly washed to remove mud and stones, and then passed through mechanical slicers that slice them into thin shreds called cossettes. They are then covered with hot water to extract the sugar. Extraction is done even more quickly and more effectively by a continuous counter current extraction with water. The juice from the extraction process is treated with lime or calcium hydroxide and then with carbon dioxide. The lime removes impurities as a precipitate, and the carbon dioxide is used to precipitate the calcium hydroxide as calcium carbonate ($CaCO_3$). The juice is then filtered and again treated with carbon dioxide to precipitate residual calcium hydroxide. After a second filtration, the extract is treated with sulfur dioxide to bleach out colored components in the liquid. The liquid extract is then vacuum concentrated to 60–70% soluble solids and filtered through bone charcoal. Next, the filtered liquid is concentrated in vacuum pans to form crystalline sugar. The sugar is washed as it is centrifuged, dried, screened, and packaged, as in the case of cane sugar. In some manufacturing processes for beet sugar, the liquid from the third centrifuging is used for the manufacture of monosodium glutamate, a flavor enhancer used for many food preparations, including soups, gravies, Chinese foods, and meat dishes. Extracted beet pulp and the tops are dried and used as cattle feed.

OTHER SUCROSE SOURCES

Sucrose can be obtained from the sap of a variety of palm trees, one of the most important being the date palm (*Phoenix sylvestris*). Much of this sucrose is obtained in the Middle East by primitive methods that involve boiling in open kettles, after which there is separation of crystals from molasses, or the unseparated mass may be allowed to set into a whole sugar.

In the northern part of North America, sucrose is obtained from the sap of the hard maple tree (*Acer saccharinum*). Although the maple sap is largely sucrose, it contains unique impurities that impart to it (when concentrated) a special delicate flavor that makes the natural maple syrup a valuable flavoring for certain preparations. Sucrose can also be produced from the cane of the sorghum plant, which is related to the sugar cane but resembles the corn plant.

CORN SYRUP AND SUGAR

Although corn is not a source of sucrose, the value of corn sugar as a sweetener in the food industry makes it worthy of mention. Corn syrup (mainly dextrose but with maltose and other oligosaccharides) is produced through the hydrolysis of corn starch by either of two processes. In one process, corn starch is made into a water slurry of 35–40% solids, to which hydrochloric acid is added. The mixture is then heated in steam under pressure. When the conversion of the starch to syrup reaches a certain point, the acid is neutral-ized. The acid conversion cannot be allowed to proceed unchecked; other-wise some of the dextrose recombines to form undesirable high-molecular-weight products, known as reversion products, which could impart a bitter taste to the syrup. Fatty acids are removed by flotation and the syrup is then concentrated, clarified, and decolorized. The syrup may be passed through ion exchange resins to remove salts. In the final step, the syrup is evaporated, usually under vacuum, to a particular solids content. Crystalline sugar can be produced by spray drying the syrup.

A second hydrolytic process for producing corn syrup from corn starch involves the use of amylolytic enzymes (alpha and beta amylases). Beta amy-lase is specific in its action, attacking starch molecules at their nonreducing ends and causing progressive breaks in the molecule at 12-carbon intervals, with the resultant release of units of maltose (a 12-carbon sugar). Thus, by this conversion, the corn syrup will have a high maltose content. Other en-zymes, glucosidases, may also be used to supplement either of the two con-version processes. In this case, the syrup will contain significant amounts of glucose.

Corn syrups are divided into five commercial classes, depending on their DE value (dextrose equivalent value). By this classification scheme, pure dextrose is given a value of 100 DE.

Type	DE Value
Low conversion	28–38
Regular conversion	38–48
Intermediate conversion	48–58
High conversion	58–68
Extra high conversion	68–100

In addition to classifying syrups by their DE values, they are also classified by their solids contents.

Corn syrup and corn sugar are used to a large extent in the food industry. They are used to supplement sucrose because they are less expensive, while at the same time nearly as effective as sucrose in sweetening characteristics. In addition, they inhibit crystallization of sucrose, especially when their malt-ose content is high. They are especially useful in the baking and brewing in-dustries because of the quick and complete fermentability of dextrose. Their use in preserves minimizes oxidative discoloration, and other unique proper-ties make them useful in many other applications. Corn starch is also used to produce a high-fructose corn syrup (see Chap. 5).

24

Fats and Oils

Fats and oils are classified as lipids, which comprise an important category of nutrients for humans; the other two important categories of nutrients, of course, are proteins and carbohydrates. As the reader may recall from Chapter 9, lipids are esters of glycerol and fatty acids, and fatty acids are mostly long, straight, hydrocarbon chains, with varying degrees of hydrogen saturation of the carbon atoms, having a carboxyl group linked to one of the end carbon atoms. The esterification reaction may be reversed with the addition of alkali, which results in a combination of the fatty acids with the alkali to form soap, a reaction called saponification.

$$
\begin{array}{llll}
CH_2OOCR^1 & & CH_2OH & N_AOOCR^1 \\
| & & | & \\
CHOOCR^2 & + \quad 3N_AOH \longrightarrow & CHOH & + \quad N_AOOCR^2 \\
| & & | & \\
CH_2OOCR^3 & & CH_2OH & N_AOOCR^3 \\
\end{array}
$$

| Lipid | Alkali | Glycerol | Soaps |

The specific gravity of lipids is less than that of water, and these compounds are generally insoluble in water; therefore, they float in water. They are soluble in a variety of organic solvents (e.g., ether). They may be suspended in water as a stable emulsion in the presence of emulsifying agents (e.g., bile salts, alkali) that function by lowering the surface tension and by coating the lipid particles, preventing their coalescence.

The members of the fats and oils may differ from one another quite distinctly in physical, chemical, and dietary properties (melting points, caloric value, reactivity, mineral content, etc.). Some of the properties can be used to identify specific fats. For example, fats can absorb halogens at the point of unsaturation (a point of unsaturation where two neighboring carbon atoms in the chain each have only one hydrogen atom attached). Thus the iodine number of a fat refers to the amount of iodine (iodine being a halogen) in grams that 100 g of the fat can absorb. The saponification value of a fat refers to the amount of potassium hydroxide in milligrams that is neutralized by saponification of 1 g fat.

The fatty acids occurring in natural fats may contain 4–26 carbon atoms (generally an even number—see Table 24-1), and they may or may not be completely saturated with hydrogen. The general formula for saturated fatty acids is $C_nH_{2n}O_2$. For unsaturated fatty acids, the number of H atoms is less than $2n$ (e.g., H_{2n-2}, H_{2n-4}, etc.). Most fatty acids are straight chains, although a few may contain a ring of carbon atoms in the straight chain. An example of this type is chaulmoogric acid, which has been used in the treatment of leprosy, and is obtained from the chaulmoogra tree of east India.

Chaulmoogric acid

The unsaturated oils, such as some vegetable oils that are liquid at room temperature and are subject to oxidation (a deteriorative process), may be transformed to a solid at room temperature and at the same time stabilized against oxidative spoilage by hydrogenation. In hydrogenation, hydrogen is

TABLE 24-1.   Common Names of Saturated
Fatty Acids

Name	No. of C Atoms
Butyric acid	4
Caproic acid	6
Caprylic acid	8
Capric acid	10
Lauric acid	12
Myristic acid	14
Palmitic acid	16
Stearic acid	18
Arachidic acid	20
Behenic acid	22
Lignoceric acid	24
Cerotic acid	26

linked to unsaturated carbon atoms, though the process generally is not allowed to go to complete saturation. An example of a hydrogenation process follows.

$$C_3H_5(C_{17}H_{33}COO)_3 \ + \ 3H_2 \ \rightarrow \ C_3H_5(C_{17}H_{35}COO)_3$$

Liquid lipid (oil)   Solid lipid (fat)

Since the fatty acid part of fat molecules is the largest part, the fatty acids influence the properties of the fat, and the chemistry of fats and oils consequently is governed by the chemistry of the fatty acids they comprise.

Fats and oils have smoke-, fire-, and flash-points that define their thermal stability when heated in the presence of air. The smoke-point is reached when the temperature is sufficient to drive out decomposition products that can be seen as a smoke. As the temperature is increased to the flash-point, the decomposition products can be ignited but do not perpetuate fire. When the temperature is increased to the fire-point, the decomposition products will perpetuate a fire.

Lipids contribute to the diet in many ways. They are a primary source of energy, possessing more than twice the calories occurring in either proteins or carbohydrates. They act as vehicles for the fat-soluble vitamins A, D, E, and K and are important in the absorption of calcium, carotene, and thiamin. They also provide certain essential fatty acids that are required but cannot be produced by the body. Fatty acids, in the form of phospholipids, are essential to the body. These include phosphoglycerides (e.g., lecithin), phosphoinositides (e.g., diphosphoinositide), and phosphosphingosides (e.g., sphingomyelin).

Essentially, solid fats are of animal origin, and oils or fats, liquid at room temperature, are of vegetable origin. There are some exceptions, however. For instance, coconut oil is solid at ordinary room temperatures, having a melting point of 75°–80°F (23.9°–26.7°C). On the other hand, fish fats or oils are liquid at room temperature. Generally, the reason that some fats are solids and others are liquids at room temperature has to do with the percentage of saturated or unsaturated fatty acid in the fat molecules composing the fats. Stearic acid: CH_3—$(CH_2)_{16}$—$(COOH)$, is a saturated fatty acid. Linoleic acid: CH_3—$CH_2)_4$—$CH{=}CH$—CH_2—$CH{=}CH$—$(CH_3)_7$—$COOH$, is an unsaturated fatty acid. It should be noted that these two fatty acids have an equal number of carbons but that all the carbons in stearic acid have been saturated with hydrogen or have taken on all the hydrogen that they can accept, while 4 of the carbons in linoleic acid are unsaturated or could each accept one more hydrogen. Oleic acid: CH_3—$(CH_2)_7$—$CH{=}CH$—$(CH_2)_7$—$COOH$, which has only 2 carbons that could accept another hydrogen, has a melting point of 61°–62°F (16.1°–16.7°C). When oleic acid is present in fats, even in comparatively large amounts, the fats are generally solid at room temperature if no more unsaturated fatty acids are present.

Fats containing only saturated fatty acids of short-chain length (8 carbons or fewer) are liquid at room temperature, but generally such fats are not found in nature. However, such fats are found as components of some natural fats, such as butter made from cattle or goats' milk. It should be recognized that unsaturated fatty acids with 4 or more carbons which could accept another hydrogen are more reactive than saturated fatty acids and are especially apt to combine with the oxygen present in the atmosphere. This is especially the case when a carbon saturated with hydrogen is present between two groups of two carbons, each of which could accept another hydrogen: —CH=CH—Ch$_2$—CH=CH—. When the unsaturated fatty acids in fats become oxidized, the fat generally becomes rancid or has an off-flavor.

Butterfat, which is discussed in Chapter 16, will not be covered in this chapter. Nonedible lipid products, such as soaps, will also be omitted.

LARD

Lard, a solid fat (at room temperature), is obtained from animals (mainly hogs) by rendering (see Fig. 24–1). Rendering involves the melting out of the fat from fatty tissues and removal of the nonfat material by mechanical means. In wet rendering, the fatty tissues are heated in water with steam under pressure. After heating, the fat layer (on top) is pumped into one tank and the watery portion into another, for purposes of settling and removal of

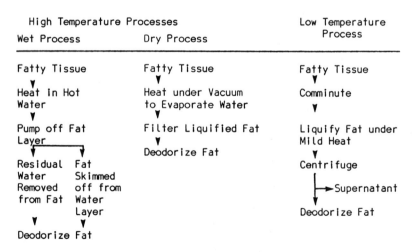

FIGURE 24–1.   Recovery of animal fats by rendering.

water in one case and skimming of the fat in the other. Dry rendering is accomplished by heating fatty animal tissues under vacuum until all of the water has been evaporated from the mass of material. The fat, while still warm enough to be liquid, is then filtered off from the residual tissues. Low-temperature rendering may be used to obtain animal fats. In this case, the tissue is first ground, then heated to a temperature only slightly higher than that of the melting point of the fat. The nonfat tissue is then removed from the fat by centrifugation. Most animal fats to be used in food materials are deodorized by blowing high-temperature steam through the liquid material before packaging. Beef tallow is rendered from the various fatty trimmings from sides or quarters of beef. Comparatively few cattle fats are used in foods today, but beef tallow has various other industrial uses.

Prime lard is rendered from fats deposited in body tissues, while ordinary lard is rendered mainly from the back fat portions, but also from the trimmings. It was once the custom to use lard in cooked foods or for cooking foods; however, its use has diminished with the increasing use of vegetable fats and oils.

Natural fats, including animal fats, tend to have some degree of organization with regard to the pattern in which the fatty acids are distributed on the glycerine molecules. This being the case, fat molecules containing three saturated fatty acids (fatty acid unable to accept more hydrogen) do not occur to any extent unless the content of saturated fatty acids exceeds two-thirds of the total fatty acids. Lard has about 40% saturated fatty acids. Interesterification of fats tends to distribute the fatty acids in a random manner as they are attached to the glycerine molecules. Interesterification usually raises the melting point of fats and oils. While the melting point of such fats as beef oleo and lard are not raised by interesterification, their characteristics and behavior in foods are changed. Interesterification can be brought about by heating the fat to the desired temperature, then adding a catalyst (sodium methoxide is often used as the catalyst). When the reaction is judged to be complete, phosphoric acid (about 85% strength) is added to destroy the catalyst. Natural lard occurs as clusters of crystals that grow larger as the lard is aged. Interesterification of lard changes the structure in such a manner that the crystals exist as finely dispersed particles. The grain of the lard is, therefore, much finer than that of the natural product. Fine-grain, interesterified lard has good creaming qualities and is desirable for the production of cakes and icings. On the other hand, the coarse-grained, natural lard has properties that make it better suited for the manufacture of flaky pastries and pie crusts.

OILS

There are many oils, most of which are of vegetable origin. Included among these are coconut oil and palm kernel oil, in both of which the fatty acid composition consists of 45–80% lauric acid, a 12-carbon saturated acid. Other vegetable oils include cottonseed, peanut, olive, sesame, corn, soybean, and canola. These oils contain a preponderance of the unsaturated acids—linoleic (18 carbons, with 4 carbons containing 1 less hydrogen than they can accept, or 2 double bonds), or oleic (18 carbons, with 2 carbons containing 1 less hydrogen than they can accept, or 1 double bond). Remember that each carbon in the chain, except for the end carbons, can accept two H atoms ($—CH_2—CH_2—CH_2—CH_2-$). Also among the oils are the marine oils (chiefly whale oil or menhaden oil), which contain some fatty acids with 20, 22, 24, or 26 carbons, and many of the fatty acids have 3, 4, or 5 double bonds (6, 8, or 10 carbons that could accept another hydrogen).

In the extraction of vegetable oils (see Fig. 24-2), some preparation of the material may be required. When corn oil is produced, the germ must first be separated from the corn kernels. The germs are then crushed prior to extraction. Some seeds, such as cottonseed, are prepressed at low pressure to remove part of the oil prior to extraction. Other seeds are crushed or flaked before subjecting to the extraction process. Soybeans are cut into thin flakes and extracted with a solvent. The extraction is started with solvent that has already taken up a high level of oil and is finished off with fresh solvent. In order to obtain the extracted oil, the solvent (which has a much lower boiling point than the oil) is distilled off and recovered for reuse in the extraction of more oil. Oil from olives and cacao beans is obtained by pressing the cooked pulp or beans. An expeller, which subjects the cooked material to high pressure, is used to squeeze out the oil. Oil from seeds may also be extracted in

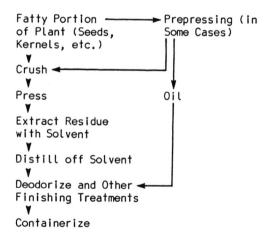

FIGURE 24-2.   Recovery of plant oils.

this manner. Due to the pressure used in expelling oil this way, the temperature of the press cake may rise above 250°F (121.1°C). Expressed oils are usually darker than solvent-extracted oils.

Extracted or expelled oils contain phospholipids, gums, and other materials that are soluble in oil but settle out when wet with water. The natural oil may, therefore, be degummed by mixing with water and centrifuging to separate out the water and the insoluble material. If oil is to be deodorized, it must first be subjected to several degumming operations; otherwise the oil will become cloudy and difficult to filter.

Oil is usually refined prior to sale as a food product. This is done by mixing a concentrated aqueous solution of sodium hydroxide or sodium carbonate with the hot crude oil, and centrifuging out the separated gums and soaps. The oil is then washed with water to remove traces of soaps, and then dried under vacuum. Oils may be bleached prior to sale for use as food products. Neutral clays, sulfuric acid clays, or charcoal may be used in bleaching. Certain yellow colors or green chlorophyll colors may be removed by filtering oils through clays. The natural yellow color of oils (carotenoids) may be removed with activated charcoal or by heating to high temperature. In bleaching, the oil is mixed with the clay or charcoal and heated under vacuum. After sufficient time has elapsed to provide for contact of the oil and bleaching material, the oil is filtered off from the treatment material. Oils are often winterized to remove the saturated fats, in this case, by cooling and holding at 40°F (4.4°C), then filtering to remove the solid fats.

HYDROGENATION

Large quantities of oil are hydrogenated, usually for purposes of forming fats that are solid at room temperature. During hydrogenation, hydrogen is attached to those carbons that are still deficient in this element. Also, during hydrogenation, the more unsaturated fatty acids in the oils are the first to add hydrogen (first those with 3 double bonds or 6 unsaturated carbons, followed by those with 2 double bonds or 4 unsaturated carbons). The result is that in a fully hydrogenated fat, the only fatty acids that may remain unsaturated have only 1 double bond, or 2 carbons, each of which can accept 1 hydrogen atom. Hydrogenation raises the melting point of the fat, but, in addition to this, the fat is changed. For example, oleic acid (one double bond) in the fat has been changed to elaidic acid, which has the same formula as oleic acid and still has one double bond, but the spatial distribution of the atoms differs as to the type of symmetry. Oleic acid is the "cis" form of the molecule and elaidic acid is the "trans" form of the same molecule. Since the melting point of elaidic acid is much higher than that of oleic acid, the melting point of the fat is raised. Oils are usually not fully hydrogenated when solid fats are produced, and in the preparation of margarine, some polyunsaturated fatty acids are left. Soybean oil, which may be used for frying, is slightly hydrogenated to eliminate linolenic acid (3 double bonds); otherwise, the oil would develop a fishy flavor when heated. This is probably due to a primary or intermediate stage of oxidation (see Chap. 2 for health implications of hydrogenation).

In hydrogenation, the oil is placed in a container and the catalyst (usually finely divided metallic nickel) is added. The oil is then heated under vacuum to 200°–400°F (93.3°–204.4°C). When the proper temperature is attained, the vacuum is discontinued, and hydrogen, under a pressure of 5–50 psi (0.35–3.52 kg/cm²), is forced through the oil. The mixture is whipped, to expose as much oil surface to the gas as possible. Hydrogenation is allowed to proceed to the desired point as determined by periodic tests made on the material. After hydrogenation, the material is cooled to a point where it is still liquid, then filtered through bleaching clay to remove the nickel catalyst and nickel soaps. Fats are ordinarily cooled in a heat exchanger after filtering. This is done to retain a homogeneous material, since, if allowed to cool slowly, the harder fats would crystallize out at the bottom of the mass, the more liquid fats solidifying at the top. After cooling, the fats are pumped through a unit that whips them. This is done to prevent large crystals from forming and to maintain a smooth creamy texture. The whipped fat (shortening) is then packaged in containers of various sizes (1–100 lb [0.5–45.4 kg]), depending on whether the product is to be sold at retail or to be used by a food product manufacturer.

After packaging, the fat must be tempered. This is done by holding it, in its containers, at 80°–85°F (26.7°–29.4°C) for a period of 24–72 hr. Tempering is done to provide suitable creaming properties in the shortening. Edible fats and oils are used as bakery shortening to make bread, cakes, icing, and pastries; as a frying vehicle used in shallow- or deep-fat frying; for ice cream–like foods; as oil for salads; for the addition to canned fish products (sardines, tuna, etc.); for the manufacture of margarine; as special coatings for meat; for greasing pans used in bakeries; and, in the home, for baking.

MARGARINE

Large quantities of margarine are manufactured. Actually, margarine has largely replaced butter, both in the home and in the manufacturing of foods. By law, margarine may contain edible fats or oils, whole milk, skim milk, cream, or reconstituted milk solids cultured with bacteria (for flavor) or combinations of these materials; also, emulsifiers (mono- or diglycerides or lecithin), citric acid or citrates to tie up metals that accelerate oxidation, salt or benzoates or both (to inhibit bacterial spoilage), vitamins A and D, artificial coloring (carotene or annato), and artificial flavoring (distillates from cultured milk or cream). The amount of fat present in margarine must be at least 80% of the finished product. All the above ingredients are not necessarily included in margarine, but some combination will be used. Blending of the materials is carried out in two steps. All the fat-soluble ingredients are mixed with the liquid fats in one container, the water-soluble materials in another. The two batches are then mixed to form a loose emulsion with the aid of a high-speed agitator that whips and beats the mixture. The emulsified material is then solidified in a heat exchanger, after which it may be kneaded. In any case, the cooled material is extruded into sheets or bars; then the extruded material is cut to length, wrapped, and packaged for shipment.

LIPID EMULSIFIERS

The mono- and diglycerides used as emulsifiers are made by heating fats or oil and glycerine, with some sodium hydroxide, under vacuum at approximately 400°F (204.4°C). Under these conditions, some of the fatty acids, attached to the glycerine in the fat, migrate and attach to the free glycerine present. Commercial monoglycerides consist of about 50% monoglycerides (1 fatty acid attached to the glycerine molecule), 40% diglycerides (2 fatty acids attached to the glycerine), and 10% triglycerides or fats (3 fatty acids attached to the glycerine). Pure mono- or diglycerides can be obtained by distillation.

SALAD DRESSINGS

Salad dressings include mayonnaise, and other products that differ from mayonnaise mainly in that they do not contain sufficient oil to form a true emulsion. Mayonnaise is made from vegetable oil (cottonseed or corn), vinegar, sugar, salt, mustard, white pepper, and egg yolk. The proportion of components may vary among different formulations. In popular usage, mayonnaise is not called a salad dressing. Salad dressings other than mayonnaise are made from vegetable oils, vinegar, spices, and in many cases, starch. The oil content in salad dressings—about 40%—is about one-half the amount used in mayonnaise.

LIPID SUBSTITUTES

The trend toward lowering dietary intakes of lipids has led to the formulation of a variety of products that can be used as substitutes for fats and oils in the production of a large number of food products that normally contain fats or oils. Some of these foods include baked goods, frozen desserts, and salad dressings, but the applications for lipid substitutes are expected to grow significantly as the relevant technology is expanded and improved.

One of the lipid substitutes is a product called Simplesse. It is made from egg white and milk protein by a patented process called microparticulation. Another fat substitute is Oatrim. It is made from oat bran or oat flour. Other fat substitutes include nondigestible synthetic fats such as olestra, a class of sugar compounds from sucrose and naturally occurring fatty acids having 8–12 carbon atoms. Olestra is intended as a partial fat substitute in frozen desserts, shortenings, and cooking oils.

Esterified propoxylated glycerols (EPG) are a family of propylene oxide derivatives that are similar to natural fats but are not digestible. The use of EPG is as a total or partial substitute for fat in table spreads, frozen desserts, salad dressings, and bakery products.

Dialkyl dihexadecymalonate (DDM) is a minimally digestible fatty alcohol ester of malonic and alkylmalonic acids. Its use is a substitute in high-temperature cooking oils for producing potato and tortilla chips.

Carbohydrate-based fat substitutes include the gums (hydrophilic colloids), polydextrose (a polymer of dextrose with small amounts of sorbitol and citric acid), and a number of other starch derivatives having low caloric values and recommended as partial fat substitutes in a variety of fat-based food products.

Part V

Food Science
and the Culinary Arts

25

Equipment Used in Food Preparation

When considering tools of the trade in culinary arts, we must also include relevant scientific principles, a description of the components of this equipment, and how this equipment will function under certain conditions common to food processing and preparation. Here, we will discuss cutting tools, heating utensils, and sources of heat and equipment (stoves, etc.) to be used.

CUTTING EQUIPMENT

Under this heading will be included equipment that is used for making general cuts as well as tools used for making specific cuts such as chopping and thin slicing.

There are a variety of knives available for general cutting purposes. When choosing knives, there are a number of things that must be considered. Among these are the type of knife, characteristics of the blade, durability, characteristics of the handle and, of course, cost.

Of the four most popular types of blades, the two most common ones to choose from are the carbon and the stainless steel varieties. Both are actually made from steel (an alloy of iron, carbon, and smaller portions of other elements), but the major difference is that the stainless steel type contains less carbon, more chromium, and often nickel. Other alloys have also been used to develop a high-carbon stainless steel blade and a third type, a superstainless steel blade. The latter contains more chromium and nickel in its plating alloy to give it a silvery look.

Each blade has its strengths and weaknesses. The high-carbon blade will sharpen most easily and will hold a very sharp edge. Unless it is wiped immediately after use, however, it will rust or, if working with acid foods (e.g., citrus fruits or tomatoes), the acid may react with the metal, forming stains from which color and off-odor may be transferred to other foods. The stainless steel and superstainless steel blades have the advantage of not staining or rusting and are the least expensive. Both, however, are difficult to sharpen and will not hold a sharp edge. With the exception of expense, a fourth type of blade, the combination stainless steel/carbon, seems to contain the best combination of positive attributes. It does not stain or rust and it takes and holds a fairly good edge.

The choice of blade is based on the needs of the chef or processor, but all the pros and cons must be weighed before investing. Once you choose the type of steel, the type of knife to be used must be carefully considered. In processing plants, a single type of knife may be sufficient (e.g., a 6- or 8-inch utility knife for boning hams), but a chef will need different knives for different jobs. The three most often chosen are a 3- or 4-inch paring knife, an 8-inch chef's knife for chopping, and an 8-inch nonserrated utility knife (see Fig. 25-1). A 10-inch steel for honing (to keep a sharp edge) would be needed in both the processing plant and kitchen. All knives, regardless of type, should be honed on a steel before each use session. Remember, more people are cut with dull knives than with sharp ones. If a knife is sharp, people tend to be more careful and it does not require as much energy to use. If a knife is dull, it is harder to work with, requires more force, and is more likely to slip. The latter two consequences of using a dull knife generally are the reasons that cutting injuries occur.

The next part of the knife that must be considered is the handle. It is claimed by some that wooden handles are less likely to slip. From a sanitation point, however, plastic handles are superior. Plastic can be molded so that the surface is not smooth but can still be cleaned and sanitized properly. If handled correctly, the slight difference in slipperiness is not noticeable and important differences in sanitary attributes will be gained. Wood will absorb water with food residue, creating an environment suitable for the growth of bacteria (see Chap. 7). Wood has other disadvantages. Wooden handles will eventually shrink after use and frequent washing. This will cause separation from the rivets, creating small crevices in which food and bacteria can accumulate.

The cutting surface on which the knife is used is important in maintaining its sharpness. Hard surfaces such as stainless steel, marble, glass, and enamel will dull a knife quickly. Other surfaces that would least dull a knife, such as a soft wood, do not meet the sanitary code for cutting boards. Hard wood cutting boards are still used in many establishments, but they, like the aforementioned knife handles, will absorb water, and when a crevice develops through use, a growth environment with moisture and food could be created. The best cutting surface to keep the knife sharp and to meet sanitary recom-

Paring   knife

Utility   knife

Chef's   knife

Sharpening   steel

FIGURE 25-1.   Basic tools for handcutting foods.

mendations is unmolded white polyethylene or an equivalent. Plastic boards do not absorb water, making them much easier to keep sanitary. Cleaning and sanitizing of cutting boards and knives should be performed after each use. The danger of cross-contamination exists if this is not done. Cross-contamination occurs when raw foods that contain microbes or parasites are prepared with equipment that will later be used in the preparation of cooked foods or foods that will be eaten raw. The equipment may be *cleaned* after the first use but not *sanitized!* Remember, something can be clean (free of visible dirt) without being sanitary (free of pathogens). To assure sanitary conditions, carefully follow recommended methods described in Chapter 3 after each use and especially if using the same equipment for raw and prepared foods.

For fast chopping, thin slicing, and mixing, there are a number of commercial food processors, choppers, and slicers on the market. In these tools, the blades are all made from stainless steel for two reasons. First, they are the easiest to keep clean and stain-free. Because of their contoured shape in food processors, it would be difficult to remove stains from a high-carbon steel blade. This would significantly raise the risk of a cutting injury. Second, even though stainless steel does not hold the edge as well as high-carbon steel, there is no great loss here because these blades are not subjected to the dulling that is encountered by cutting knives (cutting surfaces, bone, and other hard tissues). Also, the high speeds at which food processors operate allow them to cut and chop even if they have lost some of their original sharpness. The slicers, however, do not operate at very high speeds. Their slicing ability is maintained due to the serration of their cutting edges.

The general rules of sanitation apply to this equipment. Purchase equipment that is easily cleanable and has National Sanitation Foundation (NSF) approval. The NSF is a nonprofit research and testing organization that evaluates foodservice equipment and materials. The food processors should be disassembled, cleaned, and sanitized as described in Chapter 3 after each use. Slicers may be in a location where they will be used periodically over a long period of time (deli, sandwich shop, etc.) and it would not be practical to disassemble, clean, and sanitize after each use. In these cases, remember the growth patterns and requirements of bacteria (see Chap. 7) and prevent them from getting the opportunity to grow and reproduce in large numbers. Use small amounts of food to be sliced and keep the rest at temperatures out of the "danger zone" (less than 45°F [7.2°C] or more than 140°F [60°C]) until ready for use. The slicer should be disassembled, cleaned, and sanitized every 3–4 hr or whenever you switch from raw to prepared foods (remember cross-contamination).

Be sure to purchase slicers that are easily disassembled and these precautionary sanitation measures will take only a few minutes. The same considerations mentioned with knives (type, frequency, and capacity of the task to be performed) apply when choosing the proper food processor or slicer. Be sure to select one with enough horsepower in the motor and, with food processors, capacity in the bowl. Also, belt-driven models can balk and slip when processing more difficult products (i.e., chopping meat). It is better to invest the extra money and buy the models that have the motor's drive shaft directly rotating the cutting blade (direct drive).

HEATING UTENSILS

The way heat reaches food is varied. It involves phenomena described as radiation, conduction, and convection. In radiation, units of energy described as quanta travel as electromagnetic waves and are a source of heat. These infrared rays, known as radiant energy, go directly from the source to the object heated, unassisted by another medium. Sources of radiant energy in food preparation are the broiler, toaster, coals in a charcoal pit, a gas flame, and the coils of an electric stove. It should be noted, however, that all objects with any space around them, even cold ones, emit radiant heat.

In conduction heating, the transfer of heat occurs by contact, from molecules at any temperature to adjacent molecules at lower temperatures. Thus, the heated molecules of a hot plate heat the molecules of the lower surface of a pan bottom, which in turn heats adjacent molecules until heat from the upper surface of the pan transfers heat to the food with which it is in contact. Thereafter, the food is heated by conduction (contact) and convection (heated fluid in motion described below).

In convection heating, a fluid (gas or liquid) undergoes rise and fall patterns. In this manner, the spread of heat throughout a container is accelerated as opposed to heat transfer by conduction only. Most cooking is done in pots and pans, and the transfer of heat always involves conduction and usually convection.

When food in a pan is heated on a stove, energy from the heating coil or gas flame is transferred directly to the pan by conduction because they are in direct contact and heat is transferred from one molecule to another throughout the pan. The hot pan will transfer heat by conduction to the food. In liquid foods, water molecules are heated and a portion of them get hot and become less dense than cooler water molecules, which have not yet been warmed. The heated, less dense water rises while the cooler, more dense molecules will flow down toward the heat source, and a circular flow of energy transfer (top to bottom and bottom to top) is developed (see Fig. 10-4). This movement, called convection, allows faster transfer of heat from molecule to molecule (through conduction) because the cooler ones come into contact with the hotter ones more often. Convection heating is also attained when heat arrives by air, as in an oven, or in deep-fat frying. More on conduction and convection is described in Chapter 10.

When choosing pans, especially those for stove-top cooking, one must consider heat distribution. If heat cannot spread quickly through the entire bottom of a pan, hot and cold spots will develop. These will cause uneven cooking and may even burn a portion of the food and not thoroughly cook others.

The fastest heat conductor among the most popular pan materials is copper with aluminum not far behind. Cast iron and carbon (rolled) steel (used in traditional woks and crepe pans) are next with stainless steel still slower. The slowest of all are glass, porcelain, earthenware, and pottery. The thickness of the material is also a factor in heat transfer. The thicker the gauge, the more evenly the heat distribution throughout the pot or pan's interior surface. Each substance has its advantages and disadvantages and some of these are as follows:

Tinware (tin-plated iron or steel)

Advantages: It has fair conductivity.
Disadvantages: It will mar and then rusts quickly. It turns dark after use and is affected by acid foods.

Aluminum

Advantages: It heats quickly and has good heat diffusion and heat conduction, and in heavy gauges, heats relatively evenly. Light-gauge aluminum, however, will develop hot spots.
Disadvantages: It pits and will discolor food. This is seen when stains on the pan develop when foods such as potatoes are cooked or the pan is washed with a high-alkali cleanser. When acid foods, such as tomato sauce, are cooked in the stained pan, the color will be absorbed. To avoid this, the stain may be removed by boiling in a weak food acid solution like cream of tartar (2 teaspoons to 1 quart of water) for 5–10 min.

Copper

*Advantages:*It heats very quickly and is best in the heavier gauges because it gives a quick, even heat distribution when kept clean.
Disadvantages: It stains easily and must be well tinned or lined with stainless steel on surfaces contacting foods, since copper will leach into acid foods and could prove poisonous. Copper is also a catalyst and may enhance spoilage.

Cast Iron and Carbon-Rolled Steel

Advantages: They are sturdy and can withstand high temperatures without warping.
Disadvantages: They rust easily and can discolor food. The pans should be "seasoned" before using for the first time. This can be done by rubbing with vegetable oil and heating in an oven at 300°F (149°C) for 30–60 min (some recommend 450°F [232°C] for 30 min.). What happens here is the microscopic jagged peaks in both nonstainless iron-based metals

are coated with oil and appear to be smoothed, which helps to keep water from seeping in and creating rust.

Stainless Steel

Advantages: This is the easiest to keep clean and it does not stain or impart impurities to food. In heavy-gauge material, pots and pans are sturdy.
Disadvantages: It has poor heat conductivity. This can be remedied by getting lighter gauges but then the development of hot spots could be a problem. Also, by constructing the pan so that the bottom thickness is decreased and clad with copper underneath, heat transfer is improved.

Glass, Porcelain Enamel, and Earthenware

Advantages: If the gauge is heavy enough and they are covered, they hold heat well (especially earthenware) and will keep food warm during service.
Disadvantages: They break if dropped or hit by a hard object. They have poor heat conductivity, and due to this poor conductivity, they can break easily with quick temperature changes. When very hot water, for example, is poured quickly into a cold glass container, the bottom of the container will expand. Because conduction is poor, the top will not expand as rapidly, resulting in a structural stress that causes the glass to crack. The porcelain enamelware may chip and, unless treated to resist acid, the glaze can react with the acid. With the high degree of breakability, there is a danger of chips entering food. There are treated glasses such as Pyrex and Corningware that are less vulnerable to heat and breakage but they too have their limits.

There are also pans available with nonstick surfaces. These are coated with polytetrafluoroethylene (a solid, chemically inert [will not react with or absorb other substances] plastic that is baked on the surface). The plastic, better known as Teflon (the trademark of one manufacturer of this substance), covers the jagged peaks of the metal, denying the food the opportunity to cling to them. The metal usually used in these pans is aluminum.

Cleaning and sanitizing of pots and pans can be achieved as described earlier. With pans that have been seasoned, some cookbooks recommend never washing with soap or detergent. This advice can lead to off-odors and off-flavors from oxidizing fats (see Chaps. 8 and 9) and bacterial growth. Methods of cleaning and sanitizing described earlier will not destroy the seasoned pan. The only difference is that the pans should be dried with a disposable towel to remove excess oil. If pans get scratched with a metal utensil, they should be reseasoned the next time they are used for frying by the method described earlier.

The choice of cooking utensils depends on individual needs but the best general recommendation is to choose a pan of fairly heavy gauge, the bottom of which will diffuse heat evenly.

TYPES OF HEAT AND HEAT SOURCES

When choosing a source of heat and method to be used for food preparation, a number of things must be considered. First, the function of heat itself should be considered because heat changes the flavor, aroma, and color of foods. They may be either depleted or intensified, which can enhance palatability and appearance of food or, if not carefully controlled, lower the quality appreciably. Heated food also may become more chewable, disgestible, and, due to its increased temperature, have a higher appeal. Texture changes are quite evident as heat is increased and proteins coagulate. Foods may become more firm or the proteins may play a role in the processes of emulsification (Chap. 15), gelatinizing (Chap. 15), or leavening (Chaps. 20 and 26). Heat also plays a role not often mentioned with regard to cooking: its effect on the microorganisms that are present. Water activity levels may be lowered (see Chap. 11) and pathogenic and spoilage bacteria can be destroyed, thus preserving the food (see Chap. 10). Care must be taken, however, when heating and holding food in the warm or hot state. As mentioned in Chapter 3, improper heating can lead to rapid microbial growth, resulting in food spoilage or poisoning.

The functions you wish to achieve determine whether to use moist heat or dry heat. Heat transfer in food has been discussed earlier in this chapter and methods to achieve this are numerous.

With moist heat, food is heated by convection currents in hot water. There are advantages to this method. Foods that are naturally tough, such as meats with a large amount of connective tissue or plants with generous amounts of fiber, can become quite tender using moist heat. The water medium prevents drying of the product. The cooking temperature is quite easy to maintain and hold. Remember, water boils at about 212°F (100°C) and will not get much hotter or cooler. Many natural juices and nutrients in foods prepared with moist heat migrate into the cooking medium and can be incorporated into sauces or gravies. Some moist-heat methods are boiling/simmering/poaching, steaming, and pressure-cooking.

Boiling, simmering, and poaching are very similar. Boiling rapidly does not raise the temperature of the water. The extra energy incorporated to cause the rapid boil is lost as the water changes phases from liquid to gas (steam). Rapid boiling can adversely affect the texture of some foods (e.g., vegetables in a stew) but is desirable in others such as pasta to help keep it from sticking together. Simmering is probably the most important form of moist heat. The temperature is controlled so that some of the water molecules are converting to steam but a rapid boil is not obtained. As the heat from the boiling water molecules is being transferred to the food, the temperature of the total product is lower than 212°F (100°C). Simmering temperatures should be at least 140°F (60°C) to ensure safety from pathogenic microorganisms (see Chap. 6) and commonly go as high as 160°F (71.1°C). This method protects fragile foods and tenderizes tough ones. Poaching is an interesting application of moist heat. The temperature of the water is just below boiling and the method incorporates basting or self-basting. Food is placed in simmering water and basted with the cooking liquid. Self-basting can be achieved by using a lid, so that as steam condenses on the lid, it performs this action.

Steam is less dense than water and will make less frequent contact with the food. To compensate for this loss of efficiency, steam has a gain in energy. The vaporizing molecules are more energetic than those in the liquid phase and the pressure produced in a closed container will raise the temperature slightly.

As mentioned in Chapter 10 on thermal processing, higher temperatures can be achieved by boiling water under pressure. Pressure cooking incorporates this concept and can lower the cooking time significantly. Flavors and nutrients that may be destroyed by long periods of simmering or boiling are preserved to a higher degree in pressure cooking. This holds true especially for vegetables. Some meats are cooked with moist heat because they are not very tender.

Dry heat may be generated in a number of ways but all employ temperatures higher than those used in moist heat. Certain cooking goals, such as browning, searing, and crisping, can only be achieved at these elevated temperatures. Dry heat cooking methods include roasting/baking, broiling/toasting, pan-frying, deep-frying, and microwaving.

Roasting and baking basically describe the same method. The difference exists in the actual definition. If a whole bird or piece of meat (other than a ham or minced-meat preparation) is heated that will later be divided to serve, the process is defined as roasting. Whether called baking or roasting, radiant heat of the oven, convection of air, and heat from the pan is conducted and convected throughout the food. Moisture is lost from food as vapor and is circulated in the oven, thus somewhat moistening the "dry" environment. Temperatures vary, but rarely get much above 400–500°F (204.4–260°C). Some baking and roasting methods use high temperatures at the beginning to sear the outer surface, thus sealing in juices, then lower the temperature to more evenly distribute the heat throughout the food without overcooking outer layers before the internal surfaces cook.

Broiling and toasting are controlled versions of the oldest culinary technique, roasting over an open fire or glowing coals. Broiling and toasting depend largely on infrared radiation. All heat sources used in broiling and toasting emit visible light so they are intense radiators of infrared energy. Nickel-chrome alloys used in electrical appliances reach temperatures of 2000°F (1093.3°C) and a gas flame is about 3000°F (1648.9°C). Oven wall temperatures rarely exceed 500°F (260°C). The production of these extremely high temperatures is the great advantage of broiling but, at the same time, is the major problem. The development of intense, familiar flavors and colors in broiling result from the high-temperature cooking, but there is a huge disparity between the rate of radiation at the surface and the rate of conduction, via water, within the food. This explains the "burned" steak that is cold in the middle. Infrared radiation weakens quickly with distance because the rays spread out in all directions and become less concentrated. Thus, the skilled broiler cook can find the ideal distance from the heat source where the radiation and conduction can produce a rare, medium, or well-done steak whenever desired.

Pan-frying depends mostly on conduction and convection. Oil is often added to the pan and it serves several purposes. It brings the uneven surface of the pan into more uniform contact with the heat source, it lubricates and prevents sticking, and it supplies flavor. The problems encountered with broiling (burned outside and cold middle) can occur in pan-frying. Cooks will sear the surface at high temperatures and then lower the temperatures to allow the heat to penetrate by conduction and convection more evenly.

Deep-frying resembles pan-frying except that it uses enough oil to immerse the food completely. As a technique, it is similar to boiling but the temperature of the oil can get twice as hot as boiling water and therefore this method is much more rapid and can brown foods. The type of oil that is used determines many attributes of the final product, such as flavor, color, and amounts of saturated fats and cholesterol absorbed by the fried food (see Chap. 2). Temperature of the oil is important and a frying thermometer should be used. If the oil is too cool when food is added, the food will cook slowly and will absorb more oil, becoming greasy. If the oil is heated too high, smoking will be produced, which indicates the oil is breaking down and will be no good for reuse. Also, if the oil is too hot, the same problem could develop that developed with other high-temperature methods: The outside may burn while the inside is still raw. Frying is certainly an art and results usually improve with practice.

Microwave heating and how it works is described in Chapter 10. It is included in the "dry" heat section because water is not used as the cooking medium. Actual heat, however, is not really generated by the oven or the microwaves themselves. The water molecules in the food vibrate when exposed to microwaves and this movement generates heat. The microwaves only penetrate a couple of inches into most foods, so the term "heating from the inside out" is not totally correct. This penetration is much greater, however, than traditional heating where the energy is absorbed almost entirely on the surface. Once the microwaves have activated the water molecules in the outer 2 inches, further heating is accomplished by conduction as mentioned previously. Nonwater-containing materials such as paper, glass, and plastic will not get hot unless they contain food that heats them through conduction. There are advantages and disadvantages to microwave cooking. The main advantage is speed. Cooking time can be cut by 50–75%. Microwave heating uses electrical energy more efficiently, therefore costing less. With the generation of steam from within, baked goods may rise higher, and with temperatures not getting much above that of boiling water (212°F [100°C]), there is less splattering.

There are several disadvantages to microwave cooking. Only "microwavable" containers may be used. These include glass and Corningware because microwaves can penetrate through them. No metal containers or metal foil can be used because microwaves cannot penetrate and will be reflected. Microwave cooked meat can have a drier texture. This is due to the fact that the quicker heating can cause greater fluid loss. This also makes it harder to control the doneness of a roast. Even-heat penetration in microwave cooking has been a problem. In larger casseroles, roasts, and whole poultry, cold spots may develop, leaving a possible microbial safety problem. To avoid this, use thermometers and check in several places, making sure that you have reached at least 160°F (71.1°C) for beef, 170°F (76.7°C) for veal, pork, and lamb, and 185°F (85°C) for poultry. Stirring, rotating, deboning meat, and allowing food to "rest" after microwaving will also help to avoid cold spots. Covering your cookware will trap escaping steam and use this energy in the heating process.

Foods do not brown in the conventional microwave oven. Some manufacturers have incorporated heat sources or a convection fan to raise the temperature for browning and development of flavors that accompany the process. Packaging technology has also helped to solve the browning problem. Heat-susceptor packages contain thin, gray strips or discs of metalized plastic. These absorb microwave energy and can reach temperatures sufficient to brown and crisp foods. Safety of microwave ovens is always a concern because microwaves can penetrate body tissue, resulting in injury such as cataracts. Accordingly, it is important to be sure the door is checked for tight fit and the seal is not damaged. The seal should be conscientiously cleaned and free of spills and splatters. Microwave leak testers can be purchased to check the door and seal. This is extremely important for people who have coronary pacemakers because the microwaves can alter their proper function.

Equipment to cook food on or in basically includes three choices: microwave ovens, gas appliances, or electric appliances. There are advantages and disadvantages of each. The advantages and disadvantages of microwave ovens were mentioned but there are differences among microwave ovens. The power potential, expressed as watts, may vary. Some ovens may have a wattage as low as 400 while others operate at 700 watts. The required heating time will vary. Ovens having the lower wattage require longer cooking times. Gas and electric cooking also have advantages and disadvantages. For stovetop units, gas has the advantage. This is primarily due to the quickness with which temperature adjustments may be made and the range of actual cooking temperatures available. Electric burners take several minutes to reach temperature and to cool, and you are limited to the settings (e.g., low, medium, high) on the dial. Electric ovens and broilers, however, seem to have the advantage over gas. Ovens reach desired temperatures more quickly, maintain a relatively steady temperature and, generally, are more accurate. Some electric ovens can also reach very high temperatures (1000°F [537.8°C]), which allows them to "self-clean." At these high temperatures, organic compounds (most food and grease that accumulates in ovens) will be burned (oxidized) to carbon dioxide and water (steam), which is exhausted. What remains is a white ash that consists of the inorganic portions of food (i.e., calcium, sodium, and other minerals). This ash can be easily wiped away with a damp cloth after the oven has cooled. A combination of gas and electric would probably be best but the choice of one or the other will probably have to be made. Weigh the pros and cons, determine what the needs are, and the best choice can be made.

26

Food Preparation:
An Important Application
of Basic Chemistry
and Physics

When food is prepared for consumption, many of its characteristics, such as texture, appearance, taste, and nutritional value, are altered. These result from changes in the physical and chemical structure of foods. An understanding of the basic physical and chemical nature of food is an invaluable tool for chefs, bakers, and anyone involved in food preparation, and this knowledge enables one to control quality more effectively. A change in methodology or substitution of an ingredient may improve the final product or save in time and money. This chapter will give short explanations of why certain changes occur in a variety of foods.

MEAT

The basic quality factors of any food are appearance, texture, and flavor. A high-quality meat looks good, is tender, and tastes and smells good. The composition, structure, and method of storage and preparation will determine the quality. Chapter 15 discusses different types of meats and how they are processed.

The composition of meat varies among different species and within the same species. The protein contents vary but usually fall between 15% and 20%; the fat contents are more inconsistent, having a range from 5–40%. Nutritionally, the protein from meat is of high quality and the percent calories from fat varies depending on the cut and species. Also, meat contains cholesterol and saturated fats, and it is recommended by nutritionists to limit the amount of fatty meats consumed. The lean tissue of meat contains mainly water and protein. The protein consists of bundles of muscle fibers,

369

which are the basic structural unit of lean tissue. Other protein materials include connective tissue, which holds the muscles together, and the oxygen-containing pigments and enzymes associated with muscle fibers.

The texture of meat or its degree of tenderness depends on a number of factors. The amount of fat in the connective tissue within the muscle is thought by some to be an accurate measure of tenderness. It certainly gives the impression of tenderness and juiciness, because when melted, it lubricates the lean, but it is not considered a reliable predictor of tenderness. Tenderness appears to depend on two factors: the nature of the connective tissue and the condition of muscle filaments after slaughter. The nature of the connective tissue is closely related to the age of the animal. Young animals have collagen that is more water-soluble and more heat-labile than in older animals. When cooked, the collagen degrades and does not contribute to toughness. As the animal gets older, the collagen becomes more heat-stable and therefore is not broken down by cooking as readily. Muscles that have done much work have been shown to contain even more of the heat-stable collagen. Meat that is not affected by collagen may also become tough through the condition of muscle fibers.

A few hours after slaughter, meat goes into rigor, a condition that leaves the muscles rigid and inelastic. Aging the meat after slaughter allows the rigor to pass and the muscle to become soft and pliable again, and aging allows time for innate enzymes to tenderize the meat. The temperature of aging is held at 34°–38°F (1.1–3.3°C.) to prevent microbial growth and at about 70% relative humidity to prevent drying. The optimum period is about 11 days for beef and 1 day for pork. This can be quickened for beef by raising the temperature to 70°F (21.1°C) for 2 days at a relative humidity of 85–90% under ultraviolet light to control microbial growth. This fast-aged beef is usually what is sold at retail markets.

Cooking methods and tenderness are discussed in Chapter 25 but, basically, moist heat and slower cooking temperatures lead to more tender meat. Other ways to make meat more tender are to marinate it or to apply commercial meat tenderizers. The acid in the marinade from vinegar (acetic), lemon juice (citric), or wine (tartaric) chemically softens the collagen and the meat tenderizers soften the connective tissue through enzymatic action (see Chap. 8). Another method to help tenderize is to cut across the grain and in thin slices. This helps to shorten the fiber lengths, thus making chewing easier. Grinding, scoring, and pounding also help to tenderize in the same way, although scoring only affects the surface.

Appearance in meat is due mainly to the color developed during cooking or in a curing process. The pigment responsible is not hemoglobin in blood and the liquid from a rare steak is not blood, because most of this blood is removed through the arteries at slaughter. The red color is due to the pigment myoglobin, which is in muscles and stores oxygen. With heat, the pigment color changes and can be used as an index of doneness. To cook a steak rare, it is heated to an internal temperature of 140°F (60°C) and the pigment is bright red with a thin layer of denatured myoglobin, which is brown in color. Many cooks do not heat rare meat to this level but it has been shown that this temperature will ensure the destruction of *Salmonella* and thus is the basis for this recommendation (see Chap. 6). Medium rare, reached at 160°F (71.1°C), has a pink color because more of the myoglobin has been denatured. Well-done meat is cooked to 170°F (76.7°C) and it will be brown-colored throughout. When sugars are present, as in cured meats, a brown pigment is also produced from a reaction of the sugar and the protein (see Chap. 9). This also happens when cooking liver because of its glycogen content. The pink color in cured meats, like ham, results from myoglobin combining with nitric oxide from the sodium nitrite that is in most cures (see Chap. 15).

The amount of myoglobin in the muscles also determines color of meat in poultry. The muscles, which require more oxygen because they will be exercised more, like the leg muscles, will become darker during cooking while the others, like the wings and the breast, which do little work in poultry, will be white. Game birds, on the other hand, will have dark meat in the wings and breast because these muscles are used more and need more oxygen.

Flavor in meat depends on a number of factors, but, generally, well-exercised tough meat is more flavorful than that which is more tender and less exercised. Cooking decomposes some factors in lean meat to give the basic cooked meat taste. It seems that a long cooking time is needed to develop a full, meaty flavor, since tests done on meats prepared by quicker methods (i.e., microwave and pressure saucepans) did not have as desirable flavors as those prepared in the conventional manner. The meat closer to the bone also contains more flavor because it is in the most favorable position to absorb flavorful compounds from bone, which are also used to give stocks their rich flavor. The aroma from heated adipose tissue (fat) with some water-soluble components distinguish the aroma of different species such as beef, pork, and lamb. Another flavor that may be familiar is that of reheated meat that has been refrigerated. This warmed-over flavor is a result of oxidative rancidity (see Chap. 9). Meats with the relatively higher amounts of polyunsaturated fatty acids (see Chap. 24) such as pork are more susceptible to this flavor development.

DAIRY PRODUCTS

All dairy products are made from fluid milk that is either chemically or physically altered. Chapter 16 discusses how milk is handled, processed, and used in different products. In food preparation, milk and milk products can be added to many foods to improve texture, appearance, and flavor. Whole milk contains a complete protein, some carbohydrates, and fat of about 3.8% (individual states control what the fat content of whole milk will be). It also contains about 88% water so the percent calories from fat in whole milk is quite high (over 50%). Milk contains saturated fats and cholesterol.

Although it is recommended to drink milk daily, a large proportion of it should be skim milk. When cooking with milk, a few problems exist, but these can be corrected when the causes of the problems are understood. One problem is the tendency for the proteins in milk, as with many other proteins, to coagulate when they are heated. When milk is heated, water is being evaporated at the surface; the protein content is concentrated, and it complexes with calcium salts, coagulates, and forms a film. When the film is removed, much high-quality protein is lost. This can be avoided if evaporation is slowed down by covering the pan, whipping up a little foam, lowering the heat, or stirring.

Another problem is scorching. Milk proteins are relatively dense, and casein and whey proteins will fall to the bottom, stick, and burn. The best ways to avoid this are to use gentle heat, such as that from a moderate flame, or by using a double boiler or by stirring during the application of heat. Milk can also become more susceptible to curdling in the presence of any acids from fruits and vegetables or phenolic compounds in foods like potatoes or tea. Fresh milk and careful control of the cooking temperatures are the best defenses.

Heat also affects the flavor and color of milk. Some protein derivatives, such as hydrogen sulfide and methyl sulfide, contribute to the flavor of cooked milk. Heated milk fat also gives a compound (delta decalactone) that gives the flavor found in foods cooked in butter.

Other milk products are produced without heat. Butterfat is separated from whole milk and concentrated in varied amounts to make cream, which exists in three major grades: light cream, light whipping cream, and heavy whipping cream (see Chap. 16). The names of the cream and their actual weights are inversely proportional. The heavy cream, because of its higher fat content, is actually lighter in weight than the others and the light cream is the heaviest. Half and half is an intermediate between milk and cream and contains at least 10.5% butterfat. Whipped cream is a favorite among bakers and chefs alike. It is made when air is whipped into the liquid, some proteins are caught in the walls of the bubbles, and the imbalance of forces here causes the proteins to distort from their normal shape. They react with each other and form a thin film of coagulated molecules. This film gives the liquid foam a solid, delicate reinforcement. The foam in cream is much stronger than that in milk because of the higher fat content. The fat globules apparently cluster in the bubble walls where surface forces rupture some of their membranes. The soft fat now sticks together, forming a quasirigid but delicate network that reinforces the foam. This cannot be formed by protein alone. Cream whipped to optimum volume is soft and glossy but there is some leakage. A stiffer cream can be achieved with more whipping but care must be taken not to overdo it, because the stiffness indicates clumping of fat globules, and if whipping is continued, butter will be formed.

The temperature of the equipment and cream used is important. Cool equipment is much better because the fat globules get soft when their temperature rises 5°–10°F (2.8°–5.6°C) and they will be deformed by the weight of the foam, and the whole structure will be weakened. The bowls used should be cooled in a freezer for 20–30 min. Cooling the cream itself in the freezer is a good idea, especially in the summer, but it should not be allowed to freeze. The water leaves the solution to form ice and prevents the even dispersion of fat, and a good foam will be difficult to achieve. To attain a sweet whipped cream, add the sugar near the end of the process. Sugar decreases the potential volume of the cream because it probably interferes with the clumping proteins on the fat globule membranes. If a thicker cream is desired, gelatin (adding more protein) or lemon juice (adding acid to denature protein) may be added.

POULTRY AND EGGS

The handling and processing of poultry and eggs are discussed in Chapter 17. In the kitchen, the basic guidelines for cooking meat can be used for poultry, with some changes depending on the tenderness and fat content of the bird, which are mainly determined by age. Older birds are cooked by methods suitable for tough cuts of meat (see Chap. 25). Poultry, like beef and pork, is a good source of protein but contains less fat, especially if the skin is removed. White meat is less fatty but the dark meat is more flavorful (see "Meat" section). Poultry is a good addition to any diet attempting to reach the recommended 30% or less calories from fat. Young chickens of either sex are called broilers if they weigh about 2.5 lb (1.1 kg) and fryers if they weigh 2.5–3.5 lb (1.1–1.6 kg). Roasters of either sex are 8 months old and weigh 3.5–5 lb. (1.6–2.3 kg). Capons are castrated males and weigh 6–8 lbs. (2.7–3.6 kg). Fowl are hens aged 10 months or more and stags and cocks are males too old to roast but they add flavor to any stew-type meal.

Much of the poultry sold contains viable *Salmonella* organisms (see Chap. 6), so it is essential to clean and sanitize any cutting boards or utensils and to wash one's hands after handling poultry to prevent cross-contamination. After choosing the method of cooking, doneness of poultry can be determined in a number of ways, but use of a thermometer to measure internal temperature is the most reliable. All poultry is cooked to the well-done stage.

Temperatures in the thigh and breast muscles are the best indicators of doneness, and tests have shown that, cooked in a 325°F (162.8°C) oven, optimum tenderness was reached at 170°-175°F (76.7°-79.4°C) for white meat and 175°-180°F (79.4°-82.2°C) for dark meat. If a stuffed bird is cooked, the stuffing must be cooked to at least 165°F (73.9°C) to assure destruction of all pathogens. For appearance, the bird may be browned by raising the temperature at the end of the cooking period or by basting with butter (see browning in Chap. 9). The flavor in poultry, as in meat, intensifies with the age of the animal. Chemicals called volatile carbonyls (see Chap. 9) are responsible for the "chicken" aroma, and without them, a beeflike aroma exists. Cooked chickens and turkeys contain fat that is susceptible to oxidative rancidity and may, in some cases, account for a warmed-over flavor as described in the "Meat" section.

The egg (also discussed in Chap. 17) is an interesting mixture of chemicals that can be changed in appearance, texture, and flavor by addition of heat or chemicals or by physical manipulation. Nutritionally, eggs have the most complete protein. The egg white is almost all water and protein (see Chap. 17); the yolk contains a number of nutrients including fat and cholesterol. It is recommended to limit whole egg consumption to 3 to 4 per week, but egg white consumption is not limited.

The behavior of the egg in the kitchen is mostly a matter of protein chemistry and, in particular, the chemistry of coagulation. Albumen proteins are long chains of amino acids (see Chap. 2) that are folded into a globular shape. Each protein holds its shape by a number of bonds between parts of its chain. Different molecules are prevented from bonding to each other because, due to the environment in the albumen, a net negative charge is attained by each, thus resulting in their repelling one another. Acidity, salt, temperature, and even air bubbles can disturb this and cause the molecules to join together or coagulate. The perfect example is when an egg is cooked. The addition of heat disturbs the bonds in the individual molecules and the proteins unfold. As the heat is increased, the unfolded molecules are now longer and have more areas exposed that may bond with other unfolded proteins. When this happens, water in the white of the egg may be trapped in the mass and the liquid has suddenly become a solid with the ability to deflect light rays, turning it from clear in appearance to white (see Fig. 26-1).

The chemistry of the egg can be examined further in the different cooking processes. Eggs are prepared in a number of ways, including boiled in the shell, poached, fried, scrambled, and as a component in custards. Eggs can be boiled either soft or hard, depending on the length of time they remain in the cooking water. Soft-boiled eggs are not recommended since *Salmonella* have been found in the yolk of supposedly "safe," uncracked eggs (see Chap. 6). The temperature of cooking will determine the quality of the fully

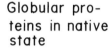

Globular pro-   Proteins unfold   Proteins form
teins in native   under heat or   intermolecular
state   other stress   bonds resulting
                                              in a coagulum

FIGURE 26-1. Molecular depiction of coagulation in eggs.

cooked egg. If high temperatures at or near boiling are used, the white may become very rubbery (see protein coagulation in this chapter) before the yolk is completely cooked. To avoid this, cook at lower temperatures (185°F [85°C]) even though it will take longer (25–35 min as opposed to about 12 min. in boiling water); the white will not be rubbery and the yolk will be fully cooked. Due to the expansion of air in the egg being boiled or just the temperature change, the shell often cracks and some of the white oozes into the water and cooks. To avoid this, use a little chemistry and coagulate the white before it leaks out. This can be done by adding salt or vinegar to the cooking water; the proteins are denatured and coagulate at the crack. The problem can also be solved by physics. Puncture the shell at the large end where the air pocket is so that the expanding air during heating can escape.

Another problem in boiled eggs is the development of a green-gray color on the surface of the yolk. This is a result of more chemistry; a harmless chemical called ferrous sulfide is formed from iron in the yolk and sulfur from the protein in the white. When the protein is heated, some of its sulfur atoms are liberated and combine with hydrogen, forming hydrogen sulfide which, in small quantities, gives cooked eggs a pleasant odor but, in large quantities, smells like rotten eggs. As this forms, it spreads and reaches the yolk where it finds the iron and forms the darkly pigmented ferrous sulfide. To limit the amount of hydrogen sulfide formed, cook the egg only long enough to harden the yolk and then place it in cold water. This lowers pressure of the gas in the outer regions of the white (cool gasses generate less pressure) and cool protein loses less sulfur. Peel the eggs as soon as they are cooled to stop gas diffusion toward the yolk.

To prepare poached eggs, remove them from the shell and drop them in hot water. The proteins begin to coagulate immediately and usually form their final shape. To control this shape, use egg poachers to eliminate too much spreading of the white. Hot water can be used to "baste" the egg to fully cook the yolk as recommended earlier.

To prepare fried eggs, place them on a hot pan to prevent spreading of the white. The pan should have a nonstick surface (see Chap. 25) or be coated with a layer of fat or oil to prevent sticking. The cooking temperature should be about 280°F (137.8°C). If the temperature is too hot, the egg will splatter; if it is too cold, the white will spread undesirably. Sunny-side-up eggs are not recommended due to the possible presence of *Salmonella,* but if fresh eggs from a reputable dealer are used, the chances of infection are small. To avoid runny eggs, add water to the pan and cover it to allow the heat from the steam to coagulate the protein at the egg's surface.

To make scrambled eggs, the yolk and white may be combined with a small amount (1 tbsp) of milk, cream, or water. The mix should be heated slowly and turned when it starts to coagulate on the sides and bottom of the pan. This removes the cooked portion from the heat and exposes the uncooked portion, thus evenly distributing the heat and not overcooking any part of the egg. If scrambled eggs are overcooked, liquid is expelled and evaporated, leaving a shrunken, dry product. If an omelet is desired, the egg mixture is added to an oiled pan, and when the bottom coagulates, lift just enough to allow the uncooked portion to flow and contact the pan. The omelet should stay in one piece and take the shape of the pan. Low-cholesterol scrambled eggs and omelets can be made by removing some or all of the yolks.

Custards are mixtures of egg, sugar, and milk with salt and vanilla often added for flavor. One whole egg or two egg yolks supply enough coagulable protein to gel 1 cup of milk. Mix the egg, sugar, and salt, then add scalded milk (the milk is scalded to shorten cooking time and add flavor, see section on dairy products). When the mixture is heated, the egg protein is denatured and unites to form a network that traps the fluid milk, forming a delicate gel. Custards are baked in a moderate oven (350°F [176.7°C]) in a utensil that is placed in a pan of hot water. This gives a more even distribution of heat and the water molecules are in contact with the pan, thus conducting heat more evenly than hot air, and the temperature of the water will never get higher than 212°F (100°C) (see Chap. 25). The temperature needed here to form a gel is greater than that to merely coagulate protein because the egg protein is diluted with milk. When the custard gels, it should be removed from heat and placed in cold water. Overheating custards results in shrinkage of the gel and development of pores that fill with watery serum.

Eggs can also be whipped and will entrap air, forming a foam (see foam formation in "Dairy Products" section). The proteins in the albumen are responsible for this, but the yolk will ruin it. Lipoproteins (formed by combining proteins and fats) in the yolk interfere with the foaming potential of the proteins. The foam made from egg whites has a unique property in that it can be stabilized by cooking. Ordinarily, when a foam is heated, the trapped air and other gases in the formed bubbles expand and break the bubble walls, collapsing the foam. One protein in the egg albumen (ovalbumen) makes up more than half of the albumen proteins, and it does not unfold much during whipping but does coagulate readily when heated. What happens here is the coagulated ovalbumen creates a solid network in the bubble walls that resist collapse when air escapes or when water evaporates. This enables the baker to utilize chemistry and physics principles again and form a solid foam from a liquid one.

FISH AND SHELLFISH

Fish and shellfish handling and processing are covered in Chapter 18. Fin fish is prepared in a number of ways including broiling, baking, frying, steaming, and poaching (see Chap. 25). The moist cooking methods are appropriate for lean fish while the fatty varieties are self-basting and may be broiled or baked. Assessing doneness in fish can be accomplished with a thermometer by inserting it into the thickest portion. Fish is edible when the internal temperature reaches 140°F (60°C), but at 150°F (65.6°C), tissues start to break down, allowing juices and flavor to escape. Fish is no longer translucent and flakes easily when done due to the unique structure of fish muscles.

The muscles in mammals and birds are composed of very long fibers arranged in longitudinal bundles. Fish muscle, on the other hand, consists of rather short fibers separated by large sheets of very thin connective tissue. The connective tissue is delicate and can be converted to gelatin with heat quite easily. The quantity of connective tissue in fish is also less (about 3% of their weight) than that of land animals (about 15% of their weight). In appearance, many fish have very little pigment in their muscle tissue. It was shown earlier that, in mammals, the white and dark meat was influenced by the amount of myoglobin in the muscles—the muscles that worked harder needing more. Fish contain about 40–60% of their body weight in muscle tissue (more than mammals) yet much of their flesh is still white. This is explained when the chemistry of the muscle fibers is understood. One of the basic muscle proteins, myosin, exists in several different forms, including red and white muscle myosin. Mammals have muscles that are needed for functions, such as standing, which require endurance. These muscles need more oxygen and have more red myosin. Fish, with their specialized muscles needed for quick spurts, need less oxygen and therefore have more white muscle myosin. Those fish with more pigment either have a need for more red muscle myosin with its myoglobin or have pigments from another source.

Salmon, which contains a carotenoid (see Chap. 9 and 24) derived from its diet, is an example of such a fish. Many types of fish taste very bland but the fatty varieties and the darker-flesh species are more flavorful.

Shellfish are divided into two major groups: molluscs and crustacea. The molluscs include clams, oysters, scallops, and mussels. These are prepared in a number of ways and some are eaten raw. If you choose to eat raw shellfish, be sure that they are alive (shell is closed tightly) and have been harvested from inspected waters. Consumption of raw shellfish from contaminated waters can lead to serious food poisoning (see Chap. 6). When steaming or boiling shellfish, be sure the shells open completely when cooked. They open because, when the fish is cooked, the muscle that holds the shells together can no longer function. If the shell does not open, the fish was probably dead before it was cooked. The second group of shellfish, the crustacea, includes lobsters, shrimp, and crabs. These are processed in a number of ways described in Chapter 18 and are often received at the restaurant in this form. Lobsters are the exception and must be cooked while still alive. This is due to a very strong enzyme in their digestive tract that is also described in Chapter 18.

CEREAL GRAINS

Cereal grains have gained more recognition in their importance in a well-balanced diet. Their handling and processing is discussed in Chapter 19. Cereal grains have proteins, carbohydrates, and fats and are a good source of many vitamins and minerals (see Chap. 2). Grains are used for cereals that must be cooked or for those that are dry and ready to eat. In preparation of cooked cereals, skim milk may be used to give a balanced protein source and lower fat and calorie consumption. Dry cereals are completely precooked and are eaten with the addition of cold milk. Here, again, skim milk is recommended. Grains are also the main source of carbohydrates in the brewing and liquor industry. Enzyme activity in the grains breaks the complex carbohydrates into simple sugars, which are fermented into ethyl alcohol and carbon dioxide by yeast. In beer and ale, hops are used to develop the bitter flavors common to beer and ale. With other alcoholic beverages made from grains, a relatively weak alcoholic beverage is boiled and the alcohol condenses and is collected in the distillation process. Different strengths are made by mixing the different liquids. Aging is done with some liquors to produce desired flavors.

In addition to these uses, grains, especially wheat, are also used for flours in baking (see "Bakery Products" section of this chapter) and to make pasta products. Pasta is made from the hardest of wheats (durum) and has a higher protein and gluten content than other wheats, giving it the capability of producing a very stiff dough. Pasta has two main ingredients: water and either flour or semolina (a coarser flourlike product). Semolina is the choice for commercial pasta makers for it has large chunks of protein and little starch. A dough made from it requires less water than flours, and pasta dough contains only about 25% water as compared to about 40% in bread dough.

In pasta making, after the dough is made, it is extruded into various shapes. The gluten matrix (see "Bakery Products" section of this chapter) of semolina is stronger than that of flours and can withstand the pressure of extraction into spaghetti rods or other shapes of pasta. The dough is then dried to about 10% moisture. This process is sensitive and requires much care to assure the timing and temperature are perfect to dry thoroughly but not too quickly. If the temperatures are too high, the pasta will become rigid on the surface and the escaping inner moisture will cause cracking when it is removed later in the drying process. Up to 5.5% egg solids by weight may be added to pasta to produce egg noodles. The main purpose for the addition of eggs is for color and flavor.

BAKERY PRODUCTS

A number of bakery products are explained in Chapter 20. In this section, the chemistry of baking will be discussed and the actions of some of the important ingredients are examined. The subjects covered are flour, leavening agents, shortening, emulsifiers, and other ingredients. Nutritionally, some bakery products such as bread are considered staples in many diets and supply a source of protein, complex carbohydrates (see Chap. 2), vitamins, minerals, and fiber while adding little fat. Others, however, are used mainly as desserts and add more enjoyment to a meal or snack than nutrition. The appearance, texture, and taste of baked items are of great importance and quality, and type of ingredients and methods of preparation controlling the chemical and physical reactions determine the final results. The baker truly exploits the sciences of chemistry and physics.

Flour is the main ingredient in most bakery products and the understanding of some protein chemistry will explain why some flours are good for certain products and not for others. The key word here is *gluten*. Gluten is a combination of two proteins, gliadin and glutenin. Wheat is unique among the grains, because it is the only one whose endosperm proteins will interact to form a gluten strong enough to produce raised breads. Other grains such as rye can produce a weak gluten. Gluten is both plastic and elastic, that is, it can change its shape under pressure yet will return to its original shape when pressure is removed. Gliadin and glutenin molecules are large proteins and their interaction with each other and water is extremely complicated but can be explained fairly simply. Gliadin molecules tend to form compact ovallike balls while glutenin molecules are somewhat longer and more extended. Mix these together and the side chains or R-groups (see Chap. 2) will react, cross-linking the proteins into a tangled mass. The gluten formed does not dissolve in water (the reason why, in raw dough, it survives chewing) but does absorb about twice its own weight in water due to hydrogen bonding (a weak attraction-type bond between hydrogen and other chemical components such as those in sugars, salts, and proteins). This formation of gluten explains why dough is so elastic, why kneading toughens it, and why overkneading breaks it down.

When flour is first mixed with water, the proteins begin to unfold somewhat and water tends to separate and lubricate them by forming hydrogen bonds. At first, the mixture is a thick liquid, but as it is mixed, the proteins are drawn together into visible filaments. Kneading both compresses and stretches the protein–water complex. The constant movement and stress force the long molecules into a more orderly pattern that can form more regular bonds between different molecules, and the cross-linking causes the mixture to be less easily deformed. The dough now is stiff with a smooth, shiny surface. At this point, the dough is much more elastic because the proteins have been elongated and unfolded to a large extent but many kinks still exist due to attractions and bonds between side groups (R-groups) of the same molecule. This explains why dough can be stretched; the kinking bonds will resist but will eventually be broken. When the stress is removed, however, they will reassert themselves and return the dough to its original shape.

If dough is overdeveloped, the bonds, called disulfide or sulfur-to-sulfur bonds, which are important in cross-linking and kinking, are broken and a sulfur molecule can combine with a hydrogen molecule, forming a chemical called a thiol (see Fig. 26–2). The presence of thiol interferes with the sulfur bonds, rekinking after pressure is removed. The result is a broken dough, which is a thick fluid with no elasticity. It is hard to break a dough by hand but it can be done with mechanical mixers or food processors. Other components of flour that contribute to successful dough and batter formation are starch, lipids, other carbohydrates, and enzymes. Starch has two major functions in batters and doughs. Starch granules help form the mechanical structure of baked products by contributing a semisolid phase and by regulating the location of water in the cooking dough. In yeast-raised products, the damaged starch granules from the milling process are attacked by enzymes, forming sugars that yeast use for nutrients. Lipids are not present in large amounts (only about 1% of the weight) but play an important role. It is thought that lipids form bonds with both gliadin and glutenin and help bind these in the formation of gluten as well as bind the gluten to starch molecules. Lipids are thought to play one more important role: They seem to exist in very thin sheets that separate gluten layers. This helps slippage and plasticity in the dough.

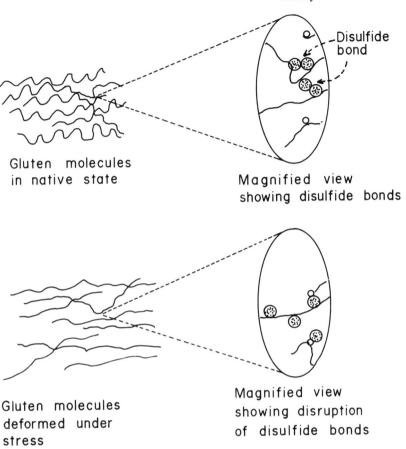

FIGURE 26-2.   Effect of disulfide bonding in gluten molecules.

Most baked products are leavened to make them light, porous, and more palatable and they may be made from a batter or dough. The major difference in these is the amount of water they contain. The batters, which contain more water and have much more fluidity, are usually poured, whereas the doughs, having less water, are stiff but can be worked by hand. The major leavens are steam, air, and carbon dioxide. Examples of steam-leavened products are cream puffs, popovers, and the flakes in pie crust that result from the vaporization of water from the mix. In air leavening, air is incorporated into batters in the preparation stage almost incidentally. When the product is cooked, the air expands and acts as a leaven. Carbon dioxide can be incorporated by yeast fermentation or chemically. With yeast, a source of sugar must be present and the temperature must be correct for the yeast to grow and reproduce (see Chap. 7). Yeast produces enzymes that convert glucose to carbon dioxide (CO_2) and ethyl alcohol (see section on "Cereal Grains"). The alcohol is of little use here and will be essentially eliminated in the cooking process, but the CO_2 acts as a leaven and the gluten, starch, lipid complex described earlier will hold the CO_2 and allow the product to rise. Chemically, carbon dioxide is usually produced by baking soda (sodium bicarbonate) or baking powder, which is sodium bicarbonate in combination with a food acid such as tartaric acid (usually in its salt form, potassium acid tartrate or cream of tartar). The baking soda requires heat to react but the baking powder will react when water is added. The reactions of these are fairly simple and are shown below.

Baking soda:

$$2NaHCO_3 \xrightarrow{\text{heat}} Na_2CO_3 + CO_2 + H_2O$$

| sodium bicarbonate | sodium carbonate | carbon dioxide | water |

Baking powder:

$$NaHCO_3 + KHC_4H_4O_6 \xrightarrow{H_2O} KNaC_4H_4O_6 + CO_2 + H_2O$$

| sodium bicarbonate | potassium acid tartrate (bitartrate) | potassium sodium tartrate | carbon dioxide | water |

Shortening is a fat or oil that "shortens" or breaks up the gluten. This is shown in pastries where the dough is folded and rolled, giving alternating fat and gluten layers. This weakens the gluten and yields a flaky product. Solid fats work much better here since they do not seep into the dough. Heat generated in working the dough could melt the fats; therefore, it is recommended in many pastry recipes to keep the shortening in the freezer prior to using. In a batter the fat has another role. It is usually "creamed" with sugar first and the sharp sugar crystals are cut into the solid fat, creating air cells that help in the leavening process. Also, fat in batters helps in the cooking process. It separates starch granules from coagulated protein and also makes the cake seem moister and smoother. The role of fat in yeast-leavened products was discussed earlier.

Emulsifiers (see Chap. 24) are added in commercial shortenings and cake mixes for they, because of their polar and nonpolar ends, have the ability to combine with lipid and water at the same time. This property enables them to prevent small fat droplets from joining and forming larger droplets, which would separate from the water phase and break the emulsion. In cake mixes and commercial shortenings, this property of insulating lipid droplets is used to prevent the fat from interfering with the protein–air foam and maintains maximum air capacity. In sweet cakes, sugar tends to lower air capacity, but with the incorporation of emulsifiers, the sugar does not coalesce with the small, insulated fat droplets and the air capacity is kept, and lightness and volume can be achieved.

A few other ingredients often added to doughs and batters are salt, sugar, milk, and eggs. Salt is added for taste but has other functions. It inhibits yeast activity somewhat and too much will be detrimental to the optimum leaven. Salt also can toughen gluten by forming bonds with side chains on protein molecules. (Remember, salt ionizes completely in solution as described by the simple formula: $NaCl \rightarrow Na^+ + Cl^-$). This can help the amateur bread maker who is forced to use the softer wheat flours. Salt also inhibits protein-digesting enzymes that can soften the gluten and inhibit its carbon dioxide–holding capacity.

Sugar, as mentioned earlier, acts as food for yeast, but if too much is added, it can also lower water activity (see Chap. 7 and 11) and inhibit fermentation. Sugar can also affect the development of gluten by competing with the protein for water. This helps explain why it takes longer for these doughs to form and develop, but the final product, such as sweet bread, is moister and more tender. Added sugar will also enhance browning reactions (see Chap. 9) and will result in a darker crust.

Milk and eggs add three major ingredients: water, protein, and lipid. The moisture content of the added milk and/or eggs affects the amount of plain water to be added to the flour to develop the dough. The proteins will coagulate and add to the structure, and beaten egg whites, as mentioned earlier in the ''Poultry and Eggs'' section, can incorporate much air into a product. The lipids from milk and eggs have the same effect as added shortening. It is recommended to heat or scald milk (198°F [92.2°C]) for 1 minute to denature the serum proteins that can cause stickiness in dough. (This is a result of their interaction with flour proteins.) It must be noted, however, that scalded milk must be cooled prior to adding to the mixture to avoid damage to the heat-labile yeast. Finally, eggs will add color to products.

VEGETABLES

A botanist defines a fruit as the part of the plant that contains seeds (the ovary). By this definition, tomatoes, eggplants, cucumbers, and squash are fruits. According to the U.S. Department of Agriculture and most chefs and cooks, however, the definition of a vegetable is a plant food that is usually eaten as part of a meal's main course. This is the definition accepted by the majority of the population.

Vegetables are an important addition to any diet. They contain complex carbohydrates and fiber, some proteins, and, generally, very little fat. They also are a rich source of vitamins and minerals. Many varieties of vegetables are discussed in Chapter 21. When vegetables are prepared for service, some nutrients may be lost by leaching out into the cooking water, or by changes to structure due to heat (as with thiamin and vitamin C), or by oxidation during cooking (vitamin C). Some basic rules for cooking vegetables to minimize loss of nutrients are:

1. Bring water to a full boil before adding vegetables. This limits oxidation by inactivating an enzyme (ascorbic acid oxidase) that catalyzes oxidation. Boiling also eliminates oxygen from cooking water in which it has dissolved and from the vegetables.
2. Return water to a boil as fast as possible after vegetables are added for the same reasons listed in number one.
3. Cook in just enough water to cover and avoid scorching. Putting a lid on the pan limits the amount of water needed and speeds cooking time, because the lid tends to increase the vapor pressure above the water, hastening the rise in temperature and shortening the time it takes to produce steam.
4. Cook until just barely done. Don't overcook.
5. Serve immediately.

Microwave heating may limit losses of nutrients due mainly to the shorter cooking time and lesser amounts of cooking water used. Methods for vegetable cookery include baking, boiling, steaming, pan-frying, stir-frying, and microwaving. These are discussed in Chapter 25.

Texture in vegetables depends on two factors: the character of the cell wall and the amount of water in the tissues. The major component of cells walls is cellulose (see Chap. 2), which is the backbone of the structure and is made up of a long polymer of glucose. The special way in which the glucose molecules are attached to one another differentiates cellulose from starch and makes it indigestible to humans. Other components including hemicellulose, which is also a long-chain polymer that is slightly different from cellulose, and pectin, which is also similar to cellulose but consists of a chain of galacturonic acid molecules, also contribute to texture. Pectin is more prominent in some fruits (see Chap. 22).

The second important factor in texture is inner water pressure or turgor of the individual cells. Water is contained in three major areas of the plant: the cytoplasm within the cell, the vacuoles (saclike spaces within cells), and the cell wall itself. These areas are separated by permeable membranes and water can cross them to attain equilibrium in the relative amounts of water and dissolved molecules and ions in each area. A drop in water content outside the cell will draw water out and vice versa. When a cell reaches its limit in water content, the vacuoles press against the cytoplasm, which presses against the cell membrane and wall, resulting in a firm texture we describe as crispness. When one bites into a crisp, raw vegetable, there is initial resistance, then a release of juices and flavor. Cooking the vegetables denatures the cytoplasm and cell membrane, which contain much of the plant protein. The cells no longer retain water and become limp. The tenderness of a cooked vegetable depends on this loss of water and also on the effect of heat, which changes pectin from an insoluble to a soluble form. The hemicellulose mentioned earlier is also partially dissolved and the resulting texture is softer than the fresh vegetable, and overcooking can produce a mushy product.

Appearance in vegetables has much to do with pigments responsible for the bright colors. An understanding of the chemistry of these pigments will help to explain the color changes that occur during cooking. Pigments may be either fat- or water-soluble and include chlorophyll, carotenoids, anthocyanins, and anthoxanthins. Chlorophyll, the major green pigment in plants, is fat-soluble but can leak into water during cooking. When vegetables are first plunged into boiling water, the green color seems to intensify. This is possibly due to the expulsion of intercellular air and the resulting more transparent plant tissue. As cooking continues, however, some organic acids (see Chap. 5) will leach from the cells into the cooking water and contact the chlorophyll. When this happens, the magnesium, which is in the chlorophyll molecule, is displaced by hydrogen from the organic acids. The resulting compound is called pheophytin and has a drab green appearance. This color change can be lessened by cooking with the cover off for the first few minutes to allow for escape of some volatile acids; limiting cooking time will also help.

Cooking in an alkali, such as sodium bicarbonate (baking soda), will help to retain green color because another bright green compound, chlorophyllin, is formed. The texture of these vegetables tends to be more mushy, however, because the alkali breaks down hemicellulose in the cells. Many water-soluble vitamins are sensitive to the change to an alkaline pH (see Chap. 5) and will be destroyed when cooked in this medium. Carotenoids are the yellow, orange, and red-orange fat-soluble pigments present in winter squash, carrots, and sweet potatoes. They are not affected as much as chlorophyll, but the color shifts slightly from orange toward yellow when exposed to boiling water for 2–3 min. Being fat-soluble, they can be absorbed by fats as in a beef stew, resulting in a fat that seems to turn orange.

Anthocyanins include the blue, red, and purple colors in plants such as berries, grapes, and red cabbage. They are all water-soluble and are changed in cooking. An example is red cabbage, which will turn blue when cooked. This can be avoided if acid (e.g., vinegar, wine, or lemon juice) is added to the cooking water. These pigments are also very sensitive to pH changes. To test sensitivity, add some baking soda to cranberry juice. You will get production of carbon dioxide (see "Bakery Products" section) but the resulting color may surprise you. To return the color to red, the pH must be lowered to below 7 by the addition of acid. Flavonoids are near-colorless compounds and often are not noticed. If they are heated in an alkaline medium, they will turn to a yellowish color. Vegetables that contain flavonoids, such as turnips and cauliflower, will turn pink when cooked in a covered pan over a long period of time. By one theory, the pink color is believed to result from a combination of heat and acidity, with hydrogen sulfide released from the vegetables as the reducing agent. By another theory "pinking" in cauliflower is due to a change in leucoanthocyanins, while with turnips, the color change is due to a carotenoid cis-trans rearrangement.

Vegetables contain little acid or sugar; therefore, their flavor is due to aromatic components they contain. Vegetables have relatively mild odors when raw, but if they are heated or cut up, the odors intensify. As the temperature increases, the substances become more volatile. An example is cooked cabbage. When the tissues of vegetables are ruptured, enzymes are released and can catalyze the production of new compounds. Good examples are when garlic is crushed or when onions are cut, with the resulting compounds causing irritation to eyes.

FRUITS

Fruits, as well as having attractive colors, are an important part of a well-balanced diet as they add flavor, vitamins, minerals, carbohydrates (for energy), fiber (both water-soluble and insoluble), and almost no fat to the diet and can be used to replace or supplement fatty choices for desserts or snacks. A variety of fruits is described in Chapter 22. Fruits are eaten raw, canned, frozen, or dried (see Chaps. 10, 11, and 13) and may be cooked in a variety of ways. Fruit products are also popular choices in the form of jams, jellies, preserves, juices, and fillings for bakery items (see Chap. 22). As with all foods, appearance, flavor, and texture are important quality attributes.

Texture in fruits is dependent on cell integrity and amounts of water in their tissue. This is described in the "vegetables" section of this chapter. Fruits, however, contain more pectin than do vegetables and this adds to their crispness. Mature but ripe fruits contain relatively high amounts of protopectin, a precursor of pectin that is water-insoluble. As the fruit matures further, more water-soluble pectins appear and the texture softens. This is thought to be a result of the action of groups of enzymes called pectinases and polygalacturonases.

Fruits, like vegetables, are made up of three major types of tissues: dermal (protective), vascular (food- and water-conducting; supporting), and parenchyma (soft tissue in the pulp). The latter make up most of the edible parts. Some fruits, such as apples, also contain a fair amount of intercellular air spaces. These are formed when three or more cells adjoin and do not fit together perfectly. This texture makes "bobbing for apples" possible as the amount of air in these spaces allows apples to float. The texture of fruit is depreciated greatly when cooked, due mainly to the breakdown of cellulose and hemicellulose, and conversion of pectin from its water-insoluble to water-soluble state. To minimize the loss of texture, fruits are often cooked in sugar syrups which, by their water attraction, help to strengthen the deteriorating cell walls and restore some turgor.

Appearance in fruit depends much on its color. A discussion of pigments is included in the "Vegetables" section of this chapter. As mentioned in Chapter 11, much care must be taken to avoid browning in fruits. A big problem exists with the light-colored fruits (e.g., apples, bananas, pears) that contain phenolic compounds and the enzyme polyphenoloxidase. When fruit is undisturbed, no discoloration occurs, but when it is cut or crushed, the enzyme can interact with the compounds and a brown pigment is produced. Some ways to stop this in most fruits (the skin of bananas is an exception) are chilling below 40°F (4.4°C), which will slow the enzyme action (see Chap. 8), and boiling or blanching, which will destroy the enzyme but affects texture adversely. Chloride ions in salt will inhibit the action, but they have a detrimental effect on taste. Acids, such as those from lemons, will slow the enzyme action. The use of sulfur products, which is usually done commercially will stop the reaction. A percentage of the population (asthmatics, especially) is allergic to sulfur, so much care must be taken in this process, and the use of the sulfur must be declared on the label.

As with other foods, flavor in fruits depends on taste and aroma. Taste is determined mainly by the amounts of acid and sugar in the fruits. When preparing fruit products, such as jams, jellies, and fruit fillings, the amounts are controlled by the food processor, and the U.S. Department of Agriculture has established standards of identity for many fruit products. The stages of maturity, storage practices, and species of fruit will determine the taste in fresh fruit. Aroma, the other characteristic in flavor, is due to a complex mixture of volatile chemicals that are often very unstable.

SUGAR

Sugars make up the simplest group of carbohydrates (see Chap. 2) and are used by the body for energy. Sucrose, or table sugar, obtained from sugar cane or beets, is the most common sugar used and the size and number of crystals formed determine the many types of candies that are made. This is controlled by the addition of agents to the sugar syrup, which interfere with the formation of crystals. Other sugars such as glucose or fructose have different structures and therefore cause the formation of many small sucrose crystals rather than a few large ones. If enough interfering substances are added, a noncrystalline candy can be made, such as lollipops, which have about 25% corn syrup in the formula. Fat and proteins from milk also act as interfering substances in products such as fudge where a less crystalline, smoother texture is desired.

Caramels, toffee, and taffy are other examples of candies with little or no crystallization of sucrose. It is prevented by a high portion of corn syrup in taffy, high fat content in toffee, and both in caramel. The chemistry of browning, as discussed in Chapter 9, comes into play in caramel as the sugar and protein from milk play a role in the color development. Fondant is another type of candy that is an important ingredient in making the huge variety of fillings for chocolates and chocolate candy bars. Fondant is made from sucrose syrup that is heated to dissolve the sugar and cooled to saturation at 104°F (40°C). Air is then beaten into the syrup, which increases the number and decreases the size of sugar crystals, resulting in a mixture that is smooth and pliable. Fondants can have sugar contents of about 88%.

Brown sugar is a mixture of molasses (see Chap. 23) and refined, white sugar. All of these sugars have unique tastes and are used in a number of culinary preparations including sauces, syrup, and candies. Invert sugar is made enzymatically converting sucrose to glucose and fructose (see Chap. 23) or by heating sucrose syrup in the presence of a weak acid such as citric. Invert sugar is sweeter and more water-soluble than sucrose, so it is used in baked items such as cookies and cakes. The final products tend to be softer and moister.

FATS AND OILS

Fats and oils are lipids (see Chaps. 2 and 24) and are important in designing a well-balanced meal plan. The effect of heat on fats and oils is of great importance to culinary science and again can be explained if the properties and chemistry of fats are understood. Included are melting points, smoke points, deterioration, and use as a cooking medium. Most fats do not have sharply defined melting points but they soften over a range of 10°–20°F (5.6°–12.5°C). The reason is the presence of a number of different triglycerides in a given fat. As the temperature rises, different ones melt. The length and degree of unsaturation in the fatty acid components greatly determine the melting point. It is this response of fats to temperatures that facilitates the spreading of melting butter on toast and basting with melting fats.

Fats and oils have much higher boiling points than does water because of their large molecular size. Fats are nonpolar so they do not form hydrogen bonds. They do, however, form weaker bonds (van der Walls bonds) all along their large molecules. It takes relatively high temperatures (500°–750°F [260°–398.9°C]) to break all of them and convert the liquid to a gas. The smoke point is defined as the point when visible gaseous products are produced from fat breakdown. This point seems to depend on the initial amount of free fatty acids in the oil or fat. The amount of free fatty acids is generally much lower in vegetable oils (smoke point of about 450°F or 232.2°C) than in animal fats (smoke point of about 375°F or 190.6°C). Other materials in the fats, such as carbohydrates, proteins, and emulsifiers, will lower the smoke point. As the fat or oil is used, the smoke point lowers due to breakdown of the fats and the buildup of other materials. Caution must be taken when smoke appears because it is a warning that the ignition point is nearing. Many restaurant fires result from overused cooking oil.

Other factors that can deteriorate fats and oils are absorption of odors and rancidity (see Chap. 9). When using fats and oils as a cooking medium, smoke point, absorbed odors, and rancidity all must be observed closely or one risks a fire or the transmission of off-flavors and odors to the foods. Foods are cooked in fats by sautéeing and deep-fat frying (see Chap. 25). Liquid fats and oils are better heat conductors than air, and foods heated in fat are not only cooked but also browned due to caramelization and the sugar-protein reaction (see Chap. 9). Texture is important as these fried foods must be crisp.

A number of changes take place in fats as they are used. The color gets darker, the smoke point is lowered, as is the ignition point, viscosity increases, foams start to form, and the amount of fat absorbed by the food increases. All of these changes are warnings that the fat is getting old and continued use will lead to an increase in probability of fire and to a reduction in food quality. It is important for the chef or cook to watch for these warnings. Cooking oils and fats must be changed regularly.

27

Food Labels

All labels associated with foods should be read at the time of procuring any food, because the contents of labels consist of important criteria for the selection of foods. These include basic information; a list of ingredients; in some cases, quality grades; nutritional information; shelf-life data; and other important information. Authority for the regulation of food labels lies with the Food and Drug Administration (FDA). See Chapter 4 for more on the FDA.

BASIC INFORMATION

The amount and type of information on food labels differ among various food products, but all labels must bear the name of the product, the net contents (net weight or liquid measure), and the name and address of the manufacturer, packer, or distributor. The net weight includes the liquid in which the food is packed. Canned vegetables are usually packed in a brine and canned fruits are usually packed in a syrup (see Chaps. 21 and 22). The inclusion of net contents in a label is important to consumers, so that they can ensure that they buy enough to satisfy their needs and to make purchasing judgments related to unit costs (e.g., buying a large package may yield significant savings in unit cost). They can also use unit cost to select the most economical product from among different brands of similar quality.

In some cases, the packaging and labels of some foods may give a false impression of what they really are. For example, a product may be packed and labeled similarly to ice cream, but it may not contain the minimum proportion of dairy fat (butterfat), making it ineligible and illegal under the standards set by the FDA to be labeled as ice cream. Many foods are covered by standards of identity, another authority of the FDA. Thus, there is a standard for ice cream, one for fish sticks, one for mayonnaise, one for ketchup, and so on. In order to prevent deception of consumers, the FDA has ruled that such foods be labeled under another common name that will provide consumers with an accurate knowledge of the product. Such a common name could be "low-fat frozen desert" if the product contains less than the minimum required amount of dairy fat, or "mellorine" if the dairy fat is substituted with a nondairy fat such as vegetable fat. In either case, the consumer will not be deceived into thinking that the product is standard ice cream.

Another labeling requirement covers foods in which components of a recipe are missing, such as may occur in the case of some prepared entrees. The name of such foods must include the name(s) of the important ingredient(s) in descending order by weight. Thus, in a chicken entree, chicken meat must be the major ingredient, and in fish sticks, fish, not the breading, is the major ingredient. And in frankfurters and beans, frankfurters comprise the major ingredient and beans must be the second major ingredient in descending order by weight. If the weight of the beans exceeds that of the frankfurters, the product must be labeled "beans and frankfurters." Furthermore, the labels of such products must identify the entree to be prepared, and the ingredients that must be added to complete the recipe. For example, in dried macaroni and cheese dinners, addition of the milk and butter must be included.

Another label requirement is the inclusion of the word *imitation* when a product resembles a standardized product but does not have an equal nutritional value. Thus, a product manufactured as a no-cholesterol substitute for eggs must be labeled as "imitation eggs" if its nutritional value is not equivalent to that of eggs. If the product is formulated to have an equal nutritional value, but is missing a major ingredient (in this case, it would be egg yolk), then the product need not be labeled "imitation," but it must be given a new name. "Eggbeaters" is the trade name of one such product currently on the market.

INGREDIENTS

A list of ingredients must be included on the label of many foods. However, foods covered by standards of identity (e.g., mayonnaise) do not have to list those ingredients that are mandatory in accordance with the standard by which a particular food is covered, and they may or may not be listed. However, a manufacturer may list optional ingredients that are specified as such in the relevant standard. The order in which ingredients are listed must start with the major ingredient (by weight) and continue with the remaining ingredients in descending order. Any additive used in a food product must be listed. For more on additives, see Chapter 5. Most colors (FD&C yellow number 5 is an exception) and flavors do not have to be listed by name. They may simply be listed as "artificial flavor(s)" or "artificial color(s)."

GRADES

Many foods carry a grade label that certifies their level of quality. All foods, except seafoods, are graded by the U.S. Department of Agriculture (USDA) and by health agencies of the individual states that are authorized by the FDA to do so. Seafoods are presently graded by the U.S. Department of Commerce (USDC). See Chapter 4 for more on the USDA and USDC. The grades, in all cases, are based on organoleptic (appearance, odor, taste, and texture) criteria as well as on physical and production characteristics. More importantly, for seafoods, the grades and inspection sticker certify that the food is safe and wholesome and produced under the sanitary standards as recommended by the FDA. The grades assigned to different foods may vary. Thus, meats are graded prime, choice, and select in descending order of quality. Seafoods are graded A, B, or C in descending order of quality.

Grading is not mandatory since all graded products are already inspected for safety. Grading is usually requested by the producer or distributor. One class of perishable foods presently not under mandatory inspection includes finfish. Consideration has been given, however, to make the inspection of finfish mandatory, and it should not be unexpected that this will eventually happen. For the present, certification of the wholesomeness of finfish is only assured when the product carries the USDC inspection sticker, which is normally accompanied by the USDC grade sticker.

While grades are not dependent on the nutritional quality of foods, the FDA has established standards that require certain levels of vitamins A and D when these vitamins are added to milk.

NUTRITION

With the growing tendency of consumers to control the consumption of various dietary components, there is a growing proclivity to read food labels mainly for the nutritional data. This puts an emphasis on the part of the label that lists the nutritional data, and it behooves manufacturers who want to remain competitive to list all of the nutritional information possible. That is why nutrition information appears on labels even though it is not required. Under FDA regulations, nutrition information is required only on the labels of food for which a nutritional claim is made or to which a nutrient has been added, but changes have been proposed.

Nutritional information includes the size of one serving, calories, protein, carbohydrate, fat, and sodium per serving and the U.S. Recommended Daily Allowance (USRDA) of protein and five specified vitamins (A, C, B_1, B_2, and niacin) and two specified minerals (iron and calcium). Other vitamins and minerals are listed when they contribute at least 2% of the USRDA per serving. The listing of other components such as cholesterol and fatty acid content is optional, except when a claim is made for their reduced contents. USRDAs are the amounts of each nutritional component (e.g., protein, vitamins) required daily to maintain health. Thus, the entire food (and supplements) intake for any given day should supply a body with 100% of the USRDA. A table that supplies this information (see Chap. 2) specifies the requirements for infants, children, female adults, and male adults.

The FDA has established nutritional guidelines for some foods and has proposed them for other foods. The guidelines specify the minimum level of nutrients that should be in a particular food product (e.g., prepared dinners, pizzas, and breakfast cereals). Manufacturers are not required to follow any of the guidelines, but if they do, they can then state on the label that the product "provides nutrients in the amounts appropriate for this class of food as determined by the U.S. government." The reader will note that the units used in the nutrition information labels on foods and nutrient supplements and the nutrition data in tables include abbreviations of metric and other units. The appendix in the back of the book has been included as a place of reference for the conversion of these units to the English equivalents and also for a definition of abbreviations.

OPEN DATING

Open dating is the practice of showing a date on packaged foods that carries information permitting the consumer to ascertain the date beyond which the quality of the product may be expected to fall below normal levels. This information may appear on the label, but in many cases, it is simply stamped on the label or elsewhere on the package. One example of open dating is the "sell by" or "pull" date. This defines the last day that the product should be sold. It is the type used for perishable products such as dairy and meat products. Another example of open dating is the expiration date. This defines the last day that the product should be used or eaten. It is the type used for dried yeast and baby foods. Another type of open dating is the freshness date. This defines the last day that the product will retain its fresh quality. This type is used largely for bakery products. From the consumer's point of view, the least important type of open dating is the pack date. This defines the date when the food was manufactured, processed, or packaged. This type of dating is used for nonperishable foods such as canned foods and some packaged foods. However, this date has little meaning to the consumer unless he or she has information on the expected shelf-life of the product. It does have a practical value similar to code dating (see next section).

OTHER INFORMATION

Other information that may be found on the package of foods includes code dating, the universal product code, legal symbols, and religious symbols.

Code Dating

Code dating is usually used for products having long shelf-lives such as canned foods, but it may be used on other packaged products. This type of dating, as the name implies, is in code. The code supplies information regarding the date when the product was packaged as well as the place where it was packaged. This information serves a number of purposes, but a major purpose is to facilitate a recall of the product should circumstances make such an action necessary.

Universal Product Code

Most food labels carry the universal product code (UPC). The value of the UPC is associated with the use of computers. The UPC is readily recognized by a block of vertical parallel lines of different widths and a line of numbers at the bottom of the block. The UPC is specific for each food product and is used to read the product description and price when computerized checkout equipment is used. The computer can yield information on the rate of sales, thus maintaining a status of the inventory, which in turn reveals when and how much product must be procured to maintain a desired inventory level. The ordering can be done automatically if the computer program provides for this service. Furthermore, one can determine the contribution of the product to net profit, its profit per unit space, and so forth. As can be seen, the UPC has a significant industrial value, with the potential to be even more valuable.

Legal Symbols

The legal symbols that may appear on labels are ® and ©. The symbol ® means that the trademark used on the label is registered with the U.S. Patent Office. The © means that the literary and artistic content of the label is protected under the copyright law of the United States and that copies of such labels have been filed with the Copyright Office of the Library of Congress.

Religious Symbols

Two religious symbols that may appear on food labels are relevant to Jews. When the letter K appears inside the letter O, it means that the food is kosher, signifying that it complies with Jewish dietary laws and that it was processed under the supervision of a rabbi. When the letter U appears inside the letter O, it means that the product complies with Jewish dietary laws and is authorized by the Union of Orthodox Jewish Congregations of America, more familiarly known as the Orthodox Union.

Appendix

Weight

1 oz = 28.35 g and 1 g = 1,000 mg = 1,000,000 mcg = 0.035 oz
1 lb = 0.454 kg and 1 kg = 1,000 g = 2.205 lb
1 ft^3 water weighs 62.4 lb = 28.3 kg
1 ton = 2000 lb = 0.893 long tons = 0.907 metric tons

Volume

1 oz = 29.573 ml and 1 ml = 0.034 oz
1 qt = 0.946 l and 1 l = 1,000 ml = 1.057 qt
1 gal = 3.785 l = 231 in^2 and 1 l = 0.264 gal
1 cup = 8 oz = 236.8 ml = 16 tbsp = 48 tsp
1 tbsp = 3 tsp = 0.5 oz = 14.8 ml
1 tsp = 4.93 ml
1 ft^3 = 7.48 gal = 0.03 m^3
1 stick butter or margarine = ¼ lb = ½ cup = 8 tbsp

Length

1 in. = 2.54 cm and 1 cm = 0.3937 in.
1 ft = 30.48 cm = 0.305 m and 1 m = 100 cm = 3.28 ft
1 yd = 0.914 m and 1 m = 1.09 yd

Area

$1 \text{ in}^2 = 6.5 \text{ cm}^2$
$1 \text{ ft}^2 = 0.092 \text{ m}^2 \text{ and } 1 \text{ m}^2 = 10.76 \text{ ft}^2$
$1 \text{ yd}^2 = 0.835 \text{ m}^2 \text{ and } 1 \text{ m}^2 = 1.19 \text{ yd}^2$
$1 \text{ acre} = 0.4 \text{ ha}$

Other

1 I.U. = 0.3 R.E. units of vitamin A (see Chap. 2)

ABBREVIATIONS

kg	=	kilogram(s)	gal	=	gallon(s)
g	=	gram(s)	qt	=	quart(s)
mg	=	milligram(s)	tbsp	=	tablespoon(s)
µg	=	mcg = microgram(s)	tsp	=	teaspoon(s)
l	=	liter(s)	yd	=	yard(s)
ml	=	milliliter(s)	ft	=	foot (feet)
m	=	meter(s)	in	=	inch(es)
cm	=	centimeter(s)	IU	=	international unit(s)
lb	=	pound(s)	RE	=	retinol equivalent unit(s)
oz	=	ounce(s)	ppp	=	parts per million
ha	=	hectare	ppm	=	parts per million

Suggested Readings

Charley, Helen. 1982. *Food Science.* New York: Wiley.

Clydesdale, Fergus, and Frederick Francis. 1985. *Food Nutrition and Health* Westport, Conn.: AVI.

Considine, D. M., and G. D. Considine (editors). 1982. *Foods and Food Production Encyclopedia.* New York: Van Nostrand Reinhold.

DeMan, John. 1990. *Principles of Food Chemistry.* New York: Van Nostrand Reinhold.

Division of Microbiology, Center for Food Safety and Applied Nutrition, U.S. Food and Drug Administration. 1984. *Bacteriological Analytical Manual.* Arlington, Va." Association of Official Analytical Chemists.

Dziezak, Judie D. 1987. Microwave foods—Industry's response to consumer demands for convenience. *Food Technology* 41(6):51-62.

Federal Register. 1990. *21 CFR Parts 101, 104, and 105—Food Labeling; Reference Daily Values, Mandatory Status of Nutrition Labeling and Nutrient Content Revision; Serving Sizes; Proposed Rules.* 55(139).

Fruits and vegetable processing—Past, present, and future. 1990. *Food Technology.* 44(2):91-104.

FSIS Directive. 1989. *Grademark Labeling on Meat and Poultry Products.* Washington, D.C.: Food Safety and Inspection Service.

Gorga, C., and L. J. Ronsivalli. 1988. *Quality Assurance of Seafoods.* New York: Van Nostrand Reinhold.

Grosser, Arthur E. 1981. *The Cookbook Decoder.* New York: Beaufort Books, Inc.

Guthrie, R. K. 1988. *Food Sanitation,* 3rd ed. New York: Van Nostrand Reinhold.

Hall, C. W., A. W. Farrell, and A. L. Rippen. 1986. *Encyclopedia of Food Engineering,* 2nd ed. New York: Van Nostrand Reinhold.

Hamill, P. V. V., T. A. Drizd, C. L. Johnson, R. B. Reed, A. F. Roche, and W. M. Moore, 1979. Physical growth: National Center for Health Statistics percentiles. *Amer. J. Clin. Nutr.* 32:607-629.

Hillman, Howard. 1983. *Kitchen Science.* Boston:Houghton Mifflin Company.

Integrated microwave packaging. 1990. *Food Engineering* **62**(4):50.

Jackson, E. B. 1989. *Super Confectionary Manufacture.* New York: Van Nostrand Reinhold.

Jay, James. 1986. *Modern Food Microbiology.* New York: Van Nostrand Reinhold.

Josephson, E. S., and M. S. Peterson (editors). 1983. *Preservation of Foods by Ionization Radiation,* vols. I, II, and III. Boca Raton, Fla.: CRC Press Inc.

Lee, F. A. 1983. *Basic Food Chemistry.* New York: Van Nostrand Reinhold.

Lewis, Richard. 1989. *Food Additives Handbook.* New York: Van Nostrand Reinhold.

Liebman, Bonnie. 1990. Trans in trouble. *Nutrition Action* **17**(8):7.

Lopez, Anthony. 1981. *A Complete Course in Canning,* vols. I AND II. Baltimore: The Canning Trade.

Lovell, R. T. 1988. *Nutrition and Feeding of Fish.* New York: Van Nostrand Reinhold.

Luh, Bor, and Jasper Woodroof. 1988. *Commercial Vegetable Processing.* New York: Van Nostrand Reinhold.

McGee, Harold. 1984. *On Food and Cooking.* New York: Macmillan Publishing Company.

Marriot, N. G. 1985. *Principles of Food Sanitation.* New York: Van Nostrand Reinhold.

Martin, R. E., and G. J. Flick, Jr. (editors). 1989. *The Seafood Industry.* New York: Van Nostrand Reinhold.

National Research Council. 1989. *Recommended Dietary Allowances:* Washington, D.C.: National Academy of Sciences.

North, M. O., and D. D. Bell. 1989. *Commercial Chicken Production Manual,* 4th ed. New York: Van Nostrand Reinhold.

Parkhurst, C. R., and G. J. Mourntney. 1987. *Poultry, Meat and Egg Production* New York: Van Nostrand Reinhold.

Plastic packaging of foods—Problems and solutions. 1990. *Food Technology* **43**(12):83–94.

Potter, N. N. 1986. *Food Science.* New York: Van Nostrand Reinhold.

Richardson, T. R., and J. W. Finley (editors). 1985. *Chemical Changes in Food During Processing.* New York: Van Nostrand Reinhold.

Rombauer, Irma S, and Marion Rombauer Becker. 1974. *Joy of Cooking,* vols. 1 and 2. New York: The New American Library.

Ronsivalli, L. J., and D. W. Baker. 1981. Low temperature preservation of seafoods: A review. *Marine Fisheries Review* **43**(4):1–15.

Roth, L. O., F. R. Grow, and G. W. A. Mahoney. 1975. *An Introduction to Agricultural Engineering.* New York: Van Nostrand Reinhold.

Ryser, Elliot T., and Elmer M. Marth. 1989. "New: food-borne pathogens of public health significance. *Journal of the American Dietetic Association.* **89**(7):948–954.

Schultz, H. W. 1981. *The Food Law Handbook.* Westport, Conn.: AVI.

Simplesse. 1989. *Food Engineering* **61**(3):71–72.

Stadelman, W. J., and D. J. Cotterill (editors). 1986. *Egg Science and Technology,* 3rd ed. New York: Van Nostrand Reinhold.

Staff Report. 1989. Top 10 food science innovations 1939–1989. *Food Technology* **43**(9):308.

Stefferud, A. (editor). 1962. *After a Hundred Years, The Yearbook of Agriculture.* Washington, D.C.: Superintendent of Documents.

Sultan, William. 1989. *Practical Baking.* New York: Van Nostrand Reinhold.

The Educational Foundation of the National Restaurant Association. 1985. *Applied Foodservice Sanitation.* New York: John Wiley and Sons.

Tiexeira, A. A., and C. F. Shoemaker. 1988. *Computerized Food Processing Operations.* New York: Van Nostrand Reinhold.

Unique aseptic design. 1990. *Food Engineering* **62**(1):95–96.

USDA. 1989. *HACCP Principles for Food Production.* Washington, D.C.: Food Safety and Inspection Service.

U.S. Department of Health, Education, and Welfare. 1978. *Grade "A" Pasteurized Milk Ordinance.* Washington, D.C.:U.S. Government Printing Office.

U.S. Dept. of Health and Human Services, Food and Drug Administration. 1976. *Food Service Sanitation Manual.* Washington, D.C.

Weiss, T. J. 1982. *Food Oils and Their Uses.* New York: Van Nostrand Reinhold.

Williams, Sue Rodwell. 1989. *Nutrition and Diet Therapy.* St. Louis: Times Mirror/Mosby College Publishing.

Wong, N. P. (editor). 1986. *Fundamentals of Dairy Chemistry,* 3rd ed. New York: Van Nostrand Reinhold.

Woodroof, J. G. 1990. 50 years of fruit and vegetable processing. *Food Technology* **44**(2):92–95.

Woodroof, Jasper, and Bor Luh. 1986. *Commercial Fruit Processing* Westport, Conn.: AVI.

Index